Colloquial

Arabic
of the Gulf

THE COLLOQUIAL SERIES
Series Adviser: Gary King

The following languages are available in the Colloquial series:

Afrikaans	German	Romanian
Albanian	Greek	Russian
Amharic	Gujarati	Scottish Gaelic
Arabic (Levantine)	Hebrew	Serbian
Arabic of Egypt	Hindi	Slovak
Arabic of the Gulf	Hungarian	Slovene
Basque	Icelandic	Somali
Bengali	Indonesian	Spanish
Breton	Irish	Spanish of Latin America
Bulgarian	Italian	Swahili
Burmese	Japanese	Swedish
Cambodian	Kazakh	Tamil
Cantonese	Korean	Thai
Catalan	Latvian	Tibetan
Chinese (Mandarin)	Lithuanian	Turkish
Croatian	Malay	Ukrainian
Czech	Mongolian	Urdu
Danish	Norwegian	Vietnamese
Dutch	Panjabi	Welsh
English	Persian	Yiddish
Estonian	Polish	Yoruba
Finnish	Portuguese	Zulu (forthcoming)
French	Portuguese of Brazil	

COLLOQUIAL 2s series: *The Next Step in Language Learning*

Chinese	German	Russian
Dutch	Italian	Spanish
French	Portuguese of Brazil	Spanish of Latin America

Colloquials are now supported by FREE AUDIO available online. All audio tracks referenced within the text are free to stream or download from www.routledge.com/cw/colloquials. If you experience any difficulties accessing the audio on the companion website, or still wish to purchase a CD, please contact our customer services team through www.routledge.com/info/contact.

Colloquial
Arabic
of the Gulf

The Complete Course
for Beginners

Clive Holes

Routledge
Taylor & Francis Group

LONDON AND NEW YORK

First published 1984
Reprinted 1986, 1992, 1994, 2000, 2004, 2005
by Routledge

This edition first published 2010
by Routledge
2 Park Square, Milton Park, Abingdon, Oxon, OX14 4RN

and by Routledge
711 Third Avenue, New York, NY 10017

Routledge is an imprint of the Taylor & Francis Group, an informa business

British Library Cataloguing in Publication Data
A catalogue record for this book is available from the British Library

Library of Congress Cataloging in Publication Data
Holes, Clive, 1948–
   Colloquial Arabic of the Gulf : the complete course for beginners /
Clive Holes. — 2nd ed.
      p. cm.
   Includes bibliographical references.
      1. Arabic language—Dialects—Persian Gulf Region—
Grammar.   2. Arabic language—Dialects—Arabian Peninsula
—Grammar.   3. Arabic language—Textbooks for foreign
speakers—English.   I. Title.
PJ6853.H64 2009
492′.770916535—dc22   2009002438

ISBN: 978-1-138-95812-8 (pbk)

Typeset in Helvetica
by Florence Production Ltd, Stoodleigh, Devon

Contents

Introduction

Who is this book for?

This book has been written for anyone who needs to acquire a solid working knowledge of the educated colloquial Arabic spoken in an area extending from Basra in southern Iraq, down through Kuwait, Bahrain, eastern Saudi Arabia, Qatar, the United Arab Emirates and Oman. No previous knowledge of Arabic is assumed. The emphasis is on the acquisition of a *working* knowledge; therefore, language items needed at the major points of social contact between Gulf Arabs and Western residents are given pride of place. Teachers, engineers, businessmen, military personnel and others who need to be able to communicate in spoken Arabic in schools, offices, shops, markets and the workplace should find this book highly useful. Grammatical explanation is given only where it serves some clarificatory purpose, and much of the book is given over to examples and exercises of a type that the writer hopes the learner will find relevant in coping with day-to-day living in the Gulf. Some texts deal with the customs and beliefs common to the area, and in each unit there is a Cultural point that gives further useful background information on culture, society and history. There is also a simple introduction to reading Arabic road signs, shop signs and other basic types of 'public text' written in Literary Arabic.

What is 'Gulf Arabic'?

It is estimated that Arabic is spoken as first language by some 250–300 million people, living in a vast geographical area that extends from Morocco to Oman along a west–east axis, and as far south as northern Nigeria and southern Sudan. Pockets of Arabic speakers can be found in such far-flung places as Central Asia and Zanzibar. Clearly, in such a large area, there is bound to be considerable dialectal diversity, comparable to the differences between what in Europe are considered separate but related languages: Italian and Spanish, Polish and Russian or Dutch and Standard German. The factor that unites the speakers of this Babel of dialects is the Arabic literary language, which shows relatively little regional variation, and is used for all written communication throughout the Arab world. The subject of this book is the educated spoken (not written) Arabic of one fairly large area – the Arabian Gulf – in which, despite dialectal variants that may be specific to the particular states that lie along it, there is such a commonality of usage that it is possible to describe a single set of language forms that will be completely understood in every part of it. This set of language forms is what will henceforth be referred to as 'Gulf Arabic' – a variety of Arabic that refers not so much to the Arabic spoken in any one state, but to a variety that is increasingly used by Gulf Arabs from different Gulf states when they converse with each other and with outsiders. In its sound system, grammar and vocabulary, 'Gulf Arabic' represents a kind of distillation of the common features of all Gulf dialects, while avoiding the peculiarities of any one area. It also shows the influence of Literary Arabic in its vocabulary, because its users tend to be educated. From the foreigner's point of view, this type of spoken Gulf Arabic is likely to be the most useful. Most of the data and examples that were collected for this book come, in fact, from Bahrain – but, where justified, a note of important alternative forms is made.

The Western resident will find that even a modest knowledge of Gulf Arabic will hugely repay the effort expended to acquire it. The Arabs are extremely proud of their linguistic heritage, and feel flattered and impressed by Westerners interested enough to have tried to learn their language. From a personal point of view, too, it is very satisfying to be able to make sense out of the babble of unintelligible speech that surrounds one from the moment of arrival at the airport. Apart from its practical value, Gulf Arabic provides a good jumping-off point for the further study of the Arabic language and its culture, should the learner feel inclined. Linguistically, Gulf Arabic is relatively close to Literary Arabic, while, culturally, what remains of Bedouin society provides a modern-day insight into the values and social conditions that gave birth to Islam.

How to use this book

The pronunciation guide

When learning to speak any language, it is important to get a feeling for what it should sound like, and to imitate the sounds and rhythms of the language as closely as possible, however odd they may seem at first. To help you in this, some preliminary pronunciation exercises have been provided at the beginning of the audio that accompanies this course. Before you begin to work through the course proper, play through these exercises several times with the written version of them in front of you. The first time you play the audio, just listen carefully, and mentally repeat the Arabic to yourself. Then listen again and repeat aloud. It doesn't matter at this stage that you don't understand the words – the idea is simply to get used to what the consonants and vowels of Gulf Arabic sound like.

The audio

A large amount of the Arabic exercise material has been recorded. Exercises with audio are marked ⌒. These exercises, at the same time as providing a model of Gulf Arabic speech for those learning the language outside the area, can be exploited in a number of ways (e.g. as practice in listening comprehension without the help of the written version). If you don't have the audio to hand (or even if you do), it's a good idea to get hold of a native speaker of Arabic from the Gulf to help you with pronunciation.

Above all, remember that it is pointless mastering the grammar and vocabulary of this fascinating language if you cannot make a passable shot at pronouncing it correctly. The difficulties in this have been greatly exaggerated. Whenever you possibly can, practise speaking the language to Gulf Arabs. Get them to correct your pronunciation and use of words ruthlessly. But one word of warning – impress on those who help you that it is *Gulf* pronunciation, grammar and vocabulary that you are trying to master, *not* Literary Arabic or some other well-known dialect of Arabic, such as Egyptian.

The units

Work through the units in the order they are presented. Each unit contains a number of grammatical points, and is structured so that, at the end of each piece of grammatical explanation and example, there are related exercises for practice. Before you move on to the next grammatical point in the unit, complete the exercises for the point you think you've mastered. These exercises generally provide generous practice on the point just covered together with material 'recycled' from previous units.

At the end of each unit there is a Vocabulary of all the new words that occur in that unit – you will need to consult this as you do the exercises. Many of the exercises involve translation. When you have checked your answers to an exercise in the 'Answer key', it is a good idea (and it doubles up on practice!) to use the key as an exercise itself, and translate it back into the other language. Try as far as possible to learn the vocabulary – at least those words you consider most useful for your purposes – as you go along. Vocabulary learning is always the most difficult part of learning a language (even one's own), and this is particularly true of an 'exotic' language like Arabic. The vocabulary in the book (about 1,500 words) should suffice for all practical purposes.

A couple of hints on vocabulary learning: try writing down individual words on small pieces of paper or cards, Arabic on one side and English on the other, with perhaps an example of the Arabic word in use in a phrase or sentence on the Arabic side (see facing page). A pack of 50 or so of these, secured with an elastic band, can be fitted easily into handbag or pocket and gone through in any idle moment.

Another possibility is to group words in your own vocabulary book according to useful criteria or 'areas of life' – 'jobs', 'food', 'the office', for example. Such an arrangement provides a ready way of revising

Arabic side	**English side**
glaas pl. -aat	glass
glaas chaay	a glass of tea
gaam imperf. **yigúum**	to get up; to start
1 **gaam u raaH** 2 **gaam yáakil**	1 He got up and went 2 He started to eat

and associating words in groups according to whatever factors are important for the learner, and they are a great help to the memory. The Vocabularies at the end of each unit are arranged alphabetically so as to make looking words up easier – but this ordering is *not* meant to be a recommendation about how to learn them!

Each unit contains a section entitled Cultural point about Gulf history, culture and society, which is designed to give you useful background information about the people whose language you are learning. This also contains useful linguistic material that cannot easily be accommodated in the body of the unit.

Finally, although this book is an introduction to the spoken Arabic of the Gulf, for those who would like to acquire a very basic reading knowledge of Arabic sufficient to allow them to read the words on Gulf road and shop signs, banknotes, stamps, business cards and other realia, there is a section at the end of every unit, Reading Arabic, which contains examples of such materials and advice on how to read them. These sections need to be studied in conjunction with the short introduction to the Arabic script, which forms Appendix 2.

The appendices and glossaries

Appendix 1 provides a quick means of reference on a number of knotty points of potential confusion to the learner of Gulf Arabic. Like speakers of all languages, Gulf Arabs show variability in their speech. Just as the same Cockney speaker of English may say 'bo'le' or 'bottle' (depending perhaps on whether he or she is trying to 'talk proper'!), so Gulf Arabs vary between different pronunciations of the same word. The word for 'child', for example, may be pronounced by the same speaker as **jáahil** or **yáahil**, where **j** and **y** are both acceptable and commonly used; 'I filled' may be **tirást** or **trást**, in one case with an **-i-** and in the other without; 'she told me' may be **gáalat lii** or **gaalát lii**, involving variation in which syllable is stressed. In all these cases, and many more, there is no change in meaning signified by the variation – indeed the speakers themselves are seldom aware of it. But to a foreign learner this apparent instability can be confusing. It is, however, something that one has to learn to live with, and it is reflected in this book in the fact that I have *deliberately* allowed variation of the types exemplified in the appendices to occur in the body of the text – to do otherwise would be to falsify the facts of the language and imply consistency where its opposite is the rule. Appendix 1 gives you a quick check on the main points in the language where variation occurs, and should be regularly consulted until you are clear on where possible confusion may arise.

Appendix 2 provides a very brief introduction to the Arabic script, which, taken in conjunction with the Reading Arabic sections at the end of every unit, should enable you, with perseverance, to master the basics of reading simple signs.

Finally, there are Arabic–English and English–Arabic glossaries of all the Gulf Arabic words that appear in the book.

How long will it take to learn?

The answer to this question depends on many factors – among them how thoroughly you want to learn the language, whether you are a quick learner of languages in general, etc. As an average figure, I should say you should spend between three and five hours per course unit, all of this preferably within the same week at a rate of up to an hour per day. Some units, particularly from Unit Seven on, may take somewhat longer than this rough estimate. In addition, there are three 'Review units' that, if you have properly mastered the material in the five regular units that precede each of them, you should be able to cover in between one and two hours. Given a modicum of application, it should be possible for the average learner to acquire a basic working knowledge of Gulf Arabic from this course in about six months. It cannot be too strongly emphasised that, in language learning, as in the acquisition of any skill, practice is everything: take every opportunity you can to talk to and listen to Arabs, however little you understand at first.

Abbreviations used in the text

act. part.	active participle
adj.	adjective
adv.	adverb
coll.	colloquial
conj.	conjunction
def.	definite
f.	feminine
fig.	figurative use
imp.	imperative
imperf.	imperfect (tense)
indef.	indefinite
intrans.	intransitive verb
lit.	literally
m.	masculine
n.	noun
p.	past (tense)
pass. part.	passive participle

pl.	plural
prep.	preposition
pron.	pronoun
sing.	singular
syn.	synonym
trans.	transitive verb
v.	verb
v. n.	verbal noun
*	signifies that a noun ending in **-a** is feminine and has a final 'hidden' **t**
<	is derived from
~	indicates that, although the words either side of ~ are separate items, they are run together in normal speech as if they were one word

Pronunciation guide

This guide is intended to help you acquire a reasonably accurate Arabic pronunciation, and to introduce you to the system of spelling used in the book. It should be used in conjunction with the accompanying audio and/or the help of a native speaker of Gulf Arabic. The pronunciation model aimed at is that of an educated speaker.

Consonants

The consonants have been divided into three groups: Group 1 contains those (a majority) that should give you no trouble – they are more or less identical to English equivalents; Group 2 contains those that, from some point of view, are slightly different from their standard English equivalents, but that are similar to sounds found in regional English accents or in well-known European languages; Group 3 is the difficult group that contains sounds not found in English or common European languages, and that usually take some time to master.

Group 1

Letter	Hints on pronunciation
b	'b' in 'bottle'
p	'p' in 'apple'
ch	'ch' in 'church'
f	'f' in 'foot'
g	'g' in 'gap'
h	'h' in 'hit'; in Arabic, unlike English, **h** can occur as the last sound of a word
j	'j' in 'jet' or 'g' in 'barge'

k	'ck' in 'tack' or 'c' in 'car'
m	'm' in 'miss'
n	'n' in 'nap'
s	's' in 'see', 'c' in 'ice'
sh	'sh' in 'shoot', 'cash'
w	'w' in 'how', 'win'
y	'y' in 'boy', 'yet'
z	'z' in 'zither', 'haze'

Group 2

'   the glottal stop. This sound is heard in the Cockney pronunciation of 'butter' ('bu'er') or the Glaswegian pronunciation of
'water' ('wa'er'), where the 't' drops and is replaced by a catch
in the voice. In Arabic, this sound can occur at the beginning
as well as in the middle of a word, as it does in German (e.g.
in words such as *'Achtung'*).

d, t   These sounds are similar to 'd' and 't' in English 'day', 'tag',
except that the point of contact of the tongue-tip is the back
of the upper teeth, not the gums as in English.

th   'th' as in 'thin', 'bath'.

dh   'th' as in 'the', 'soothe'.

l   'l' as in English 'limb', 'bill' (i.e. 'light' l). In a few Arabic words,
the commonest of which is **alláah** 'God', the l is 'dark' like the
'l' in 'field'.

Group 3

gh   Parisian 'guttural' 'r' as in 'grand'. Sounds similar to the sound
of gargling.

x   Scottish 'ch' in 'Loch Ness'.

H   This and 9 are probably the most difficult sounds in Arabic for
Europeans. H is a voiceless sound similar to the hoarse
expulsion of breath sometimes made by people breathing on
spectacle lenses before cleaning them! It is produced from the
extreme back of the throat (the pharynx), and there is a feeling
of constriction in the muscles of the throat when producing
this sound.

9	**9** is the voiced counterpart of **H**. Like **H**, it is produced by constricting the passage of air at the back of the throat, but in this case the vocal chords vibrate. **9** is like the sound made by someone being strangled.
r	Like the Italian trilled 'r' in 'ragazza'.
S, T,	**S, T, D** and **DH** are the so-called 'emphatic' consonants. The
D, DH	position of the tongue is as for their non-emphatic counterparts **s, t, d** and **dh**, but the tongue should be flattened and broadened in the mouth so that the mouth cavity feels 'filled'. At the same time, there is a feeling of muscular tension in the mouth and constriction (as for **H** and **9**) at the back of the throat. The result is a duller, heavier sound for **S, T, D** and **DH** compared with **s, t, d** and **dh**. Consonants in neighbouring syllables tend to become 'emphatic' under the influence of these sounds.
q	This sound, which is not common in the colloquial speech of Kuwait, Bahrain, Qatar, Saudi Arabia and the UAE, is, in these countries, an 'educated' variant of **g**. It is a voiceless sound similar to the final consonant in 'hock', except that it is produced from further back in the mouth – from the uvula, to be exact. The exception is Oman, where **q** is pronounced as the normal dialect form by ordinary Omanis who live in the Capital Area, in the mountains of the interior, and in Salala in the south, exactly as it is in Classical Arabic, that is, as a uvular **q**. However, the desert Omanis pronounce the sound as a **g**, as in the rest of the Gulf.

Pronunciation practice: consonants (Audio 1; 2)

Using the accompanying audio, practise pronouncing the consonants in initial, medial and final position. In words of more than one syllable, the stressed vowel is marked superscript, for example **á**.

	Initial	Medial	Final
Group 1			
b	bas	gábil	gálab
p (often replaced by b)	pánka	(does not occur)	
ch	chalb	bíchar	sámach

	Initial	Medial	Final
f	faar	safíir	sálaf
g	gaal	bágar	báayig
h	húwa	sáahir	kárah
j	jíbin	hujúum	thalj
k	karíim	búkra	tárak
m	múslim	jamíil	sáalim
n	nínsa	sánad	gálan
s	samíir	jáasim	naas
sh	shaaf	fáshal	mish
w	wálad	náwas	gáalaw
y	yáahil	shíyar	dáray
z	ziyáara	kaazíino	báariz

	Initial	Medial	Final
Group 2			
'	'ákal	sá'al	(does not occur)
d	dazz	bádla	faríid
t	tigúul	bítri	mukaanáat
th	thalj	thaláatha	turáath
dh	dhii	háadhii	fuláadh
l ('light')	libáas	sálaf	jamíil
l ('dark')	laTíif	alláah	gábil

	Initial	Medial	Final
Group 3			
gh	ghásal	bághal	bálagh
x	xáali	náxal	taaríix
H	Harb	báHar	fáraH
9	9áraf	ba9íir	dáfa9
r	rayyáal	baríid	kathíir
S	SabáaH	báSal	xaláaS
T	Tabíib	báaTil	balaalíiT
D	Dárab	ráDi	'arD
DH	DHúhur	HáaDHra	HáafiDH
q	qur'áan	mínTaqa	faríiq

'Doubled' consonants (Audio 1; 3)

Consonants sometimes occur 'doubled' in Arabic: that is, the same consonant occurs twice in a word without an intervening vowel. It is important when pronouncing such doubled consonants to increase the length of time over which the consonant sound is produced to approximately twice that of the single consonant. Thus **sállaf** 'to lend' is pronounced as two syllables **sal-laf**. Try the following contrastive exercise:

Single	Doubled
dáxal	dáxxal
sálaf	sállaf
mára	márra
fáham	fáhham
HáSal	HáSSal

Now practise pronouncing the following words, which contain 'doubled' consonants **(Audio 1; 4)**:

mu9állim	mudárris	muHássin	mulábbas
dáshsha	dázza	Hággah	Sáxxa
rayyáal	gaSSáab	baggáal	shaghgháal

Vowels

Gulf Arabic vowels present no particular problem to an English speaker. There are three types of vowel: short vowels, long vowels and diphthongs:

short	**a i o u**
long	**aa ii oo uu**
diphthongs	**ay aw**

As the name implies, a long vowel (like a 'doubled' consonant) lasts longer than a short one: in English, 'cat' contains a short 'a' and 'cart' contains a long one. This distinction in vowel length is made in the spelling system used in this book by writing the long vowels as a doubled version of the short vowel. The precise phonetic value of any vowel (what it sounds like) depends to a large extent in Arabic on the consonants that surround it, and on its position in the word. There is also a certain amount of dialectal variation within the Gulf area. The notes below reflect the commonest type of pronunciation.

Letter	Hints on pronunciation
a	Like the 'e' in Southern English 'bed', this value of **a** usually occurs between any two Group 1 or 2 consonants, for example **jábal, cham, sámach**. It occurs at the end of words whose last consonant is from Group 1 or 2: **sána, dálla**.

Like Northern English 'a' in 'cat'. This value of **a** occurs wherever **gh, x, H, 9** or **q** precedes or follows **a**: **baHar, xast**. Finally, after these same consonants, the same value of **a** occurs: **lúgha**.

Like the vowel in English 'sob'. This value occurs whenever **a** precedes or follows **S, T, D** or **DH**, and in a few words when it occurs next to **r** or 'dark' **l**: **Tabíib, maHáTTa, rabb**.

aa	In Bahrain and Qatar **aa** almost always has the sound of the vowel in English 'father' (= a 'back' vowel), whatever the consonant environment. In other parts of the Gulf, it only has this back vowel when **S, T, D** or **DH** occur next to it – otherwise it is similar to the vowel in southern English 'pair' (= a 'front' vowel), for example **Saab** is pronounced the same in all dialects, but **baab** in Bahrain has a 'back' variety of **aa**, but in eastern Saudi Arabia and Kuwait, it has a 'front' variety.
i	Similar to 'i' in 'bit', unless at the end of a word. When **i** occurs next to one of the consonants **S, T, D** or **DH** it has a rather 'dull' sound. Thus **i** in **Tibb** 'medicine' sounds somewhat like the southern English pronunciation of the vowel in 'tub'. At the end of a word, **i** has the value of 'e' in 'be', for example in **báyti, gúuli**.
ii	Similar to the long vowel in 'seem'.
o	In the middle of a word, **o** sounds like the vowel in 'cot': **9ógub**. At the end of a word, it is like the 'o' in 'so': **kaazíino**.
oo	Like the long vowel in the Welsh pronunciation of 'no', or an extended version of the southern English vowel in 'bore'.
u	Like 'u' in northern English 'pub', 'cup'.
uu	The 'oo' vowel in English 'boo' is similar.

| **ay** | Like the diphthong in English 'bay', or, in some speakers' speech, more like the pure vowel in the French 'clé' ('key') but longer. |
| **aw** | Like the diphthong in 'mouth'. |

Pronunciation practice: vowels (Audio 1; 5)

Vowel	Consonant environment	Examples		
a	Group 1 and 2 consonants only	chalb	sámach	thalj
		fársha	'ákal	dazz
	gh x H 9 q	ghásal	náxal	9áraf
		báHar	bálagh	qámar
	S T D DH and sometimes r and l	Sábar	Dárab	báTal
		alláah	DHábi	rabb
aa		gaal	raaH	shaaf
		káatib	rayyáal	Sáafi
i (non-final)	non-emphatic	bint	siff	Híbir
	emphatic	Tibb	Sífir	Dírba
i (final)		bínti	Tábxi	búsTi
ii		Hiin	siim	fiik
o		9ógub	lo	kaazíino
oo		yoom	thoor	góola
		Soob	HooD	Soot
u		hum	kúbar	múhub
		Subb	Tub9áan	yíDrub
uu		byuut	yigúul	yiruuHúun
		Sufúuf	xuTúuT	maHDHúuDH
ay		bayt	baHráyn	sayf
		Tayr	bayD	Sayf
aw		náwas	gáalaw	9áwwar
		xálliSaw	HúrDaw	HífDHaw

Syllable types and stress

The stressed syllable in individual words of more than one syllable is marked superscript (e.g. á) throughout the text. When words are strung together to form sentences, these word stresses are maintained, but, obviously, the meaning that speakers wish to give their sentences leads them to stress some words more than others. An exhaustive treatment of sentence stress is beyond the scope of this book, but you will not go far wrong if you simply copy, quite slavishly, the examples given in the exercises. Gradually, you will acquire a feel for the rhythmic patterns of Arabic sentences through listening and practice. Word stress in Arabic depends on syllable structure. There are two kinds of syllable: short- (sh) and long (lo). In the examples below, C and V stand for 'consonant' and 'vowel'. In general, all Arabic syllables must start with a C, and all syllables must have a V in them.

		Example	*Syllable structure*	
Short syllables:				
CV or CCV	smícha	smi-cha	CCV-CV	(sh-sh)
CVC	Híjra	Hij-ra	CVC-CV	(sh-sh)
	sábab	sa-bab	CV-CVC	(sh-sh)
	shírbat	shir-bat	CVC-CVC	(sh-sh)
Three-syllables (all short):				
	báraka	ba-ra-ka	CV-CV-CV	(sh-sh-sh)
	warágtik	wa-rag-tik	CV-CVC-CVC	(sh-sh-sh)
	sim9áthum	sim-9at-hum	CVC-CVC-CVC	(sh-sh-sh)
	sharábna	sha-rab-na	CV-CVC-CV	(sh-sh-sh)
Long syllables:				
CVV or	gáalat	gaa-lat	CVV-CVC	(lo-sh)
CCVV	shgáalat	shgaa-lat	CCVV-CVC	(lo-sh)
CVVC or	guulúuh	guu-luuh	CVV-CVVC	(lo-lo)
CVVCC	muDáadd	mu-Daadd	CV-CVVCC	(sh-lo)
	baHráyn	baH-rayn	CVC-CVCC	(sh-lo)
CVCC	simá9t	si-ma9t	CV-CVCC	(sh-lo)

From these examples it can be seen that stress is assigned on the following basis:

1 If the word contains one long syllable only, that syllable must be stressed: **gáalat, shgáalat, muDáadd, baHráyn, simá9t**.

2 If the word contains two long syllables, the last one is stressed: **guulúuh**.

3 If the word contains no long syllable, then:
   (i) the ante-penultimate syllable is stressed in words of three or more 'open' syllables (i.e. that end in a vowel): **báraka**;
   (ii) the penultimate syllable is stressed in words of two syllables: **smícha, Híjra, sábab** and in three-syllable words if the penultimate syllable is 'closed' (i.e. ends in a consonant): **warágtik, sim9áthum, sharábna**.

These rules may appear unduly complicated at this stage, and there is no point in learning them by heart – a 'feel' for where stress should occur will come with practice. There is in fact a certain amount of variation in the placement of stress in certain words and types of phrase in any case (see Appendix 1(E)).

Stress exercise (Audio 1; 6)

Two short syllables:

Híjra, sím9at, shísmik, Hílba, fítna, gálam

Three short syllables:

1 all 'open'

báraka, xálaga, HáTaba, wáraga, gálami

2 penultimate 'closed'

simá9na, Darábtik, Hijráthum, tirástah, shuwándar

Two syllables, first one long:

ráayiH, káanaw, sháafat, máaltik

Two syllables, both long:

guulúuh, shaafóok, xaayfíin, HaaTTíin

Two syllables, second one long:

mudíir, baHráyn, ghashmárt, 9ishríin

Three or more syllables, at least one long:

kuwaytiyyíin, balaalíiT, yismaHúun, mudarrisíin, tistahlikíin, insiHáab, shifnáahum, Haddáada, isti9laamáat, mu9taqadáatah

Unit One

In this unit you will learn about:

- expressions of quantity, e.g. 'a bottle of milk', 'a dozen eggs'
- orders and requests, e.g. 'Come here!', 'Go!'
- how to say 'Please', 'Thank you' and 'Be so kind'

Language point

1.1 Expressions of quantity

Look at the way the Arabic words for 'cup', 'glass', 'tea' and 'coffee' are combined to form phrases:

glaas	'glass'	**chaay**	'tea'
finjáal	'cup' (Arab-style)	**gáhwa**	'coffee'

glaas chaay	'a glass of tea'
finjáal gáhwa	'a cup of coffee'

Now memorise the following words:

sandawíich	'sandwich'	**burtugáal**	'orange'
dárzan	'dozen'	**láHam**	'meat'
nuSS dárzan	'half-dozen'	**símich/samak**	'fish'
káylo	'kilo'	**Halíib**	'milk'
nuSS káylo	'half-kilo'	**bayD**	'eggs'
búTil	'bottle'	**jíbin**	'cheese'

Exercise 1.1

Translate the following phrases:

1 a half-kilo of meat	4 a kilo of fish
2 a bottle of milk	5 half-a-dozen oranges
3 a dozen eggs	6 a cheese sandwich

In phrases of quantity of this type, no Arabic words for 'a' and 'of' are needed. Note that, when the first word of the phrase ends in **-a**, for example **gúT9a** 'piece, chunk', a final **-t** is added to it before the second word. This **-t** is in fact a so-called 'feminine' ending, and most Arabic nouns ending in **-a** have this 'hidden' **t**, which shows up in 'quantity' phrases (and other types that we shall meet later). Such words are marked * in the Vocabularies. Here are some examples of phrases involving **-t**:

gúT9a	'a piece'	**gúT9at láHam**	'a piece of meat'
nítfa	'a bit'	**nítfat xúbuz**	'a bit of bread'
Hábba	'a grain'	**Hábbat 9aysh**	'a grain of rice'

Words like **bayD** 'eggs', and **símich** 'fish' are called 'collective' nouns: that is, they denote 'eggs' or 'fish' in general. If we wish to talk about 'one egg' or 'a fish', we add the **-a** feminine ending to form the so-called 'unit noun':

bayD	'eggs'	**báyDa**	'an egg'
símich	'fish'	**símicha**	'a fish'
xúbuz	'bread'	**xúbza**	'a loaf'

Language points

1.2 Orders and requests

In Arabic, as in English, we can ask people to do things by giving them one-word orders. For example, when addressing male speakers, the following forms are used:

9aT	'Give!'
jiib	'Bring!'
saww	'Make!'

| **ruuH** | 'Go!' |
| **ta9áal** | 'Come here!' |

If the person addressed is female, an **-i** is added:

9áTi	'Give (f.)!'
jíibi	'Bring (f.)!'
sáwwi	'Make (f.)!'
rúuHi	'Go (f.)!'
ta9áali	'Come (f.) here!'

If there are several people addressed, a **-u** is added:

9áTu	'Give (pl.)!'
jíibu	'Bring (pl.)!'
sáwwu	'Make (pl.)!'
rúuHu	'Go (pl.)!'
ta9áalu	'Come (pl.) here!'

To say 'give me!', we add the suffix **-ni** ('me') directly to these command words, which become **9áTni, 9aTíini, 9aTúuni** respectively. Note that the feminine ending **-i** and the plural ending **-u** is lengthened (and hence stressed) when **-ni** is suffixed to it.
    To say 'bring me!' or 'make (for) me!' we need to add not **-ni** but **lii** (or **líyyi**) ('to, for me') to the command words. Compare:

9áTni/9aTíini/9aTúuni   'Give me!'

and

saww/sáwwi/sawwúu lii (or **líyyi**)   'Make (for) me!'

The word **yállah!** is often added to give an extra note of urgency, e.g. **yállah, ruuH!** 'Just go, will you!', **yállah, saww!** 'Go on, do (it)!'.

1.3 'Please', 'Thank you', 'Be so kind'

Orders of the kind shown above are made more polite by adding the Arabic equivalent of 'please': **min fáDlik** (or **min fáDlak**) to men, **min fáDlich** (or **min fáDlach**) to women, and min **fáDlakum** to several people. Thus:

| **saww lii finjál gáhwa min fáDlak** | (to a man) |
| **sáwwi lii finjáal gáhwa min fáDlich** | (to a woman) |

The normal way of politely addressing a person by name, or calling his or her attention is to use the word **yaa** ('oh') followed by his or her name:

yaa 9áli, jiib lii nuSS káylo símich min fáDlak.
'Ali, bring me half-a-kilo of fish please.'

yaa záhra, 9aTíini nítfat xúbuz min fáDlich.
'Zahra, give me a bit of bread please.'

If you don't know the names of people you are addressing, call them **naas** 'people':

yaa naas, ta9áalu min fáDlakum!
'Come over here please, people!'

The commonest way of saying 'thank you' in Arabic is **shúkran**. But there are other ways that are typical of Gulf Arabic. You can say **ahsánt** to a man (literally 'you have done well'), **ahsánti** to a woman, and **aHsántu** to several people. This is usually said when someone has done you a favour or a good turn.

When you wish to invite someone politely to do something, or offer or pass something to them (a cigarette, a newspaper, a seat, etc.), it is polite to use a word that means 'be so kind!'. This is **tafáDDal!** to a man, with the usual **-i** added when addressing a woman and **-u** for the plural; for example, when offering a group of people some tea:

tafáDDalu chaay!
'Please (pl.) have some tea!'

 Exercise 1.2 (Audio 1; 7)

Read aloud and translate the following requests:

1 yaa áHmad, saww líyyi glaas chaay min fáDlak.

2 yaa láyla, 9aTíini nítfat símich min fáDlach.

3 yaa mHámmad, ruuH jiib lii gúuTi jigáara min fáDlik.

4 yaa 9abdállah, 9áTni finjáal gáhwa min fáDlik.

5 yaa sálwa, rúuHi jíibi líyyi dárzan burtugáal min fáDlich.

Exercise 1.3

Ask a man to do the following:

1 to bring you half-a-kilo of meat
2 to give you a bit of cheese
3 to go and make you a cheese sandwich

Ask a woman to do the following:
1 to make you a cup of coffee
2 to go and get you a glass of milk
3 to go and bring you a dozen eggs

Exercise 1.4

Imagine you are shopping and ask politely for the following items. Use
the Vocabulary for this unit to help you.

Male shopkeeper	Female shopkeeper
1 a box of matches	8 a bag of potatoes
2 a packet of salt	9 a kilo of onions
3 a bottle of cooking oil	10 a packet of soap
4 a bit of lettuce	11 a quarter-kilo of sugar
5 a half-kilo of rice	12 a kilo of dates
6 a packet of butter	13 a piece of meat
7 a quarter-kilo of tomatoes	14 a glass of water

Vocabulary

aHsant/i/u	thank you; much obliged	chiis	bag
báSal	onion(s)	dárzan	dozen
baTTíix	watermelon(s)	díhin	cooking oil
bayD	egg(s)	min fáDlik/ch/kum	please
burtugáal	orange(s)	finjáal	(small) coffee cup
búTil	bottle	gáhwa*	coffee
chaay	tea	glaas	glass
chibríit	matches	gúT9a*	piece

gúuTi	box; packet; tin	saww/i/u	make; do!
Hábba*	grain	símich	fish
Halíib	milk	shákkar	sugar
jíbin	cheese	shúkran	thank you
jigáara*	cigarette	shwáyya*	a little; a bit
jiib/i/u	bring!	tafáDDal/i/u	be so kind!
káylo	kilo	támar	dates
láHam	meat	TamáaT	tomato(es)
maay	water	ta9áal/i/u	come here!
milH	salt	uu or wi	and
nítfa*	a bit	xast	lettuce
nuSS	half	xúbuz	bread
putáyta	potato(es)	yaa	hey; oh
rub9	quarter	zíbid	butter
ruuH/i/u	go!	9aT/i/u	give!
Saabúun	soap	9aysh	rice
sandawíich	sandwich	9ínab	grape(s)

 ## Cultural point

In the Cultural points of each of the 20 units of this book, aspects of the history, culture and everyday life of the Gulf that are not dealt with in the grammatical sections will be explored, as far as possible through examples of how these practices are expressed in Gulf Arabic, such as dress, marriage, cooking, religious festivals and sport.

The Gulf States and the GCC

With the exception of Oman, whose independence dates from the expulsion of the Portuguese in 1650, the Gulf States, or **dúwal al-xalíij** as they are known in Arabic, all gained their political independence relatively recently: Kuwait in1961, Bahrain, Qatar and the United Arab Emirates (UAE) in the 1970s when the various treaty relationships each of them had with the United Kingdom came to an end. Their names, as pronounced in spoken Gulf Arabic, are **il-kwáyt** (or **l-ikwáyt**) 'Kuwait' ('**A**' on the map, see page 7), **il-baHráyn** 'Bahrain' ('**C**'), **gáTar** 'Qatar' ('**D**'), **il-imaaráat** 'the Emirates' ('**E**') and **9umáan** 'Oman' ('**F**'), which is also known to Omanis as **is-sálTana** 'the Sultanate'. The Kingdom

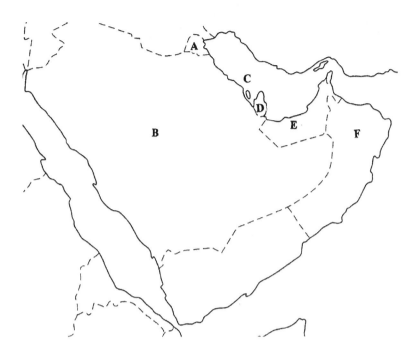

of Saudi Arabia ('**B**'), formed in 1932, part of whose coastline is on the Gulf, is usually known colloquially as **is-sa9úudiyya**, although among themselves Saudis often simply refer to it as **il-mámlaka** 'the kingdom'. However, this term is now potentially ambiguous since Bahrain also became a kingdom in 2002.

Contrary to popular belief, not all the Gulf States are oil-rich: Bahrain, although it was the first Gulf country to strike oil in the 1930s, never had much oil and now earns a large proportion of its export receipts from refining the oil production of other Gulf countries, as well as producing aluminium; and, in 2005, only about 6 per cent of the GDP of Dubai, one of the seven emirates that make up the UAE, was derived from oil and gas, its main high earning activities being trade, re-export and financial services.

Despite their differences, the Gulf States share many things – a dialect of Arabic that differs little from Kuwait in the north to the UAE in the south (though there are some marked differences in Oman); a similar economic history, in which a dependence on pearl production until 1930s shifted to oil; a long tradition of maritime trade with India, East Africa and the Far East; and a shared set of social and cultural values. In 1981, the Gulf States joined together to form the Gulf Cooperation Council (GCC), known in Arabic as **májlis at-ta9áawun al-xalíiji**. This is basically a trade bloc that aims to increase inter-state cooperation in finance, trade, tourism and scientific research, and to present a common 'Gulf approach' to problems of mutual concern. Yemen is not at the moment part of the GCC, but has applied to join.

 ## Reading Arabic

Below you will find the names of some Gulf States and cities written in the Arabic script. Using the introduction to the Arabic script in Appendix 2, try to match the Arabic names to the English equivalents.

 ## Exercise 1.5

Many Gulf place names consist of the definite article ال 'the' followed by the name. Here are some examples. Match them correctly to the English names on the right, which are jumbled up.

Arabic name	English name
1 الكويت	The Emirates
2 الرياض	Bahrain
3 الدوحة	Kuwait
4 البحرين	Riyadh
5 الإمارات	Doha

 ## Exercise 1.6

These Gulf place names do not have the definite article. Match them correctly with the English names.

Arabic name	English name
1 دبي	Qatar
2 مسقط	Dubai
3 دمام	Abu Dhabi
4 قطر	Muscat
5 ابو ظبي	Dammam

Many Arab place names, like English ones, have meanings. 'Muscat', for example, literally means 'anchorage', as does the name of its twin town 'Mutrah'. 'Al-Bahrain' means 'the two seas', and the name is traditionally explained as referring to the salt water of the sea that surrounds the Bahrain islands, and the fresh water below its land, which was once abundant. 'Al-Kuwait' means 'the little fort', while Al-Riyadh means 'the gardens' or 'the meadows'. 'Al-Doha', in Gulf Arabic, is one of the words for 'the bay'. 'Abu Dhabi' literally means 'father of the gazelle', 'father' and 'mother' in Gulf Arabic often being used to denote a place where something is found in abundance: so, once upon a time, Abu Dhabi must have been a place of plentiful game. Similarly, in Bahrain, the district of the capital city Manama (which means 'sleeping place'), called Umm il-Hasam 'the mother of pebbles', refers to part of the shoreline near Al-Jufair where once there were many pebbles to be found; and perhaps the Kuwaiti island of Umm il-Namal 'the mother of ants' was a place where there once were many ants!

Unit Two

In this unit you will learn about:

- the Arabic equivalent of 'the'
- the 'dual', which is a way of talking about two things, e.g. 'two cars'
- the plural: by using suffixes and 'broken' plurals

Language point

2.1 The Arabic equivalent of 'the'

The Gulf Arabic for 'the' is **il**, and it is placed, as in English, before its noun:

glaas	'(a) glass'	**il-glaas**	'the glass'
inglíizi	'(an) English(man)'	**il-inglíizi**	'the Englishman'
muhándis	'(an) engineer'	**il-muhándis**	'the engineer'

When **il** is placed before some nouns, its **l** assimilates to (that is, becomes the same sound as) the first letter of that noun, for example **suug** 'market' becomes **is-suug** 'the market' (not **il-suug**). When this assimilation occurs, it is important to hold the double consonant for what seems to an English ear an unnaturally long time. Assimilation of **l** occurs before nouns that begin with:

t th d dh z r s sh S D T DH n l

but does not occur before nouns that begin with:

b p ch j x H k f g gh 9 q m h w y

Thus we have **is-sayyáara** 'the car', **iT-Tayyáara** 'the aeroplane', **ir-riyáD** 'Riyad' (lit. 'the-Riyad'), but **il-baab** 'the door', **il-jaríida** 'the newspaper', **il-kwáyt** 'Kuwait' (lit. 'the-Kuwait').

Exercise 2.1

Make the following nouns definite, assimilating the **l** where necessary. Be careful about pronunciation, holding the doubled letters twice as long as single letters.

1 mudíir	boss	6 sammáach	fisherman
2 farráash	servant	7 gaSSáab	butcher
3 rayyáal	man	8 mudárris	teacher
4 poolíis	policemen	9 9áamil	worker
5 sikirtíir	secretary	10 shárika	company; firm

Language point

2.2 The 'dual'

When, in Arabic, we wish to talk about two of a thing (rather than three or more), we use a special form of the plural called the 'dual'. To form the dual of a noun, the suffix **-ayn** is added to it. Thus we have **rayyáal** 'a man' and **rayyaaláyn** 'two men', **il-baab** 'the door' and **il-baabáyn** 'the two doors'. If the noun ends in **-a**, the 'hidden' **t**, which we noted in Unit One in phrases like **gúT9at láHam** 'a piece of meat', again appears:

shárika	'a company'
sharikatáyn	'two companies'
Is-sayyáara	'the car'
Is-sayyaaratáyn	'the two cars'
gúT9at laHam	'a piece of meat'
guT9atáyn láHam	'two pieces of meat'

If the noun ends in **i**, for example **inglíizi** 'English', **-yy-** is inserted
between the **-i** and the suffix **-ayn**:

il-inglíizi   'the Englishman'   **míSri**   'an Egyptian'

il-ingliiziyyáyn 'the two Englishmen'   **miSriyyáyn** 'two Egyptians'

Exercise 2.2

Change the following nouns into the correct dual form. Remember that
the stress must fall on **-ayn** as it is the last long syllable in each word.

1	shárika	a company	8	is-sikirtíir	the secretary
2	dárzan	a dozen	9	il-muhándis	the engineer
3	gúT9a	a piece	10	is-smicha	the fish
4	baHráyni	a Bahraini	11	il-mukáan	the place
5	gúuTi	a packet	12	il-finjáal	the cup
6	jigáara	a cigarette	13	il-mikáaniki	the mechanic
7	glaas	a glass	14	il-bayt	the house

 Language point

2.3 The plural

In Arabic, nouns form their plurals (that is, more than two) in two basic
ways: by adding a suffix, or by changing the vowel pattern within the
word. In English, most nouns form their plurals by the first method –
we simply add **-s** or **-es** – and there are only a few nouns, such as
'mouse' and 'louse', that form their plurals through vowel change.
Arabic is unlike English in that a very large number of nouns – certainly
the majority – form their plurals by vowel changes rather than suffixation.
The nouns that pluralise by adding a suffix can be divided into three
groups according to the suffix used, and examples are provided below.
Nouns that pluralise by internal vowel change – the so-called 'broken'
plurals – do so according to a variety of different patterns. The problem
for the beginner is that you cannot predict by looking at the singular
of a noun which of the plural patterns applies to it: it is best to learn
what the plural of each noun is at the time you learn the singular.

At first this may seem a daunting task, but in fact the number of plural patterns in common use is relatively small, and the problem will diminish as you progress.

■ Plurals by suffixation

1 THE SUFFIX -iin

Many nouns denoting professions and occupations, particularly those that begin with the prefix **mu-**, form their plurals this way. The **-iin** suffix is only used with nouns denoting human beings, for example:

mudárris	'teacher'	**mudarrisíin**	'teachers'
muhándis	'engineer'	**muhandisíin**	'engineers'
muqáawil	'contractor'	**muqaawilíin**	'contractors'
muHássin	'barber'	**muHassiníin**	'barbers'
mikáaniki	'mechanic'	**mikaanikiyyíin**	'mechanics'
shúrTi	'policeman'	**shurTiyyíin**	'policemen'
SáHafi	'journalist'	**SaHafiyyíin**	'journalists'

Notice that, if the singular ends in **-i**, **-yy-** is inserted before the **-iin** suffix, just as it is before the **-ayn** 'dual' suffix.

2 THE SUFFIX -aat

This suffix is the feminine equivalent of **-iin**, and is used where a *wholly female* group is being referred to (**-iin** is used where the group is mixed male and female). Thus:

mudárrisa	'female teacher'	**mudarrisáat**	'female teachers'
shurTíyya	'policewoman'	**shurTiyyáat**	'policewomen'

The same suffixes are used for the plurals of nouns denoting nationality or origin:

kuwáyti	'Kuwaiti'	**kuwaytiyyíin**	'Kuwaitis'
kuwaytíyya	'Kuwaiti woman'	**kuwaytiyyáat**	'Kuwaiti women'

3 THE SUFFIX -iyya

There are a few nouns, again denoting professions or occupations, that pluralise by adding the suffix **-iyya**. Most of them are borrowings from other languages, for example:

dráywil	'driver'	draywilíyya	'drivers'
sikirtíir	'secretary'	sikirtiiríyya	'secretaries'
lóofar	'layabout'	loofaríyya	'layabouts'

4 THE SUFFIX **-aat** WITH INANIMATE NOUNS

In addition to the use of **-aat** noted above, it is also used to pluralise many inanimate nouns. Some of these have the feminine ending **-a**, while many others are foreign borrowings, for example:

sayyáara	'car'	sayyaaráat	'cars'
shárika	'company'	sharikáat	'companies'
baaS	'bus'	baaSáat	'buses'
sandawíich	'sandwich'	sandawiicháat	'sandwiches'
káylo	'kilogram'	kaylowáat	'kilograms'

■ 'Broken' plurals

A particularly striking feature of Arabic is its system of roots and vowel patterns, which constitute the 'bricks and mortar' of the language. To the root **k t b**, which has the basic meaning 'writing', different vowel patterns can be applied to form words that modify this basic meaning in (mostly) predictable ways.

For example, we can derive:

		Pattern		
kitáab	'book'	CiCaaC	=	Noun
káatib	'clerk; one who writes'	CaaCiC	=	Agent noun
máktab	'office; place where writing is done'	maCCaC	=	Noun of place
maktúub	'written; letter'	maCCuuC	=	Passive participle

Note that the root consonants always remain in the same order. To make the plural of most nouns, a new vowel pattern is applied to the root consonants of the singular form. Thus **kitáab** has the plural **kútub**, **káatib** the plural **kuttáab** (note the doubling of the middle consonant), **máktab** has **makáatib** and **maktúub** has **makaatíib**. Some of the commoner plural patterns are exemplified below.

■ Singular patterns

1 Singular CaCCaaC plural CaCaaCiiC

2 Singular CaaCiC plural CuCCaaC

These two patterns always denote jobs, professions or occupations:

farráash	/ faraaríish	'servant'
xabbáaz	/ xabaabíiz	'baker'
sammáach	/ samaamíich	'fisherman'
najjáar	/ najaajíir	'carpenter'
gaSSáab	/ gaSaaSíib	'butcher'
rayyáal	/ rayaayíil	'man'
xáadim	/ xuddáam	'servant'
káatib	/ kuttáab	'clerk'
9áamil	/ 9ummáal	'worker'
Háakim	/ Hukkáam	'ruler'
táajir	/ tujjáar	'merchant'
záari9	/ zurráa9	'farmer'

Some common patterns that apply to many different singular patterns:

■ Plural patterns

3 The plural pattern aCCaaC

wálad /	awláad	'boy'	qísim /	aqsáam	'section; department'
gálam /	agláam	'pen'	suug /	aswáag	'market'
fílim /	afláam	'film'	kuub /	akwáab	'cup'

4 The plural pattern CuCuuC

shayx /	shuyúux	'sheikh'	Saff /	Sufúuf	'class-room; row'
sayf /	suyúuf	'sword'	bayt /	buyúut	'house'
fils /	fulúus	'money'	galb /	gulúub	'heart'

5 The plural pattern CaCaaCiC

dárzan	/	daráazin	'dozen'
dáftar	/	dafáatir	'notebook'

dáxtar	/	daxáatir	'physician'
máSna9	/	maSáani9	'factory'
máblagh	/	mabáaligh	'sum of money'
máktab	/	makáatib	'office; desk'

Exercise 2.3 (Audio 1; 8)

Practise reading aloud the requests below, and translate them into English:

1 jiib lii d-dáftar!

2 ruuH il-máktab min fáDlak!

3 sáwwi líyyi sandawiicháyn jíbin min fáDlich!

4 9áTni gálam!

5 xudh is-sayyáara u ruuH!

6 ruuH il-xabbáaz uu jiib lii xubzáyn!

7 xudh il-fulúus!

8 saww lii finjáal gáhwa yaa áHmad!

9 9áTni l-akwáab!

10 ruuH il-gaSSáab uu jiib líyyi kaylowáyn láHam!

11 ruuH il-bayt!

12 ruuH il-mudíir min fáDlak u jiib lii l-kútub!

Note (nos. 1, 9, 12) that, when il follows a word ending in a vowel, its i is dropped.

Exercise 2.4

Take sentences 1, 7 and 11 in Exercise 2.3 as your model.

(a) Tell someone male to:

    1 Take the sugar!

    2 Go to the barber!

    3 Bring me a little water!

    4 Take the sandwiches!

    5 Go to the market, please!

    6 Bring me the notebooks!

7 Take two bottles of milk!

8 Go to the two Englishmen!

(b) Tell someone female to:

9 Bring the pens please!

10 Take two packets of cigarettes!

11 Go to the doctor!

12 Take a bit of rice!

13 Bring the cups!

14 Bring the two books please!

15 Go to the women teachers!

Vocabulary

baab/abwáab	door	lóofar(iyya)	layabout
baaS(aat)	bus	máblagh/mabáaligh	sum of money
baHráyni(yyiin)	Bahraini		
bayt/buyúut	house	máktab/makáatib	office; desk
dáftar/dafáatir	notebook	maktúub/	
dáxtar/daxáatir	doctor	makaatíib	letter
dráywil(iyya)	driver	máSna9/maSáani9	factory
farráash/faraaríish	servant; cleaner	mikáaniki (yyin)	mechanic
		míSri (yyin)	Egyptian
fílim/afláam	film	mudárris(iin)	teacher
fils/fulúus	money	mudíir(iin)	boss; director
gálam/agláam	pen		
galb/gulúub	heart	muhándis(iin)	engineer
gaSSáab/gaSaaSíib	butcher	muHássin(iin)	barber
Háakim/Hukkáam	ruler (of a country)	mukáan(aat)	place; spot
		muqáawil(iin)	contractor
inglíizi(yyiin)	English(man)	najjáar/najaajíir	carpenter
jaríida/jaráayid	newspaper	poolíis(iyya)	policeman
káatib/kuttáab	clerk	qísim/aqsáam	department
kitáab/kútub	book	rayyál/rayaayíil	man
kuub/akwáab	cup	sammáach/	fisherman
kuwáyti(yyiin)	Kuwaiti	samaamíich	

sayf/suyúuf	sword; seashore	shúrTi(yyiin)	policeman
sayyáara*/sayaayíir	car	táajir/tujjáar	merchant
sikirtíir(iyya)	secretary	Tayyáara*(aat)	aeroplane
suug/aswáag	market	wálad/awláad	boy
Saff/Sufúuf	classroom; row	xáadim/xuddáam	servant
SáHafi(yyiin)	journalist	xabbáaz/ xabaabíiz	baker
shárika*(aat)	company; firm	xudh, f. xúdhi	take!
		záari9/zurráa9	farmer
shayx/shuyúux	sheikh	9áamil/9ummáal	worker; labourer

 Cultural point

History (1): the Portuguese

The first of the Western powers to take an interest in the Gulf were the Portuguese in the early sixteenth century. Their main interest was to protect the newly established trade routes to their colonies in India and the Far East from Gulf pirates. Over the course of the sixteenth century they built forts in Bahrain and the southern Gulf in which they maintained permanent garrisons, finally being evicted from the Gulf for good in the mid-seventeenth century. The so-called 'Portuguese Fort' in Bahrain was in fact built on top of the ruins of earlier buildings that go back thousands of years to times when Bahrain was governed from Babylon in southern Iraq, and known as Dilmun. In Muscat, the two imposing forts of Jalali and Merani, finished in 1587, still dominate the entrance to the original harbour.

The Portuguese left little in the way of a linguistic legacy to Gulf Arabic. The only word of Portuguese origin that is still in common use today is **burtugáal**, literally 'Portugal', the name given by Gulf Arabs, and now Arabs in general, to the sweet eating orange that the Portuguese brought with them from the orange groves of the Algarve (itself a corruption of the Arabic **al-gharb** 'the west'). The much older Gulf word for 'orange', **naranj**, the source of the word for 'orange' in most European languages, came originally from northern India and in the Gulf only denotes the bitter inedible orange that is used there as a food flavouring, and that we in Europe call the 'Seville orange' and use to make marmalade. The older Gulf generations still use one or two other Portuguese borrowings, though these have now dropped out of use among the more educated younger people. In Bahrain, the word for a 'table' or 'desk', for example, used to be **mayz**, from Portuguese **mesa** 'table'. Other examples of words that the Portuguese gave the Gulf are **báaldi** 'bucket' (which is the origin of the Indian culinary term 'balti', the word having also been borrowed into Indian languages), **biib** 'pipe; small drum or cask', from Portuguese **pipa** with the same meaning, which also came into English in the expression 'a pipe (= a small cask) of port wine', and **gáTu** 'cat', which was used in the popular Gulf name for a British brand of cigarettes of the 1960s whose proprietary name was 'Craven A', but which was known in the Gulf as **abu gáTu** 'the one with the cat on' (lit. 'father of the cat') because of the black cat logo on the packet. There were once also quite a number of Portuguese terms for the parts of wooden ships in common use, but these have now been consigned, along with the ancient crafts associated with them, to Gulf museums and heritage theme parks.

Reference for further reading: Sir Charles Belgrave, *The Pirate Coast*, G. Bell & Sons, New York, 1966.

Jalali Fort, Muscat, in 2005

Reading Arabic

Many street signs in the Gulf, particularly restaurant signs, often contain English words that have simply been transliterated (rather than translated) into Arabic. Look at the two examples below, taken from shop and restaurant signs in Qatar.

In this sign, which is the name of the restaurant, 'Hollywood' is simply transliterated into Arabic, in large letters directly above the English. Reading the Arabic from right to left, we have ﻪ for 'H', و stands for 'o', ﻝ for 'll', ﻴ for 'y', و for 'w' and ﺪ for 'd'. But the Arabic word, as actually written, looks like 'Holywd'. This is because double letters, such as English 'll', are not normally written double in Arabic; and notice that the letter و can stand for English 'w' as well as vowels like 'o'. Sometimes, as in و ﺪ at the end of the word, which is simply 'wd' in Arabic, the English vowel between the 'w' and the 'd' is not represented, because short vowel sounds are not normally represented in the Arabic script.

In the other word in this sign, the word 'saloon' is transliterated into Arabic. Here the word starts with the letter ﺺ , one of the two letters in Arabic that can represent English 's'. The letter alif, ﺍ , follows it: this sign represents the 'a' sound of the English word. An ﻝ follows it for English 'l', and then we have و for 'oo' and finally ﻥ for 'n'. So the Arabic reads 's-a-l-oo-n'.

Look at another sign, this time from a baker's shop selling sweets and pastries:

The sign says 'Jolly Bee', with the English again transliterated in the Arabic version of the name above it. This time, the Arabic script is a bit more ornate (it's called 'Kufic script'). From right to left it begins with ج for 'j', then, once again, و stands for 'o', ل for 'll', and a rather ornate ي for the 'y' at the end. 'Bee' consists of ب for 'b', followed again by ي, which this time stands not for 'y', but for the 'ee' sound of 'bee'.

Exercise 2.5

Look at the list on page 22. It lists the satellite channels available in a Gulf hotel room, in English and in Arabic. In all of the ten cases where the English name has been blacked out, the Arabic equivalent on the right-hand side of the card is simply a transliteration of the English name of the channel on the left, like the 'Hollywood' and 'Jolly Bee' examples we have just looked at. The first one blacked out, Channel 4, is 'BBC'. See if you can work out the names of the English channels for numbers 5, 6, 11, 13, 15, 22, 23, 24 and 25.

English	No.	Arabic
Qatar	1	قطر
Al Jazeera News	2	الجزيرة الاخبارية
CNBC Arabia	3	سي ان بي سي العربية
▮▮▮▮	4	بي بي سي
▮▮▮▮	5	سي ان ان
▮▮▮▮	6	يورونيوز
Bloomberg TV	7	بلوم برع الاقتصادية
Dubai	8	دبي
Kuwait	9	كويت
Abu Dhabi	10	ابو ظبي
▮▮▮▮	11	ام بي سي
Future	12	المستقبل
▮▮▮▮	13	ل بي سي
ESC (Egypt)	14	المصرية
▮▮▮▮	15	روتانا سينما
Rotana Zaman	16	روتانا زمان
Al Jazeera Children	17	الجزيرة للاطفال
MBC 3	18	ام بي سي الاطفال
MBC 4	19	ام بي سي برامج
MBC 2	20	ام بي سي افلام
One TV	21	وان تي في
▮▮▮▮	22	سوبر موفي
▮▮▮▮	23	موفي تايم
▮▮▮▮	24	ستار
▮▮▮▮	25	دريم
Melody Arabia	26	اغاني عربي
Melody Hits	27	اغاني منوعة
Zee Music	28	الاغاني z
Al Jazeera Sport	29	الجزيرة الرياضية
Fox Sport	30	فوكس للرياضة
TV 5	31	تي في 5 الفرنسية
VOX	32	فوكس الالمانية
RTL	33	ار تي ال الالمانية
RAI UNO	34	راي اونو الايطالية
CCTVI	35	سي سي تي في

List of satellite channels available (for Exercise 2.5)

Unit Three

Language point

3.1 'How much?/How many?

kam or its variant **cham** is the Gulf Arabic word for 'how much/many', and it is used with *singular* nouns:

kam/chám Halíib?	'How much milk?'
kam/chám rayyáal?	'How many men?'
kam/cham káylo?	'How many kilos?'

The words **hast** (used mainly in Bahrain, now considered rather old fashioned), **aku** (used in Kuwait), and **fii** (used almost everywhere) all mean 'there is/are', and they are often used with **kam/cham** in questions:

kám sayyáara hást?	'How many cars are there?'
áku kam qisim?	'How many departments are there?'
chám 9áamil fii?	'How many workers are there?'

If the answer to such questions as these is that 'there isn't/aren't any', the negative word **maa** ('not') is used: **maa hast, máaku, maa**

fii. There is also **maa mish**, with the same meaning, used mainly in Bahrain, and there is even a fifth possibility, **maa shay**, used in Oman. The most general, least localised expression is **maa fii**. All of these phrases may occur before or after the noun. Thus, in reply to:

kám náas fíi?   'How many people are there?'

all of the following are possible negative replies:

máa haśt náas/náas máa hást
máa fíi náas/náas máa fíi
máa mísh náas/náas máa mish   'There aren't any people.'
máaku náas/náas máaku
máa shay náas/náas máa shay

Note that, although the noun that follows the word for 'how much' is in the singular (except for collective nouns such as **Halíib**, **jíbin** and **naas**, which have no singular), the noun that follows **maa hast/fii/mish/shay** or **máaku** is in the plural:

– **chám rayyáal fíi?**	'How many men are there?'
– **rayaayíil máa fíi**	'There aren't any men.'
– **aku kam gláas?**	'How many glasses are there?'
– **máaku glaasáat**	'There aren't any glasses.'

Using the singular noun in reply would mean 'there' isn't a single ...', for example **máaku gláas** 'there isn't a single glass' and **9aamil maa shay** 'there isn't a single workman'.

Exercise 3.1

Translate the following short exchanges using **maa hast/fii/mish/shay** or **máaku**:

1 – How many notebooks are there?
   – There aren't any notebooks at all.
2 – How many policemen are there?
   – There aren't any at all.
3 – How much meat is there?
   – There isn't any meat.
4 – How many women are there?
   – There are no women.

5 – How many bottles are there?
   – There aren't any bottles at all.

Exercise 3.2

Look at the following exchange:

   – **fii láHam?**   'Is there any meat?
   – **lá, máa fíi il yóom**   'No, there isn't any today.'
or
   – **áy, fíi**   'Yes, there is.'

Now translate the following exchanges, using **(maa) fii**, etc.

1 – Is there any bread?
   – Yes there is.
2 – Are there any onions?
   – No, there aren't today.
3 – Are there any people here?
   – No, there aren't any here today.
4 – Are there any teachers there?
   – Yes, there are.
5 – Are there any doctors here?
   – No, there aren't.

Language point

3.2 Prices

When asking the price of something, use **bi chám/kam** ('for how much')
rather than simple **kam/cham**. Look at these examples:

   il-xúbuz bi chám?   'How much is bread?'
                              (lit. 'the bread for how much?')

   il-láHam bi chám il-káylo? 'How much is a kilo of meat?'
                              (lit. 'the meat for how much the kilo?')

il-Halíib bi chám il-búTil?   'How much is a bottle of milk?'
is-smíit bi chám il-xáysha?   'How much is a sack of cement?'

Exercise 3.3

Translate:

1 How much is a dozen eggs?
2 How much is a bottle of cooking oil?
3 How much is a kilo of oranges?
4 How much is a packet of cigarettes?
5 How much is a bag of potatoes?
6 How much is a box of matches?
7 How much is a sack of rice?
8 How much is a bottle of Pepsi?
9 How much is a glass of tea?
10 How much is a kilo of prawns?

Language point

3.3 Numbers 1 to 10

The numbers 1 to 10 have both a masculine and feminine form in Gulf Arabic, as follows:

Masculine	Feminine	
wáaHid	wáHda	one
ithnáyn	thintáyn	two
thaláath	thaláatha(t)	three
árba9	árba9a(t)	four
xams	xámsa(t)	five
sitt	sítta(t)	six
sab9	sáb9a(t)	seven
thamáan	thamáanya(t)	eight
tísa9	tís9a(t)	nine
9áshar	9áshra(t)	ten

A peculiarity of Arabic is that feminine numbers are used to enumerate masculine nouns, and masculine numbers to enumerate feminine nouns! Nouns can be feminine either by *meaning*, for example **bint** 'girl', **uxt** 'sister', **umm** 'mother', or feminine by *grammatical category*, and ending in **-a**, for example **shárika** 'company', **sayyáara** 'car' or, in a few cases that have to be learnt by heart, by *convention*, for example **riiH** 'wind'. Here are some examples:

xáms sayyaaráat	'five cars'	**xámsa rayaayíil**	'five men'
thaláath banáat	'three girls'	**9áshra kútub**	'ten books'
árba9 niswáan	'four women'	**sáb9a mudarrisíin**	'seven teachers'

If the plural of a masculine noun begins with a vowel, the 'hidden' **t** (in brackets in the list above) is sounded for each pronunciation:

síttat awláad	'six boys'	**sáb9at áshhur**	'seven months'
(not **sítta awlád**)			

thamáanyat ayyáam	'eight days'	**thaláathat anfáar**	'three persons'

The words for 'one' and 'two' are exceptional in two ways. First, they normally *follow* the noun they enumerate and, second, they are of the same gender as the noun they follow, thus:

wálad wáaHid	'one boy'	**bínt wáHda**	'one girl'

As we saw in 2.2, we would normally translate 'two boys' and 'two girls' by using the 'dual' form **waladáyn**, **bintáyn**. Sometimes, however, **ithnáyn** and **thintáyn** are used with the normal plural of these words, thus:

waladáyn	} 'two boys'	**bintáyn**	} 'two girls'
awláad ithnáyn		**banáat thintáyn**	

Numbers are often used in conversation with the noun they enumerate omitted:

cham rayyáal hast?	'How many men are there?'
xámsa (understood: **rayaayíil**)	'Five.'

cham bint fii?	'How many girls are there?'
thaláath (understood: **banáat**)	'Three.'

aku kam mudárrisa?	'How many women teachers are there?'
thintáyn	'Two.'
cham wálad fii?	'How many boys are there?'
wáaHid	'One.'

The phrase **kam/cham wáaHid?** (lit. 'how many one?') is often used when asking about how many there are of something already referred to:

fii kútub wáayid íhni	'There are a lot of books here.'
kam wáaHid fii?	'How many (exactly)?'

 Dialogue 3.1

(Audio 1; 9)

Read and translate the following dialogue. Practise reading it aloud, paying special attention to the stressed syllables.

A hast cham káatib fish-shárika?
B tís9a kuttáab.
A uu cham sikirtíir?
B fii sitt sikirtiiríyya.
A nzáyn, hast faraaríish bá9ad?
B ay wállah, fii faraaríish thnáyn.
A uu draywilíyya ... kam fii?
B wállah, maa mish draywilíyya il-Hiin.
A nzayn ... uu fii 9ummáal?
B ay ná9am.
A cham wáaHid fii?
B 9áshra.

 Exercise 3.4

Translate into Arabic:

1 – How many boys are there in the class?
   – Nine.
2 – How many days are there in the week?
   – Seven.

3 – How many rooms are there in the house?
   – Five rooms and two bathrooms.
4 – How many engineers are there in the company?
   – There aren't any.
5 – How much money is there in the wallet?
   – Seven dinars.

Language point

3.4 Greetings

Greeting someone in Arabic can be a somewhat elaborate business, particularly in the Gulf. As in English, there are standard formulas roughly equivalent to 'How d'you do?', 'How are you?', 'Pleased to meet you', etc., but in Arabic there are a much larger number of them, and they vary with the degree of formality of the situation. We note here only the commonest and most useful expressions.

At the most formal end of the scale, especially when greeting a number of people in a group (say on entering a room or office), one says:

> **is-saláam 9aláykum**   'Peace be upon you.'

to which the reply is:

> **uu 9aláykum is-saláam**   'And peace be upon you.'

Less formally, especially with friends and acquaintances, one says:

or   **áhlan!**
     áhlan wa sáhlan!   } 'Welcome! Hello! Hi!'

to which the reply may be:

or   **áhlan biik/biich!**
or   **áhlan marHába!**   } 'Welcome! Hello! Hi!'
     yaa hála!

The last of these three has a particularly 'Gulf' flavour.

After the initial exchange, one asks about the person's health:

chayf il Haal?	⎫	(lit. 'How is the state?')
chayf Háalik/ich?	⎬ 'How are you?'	(lit. 'How is your state?')
shlóonak/ach?	⎭	(lit. 'What is your colour?')

A number of replies are possible, which may be used singly or in combination:

il Hámdu lilláah!		'Praise be to God!'
bi xayr!	⎫ 'Good!'	
zayn!	⎬	
állah yisálmik/ich!	⎭	'God save you!'

After replying to the enquiry after one's health, one then in turn asks after the enquirer's health. It is quite common for the greeting sequence to go on for some time, with the same questions about the other person's health being repeated in different forms! The following might be a typical informal sequence:

- **áhlan, áhlan yaa mHámmad!**
  Hello, Muhammad!

- **yaa hála, yaa jáasim! chayf Háalak?**
  Hello, Jasim! How are you?

- **il Hámdu lilláah, zayn! shlóonak?**
  Praise be to God! Well! How are you?

- **bi xayr, shlóonak ínt?**
  Well! How are you?

- **állah yisálmik**
  God save you!

When taking leave of someone, one normally says:

fi amáan illáah
'in the safe-keeping of God'

to which the reply is usually:

ma9a s-saláama
'farewell' (lit. 'with safety')

Dialogue 3.2

Read aloud the following dialogue and translate it.

9ind il-gaSSáab 'At the butcher's' (Audio 1; 10)

CUSTOMER is-saláam 9aláykum.
BUTCHER wa 9aláykum is-saláam.
C   il-yoom fii láHam bágar?
B   ay ná9am fii.
C   il-káylo bi cham?
B   dinaaráyn uu nuSS.
C   nzáyn, 9áTni nuSS káylo min fáDlak.
B   insháallah ... u fii shay bá9ad?
C   hast dajáaj?
B   la, dajáaj il-yoom máa mish. báachir insháallah.
C   nzáyn. fi amáan illáah.
B   má9a s-saláama.

Exercise 3.5

Using the dialogue above as a model, imagine you are **9ind il baggáal** – at the greengrocer's. Make questions along the following lines:

(a) Are there any _____ today?

(b) How much per _____ are they?

(c) Give me _____.

(d) And do you have any _____?

    1 (a) onions (b) bag (c) a bag (d) potatoes

    2 (a) apples (b) kilo (c) half a kilo (d) oranges

    3 (a) eggs (b) dozen (c) two dozen (d) grapes

    4 (a) milk (b) bottle (c) three bottles (d) cheese

    5 (a) rice (b) sack (c) four bags (d) sugar

Vocabulary

áhlan wa sáhlan	welcome	il-Hiin	now
aku/máaku (KWT)	there is/are; there isn't/aren't	Híjra*/Híjar	room
		íhni	here
alláah	God	insháallah	God willing
amáan	security	ínta	you (m. sing.)
árba9	four	ithnáyn	two
ay	yes	la	no
báachir	tomorrow	maa	not
bágar	cows; cattle	maa mish (BAH)	there isn't/ aren't
baggáal/ bagaagíil	greengrocer	mára*/niswáan	woman
bá9ad	more; as well; still; yet	márHaba	welcome
		bil-márra*	at all
bint/banáat	girl	má9a	with
búTil/bTáala	bottle	míHfaDHa*/ maHáafiDH	wallet
cham/kam	how much/ many?	naas	people
bi cham	for how much?	náfar/anfáar	person
chayf/kayf	how?	ná9am	yes
dáaxil	inside	nzayn	OK, right
dajáaj/dyáay	chicken	riiH (f.)/riyáaH	wind
diináar/danaaníir	dinar	rubyáan	prawns
fi	in; at	sab9	seven
fii/maa fii	there is/are; there isn't/aren't	saláam	peace; tranquillity
ghársha*/ aghráash	bottle	saláama*	safety
		sitt	six
yaa hála	hello, welcome	smiit	cement
hast/maa hast (BAH)	there is/are; there isn't/ aren't	subúu9/asaabíi9	week
		sháhar/áshur	month
		shay/maa shay (OM)	there is/are; there isn't/ aren't
hunáak	over there		
Haal/aHwáal	condition; state	shloon	how?
il-Hamdu lilláah	Praise be to God	tísa9	nine
		thaláath	three
Hammáam(aat)	bathroom; toilet	thamáan	eight
		umm/ummaháat	mother

uxt/axawáat	sister	**xáysha*/xiyáash**	sack
wáaHid	one	**yoom/ayyáam**	day
wáayid/waajid	a lot; many	**il-yoom**	today
xams	five	**zayn/zayníin**	good
bi xayr	good; well	**9áshar**	ten

Cultural point

Food and cooking

Newcomers to the Gulf could be forgiven for thinking that there is no such thing as 'Gulf cuisine', and it is true that the area does not have the culinary history of long-established cities such as Damascus and Beirut. Lebanese/Syrian restaurants abound in the Gulf, serving the traditional dips and salads – **HúmmuS**, **báaba ghanúuj**, **mtábbal**, etc.– for which the Levant is justly famed, as well as **shuwarma** and **kabáab** meat sandwiches. The fast food (**wájba xafíifa**) industry serves its **kayafsii** ('KFC'), **hambúrgar** ('hamburger') and **bábsii** ('Pepsi') just as it does elsewhere in the world.

But there *is* a Gulf cuisine, which can be sampled in people's homes, and which is both simple and delicious. The Gulf's age-old trade links with India have left their imprint on its food, and the staple ingredients of Gulf cooking have long been fish (**samak** or more colloquially **simach**), available in abundance in the Gulf, and rice (**9aysh**) imported from India. The traditional way of cooking fish is mixed with rice to make a dish called **machbúus** (lit. 'turned over'), in which the fish is cooked together with the rice in a large cooking pot (**gídir** or **jídir**) with many spices (**bhaaráat**). The result is a kind of spicy fish risotto. This is then 'turned over' on to a large serving tray or platter (**Siiníyya**), and eaten communally with warm, flat disks of unleavened bread (**xubz irgáag**) cooked on a hotplate or traditionally bought from a local baker (though such bakeries are now becoming a rarity), where they are baked on the inside of a clay oven (**tannúur** – the word is the same one as the 'tandour' in Indian cooking). The favourite varieties of fish are **haamúur** 'grouper' and **kán9ad** or **chán9ad** 'king mackerel'. Thus **machbúus** made with **haamúur** is called **machbúus 9ála haamúur**. And if the **machbúus** is made with meat, **láHam**, it is **machbúus 9ála láHam** and, if with chicken, **dajáaj** (also pronounced dyáay), **machbúus 9ála dajáaj** (pictured below). Such dishes are often spiced with **filfil** 'chilli peppers' and a bitter citrus fruit called **trinj** (or **trínay**) 'citron', a cross between an orange and a lemon. Other traditional savoury Gulf favourites are **Saalúuna**, a spicy curry-like stew of meat and/or vegetables, and **haríis**, a kind of meat porridge traditionally eaten during Ramadan.

Levantine sweets such as **ma9múul**, a buttery pastry enclosing dates, **kunáafa**, vermicelli baked in sugar, honey and butter and the **halwa** and **bakláawa** we know in the West are also popular and sold in many Lebanese-run bakeries. But there are also home-made Gulf sweets, such as **maHlabiyya**, a kind of highly flavoured rice-pudding, **9aSíid**, a sweet porridge made of wheat gruel, sugar and butter, and **xanfarúush**, a deep-fried confection of eggs and flour, dipped in honey or syrup. These are highly calorific, but delicious!

A particular specialty of Oman is honey, **9asal**. This is on sale in most small-town markets in the interior of the country, often in large recycled Coke bottles, and comes in a variety of colours and types. It is relatively expensive, but it is an absolutely natural product collected by the beekeepers of the Omani mountains, and is utterly delicious, especially when mixed with porridge!

Machbúus. Photo © Margarita Lacabe

The village of Misfaa al-9abriyyiin, Oman

Reading Arabic

Look at the sign below, which is the Arabic for KFC ('Kentucky Fried Chicken').

The KFC name, logo and related marks are trademarks of Kentucky Fried Chicken International Holdings, Inc., and are used with permission

The script style in the sign is a little difficult to read, and it is written in plainer style below:

دجاج كنتاكي KFC

You already know the Arabic word for 'chicken' – **dajáaj** – and the following word is another example of an English word transliterated into Arabic script: 'Kentucky'. Reading from right to left, the sign says 'Chicken Kentucky KFC'. In English, we put the word that tells us what kind of chicken it is first, here 'Kentucky (fried) chicken, but in Arabic it's the other way round: 'chicken Kentucky'. Similarly, 'Dubai airport' in Arabic is expressed as 'airport (of) Dubai'. The word for 'airport' is **maTáar**:

مطار دبي

Dubai maTáar
'Dubai airport'

Now look at the sign below:

 Exercise 3.6

Complete the gaps in the table below:

Arabic	Transliteration	Translation
الرميلة		Al-Rumeila
مستشفى	mustáshfa	
حمد	Hamad	

Unit Four

In this unit you will learn about:

- simple descriptive sentences, e.g. 'the man is old', 'the rooms are nice'
- noun-adjective phrases, e.g. 'a new palace', 'the good men'
- some other types of adjective: relative, colour and stative

Language point

4.1 Simple descriptive sentences

In Arabic, there is no equivalent of 'is' and 'are' in equational sentences of the type 'The office is big', 'The house is empty'; one simply says:

il-máktab kabíir
'the office big'

il-bayt xáali
'the house empty'

But where the noun that the adjective describes is feminine, dual, or plural the adjective must agree with the noun as in the following basic scheme:

Singular

ir-rayyáal zayn.	'The man is good.'
il-mára záyna.	'The woman is good.'
ir-rayyaaláyn zayníin.	'The two men are good.'

Dual/Plural

ir-rayaayíil zayníin.	'The men are good.'
il-maratáyn zayníin.	'The two women are good.'
in-niswáan zayníin.	'The women are good.'

It can be seen from these examples that **zayn**, and other adjectives like it, add a final **-a** when they qualify a feminine noun, and the plural suffix **-iin** (which we saw in Unit Two) when they follow dual or plural nouns. As we saw earlier, many nouns have 'broken' plurals – and the same is true of many adjectives. Substituting the adjective **kabíir** pl. **kibáar** into the above examples, we get:

Singular (m.)	**ir-rayyáal kabíir.**	'The man is old.'
Singular (f.)	**il-mára kabíira.**	'The woman is old.'
Dual	**ir-rayyaaláyn kibáar.**	'The two men are old.'
Plural	**in-niswáan kibáar.**	'The women are old.'

kibáar not **kabiiriin** is used in the dual/plural. Whether an adjective behaves in the plural like **zayn** or **kabiir** cannot be predicted from the form of the singular: as with the noun, it is wise to learn the plural form at the same time as the singular.

Note that the feminine examples given so far have involved nouns that are feminine by *meaning* (3.3). What about those (mostly ending in **-a**) that are feminine by grammatical category, such as **shárika**, **sayyáara**, **Híjra**? In the singular, such nouns behave exactly like **mára**:

ish-shárika kabíira.	'The company is big.'
il-Híjra záyna.	'The room is nice.'

But in the dual/plural, the adjective may either be plural *or* feminine singular, thus:

Dual	**ish-sharikatáyn kabíra.** ⎫	'The two companies are big.'
	ish-sharikatáyn kibáar. ⎭	

Plural	**il-Híjar záyna.** ⎫	'The rooms are nice.'
	il-Híjar zayníin. ⎭	

It is important to note that, in general in Gulf Arabic, noun duals and plurals such as 'companies' or 'rooms' – that is, inanimate objects – may be considered grammatically plural or feminine singular, and may hence have adjectives and verbs that are either plural or feminine singular. This applies *whatever* the gender of the noun in the singular.

Thus one may (not only) say **ish-sharikatáyn kabíira/kibáar**, where **shárika** is feminine in its singular form, but also **il-aswáag kabiira/kibáar** 'The markets are big', where the singular **suug** 'market' is grammatically masculine singular.

The system of adjective agreement described above is the one in general use in all Gulf dialects, but it should be noted that, in some areas, particularly Oman, there is also a feminine plural form of the adjective that is formed by adding **-aat** to the adjective when the noun it is agreeing with is feminine plural or dual, whether animate or inanimate. So, for example, instead of **in-niswáan zayníin** for 'The women are good', one often hears **in-niswáan zaynáat**, and instead of **in-niswáan kibáar** for 'The women are old', one hears **in-niswáan kabiiráat**, where a specifically feminine plural adjective form is used. Feminine plural forms in general, not only for adjectives, but also pronouns and verbs, are quite commonly used in Oman and to some extent the UAE, but if you use the forms given in the examples above, you will not be misunderstood.

Exercise 4.1

Translate the following into Arabic:

1 The kettle is old.
2 The chairs are new.
3 The houses are large.
4 The children are happy.
5 The rooms are small.
6 The two brothers are tall.

7 The woman is fat.
8 The coffee is good.
9 The milk is cheap.
10 The buses are empty.
11 The wallet is expensive.
12 The two men are tired.

Exercise 4.2

In the following sentences, substitute the nouns supplied for the noun in the model sentence, making necessary adjustments to the adjective to make it agree with the new noun. Then translate into English the sentences you have formed.

1 il-bayt jadíid. 'The house is new.'
  il-Híjra / il-buyúut / il-mudarrisáat / il-farráash
2 il-gáhwa gháalya. 'The coffee is expensive.'
  is-saayyáara / il-kútub / il-jíbin / il-chaay

3 in-niswáan aghniyáa. 'The women are rich.'
   il-mudíir / il-bintáyn / il-málika / il-waladáyn

 Language point

4.2 Noun-adjective phrases

In noun phrases such as 'a new palace', 'a spacious room' or 'good
men', the adjective *follows* the noun in Arabic, agreeing in number and
gender as described above:

gáSir jadíid	'a new palace'
Híjra wáasi9a	'a spacious room'
rayaayíil zayníin	'good men'

If these phrases are made *definite*, that is, '*the* new palace', etc., the
definite article **il** is put before *both* the noun and its adjective. Thus the
literal English translation of the Arabic for 'the new palace' is 'the-palace-
the-new':

il-gáSir il-jadíid	'the new palace'
il-Híjra l-wáasi9a	'the spacious room'
ir-rayaayíil iz-zayníin	'the good men'

Note that, where the noun ends in a vowel, as with feminine nouns like
Hijra, the **i** of the following **il** is elided.
   The defined adjective can stand alone in much the same way as in
English:

fii noo9áyn, kabíir uu Saghíir.
'There are two kinds, big and small.'

nzayn, 9áTni l-kabíir.
'OK, give me the big one.'

 Exercise 4.3

Read aloud and translate into English:

1 il-awláad iT-Tiwáal   3 baaS xáali
2 iT-Tayyáara s-saríi9a   4 ish-shams Háarra

5 buyúut 9atíija

6 il-banáat il-kibáar

7 tujjáar aghniyáa

8 9áTni l-glaasáyn il-kabíira min fáDlak!

9 máa hast kútub raxíiSa ihní.

10 fii xámsat aqsáam jíddad fish-shárika.

Exercise 4.4

Translate into Arabic, and say aloud:

1 a good mechanic	6 a cheap watch
2 the boss is late	7 the food is delicious
3 today is cold	8 the old palace
4 the new office	9 a new secretary
5 the woman is rich	10 the big problem

Language point

4.3 Some other types of adjective

■ 1 Relative adjectives

These are formed by adding **-iyy** to certain nouns. In pause position
(that is, at the end of a phrase or sentence) **-iyy** is shortened to **i**:

dáaxil	'inside'	**dáaxili(yy)**	'interior'
xáarij	'outside'	**xáariji(yy)**	'exterior'
rásam	'formality'	**rásmi(yy)**	'formal; official'
míSir	'Egypt'	**míSri(yy)**	'Egyptian'
il-kwáyt	'Kuwait'	**kwáyti(yy)**	'Kuwaiti'

The feminine and dual/plural form of the relative adjective shows **-a**
and **-iin** added to the **-iyy**:

is-sifáara l-kwaytíyya	'the Kuwaiti embassy'
il-gamáarik il-miSríyya	'the Egyptian Customs and Excise'
zuwwáar rasmiyyíin	'official visitors'

■ 2 Colour adjectives

Most adjectives that denote colours or physical conditions (blind, deaf,
dumb, etc.) are formed according to the pattern below:

Masculine	Feminine	Plural	
áHmar	Hámra	Húmur or Humráan	'red'
áxDar	xáDra	xúDur or xuDráan	'green'
ábyaD	báyDa	biiD or biiDáan	'white'
á9ma	9ámya	9umy or 9umyáan	'blind'

Here are some examples:

sayyáara Hámra	'a red car'
il-báyt il-ábyaD	'the white house'
il-9umyáan	'the blind (people)'

■ 3 Stative adjectives

There are a great many adjectives of this class that denote temporary
physical states, and that are formed as below:

Masculine	Feminine	Plural	
9aTsháan	**9aTsháana**	**9aTshaaníin** or **9aTáasha**	'thirsty'
yuu9áan	**yuu9áana**	**yuu9aaníin** or **yuwáa9a**	'hungry'
ta9báan	**ta9báana**	**ta9baaníin** or **ta9áaba**	'tired'
bardáan	**bardáana**	**bardaaníin** or **baráada**	'cold'

Thus:

sálma wáayid ta9báana	'Salma is very tired.'
ir-rayaayíil 9aTshaaníin	'The men are thirsty.'
ana bardáan il-yoom	'I'm feeling cold today.'

Note that **bardáan** refers to how a person feels; the adjective **báarid**,
from the same root, is used to describe liquids, food or things that are
cold, for example:

jíib lii báarid!	'Bring me a cold drink!' (lit. 'a cold')
il-yoom báarid	'Today is cold'
ákil báarid	'cold food'

■ 4 Adjectives that precede the noun

There are very few adjectives that precede the noun they qualify. The most important is **xoosh** 'nice, good', which is used in exclamatory phrases of the following kind, and takes no feminine or plural endings:

xóosh wálad!	'Good boy!'
xóosh dráywil ínt!	'What a good driver you are!'
xóosh sháy!	'What a nice thing!'

When George Bush senior visited Kuwait after its liberation in 1991, the Kuwaiti phrase of the moment was **xóosh boosh!** 'Good old Bush!'.

Exercise 4.5 (Audio 1; 11)

Pronunciation practice: read aloud and translate the following short description, checking unfamiliar words in the Vocabulary of this unit where necessary.

> **il-gáSir il-9atíij binyáan 9óod wáayid. lih** ('it has') **baabáyn xaarijíyya uu 9árba9a biibáan daaxilíyya. il-HiiTáan máalih** ('belonging to it') **bíiD wi d-daraaríish máalih min jáam áSfar uu ázrag.**

Exercise 4.6

Pronunciation practice: read aloud the sentence below and translate it, then make appropriate substitutions using the cue words to make similar sentences.

wállah yaa 9áli, ána ('I')	**wáayid 9aTsháan ... jiib lii**
	báarid min fáDlak
	gláas chaay
	kúub maay
	gúuTi bábsi
wállah yaa 9áli, ána ('I')	**shwáy yuu9áan ... jiib lii**
	rúuti jíbin
	sandawíich láHam
	9áysh uu símich

Exercise 4.7 (Audio 1; 12)

Read aloud and translate the following dialogue:

- chayf Háalik yaa áHmad?
- állah yisálmik. chayf Háalik ínt?
- ana walláahi il-yóom ta9báan ...
- laysh?
- li'ánn fii shúghul wáayid.

Now substitute in the dialogue for **ta9báan** and **fii shúghul wáayid** different adjectives and different reasons:

upset – because   the car has   broken down
                     TV has
                     fridge has
                     washing-machine has

happy – because   there's no work today
                     there's no school today
                     today is a holiday
                     the weather's cool

Exercise 4.8

Translate into Arabic:

1 I'm cold and hungry ... Is there any food?
2 Fatma and Ahmad are tired because there was a lot of work today.
3 The machine's broken down ... Is there a mechanic here?
4 Why is the boss angry?
5 The house is white in colour and has a green roof.
6 Give me the red shirt and the white shoes.
7 The Ministry of the Interior is a big white building.
8 The British Embassy is in the old quarter.
9 The National Bank is a small building which has (**lih**) a large black door.
10 The Egyptian ambassador is a very nice man (use **xoosh**).

Vocabulary

ábyaD/biiD	white	loon/alwáan	colour
áHmar/Húmur	red	matíin/amtáan	fat
ákil(aat)	food	mit'áxxir	late
áswad/suud	black	múshkila*/	problem
áSfar/Súfur	yellow	masháakil	
ax/ixwáan	brother	noo9/anwáa9	type; kind
áxDar/xúDur	green	qadíim	old (of things)
ázrag/zúrug	blue	qamíiS/qumSáan	shirt
á9ma/9umyáan	blind	rásmi	official
baab/biibáan	door	raxíiS	cheap
báarid	cold (weather, manner)	rúuti	bread roll
		sáa9a*(aat)	watch
bardáan(iin)	cold (feeling)	safíir/sufaráa	ambassador
binyáan	building	sagf/sugúuf	roof
dáaxili	internal; interior	samíin/simáan	fat
daríisha*/	window	saríi9/siráa9	fast, speedy
daráayish		sifaara	embassy
farHáan(iin)	happy	Saghíir/Sigháar	small; young
firíij/firgáan	quarter (of a city)	shams (f.)	sun
gáSir/guSúur	palace	shay/ashyáa	thing
gúmruk/gamáarik	Customs	shúghul/ashgháal	work; job
gháali	expensive	ta9báan(iin)	tired
gháni/aghniyáa	rich	tilivizyúun(aat)	TV
ghassáala*(aat)	washing machine	Taqs	climate; weather
ghúuri	kettle; teapot	Tawíil/Tiwáal	tall; long
Háa'iT/HiiTáan	outer wall	Tífil/aTfáal	child
Haarr	hot	thalláaja*(aat)	fridge
jaam	glass (sheet)	wáasi9	roomy; spacious
jadíid/jíddad	new		
júuti	shoes	wállah/walláahi	By God!
kabíir/kibáar	big; old	wizáara*(aat)	ministry
kúrsi/karáasi	chair	xáali	empty
ladhíidh	delicious	xáariji	external; exterior
laysh	why?		
li'ann	because	xarbáan	broken down

xoosh	nice, good	9atíij/9itáag	old; ancient (of things)
yuu9áan/ yuwáa9a	hungry	9aTsháan(iin)	thirsty
záayir/ zuwwáar	visitor	9ood	big; large
za9láan(iin)	angry; upset	9úTla*/9úTal	holiday; day off

Cultural point

Standard Arabic and Gulf Arabic

The kind of Arabic that you are learning in this book is that which is spoken on the east coast of Arabia. This kind of Arabic, like the spoken Arabic of other areas of the Arab World, is not normally written. The written form of modern Arabic, often called Modern Standard Arabic (or MSA), is what is used for virtually all written communications and official spoken ones, from road signs to news broadcasts, throughout the Arab World, and is the form of Arabic you are becoming familiar with through the Reading Arabic sections of each unit in this book.

The grammar of Gulf Arabic, like that of the other Arabic colloquials, is different from, and somewhat simpler than, MSA, though ultimately all are varieties of one language. Since this book only introduces the written language in a limited way, in order to enable you to read street signs and other such visual examples of the public use of MSA, the grammatical differences between Gulf Arabic and MSA will not be very apparent. What will be more obvious, perhaps, are differences in vocabulary.

The various Arabic colloquials reflect, in their vocabulary, the cultural and even political history through which the speakers of these colloquials have passed. So, for example, there are still quite a number of Italian words in the spoken Arabic of Libya, which was an Italian colony for the first half of the twentieth century, and a large number of French borrowings in the dialects of Morocco, Algeria and Tunisia. The Gulf has, at various times, been occupied by, or otherwise under the linguistic influence of, Persians, Indians, the British and, as we saw in Unit Two, the Portuguese. All of these groups left a linguistic legacy, though one that, because of the effects of increased education and exposure to MSA, is now on the wane. Thus it is quite common for there to be two words in use for the same thing, one an old borrowing from outside the Gulf, and one a modern neologism from MSA.

So, for example, a large number of words came into Gulf Arabic from the languages of India, from where the British ruled the Gulf for a hundred years from the middle of the nineteenth century until Indian independence in 1947. Examples of Indian borrowings in Gulf Arabic are **kráani** 'clerk', **bánka** 'fan', **júuti** 'shoes', **áalu** 'potato', **chúula** 'primus stove', **bínjiri** 'bangle' and **bíjli** 'torch'. There are also a number of common expressions that are of Indian origin, for example **síida** 'directly; straightaway; straight on', as in giving directions to a taxi driver, **rúuH síida!** 'Go straight on!', or the word **múul** 'completely; at all', often used in negative sentences, for example **maa fii múul!** 'There aren't any at all'. Because of the effect of exposure to MSA, many of these words are now dropping out of use, especially among the younger generations, so one hears **kaatib** 'clerk' instead of **kráani**, **miSbáaH** 'torch' instead of **bíjli**, **Hidháa** instead of **júuti** 'shoes'.

There was also a large influx of English words from the time when British and American employees of the oil companies began working in the Gulf from the 1930s. Not surprisingly, the type of vocabulary borrowed into Gulf Arabic from this source reflects the industrial and work-related nature of contact. Thus, from Kuwait, to eastern Saudi Arabia, to Bahrain and the Lower Gulf, words such as **bulT** 'bolt', **sháywal** 'shovel', **wilf** 'valve', **bamb** 'pump', **bayb** 'pipe', **hooz** 'hose', **sbáana** 'spanner', **smiit** 'cement', **kánkari** 'concrete', **rábil** 'rubber' and **dóozar** 'bulldozer' flooded in. Quite a number of these words for everyday things are still in common use. But others, for example those associated with modes of transport, have been replaced by neologisms. Thus **sayyáara** 'car' is much more commonly heard now than **móotir** (from English 'motor'), **baaS** (English 'bus') shows signs of giving way to **Háafila**, while **láari** (English 'lorry') is being replaced by **sháaHina**, and **láysan** '(driving) licence' by the MSA neologism **rúkhSat siyáaqa**. However, when you get a puncture, it is still referred to as a **bánchar**, and there is a verb **tbánchar** 'to get a puncture', as in **is-sayyáara tbáncharat** 'the car got a puncture'. Such words have become so much part of Gulf Arabic that many Gulf Arabs do not even realise they are borrowings.

And borrowing still goes on, of course, wherever there is cultural contact. In the modern era, Gulf Arabic has acquired **diish** 'satellite dish', **rimúut** '(TV) remote control', **forwíil** '4 WD', **jinz** 'jeans' and even, for a period in the 1970s and 1980s, **jíksan**, 'Afro hair-cut', named after the erstwhile Gulf pop idol and populariser of this hairstyle, the late Michael Jackson!

Reading Arabic

As we have seen in this unit, adjectives follow the nouns they modify. Here are some typical examples from the written Arabic you will come across in everyday Gulf life:

بريد إلكتروني

E-mail

The text in the above sign reads (right to left) **baríid iliktruuníi**, literally 'electronic mail'. The noun and adjective here are both indefinite.

As we have seen, if the noun in a noun-adjective phrase is definite, the adjective modifying it is also definite. So, in the example below, from a hotel entrance, the text reads literally 'the-entrance the-main', the word **mádkhal** meaning 'entrance' and **ra'iisíi** 'main':

Look at the writing at the top of the Omani banknote below. The three key words are, from right to left, **bank** 'bank', **markazíi** 'central', **9umaaníi** 'Omani', and the complete phrase is **al-bank al-markazíi al-9umaaníi**, literally 'the-bank the central the-Omani', or, as it is officially known, 'The Central bank of Oman'. Note that the word for 'the' in MSA is pronounced **al-** rather than **il-** as in spoken Gulf Arabic.

Exercise 4.9

Look at these nouns, some of which you already know:

máktab	office	sifáara	embassy
maTáar	airport	mámlaka	kingdom
film	film	máT9am	restaurant
madrása	school	lúgha	language
wájba	meal		

Now look at these adjectives:

dáwli	international	sa9úudi	Saudi
míSri	Egyptian	híndi	Indian
tháanawi	secondary	9árabi	Arab; Arabian; Arabic
ra'íisi	main; head	khafíif	light

Now translate these common written phrases, which combine the nouns and adjectives transliterated above, and which you will see on shop signs and notices. All of them consist of a noun and a following adjective that agrees with it in gender. The first group of phrases are definite ('The ...') and the second indefinite:

المطار الدولي   1 _____

المكتب الرئيسي   2 _____

السفارة المصرية   3 _____

4 _____	4	المملكة العربية السعودية
5 _____	5	اللغة العربية
6 _____	6	مطعم هندي
7 _____	7	فلم عربي
8 _____	8	مدرسة ثانوية
9 _____	9	وجبة خفيفة
10 _____	10	مدرسة عربية

Unit Five

In this unit you will learn about:

* numbers 11 to 1,000,000
* asking someone's age and how to reply
* telling the time
* personal pronouns: 'I', 'you' and 'my', 'your', etc.
* how to ask 'Who?' and 'What?'

Language point

5.1 Numbers 11 to 1,000,000

The numbers from 11 to 20 are formed according to a pattern that, literally translated, means 'one-ten', 'two-ten', 'three-ten', etc. Beyond 20, the pattern is 'one-and-twenty', 'two-and-twenty', 'seven-and-forty', etc.:

iHdá9shar	eleven
ithná9shar	twelve
thalaathtá9shar	thirteen
arba9tá9shar	fourteen
xamstá9shar	fifteen
sittá9shar	sixteen
saba9tá9shar	seventeen
thamantá9shar	eighteen
tisa9tá9shar	nineteen

9ishríin	twenty
wáaHid u 9ishríin	twenty-one
ithnáyn u 9ishríin	twenty-two, etc.
thalaathíin	thirty
arba9íin	forty
xamsíin	fifty
sittíin	sixty
sab9íin	seventy
thamaaníin	eighty
tis9íin	ninety
míya	one hundred

Unlike the numbers 1 to 10, those from 11 onwards do not show a gender distinction: they are indeclinable. Any noun that follows them is always grammatically singular, although its meaning is obviously plural, for example:

xáms u 9ishríin sána	'twenty-five years'
ithná9shar bínt	'twelve girls'
wáaHid u sittíin diináar u núSS	'sixty-one and a half dinars'

Note that, when a noun follows **miya**, the 'hidden' **t** of the feminine shows up, just as we had in Unit One ('expressions of quantity'):

nítfat xúbuz	'a bit of bread'

from **nítfa**, 'a bit', so we have:

míyat xúbza	'a hundred loaves'

and likewise:

míyat márra	'a hundred times'
míyat fíls	'a hundred fils'

Where **miya** stands on its own, or is part of a compound number, the **t** does not appear:

- **cham 9áamil hást fi sh-shárika?**
  'How many workers are there in the company?'

- **míya**
  'A hundred.'

Compound numerals from 100 to 200 are formed as follows:

míya u wáaHid   'a hundred and one'
míya u ithnáyn   'a hundred and two', etc.
míya u ithná9shar   'a hundred and twelve'
míya u thaláath u 9ishríin 'a hundred and twenty-three', etc.

'Two hundred' is **miyatáyn** (the dual), but there is no plural form for **míya** in '300', '400', etc. Thus:

árba9 míya u xáms u 9ishríin diináar   '425 dinars'
miyatáyn u tísa9 káylo   '209 kilos'
sítt imyát náfar   '600 persons'

Note in this last example that **míya** becomes **imyá** where it is preceded by a number ending in a double consonant: this is to avoid three consonants in a row, which is not normally allowed in Gulf Arabic. 'One thousand' is **alf**. 'Two thousand' is of course **alfáyn**, and the plural of **alf** is **aaláaf**:

síttat aaláaf sána   '6,000 years'
tís9at aaláaf kitáab   '9,000 books'

Since, as we have seen above, numbers over 11 have the noun in the singular, so **alf** remains in the singular if the number in which it appears is 11,000 or more:

iHdá9shar álf jináy istárlin '£11,000 sterling'
9ishríin álf mayl   '20,000 miles'

Years are expressed as follows:

fi sánat álf u tís9 imyá u wáaHid u thamaaníin 'in 1981'
fi sanat alfáyn u thaláath   'in 2003'

'One million' is **milyóon**, and its plural is **milaayíin**.

Exercise 5.1

Translate into Arabic:

1 50 kilos of potatoes   4 60,000 people
2 46 bags of cement   5 200,000 dinars
3 360 miles   6 in 1976

7 in 1960   9 200 sacks of rice

8 750 fils   10 39 years, 11 months

Exercise 5.2

Read aloud and translate the following dialogue:

- bi cham il-bayD il-yóom?
- xáms imyát fíls id-dárzan.

Using the same format, ask and answer questions on the price of things in the market:

1 oranges – 100 fils a kilo   6 tea – 70 fils a quarter

2 onions – 55 fils a kilo   7 dates – 900 fils a kilo

3 fish – 350 fils a kilo   8 tomatoes – 50 fils a bag

4 bananas – 175 fils a dozen   9 potatoes – 80 fils a sack

5 cabbage – 125 fils each   10 radishes – 12 fils a bundle
   ('the one')

 Language points

5.2 Age

The phrase for asking a person's age is **kam/chám 9úmrik/ch?** (lit. 'How much is your life?'). The answer is **9úmri … sána** 'I'm … years old' (lit. 'My life is … years'). Since many older Gulf Arabs are not sure exactly when they were born, one often hears exchanges of the following type:

- yáa 9áli, chám 9úmrik il-Híin?
'How old are you now Ali?'

- wállah 9úmri Hawáali sittíin sána.
'About sixty.'

5.3 Telling the time

The word for 'a watch,' 'a clock' and 'an hour' is the same in Arabic – **sáa9a**. 'What time is it?' is **chám is-sáa9a?** The answer is **is-sáa9a** ... 'It's ... o'clock.' The feminine form of the cardinal numbers is used:

is-sáa9a xámsa	'It's five o'clock.'
is-sáa9a thintáyn	'It's two o'clock.'

For 11 and 12, the indeclinable **iHdá9shar** and **ithná9shar** are used.

Times between full hours are expressed using

... **u rub9**	'quarter past ... (lit. 'and a quarter')
... **u nuSS**	'half past ... (lit. 'and a half')
... **u thilth**	'twenty past ... (lit. 'and a third')

Here are some examples:

is-sáa9a iHdá9shar u rúb9	'quarter past twelve'
is-sáa9a thaláatha u núSS	'half past three'
is-sáa9a sítta u thílth	'twenty past six'

'Quarter to ...' and 'twenty to ...' are expressed by the preposition **illa** 'except':

is-sáa9a 9áshra illa thílth	'twenty to ten'
is-sáa9a tís9a illa rúb9	'quarter to nine'

'Five to/past ...' and 'ten to/past ...' are expressed using **u** and **illa**, but the masculine form of the number is used. The word for 'minutes', **dagáayig** (sing. **dagíiga**) is not usually used in colloquial speech:

is-sáa9a xámsa u xáms	'five past five'
is-sáa9a 9áshra illa 9áshar	'ten to ten'

'Twenty-five to/past ...' involves the use of **nuSS**: one says 'and a half and five' for 35 minutes past the hour, and 'and a half except five' for 25 minutes past the hour:

is-sáa9a árba9a u núSS u xáms
'twenty-five to five'

is-sáa9a thamáanya u núSS illa xáms
'twenty-five past eight'

When it needs to be specified which part of the day is being referred to, one uses the following expressions: **is-SubH** (or **SabáaHan**) 'in the morning', **bá9ad iDH-Dhúhur** or **il-9aSr** (or **9áSran**) 'in the afternoon', **il-masáa** (or **masáa'an**) 'in the evening' and **bil-layl** 'at night' (or **láylan**). The variants ending in **-an** are more 'literary' sounding than the alternatives. These expressions are used more or less as their English equivalents, 'the evening' beginning about 5.00 p.m., and 'the morning' beginning at sunup. It is worth noting, however, that there are other modes of time-keeping in the Gulf region: the Westerner is unlikely nowadays to meet anyone who sets a watch by Muslim Suntime, according to which the day begins with sunup and ends with sundown, but he or she may well meet the words **iD-DíHa** 'the forenoon', **il-gayúula** 'noontime' and **il-mughárb** 'sunset' (= '(in the) evening'). These words refer to parts of the day that we do not normally distinguish, and are still in common use in speech: **iD-DíHa** refers to the late morning from about 9.00 a.m. to noon, while **iS-SubH** is really 'early morning'; **il-gayúula** refers to the early part of the afternoon from noon to about 3.00 p.m, and the late afternoon is **il-9áSr** (3.00 to 5.00 p.m. roughly). **il-mughárb** comes after **il-9áSr** and means the period from sundown to when daylight has faded completely. The truly black part of the night is **il-layl**. These expressions were a means of measuring the passage of time before watches were common, but are still often used.

Exercise 5.3

Translate the following phrases, which are responses to the question:

il-máw9id fis-sáa9a chám?
'At what time is the appointment?'

1 fis-sáa9a wáHda u núSS bá9ad iDH-DHúhur
2 fis-sáa9a tiś9a illa thílth SabáaHan
3 il-9áSr is-sáa9a árba9a
4 fis-sáa9a thamáanya u núSS il-masáa
5 iS-SúbH is-sáa9a sáb9a u rúb9

Exercise 5.4

Someone asks you **kám is-sáa9a?** 'What's the time? Refer to your
watch and answer:

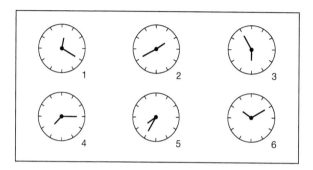

Language points

5.4 Personal pronouns

The most common forms of the personal pronouns used in the Gulf
are as below. Note that a gender distinction is made in the 2nd person
singular:

ána	I	**íHna**	we
ínta	you (m. sing.)		
ínti	you (f. sing.)	**íntu**	you (common pl.)
húwwa	he		
híyya	she	**húmma**	they (common pl.)

The forms given here are the most dialectally 'neutral', and the learner
is advised to use these. However, there is a great deal of variation
from dialect to dialect and many variants will be encountered. **ani** is a
feminine form for 'I' used by some (uneducated) women; **íntay** 'you
(f.sing.)' and **íntaw** (common pl.) may be heard as alternatives to **ínti**
and **íntu**; and **íntan** 'you (f. pl.)' and **hin** 'they (f. pl.)' are heard in the
Lower Gulf and Oman. **húwa**, **híya** and **hum** are also used for 'he',
'she', 'they' (common pl.).

Generally speaking, as will become clear from the examples throughout the following units, the 'independent' personal pronouns listed
above are used for emphasis only – in Arabic, sentences such as
'I go' or 'she sat down' consist of a verb only, which contains an ending
signifying 'I' and 'she'. The independent personal pronouns are used
when one wishes for some reason to emphasise *who* was involved in
an action, for example '*I* go (not him)' and 'it was *she* who sat down
(not someone else)'.

These independent personal pronouns are matched by a set of
'dependent' personal pronouns, which perform a function in Arabic
equivalent to that of the object pronouns and possessive adjectives in
English. Thus in Arabic 'him/his', 'us/our' and 'them/their' are translated
by the same word. In only one case does Arabic make a distinction –
between 'me' and 'my':

-i	my	**na**	us/our
-ni	me		
-ik/ak	you/your (m. sing.)	**-kum**	you/your (pl.)
-ich/ach	you/your (f. sing.)		
-ah	him/his/its (m. nouns)	**-hum**	them/their (pl.)
-ha	her/her/its (f. nouns)		

As noted previously, **-ik/-ak** and **-ich/-ach** are freely variable. These
suffixes are attached directly to verbs, nouns and prepositions:

9aT	give (m. sing.)!	**+ ni**	me	**9áTni**	'give me!'	
kitáab	book	**+ i**	my	**kitáabi**	'my book'	
9ind	with; at	**+ ik**	you (m.)	**9índik**	'you have' (lit. 'with you')	

A number of points should be noted:

1 As with other suffixes that begin with a vowel (such as the dual
  ending **-ayn**), the 'hidden' t of feminine nouns ending in **-a** shows
  up when these suffixes are attached: **sáa9ati** 'my watch', **Hijráthum**
  'their room'.
2 Where suffixes that begin with a consonant are added to **9ind**, which
  already ends with two consonants, some speakers insert **-a-** to
  make the word more easily pronounceable: **9índahum** 'they have',
  9índana 'we have'. Yet others simply drop the **-n-**: **9ídhum, 9ídna**.
  Either of these types of form is acceptable.

3 Two nouns, **ab** 'father' and **ax** 'brother', insert a **-uu-** before suffixation: **abúuk** 'your father', **axúuh** 'his brother'. The 'my' suffix with these two words is **-yi** rather than **-i**: **abúuyi** 'my father'.

4 There are a few nouns that end in **-a**, that do not have 'hidden' **t**, and that lengthen and stress the final vowel when suffixed, for example **gháda** 'lunch', **ghadáach** 'your (f.) lunch' and **9ásha** 'dinner', **9asháahum** 'their dinner'.

5 The 2nd person feminine singular in Oman and in certain areas in eastern Saudi Arabia and Bahrain is **-ish**, not **-ich**.

6 In Oman and parts of the UAE, there are 2nd and 3rd person feminine plural pronouns, **-kin** and **-hin** respectively.

In sentences of the type 'The colour of my car is red', it is quite common in Arabic to 'reverse the order' and say 'My car, its colour is red' (as in French 'ma voiture, elle est rouge'):

sayyáarti lóonha áHmar.

Similarly,

ána ísmi mHámmad.
'My name is Muhammad.'
('I, my name ...')

Sadíiqa báytha fil-muHárrag.
'Sadiiqa's house is in Muharraq.'
('Sadiiqa, her house ...')

Nouns that have a personal suffix attached to them are treated in Arabic like 'defined' nouns if they are modified by an adjective. Just as we have (4.2)

is-sáa9a l-jadíida
'the new watch'

so we have:

sáa9atik il-jadíida
'your new watch'

The omission of the definite article before the adjective in this example

sáa9atik jadíida

changes the meaning to 'your watch is new'.

5.5 'Who?' and 'What?'

There are a number of words used for 'what?' in interrogative sentences. The commonest in the northern Gulf are **shínhu** and **waysh**, which may both be abbreviated to **sh-** and directly prefixed to nouns:

waysh/shínhu shúghlik?   'What's your job?'
shísmich?   'What's your (f.) name?'

Parallel with **shínhu** we find **mínhu** 'who?' or **min** for short:

mínhu int?   'Who are you?'
min dáaxil?   'Who's inside?'

In Oman, **muu** is used for 'what?', as in **muu shúghlik?** 'What's your job?'.

Dialogue 5.1

Read aloud and translate the dialogue below.

iDH-DHurúuf ish-shaxSíyya 'Personal circumstances' (Audio 1; 13)

A ísmik il-káamil min fáDlik?
B ísmi Hsáyn mHámmad Hasan.
A nzayn ... wil-jinsíyya?
B baHráyniyya.
A uu l-Háala l-ijtimaa9íyya?
B mitzáwwij.
A 9índik yiháal?
B ay wállah. bintáyn u síttat awláad.
A síttat awláad ... wáayid! uu wayn sáakin?
B sáakin wállah fi madíinat 9íisa.
A fi ay sháari9?
B ish-sháari9 sitt u arba9íin, il-bayt rágam thaláath míya u iHdá9shar.
A nzayn, u shínhu shúghlik il-Háali?
B 9áamil fish-shárika.
A ay shárika?
B shárikat báabko.
A u cham il-ma9áash?

B kill sháhar míya u tis9íin diináar.
A ráatib zayn, wállah … u cham 9úmrik il-Hiin?
B 9úmri wállah Hawáali xams u arba9íin sána.
A 9índak shahaadáat Táb9an?
B ay ná9am. 9índi sh-shaháada l-ibtidaa'íyya.
A bas? thaanawíyya maa mish?
B la.

Exercise 5.5

Look at the following chart:

Name:	9áli	HáafiDH	Hsayn	you
Nationality:	Bahraini	Palestinian	Kuwaiti	?
Social status:	married	divorced	bachelor	?
Children:	2 boys	3 b. 2 g.	–	?
Domicile:	Manama	Doha	Salmiyya	?
Age:	23	45	27	?
Job:	plumber	contractor	engineer	?
Salary per month:	210 B.D.	2,600 Q.R.	1,200 K.D.	?
Education:	primary	secondary	university degree	?

1 Practise asking **9áli**, **HáafiDH**, etc. (**yaa 9áli** …) about the topics in the left-most column of the chart, using the question forms exemplified in the dialogue you have read.
2 Imagine you are **9áli**, etc. and make your answers.
3 Answer the questions as they relate to you yourself.

Here is some vocabulary to help you:

divorced	**mTállag**	plumber	**baybfíita**
bachelor	**á9zab**	contractor	**muqáawil**
Manama	**il-manáama**	riyal	**riyáal**
Doha	**id-dóoHa**	university degree	**dáraja jaami9íyya**
Salmiyya	**is-saalmíyya**		

Note that there are no answers for this exercise given in the Answer key.

Vocabulary

ab/ubuháat	father	ínta	you (m. sing.)
alf/aaláaf	thousand	ínti	you (f. sing.)
ána	I	íntu	you (pl.)
arba9íin	forty	ísim/asáami	name
arba9tá9shar	fourteen	ithná9shar	twelve
ay	which?	jáami9a*(aat)	university
á9zab	bachelor	jáami9i	university (adj.)
bas	only; just; but	jínay stárlin	pound sterling
baybfíita	plumber	jinsíyya*(aat)	nationality
bá9ad	after (prep.)	káamil	complete
dagíiga*/dagáayig	minute	kill	all
dáraja*(aat)	degree	layl/layáali	night
DíHa	forenoon	malfúuf	cabbage
DHúhur	noon	márra*(aat)	time; occasion
DHurúuf	circumstances (pl.)	masáa	evening
		masáa'an	in the evening
filasTíini	Palestinian	máw9id/mawáa9id	appointment; date
gayúula*	noonday heat		
gháda	lunch	mayl/amyáal	mile
híyya	she	ma9áash(aat)	salary
húmma	they	milyóon/malaayíin	million
húwwa	he	mínhu	who?
Háala*/aHwáal	condition; state	mitzáwwij	married
Háali	present; current	míya*(aat)	hundred
		mooz	banana
Hawáali	approximately	mTállag	divorced
il-Hiin	now	mughárb	evening; sunset
ibtidáa	beginning		
ibtidáa'i	elementary; primary	muqáawil	contractor
		ráatib/rawáatib	salary
iHdá9shar	eleven	riyáal(aat)	riyal
íHna	we	ruwáyd	radishes
ijtimáa9	meeting; society	sáakin	living; domiciled
ijtimáa9i	social	sáa9a*(aat)	hour; watch; clock
ílla	except	saba9tá9shar	seventeen

sab9íin	seventy	tháanawi	secondary (school)
sána*/sanawáat (or siníin)	year	thalaathíin	eighty
sittá9shar	sixteen	thalaathtá9shar	thirteen
sittíin	sixty	thamantá9shar	eighteen
SabáaHan	in the morning	thilth/athláath	one third
		wayn	where?
SubH	early morning	waysh	what?
Súrra*(aat)	bundle; bunch	xamsíin	fifty
		xamstá9shar	fifteen
sháari9/shawáari9	street	yáahil/yiháal	child
shaháada*(aat)	certificate; diploma	yууníyya*/ yawáani	sack
shaxS/ashxáaS	person	9ásha	dinner
sháxSi	personal	9áSir	late afternoon
shínhu	what?	9ind	with; at
tisa9tá9shar	nineteen		(+ pron. 'to have')
tis9íin	ninety		
Táb9an	naturally	9umr/a9máar	life (length of)

Cultural point

Currencies, bank notes and stamps

For many decades now, each of the Gulf countries has had its own currency: the Kuwait **diináar**, pl. **danaaníir** (divided into 1,000 **fils**, pl. **fluus**), the Bahraini **diináar** (also divided into 1,000 **fils**), the Saudi **riyáal**, pl. **riyaaláat** (divided into 100 **haláala**, pl. **halaaláat**), the Qatari **riyáal** (divided into 100 **dírham**), the UAE **dírham**, pl. **daráahim** (divided into 100 **fils**) and the Omani **riyáal** (divided into 1,000 **báysa** (so written, but pronounced **báyza**), pl. **bayzáat**). The names of the main denominations are all familiar to us in slightly different forms: the word **diináar** is derived from the Roman 'denarius', **dírham** from the Greek 'drachma' and the **riyáal** (often spelt 'rial') was in use as a medieval coin in several countries of Europe, and is ultimately from the same origin as the word 'royal'. But up until the late 1950s, several of the Gulf countries – Bahrain, Qatar, the UAE (then known, before

its independence, as 'The Trucial States') and Oman used Indian
currency: the 'rupee' (**rubbiya**, pl. **rubbiyaat**), which was divided into
16 'annas' (**áana**, pl. **aanáat**), which was further divided into 4 'baysa'
(Indian 'pies') (**báyza**, pl. **bayzáat**). The first postage stamps used in
the Gulf were, until Indian independence in 1947, stamps of British
India, and after Indian independence until the late 1960s, British stamps
overprinted in rupees and annas (and then, for a brief period before
the present-day currencies came in, in rupees and the revalued 'naiye
paisa' (NP) 'new baisa', which replaced the 'anna'). Here are some
examples from Bahrain, showing (left to right): a stamp of British India
of the 1930s–1940s (King George VI), three British stamps overprinted
in Indian currency from the mid-1950s (King George VI and Queen
Elizabeth II) and a stamp of the late 1950s, still in Indian currency
showing Sheikh Salman bin Hamad, the grandfather of the present
King, Hamad bin Isa bin Salman:

 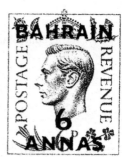 

Just as, in the UK, people continued to remember, and use in speech, the old currency denominations of 'pounds, shillings and pence' for several years after decimalisation in 1971, so, in the Gulf, people continued to use the old Indian denominations for quite some time into the 1960s and 1970s. Even today the older generation still occasionally uses them. In Bahrain, for example, instead of saying that something cost **míyat fils**, '25 fils', people would often say it cost **árba9 aanáat** '4 annas', its equivalent in the old currency; and rather than '100 fils', they would say **rubbíya** 'one rupee'. '500 fils' would be **xams rubbiyáat** '5 rupees' rather than **xams ímyat fils** '500 fils' or **nuSS diináar** 'half a dinar'. Nowadays, these old terms have all but disappeared, except in certain idiomatic expressions. So, for example, **báyza** 'baisa', the lowest denomination coin, and its plural **bayzáat** are still sometimes used as general terms for 'money', 'dough' or 'dosh' in expressions such as: **il-yoom, maa lih gíima, il-báyza** 'these days, money has no value'; **jiib il-bayzáat!** 'Give us the money!'; and **bayztáyn** 'a few quid' (lit. 'two baisas').

Look at the denominations of the Gulf banknotes below. What do they say in Arabic? Translate them into English. The first one contains a word that looks like **maa'it**, but is in fact a written variant of MSA **mi'a** = colloquial **miya**:

1   مَائةبيسَة

2   ريـالواحـد

3   دينارواحد

4   خمسةريالات

Reading Arabic

The Arabic numbers are often used alongside European ones, for example on car registration plates, but it is a good idea to be able to recognise them without that help. The numbers 1–12 are sometimes seen on clock faces.

Oddly, considering that Arabic is written from right to left, the numbers are written from left to right. So what is the number on the car registration plate below, and what country is it from?

Here are some values taken from postage stamps. What are they in English, and how would you say these values in Arabic?

Look at the sign for a coffee shop below, which tells you that it is currently 'open', and gives the times of day and night when it is open. What is the word for 'open'? And from what hour to what hour is it open? Can you read what the sign says?

Look at this sign, which gives the opening hours for a business. The
sign announces **awqáat ad-dawáam**, which literally means 'times'
(**awqáat**) of 'working' (**dawáam**). What are the times from Saturday to
Thursday (**min as-sabt ila l-xamíis**)? And when are they open on Friday
(**al-júm9a**)? They have two telephone numbers – what are they?

Review Unit I

Exercise RI.1

Read aloud and translate the following dialogue:

Polite requests

- yaa 9áli, ta9áal!
- ná9am.
- jíib lii máay báarid min fáDlik. ana wáayid 9aTsháan.
- insháallah.

Using the chart below, make as many similar polite requests as you can, in each case giving an appropriate reason.

jíib lii	cháay áHmar	9aTsháan
sáww lii	sandawíich	bardáan
bánnid	il-kandíshan	juu9áan
báTTil	il-pánka	Háarr
	id-daríisha	

Dialogue RI.1

Read aloud and translate the following dialogue.

Business diary (Audio 1; 14)

BOSS   9índi mawáa9id báachir, yaa sálwa?
SECRETARY 9índik maw9idáyn iS-SúbH ... il-máw9id il-áwwal fis-
          sáa9a tís9a wiyya zuwwáar rasmiyyíin min wizáarat
          il-xaarijíyya with-tháani fis-sáa9a iHdá9shar u núSS
          wiyya l-muhándis ir-ra'íisi min shárikat '9ántar'.

B	nzáyn, u fii shay bá9ad iDH-DHúhur?
S	la máa mísh ... 9índik faráagh.
B	u fil-masáa?
S	9índak mubáarat tánis wiyya s-sáyyid Johnson fis-sáa9a sítta u rúb9 ...

Imagine now that you are the secretary. Your boss asks you:

9índi mawáa9id il-yóom?

and you refer to his business diary below. Give him a summary of what's in store for him!

○ **Monday 4 January**

a.m.

9.00 —
9.30 *Journalist from il-jumhuurriyya (newspaper)*
○ 10.00 —
10.15 *Two students from the university*
11.00 *The contractor Ahmad 'Abdullah*
p.m.
4.00 *Tea party at the British Embassy*
● 7.30 *Dinner party at home*

Dialogue RI.2

Read aloud and translate the following dialogue.

Greetings (Audio 1; 15)

A áhlan marHába, yaa jáasim!
B yaa hála áHmad! shlóonik? insháallah záyn!
A állah yisálmik! shlóonik ínt?
B záyn walláh ... tfáDDal cháay!
A ismáH li, 9indi shúghul shwáy fil-báyt.
B shínhu yá9ni?
A wállah mushkíla! sayyáarti xarbáana.
B wállah? ána shúghli taSlíiH sayyaaráat!

A Sidj?

B ay.

A nzáyn, ta9áal wiyyáay!

Exercise RI.2 (Audio 1; 16)

Read aloud and translate the following passage.

A mother talks about her family

ána ísmi fáaTma mHámmad 9íisa. mawlúuda fil-manáama u
sáakina Haalíyyan fi firíij il-fáaDil. 9índi árba9a yiháal – bínt
wáHda isímha núura u thaláathat awláad asaamíihum jáasim,
mbáarak u baxáyt. bínti núura 9umúrha saba9tá9shar sána u
híyya Tāliba fil-jáami9a. bínt Hálwa, wállah! wíldi jáasim shúghlah
káatib fi shárikat '9ántar'. xóosh wálad hu! mbáarak shúghlah
muqáawil. 9índah flúus wáayid u sayyáara Hámra 9óoda. wíldi
th-tháalith baxáyt. 9umráh il-Híin Hawáali 9ishríin sána, bas máa
9índah shahaadáat wa la shay.

Exercise RI.3

Below is your shopping list for the weekend. First ask the shopkeeper
whether what you want is available, and then ask him for the quantity
you want.

Shopping list

Drink
  3 bottles of milk
  3 cartons of Pepsi-Cola
Food
  Packet of salt
  1 kilo lamb
  1/2 doz. oranges
  3 kilos potatoes
  1 cabbage
Other
  2 boxes of matches
  5 packets of cigarettes

Vocabulary

áwwal, (f.) úula	first	pánka(aat)	fan
bánnid!	close! (imp.)	ra'íis/ru'asáa	chief; boss (n.)
báTTil!	open! (imp.)	ra'iisi	chief; main;
faráagh	free time		principal (adj.)
firíij/firgáan	quarter	sáyyid/sáada*	Mr
	(of a city)	Sandúug/	box; chest
gúuTi/gawáaTi	packet; box; tin	Sanaadíig	
Háfla*(aat)	party; celebration	Sidj	that's true!
Háflat chaay	tea party	tánis	tennis
Hálu (f.) Hálwa	sweet; pretty;	taSlíiH	repair
	handsome	ta9áal!	come (here)!
ismáH lii!	excuse me;	Táalib/Tulláab	student
	sorry!	tháalith	third (adj.)
kandíshan	air-conditioning	tháani	second (adj.)
kartúun/	carton, large box	wild	boy; son
kawaartíin	(of soft drinks,		(often used
	beer, etc.)		instead of wálad
mawlúud	born		in phrases such
mubáara*(aat)	match; contest		as wíldi 'my son',
muxx	brain;		wíldik 'your son')
	intelligence		

Unit Six

In this unit you will learn about:

* expressions of place, e.g. 'in the house', 'near the bank'
* the past tense of verbs: basic forms, suffixed forms, negatives and interrogatives

Language point

6.1 Expressions of place

In answer to the question word **wáyn**? 'where?', some of the most common types of locational phrase are exemplified below:

Examples

fi (or **bi**)	'in', 'inside', 'at'	**fil-báyt**	'in the house'; 'at home'
9ála	'on'	**9álal-máyz**	'on the table'
fóog	'above', 'on', 'upon'	**fóog il-árD**	'above the ground'
táHt	'under'	**táHt il-kúrsi**	'under the chair'
giddáam	'in front of'	**giddáam il-báab**	'in front of the door'
mgáabil	'opposite'	**mgáabil báyti**	'opposite my house'
wára	'behind'	**wáral-mál9ab**	'behind the (football) pitch'

yánb/	'next to',	yánb il-másyid	'next to the mosque'
yamm	'beside'		
garíib min	'near to'	garíib min il-bánk	'near the bank'
ba9íid 9an	'far from'	ba9íid 9an il-madíina	'far from the town'

Exercise 6.1

Look at the street map below and complete the sentences that follow; translate the sentences.

| is-síinama | | il-mátHaf | il-bank il-wáTani | | il-mál9ab | il-baríid |

⭕ id-dawwáar   sháari9 9abdállah

madrásat ábu bakr

shárikat "9antar"   sháari9 9uthmáan   báyti   másyid

1 wayn il-mátHaf? _____ min id-dawwáar.

2 wayn il-bank il-wáTani? yamm _____, _____ sháari9 9abdállah.

3 wayn _____? wara madrásat ábu bakr.

4 wayn báytik? _____ shárikat '9ántar', fi _____.

5 il-baríid _____ shárikat '9ántar'.

6 madrásat ábu bakr _____ il-bank il-wáTani.

7 wayn il-mál9ab? _____ il-baríid fi _____.

Now translate the following questions, and answer them from the street map:

8 Excuse me, where's the post office?

9 Where's Abu Bakr school, please?

10 Excuse me, where's the Antar Company?

11 Excuse me, where's the mosque please?

12 Where's the cinema please?

Exercise 6.2

Translate into Arabic:

1 on the table	10 above the house
2 under the car	11 in the water
3 up the ladder	12 next to the new palace
4 in the cinema	13 far from Kuwait
5 in the car	14 behind al-Malik Street
6 under the sea	15 on the wall
7 on the roof	16 near the window
8 near my house	17 under the table
9 in front of the bank	

Note that the personal pronoun suffixes (5.4) can be added directly to any of these prepositions, for example **táHtik** 'below you' and **mgáabilha** 'opposite her'. A number of changes occur when the suffixes are added to prepositions ending in a vowel:

1 The 1st person singular suffix is **-i** after prepositions ending in a consonant, for example **giddáami** 'in front of me', but note the following:

after	**fi**	'in; at'	**fíyyi** or **fíini**	'in me'
	bi	'in; with'	**bíyyi** or **bii**	'in/with me'
	li	'to'	**líyyi** or **lii**	'to me'
	9ala	'on'	**9alíyyi** or **9alíi**	'on me; against me'
	ila	'to'	**ilíyyi** or **ilíi**	'to/toward me'
	wiyya	'with'	**wiyyáayi** or **wiyyáay**	'with me'
	wára	'behind'	**waráayi** or **waráay**	'behind me'

2 The other preposition + personal suffix forms are:

fi:	**fiik, fiich, fiih, fíiha, fíina, fíikum, fíihum**
bi:	**biik, biich, biih, bíiha, bíina, bíikum, bíihum**
9ála:	**9aláyk, 9aláych, 9aláyh, 9aláyha, 9aláyna, 9aláykum, 9aláyhum**
íla:	**iláyk, iláych, iláyh, iláyha, iláyna, iláykum, iláyhum**
wára:	**waráak, waráach, waráah, waráaha, waráana, waráakum, waráahum**

wíyya: wiyyáak, wiyyáach, wiyyáah, wiyyáaha, wiyyáana,
        wiyyáakum, wiyyáahum
li: lik, lich, lih, líha, lína, líkum, líhum

Many of these prepositions are used in set phrases or idioms:

fi/bi	waysh biik/fiik? shbiik/shfiik?	'What's the matter with you?' (lit. 'What is in you?')
bi	bil-lúgha l-9arabíyya/ bil-9arabi	'in Arabic'
9ála	9aláyk il-Hagg.	'You're in the wrong.' (lit. 'The right is against you.')
	9aláyk dyúun.	'You're in debt.' (lit. 'Debts are against/on you.')
li	lík il-Hágg.	'You're in the right'; 'You have the right.' (lit. 'The right is to you.')
taHt	hu sáakin táHti.	'He lives right next to me.' (lit. 'He is living under me.')
foog	máa fóogah fóog.	'The best there is.' (lit. 'There's not above it an above.')
	fóog in-náxal.	'Fantastic, marvellous.' (reply to 'How are you?') (lit. 'Above the palm trees.')

foog and taHt are also used as adverbs meaning 'upstairs' and
'downstairs':

- wayn jíHa?   'Where's Jiha?'
- foog.   'Upstairs.'

Exercise 6.3

Translate the following sentence into Arabic:

The driver's in your office, and there's a man with him.

Now substitute into this sentence the following nouns, making appropriate changes in the pronoun:

1 The servant	5 The engineers
2 Your secretary (f.)	6 The journalists
3 The contractor	7 The teacher (f.)
4 My daughter	

Translate the following exchange into Arabic:

What's the matter with you (m.)? – I'm tired, that's all!

Now substitute into this exchange the following pronouns and adjectives:

8 you (f.)	_____	thirsty
9 him	_____	upset
10 you (pl.)	_____	hungry
11 them	_____	cold

Translate into Arabic:

1 My house is right next to yours (pl.).

2 'Antar' cigarettes are the best there are!

3 I'm in debt and I don't have any money.

4 How are you? Fantastic!

5 What's wrong with the fridge? It's broken down.

Language point

6.2 The verb: past tense

■ Basic forms

In this unit we have our first encounter with the Arabic verb. For describing events that happened at a definite time in the past – that is, *completed actions* – and for certain other purposes that will be described later, the 'past tense' verb is used. The basic form of the past tense of the first group of verbs we will consider (Theme I verbs) consists of a consonant skeleton C-C-C (where C = consonant) to which one of three vowel patterns is applied: **a-a**, **i-a** or **u-a**. Thus CaCaC,

CiCaC and CuCaC are the possible Theme I basic forms. Typical examples of the three types are **shárab** 'to drink' (**sh-r-b**), **kítab** 'to write' (**k-t-b**) and **kúbar** 'to grow old/big' (**k-b-r**). In fact, although verbs are always, by convention, listed in vocabularies and dictionaries in this basic form, and translated into English as infinitives, they are in fact the 3rd person masculine singular form, and mean literally 'he drank', 'he wrote' and 'he grew old'. There is no infinitive in Arabic (though there is a verbal noun, equivalent to '(the act of) drinking, writing', etc., as we shall see later). Whether a verb has the **a-a**, **i-a** or **u-a** vowel pattern has to be learnt – there is no reliable rule that predicts it, and there is a certain amount of variation in vowel patterns from area to area within the Gulf region. The basic forms given in this book are the most common.

To this basic form of the verb are added suffixes denoting gender and number. As you will notice below, the second vowel of the vowel pattern (**a**) is dropped in certain persons of the verb. The full paradigms of our model verbs are:

shárab 'to drink'	**kítab** 'to write'	**kúbar** 'to grow old'	
sharábt	kitábt	kubárt	I
sharábt	kitábt	kubárt	you (m.)
sharábti	kitábti	kubárti	you (f.)
shárab	kítab	kúbar	he/it
shírbat	kítbat	kúbrat	she/it
sharábna	kitábna	kubárna	we
sharábtaw	kitábtaw	kubártaw	you (pl.)
shírbaw	kítbaw	kúbraw	they

Note that:

1 The 3rd person feminine and plural are of the general form CvCCat and CvCCaw. The 'v' is **i** except in CuCaC-type verbs, when it is always **u**.

2 In some areas of the Gulf, and especially in the speech of older or uneducated people, alternative forms for CvCCat/w are often heard. These alternatives have the general form iCCvCat/w. Thus, instead of **kítbat** 'she wrote', one hears **iktíbat**, and instead of **shírbaw** 'they drank' one hears **ishríbaw**. It is as well to be aware of such forms, though it might sound odd if you imitated them.

3 In Oman, and parts of the UAE, there are feminine plural forms for the 2nd and 3rd person when one is talking about a group that is purely composed of women. The 2nd feminine plural form is usually formed with **-tan,** and with **-an** for 3rd feminine plural, for example **sharabtan** 'you (f. pl.) drank', **shirban/sharban** 'they (f.) drank'. The vowel ending of the 'they (m.)' form is usually **-u**, not **-aw,** for example **shirbu** 'they (m.) drank'.

Exercise 6.4

Study the following verbs:

síma9	'to hear; listen to'	**Hámal**	'to carry'
dáxal	'to enter'	**lá9ab**	'to play'
kísar	'to break'	**tíras**	'to fill'
gá9ad	'to sit; stay'	**wúgaf**	'to stop (intrans.)'
Dárab	'to hit'		

Now translate into English:

1	sím9aw	9	Hámal	17	Darábna
2	ga9ádt	10	tirást	18	sharábtaw
3	la9ábtaw	11	kísar	19	kúbar
4	kúbrat	12	sím9at	20	la9ábti
5	tírsat	13	wugáft	21	gí9daw
6	Darábti	14	kísraw	22	kubárna
7	wúgfaw	15	Hímlaw		
8	daxálna	16	kítbat		

■ Suffixed forms

When the personal pronoun suffixes (5.4) are added to the verb forms described so far, a number of changes occur:

1 If the verb form ends in a vowel, this vowel is *lengthened and becomes stressed.* Thus:

kitábti		'you (f.) wrote'
kitábti + **ha**	**kitabtíiha**	'you (f.) wrote it (f.)'
kitábna		'we wrote'
kitábna + **ha**	**kitabnáaha**	'we wrote it (f.)'

2 If the pronoun suffix *also* begins with a vowel, the final vowel of the
   verb form is likewise lengthened but *the initial vowel of the suffix is
   dropped.* Thus:

   kitábti + ah   **kitabtíih**   'you (f.) wrote it (m.)'
   simá9na + ich   **sima9náach**   'we heard you (f.)'

3 In the case of the 2nd and 3rd persons plural, the final **-aw** changes
   to **oo** on suffixation:

   sím9aw + ik   **sim9óok**   'they heard you (m.)'
   simá9taw + ah   **sima9tóoh**   'you (pl.) heard it/him'

The paradigms below summarise the rules for forming suffixed forms
that (a) involve verb form + vowel-initial suffix and (b) involve verb form
+ consonant-initial suffix:

(a) 'to hear' + **-ik** or **-ah**		(b) 'to hear' + **-kum** or **-hum**	
simá9tik	I-you (m.)	**simá9tkum**	I-you (pl.)
simá9tah	you (m.)-him	**simá9thum**	you (m.)-them
sima9tíih	you (f.)-him	**sima9tíihum**	you (f.)-them
simá9ah	he-him	**simá9hum**	he-them
sim9átah	she-him	**sim9áthum**	she-them
sima9náak	we-you (m.)	**sima9náakum**	we-you (pl.)
sima9tóoh	you (pl.)-him	**sima9tóohum**	you (pl.)-them
sim9óoh	they-him	**sim9óohum**	they-them

Exercise 6.5

Read aloud and translate:

1 sim9óoh	5 daxalnáah	9 shirbóoh
2 tirástah	6 kisróoh	10 daxaltóoh
3 Hamálah	7 Darabnáah	
4 kisartíih	8 kitbátah	

Using the suffix **-ik**, translate into Arabic:

11 I heard you	14 he hit you	17 she carried you
12 she hit you	15 they heard you	18 we heard you
13 we carried you	16 he heard you	

Read aloud and translate:

19 Darábni	23 Darabtóoni	27 simá9ni
20 sim9óoni	24 Darabtíini	28 Himlátni
21 Dirbóoni	25 sim9átni	
22 Himlóoni	26 Hamálni	

Using the suffixes **-kum** or **-hum**, translate into Arabic:

29 I heard them	33 you (f.) carried them
30 they heard you	34 we hit you
31 he hit them	35 I filled them
32 you (pl.) broke them	36 they hit you

■ The negative (past tense)

Past-tense verbs are made negative by prefixing **maa** to the verb form.
Thus:

Darábhum	'he hit them'
maa Darábhum	'he didn't hit them'

■ Interrogatives

With a falling intonation (┐) on the syllable following the stress:

    ┐
Darábhum   'he hit them'

        ┐
maa Darábhum   'he didn't hit them'

a simple statement of fact is indicated. A question is indicated by an
intonation pattern that rises sharply (┘) on the syllable following the
stress:

    ┘
Darábhum?   'Did he hit them?'

       ┘
maa Darábhum?   'Didn't he hit them?'

When one wishes to ask a more open-ended question, the phrase **wálla la** ('or not?') with a falling intonation (┐) is used:

⌐   ┐
Darábhum wálla la? 'Did he hit them or not?'

Dialogue 6.1

(Audio 1; 17)

The following set of short dialogues is intended to give you practice in past-tense forms. Read them aloud and, referring where necessary to the Vocabulary for this unit, translate them.

1 A yáa 9áli, kitábt it-taqríir wálla la?
   B mit'ássif, yaa sáyyid Smith, máa kitábtah.
   A shlóon máa kitábtah?
   B walláahi, 9índi shúghul wáayid il-báarHa. ga9ádt fil-máktab
      Hátta s-sáa9a sítta, bas máa xalláStah.
   A záyn, máa 9aláyh.

2 A máa simá9t il-xábar?
   B shínhu?
   A sálwa níjHat fil-imtiHáan!
   B yáa saláam! u fáaTma?
   A híyya níjHat bá9ad, láakin 9abdállah físhal.
   B u ínta?
   A nijáHt!

3 A shlóon ghadáak il-yóom yaa áHmad?
   B walláahi l-9aDHíim, gháda máa fóogah fóog … 9áysh.
      u láHam u Saalúuna, u sharábna cháay áHmar.
   A xóosh sháy! u ba9adáyn?
   B ga9ádna shwáy fil-máylis u sharábna finjáal gáhwa.
   A rigádtaw wálla lá?
   B áy, rigádna shwáy il-9áSir.

4 A alló? ihní áHmad …
   B shlóonik áHmad insháallah záyn?
   A állah yisálmik, il-awláad mawjuudíin?
   B la, xírjaw is-sáa9a iHdá9shar u núSS u máa ríj9aw lil-Híin.
   A záyn, shúkran, fi 'amáan illáah.

5 A shfíich, yaa 'amíina, ta9báana?
   B áy, wáayid ta9báana. iS-SúbH ghasált ith-thiyáab, u ba9adáyn
      ghasált il-mawaa9íin il-wásxa. il-9áSir la9ábt wiyya l-yiháal
      saa9atáyn thaláath.

Vocabulary

arD (f.)	earth; floor	jidáar/jidráan	wall (interior)
il-báarHa	yesterday	kísar	to break
báHar/biHáar	sea	kítab	to write
bank/bunúuk	bank	kúbar	to grow up;
baríid	post;		grow old
	post office	láakin	but
ba9adáyn	afterwards	lá9ab	to play
ba9íid 9an	far from	li	to; for
bi	in; at; with	lúgha*(aat)	language
dáray(aat)	steps; stairs;	maa 9aláyh	it doesn't
	ladder		matter; OK,
dawwáar(aat)	traffic		no objection
	roundabout	maa9úun/	dishes;
dáxal	to enter	mawaa9íin	tableware
dayn/dyúun	debt	madíina*/múdun	town; city
Dárab	to strike; hit	madrása*/	school
físhal	to fail	madáaris	
foog	above; over;	mál9ab/	pitch; playing
	on top of; on;	maláa9ib	field
	upstairs	másyid/	mosque
gáriib min	near to	masáayid	
gá9ad	to sit; stay	mátHaf/matáaHif	museum
giddáam	in front of	mawjúud(iin)	present;
ghásal	to wash		existent
Hagg	right (n.)	máylis/mayáalis	sitting room
Hámal	to carry		(in an Arab-
Hátta	until; even		style house)
lil-Hiin	up till now	mayz(aat)	table
Íla	to; towards	mgáabil	opposite (prep.)
imtiHáan(aat)	examination;	mit'ássif(iin)	sorry
	test	náxal	palm tree(s)
jánTa*/janaTáat	bag; case	níjaH	to succeed;
			pass

rígad	to lie down; sleep	walláahi l-9aDHíim	by the great God (strong oath)
ríja9	to return; come back	wára	behind
síinama(aat)	cinema	wásix	dirty
síma9	to listen to; hear	wáTan	homeland
Saalúuna*	stew; curry	wáTani	national; belonging to one's homeland
shárab	to drink; smoke (tobacco)	wúgaf	to stop; stand
shway	for a little while	xábar/axbáar	piece of news
taHt	under; below; right next to	xállaS	to finish
		xáraj	to go out
taqríir/ taqaaríir	written report	yaa saláam	bravo!
tíras	to fill	yanb or yamm	next to; beside
thoob/thiyáab	clothes (sing. means a man's long shirt)	9ála	on; against
		9árabi/9árab	Arab; Arabic (pl. means 'Arabs')
wálla or wílla	or	9ayb/9uyúub	shame; disgrace

Cultural point

History (2): the British

British involvement in the Gulf dates from the early seventeenth century, when, in 1622, they helped the Safavid Persians to conquer the great Portuguese fortress at Hormuz, which dominated the entrance to the Gulf, and thus end a century Portuguese control. By 1650, the Portuguese had been expelled from Muscat, their last stronghold in the Gulf. But it would be another two centuries before the British took control of Gulf waters. Initially, they did so for very much the same reasons as the Portuguese in the sixteenth century – to protect the trade routes, in this case of the English East India Company, from the depredations of Gulf pirates. Even until the late eighteenth century,

British interest in the Gulf was almost exclusively commercial, but during the course of the nineteenth century, it became increasingly political, as individual European powers, as well as Ottoman Turks, struggled for supremacy. Between 1861 and 1916, the British concluded treaties with local rulers the length of the Gulf, under the terms of which the British provided security from external threats, while the rulers were largely left to rule the internal affairs of their realms themselves. There was a British Political Resident, answerable from 1873 until 1947 to the British Raj in Bombay, and based from 1946 in Bahrain, who was in overall charge of external affairs. There were also individual British Political Agents (known as the **balyóoz**) at various locations in the Gulf. One of the best known of these was H.R.P Dickson (1881–1959), British Political Agent in Bahrain in 1919–20 and in Kuwait from 1929 to 1936, later joining the Kuwait Oil Company (KOC). The original building that housed the Kuwait Political Agency, in which Dickson lived with his wife Violet, a fluent speaker of Bedouin Arabic, until his death in 1959, has now been converted into the Dickson House Cultural Centre. Dickson wrote two major books on the Gulf that he knew: *The Arab of the Desert* (1949) and *Kuwait and Her Neighbours* (1956). Some rulers engaged British advisers to help them run their internal affairs. Probably the most famous of these was Charles Dalrymple Belgrave, who was

Girls' school in Bahrain, mid-1930s

Source: Ahmad Mustafa Abu Hakima, *Eastern Arabia: Bahrain: Historic Photographs, Volume 1*, Hurtwood Press, London, 1984, p. 42

appointed adviser to the Bahraini ruler Sheikh Hamad bin Isa bin Ali in 1926, and left Bahrain, following the Suez Crisis, in 1957. He was known to all Bahrainis as **il-mustasháar** 'The Adviser' and oversaw the transformation of the country from a state of semi-feudalism to a (by the standards of the time) modern state with a public education system, a medical service and metalled roads.

Until independence for Bahrain, Qatar and the UAE in 1971, the British maintained a military presence in the Gulf whose centre was Bahrain, with an airbase at Muharraq (known to Bahrainis as **aaréf**, their pronunciation of 'RAF'), a naval base at Jufair and troops at Hamala. There were also large numbers of British people employed in the oil industry. It is this presence that explains the heavy infiltration of the Gulf dialects by many English terms for tools and modern materials, already noted in Unit Four's Cultural point.

 Reading Arabic

Look at the street map at the beginning of this unit (page 74), which contains the names of several landmarks. Match the Arabic script versions of the names of some of these landmarks below to the transliterations on the map. What do these names mean?

1	البنك الوطني	
2	مدرسة "ابو بكر"	
3	شركة "عنتر"	
4	شارع عثمان	
5	المتحف	
6	شارع عبد الله	

Look at the sign from the Merweb Hotel, Qatar (facing page). What is the Arabic word in the sign that means 'hotel'?

Look at the hotel sign below, which tells you where to park. What is the Arabic word in this sign for 'parking'?

Unit Seven

In this unit you will learn about:

- past-tense verbs beginning with a glottal stop
- past-tense verbs known as 'hollow' verbs
- reported speech, i.e. how to report that something has happened
- how to ask 'if' or 'whether'
- how to use **li'ann** 'because'
- expressions of manner, e.g. 'he went by car', 'he wrote with ease'
- further expressions of time, e.g. 'today', 'last Friday'

Language points

7.1 Past-tense verbs: verbs beginning with a glottal stop

We saw in Unit Six that the basic past-tense verb consists of a three-consonant skeleton C-C-C on to which one of three vowel patterns is superimposed. The first of a number of important subclasses of this kind of verb is that which has the glottal stop ' as first consonant. The two commonest verbs in this subclass are **'ákal** (**'-k-l**) 'to eat' and **'áxadh** (**'-x-dh**) 'to take'. These verbs behave very much like regular verbs except that, in the 3rd person feminine singular and 3rd person plural, they have exceptional forms. Their paradigms are as follows:

'akált	'I ate'	**'axádht**	'I took'
'akált	'you (m.) ate'	**'axádht**	'you (m.) took'
'akálti	'you (f.) ate'	**'axádhti**	'you (f.) took'
'ákal	'he ate'	**'áxadh**	'he took'
'ákalat/kálat	'she ate'	**'áxadhat/xádhat**	'she took'
'akálna	'we ate'	**'axádhna**	'we took'
'akáltaw	'you (pl.) ate'	**'axádhtaw**	'you (pl.) took'
'akálaw/kálaw	'they ate'	**'áxadhaw/xádhaw**	'they took'

Note that we do not get a CvCCat/w-type form in the 3rd person (like **shírbat/shírbaw** 'she/they drank'): the **-at/aw** suffixes are simply added to the stem **'ákal**, **'áxadh** without vowel changes. Optionally, the initial syllable **'a-** may be dropped in these 3rd person forms. In Oman, the forms are similar, and often lack the initial **'a-**. The Omani feminine plural forms for the 2nd and 3rd persons are respectively **káltan** and **kálan**, **xádhtan** and **xádhan**.

7.2 Past-tense verbs: 'hollow' verbs

A second, and very important subclass of past-tense verbs is the so-called 'hollow' verbs. The term 'hollow' refers to the fact that the middle consonant of the C-C-C skeleton is a 'weak' consonant – **w** or **y** – which fails to show up in the basic form of the verb. Thus the verb **gaal** 'to say' consists of the skeleton **g-w-l** on to which the vowel pattern **a-a** is superimposed, to give **gawal**. However, **w** is 'weak' when it occurs between **a-a**, and it drops out to give **gaal**. Similarly, the verb **Saar** 'to become, to happen' consists of an **S-y-r** skeleton and an **a-a** vowel pattern, which gives **Sayar**. But since **y** is weak, it drops out to give **Saar**. It is important to know whether the missing consonant in 'hollow' verbs is **w** or **y** since this determines the vowel pattern of the imperfect tense in such verbs (see Unit Eleven).

In the past tense, all 'hollow' verbs have the following characteristic paradigm:

gilt	'I said'	**gílna**	'we said'
gilt	'you (m.) said'	**gíltaw**	'you (pl.) said'
gílti	'you (f.) said'		
gaal	'he said'	**gáalaw**	'they said'
gáalat	'she said'		

So, from the verb **Saar** 'to happen; become', we get **Sirt** 'I became', etc., and from the verb **raaH** 'to go', we get **riHt** 'I went', etc. We can generalise by saying that, whenever the suffix denoting person and gender begins with a consonant, the basic form CaaC (**gaal, Saar, raaH**) is shortened to CiC- (**gil-, Sir-, riH-**) and the suffix is added:

gaal + t	→	**gilt**	'I/you (m.) said'
gaal + na	→	**gílna**	'we said'
gaal + taw	→	**gíltaw**	'you (pl.) said'

But, where the suffix begins with a vowel (or where there is no suffix), the basic form is retained:

gaal + at	→	**gaalat**	'she said'
gaal + aw	→	**gaalaw**	'they said'

In a few 'hollow' verbs, the vowel in the 'shortened' form of the stem is **u** rather than **i**. Thus, from **gaam** 'to rise; get up' we get **gumt** 'I rose' rather than **gimt**, and from **baag** 'to steal' we get **bugt** 'I stole' rather than **bigt**.

In the hollow verb, the Omani 2nd and 3rd feminine plural forms follow the normal Omani pattern, namely with **-tan** and **-an** endings. But in this particular verb, the vowel of the shortened stem in the speech of townspeople from Muscat and the Capital Area is usually **u** not **i**, and, as noted in Appendix 1(A) on variations in Omani speech, Omani townspeople have **q** where the rest of the Gulf (and Omani Bedouin) have **g**, so they would say **qult, qult, qúlti, qaal, qáalat, qúlna, qúltu, qúltan** ('you (f. pl.) say'), **qáalu, qáalan** ('they (f.) say') instead of the forms in the chart above.

In all other respects, 'hollow' verbs behave like regular verbs. Thus, when dependent personal pronouns are suffixed to them, we get such forms as the following:

jáabaw	'they brought'
jaabaw + ah → jaabóoh	'they brought it/him'
jibt	'I brought'
jibt + ah → jíbtah	'I brought it/him'

One very important 'hollow' verb is **jaa** 'to come'. This verb is conjugated as follows:

jiit	'I came'	**jíina**	'we came'
jiit	'you (m.) came'	**jíitaw**	'you (pl.) came'
jíiti	'you (f.) came'		
jaa/ja	'he came'	**jaw**	'they came'
jaat/jat	'she came'		

Note that the vowel of **jaa** and **jaat** may be shortened to **ja** and **jat**. Many Gulf Arabs also substitute **y** for **j** in this and other common words such as **jaab**: thus one hears **yiit** 'I came', etc. and **yibt** 'I brought' (see Appendix 1).

In Omani towns (see Appendix 1(A)), the dialect has a **g** where the rest of the Gulf (and Omani Bedouin) have **j** or **y** in such vocabulary items, so Muscat/Mutrah **giit** 'I came, **ga** 'he came', etc. The Omani 2nd and 3rd plural forms are **gíitaw** 'you (m. pl) came', **gíitan** 'you (pl.) came', **gáyu** 'they (m.) came' and **gáyan** 'they (f.) came'.

Exercise 7.1

Study the following 'hollow' verbs:

gaam	'to get up; rise'	**naam**	'to sleep'
gaal	'to say'	**baa9**	'to sell'
baag	'to steal'	**maat**	'to die'
shaal	'to remove'	**jaab**	'to bring'
jaa	'to come'	**raaH**	'to go'
Saar	'to become'	**Saad**	'to hunt; catch'
xaaf	'to fear'	**shaaf**	'to see'
kaan	'to be'	**zaar**	'to visit'

Translate the following into English:

1 náamaw	6 bugt	11 gáamat
2 ríHtaw	7 mitt	12 gáalaw
3 jíbti	8 Sírna	13 Sídtaw
4 záarat	9 xaaf	14 bí9na
5 shift	10 bí9taw	15 jíiti

16 Sáarat	21 sháafat	26 ráaHaw
17 gumt	22 nimt	27 jáabat
18 zirt	23 sháalaw	28 xúfti
19 maat	24 kint	29 káanat
20 jáabaw	25 gílna	30 Saad

 Dialogue 7.1

(Audio 1; 18)

This is extended translation practice. Read aloud and translate the following short dialogues.

1 A shu Saar?
   B báagaw s-sayyáara u baa9óoha!

2 A wayn ríHtaw il-báarHa? maa shifnáakum.
   B wállah, axádhna l-lansh u ríHna jazíira Saghíira. Sídna
      sámach wáayid u 'akalnáah Hagg il-9ásha.
   A xoosh shay!

3 A laysh ráaHaw l-bayt?
   B maa gáalaw líyyi, wállah.

4 A shu yíbti min is-suug?
   B ashyáa wáayid ... láHam bágar zayn u máywa u cham min
      yúuniyyat 9aysh.

5 A wayn jáasim? maa shíftah min zamáan.
   B jáasim raaH lándan Hagg il-9úTla S-Sayfíyya.
   A maHDHúuDH! cham fluus 'áxadh wiyyáah?
   B sitt imyát diináar.

6 A wayn 'axádhtaw l-9ásha il-báarHa?
   B wállah, 'axadhnáah fi máT9am lubnáani ísmah 'il-'arz', kaan
      il-'ákil ladhíidh kíllish u sharábna cham min ghárshat bábsi.

Language points

7.3 'To say that ...'

Reported speech is expressed in Arabic by using the particle **inn** 'that':

gilt lih inn jáasim raaH il-bayt.
'I told him (lit. 'said to him') that Jaasim had gone home.'

gaal líyyi inn jáasim maa 9índah ixwáan.
'He told me that Jaasim doesn't have any brothers.'

The 'dependent' personal pronouns may be suffixed directly to **inn** if the subject of the noun clause following **inn** is a pronoun:

gaal líyyi ínnik bi9t is-sayyáara.
'He told me that you had sold the car.'

gáalaw ínnich jíbti l-wálad wiyyáach.
'They said that you (f.) had brought the boy with you.'

If the suffixed personal pronoun begins with a consonant, **a** is inserted after **inn**:

gáalat ínnahum 9índahum máw9id ba9d iDH-DHúhur.
'She said they had a meeting in the afternoon.'

gaal lína ínnaha máatat min zamáan.
'He told us she'd died a long time ago.'

7.4 'To ask whether ...'

After the verb **sa'al** 'to ask', the particle **law** (variant: **lo**) 'if; whether' is used for reporting questions:

sa'álni law 9índi flúus káafi.
'He asked me if I had enough money.'

sa'álha law ínta sáakin fil-manáama.
'He asked her if you (m.) were living in Manama.'

Note that dependent personal pronouns are *not* suffixed to **law**.

7.5 li'ann 'because'

We have already noted that questions 'why?' are formed by using the word **laysh**:

laysh maa gilt líyyi ínnik bi9t is-sayyáara?
'Why didn't you tell me you'd sold the car?'

Such questions are answered by using the particle **li'ánn** 'because', which, like **inn**, may have dependent personal pronouns suffixed to it:

li'ínnik maa sa'áltni
'because you didn't ask me'

li'ínnik maa kint mawjúud
'because you weren't here'

li'ánni maa shíftik
'because I didn't see you'

li'ánni maa kaan 9índi waqt
'because I didn't have time'

As with **inn**, an **a** is inserted after **li'ann** if the suffixed pronoun begins with a consonant:

bí9tha li'ánnaha 9atíija.
'I sold it because it was old.'

Exercise 7.2

In the following exercise, you have to change direct into reported speech. A statement is made about a certain person(s) – you have to report that statement to the person(s) about whom it was made, making appropriate changes in the sentence, for example:

	'9áli raaH baghdáad.'
gaal	líyyi ínnik riHt baghdáad.
	'maa shifnáah min zamáan.'
gaalaw	liyyi innahum maa shaafook min zamaan.

1 'jáasim 'áxadh rúxSa u raaH id-dáxtar li'ánnah maríiD.'
gaal _____

2 'sálwa báa9at il-bayt il-9atíij li'ánnaha maa 9índaha fluus.'
gaal _____

3 'muHámmad jaab il-gháda wiyyáah u 'ákal mínnah shway.'
gaal _____

4 'jaw min amríika Hagg il-9úTla u jáabaw hadáaya Hagg il-yiháal.'
gaal _____

5 'fítHaw l-máxzan u sháalaw il-aaláat mínnah.'
gaal _____

6 'maa sháafatah min zamáan.'
gaal _____

7 'ana sáakin il-Hiin wara madrásat ábu bakr, garíib min báytik.'
gaal _____

8 'muHámmad ríja9 min ish-shúghul u naam min waqt li'ánnah ta9báan wáayid.'
gaal _____

9 'físhlaw fil-imtiHaanáat li'ánnahum kaslaaníin.'
gaal _____

10 'gaam u gaal 'áhlan wa sáhlan.'
gaal _____

Exercise 7.3

Change the following direct questions into indirect speech using *sá'al law* 'he asked if ...'. Imagine you are reporting the question to the person about whom it was asked, for example:

'záaraw il-qáahira?'
sa'álni law zírtaw il-qáahira.

1 'shift il-ahráam?'
sa'álni _____

2 'sím9aw il-xábar?'
sa'álni _____

3 'ríja9 min ish-shúghul?'
sa'álni _____

4 'níjHaw fil-imtiHáan?'
sa'álni _____

5 'kísar il-jaam?'
sá'alni _____

6 'báagat il-jánTa?'
sá'alni _____

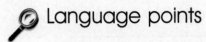

Language points

7.6 Expressions of manner

Adverbial expressions of manner are often expressed in Arabic by a preposition + noun phrase. Learn the following common phrases:

raaH	bil-baaS	'He went	by bus'
	biT-Tayyáara		by plane'
	bis-sayyáara		by car'
	bis-sáykal		by bicycle'

In these, and similar phrases that indicate mode of transport, **fi** is an alternative to **bi**:

kítab	bi-súr9a	'He wrote	quickly'
	bi-búTu'		slowly'
	bi-suhúula		with ease'
	bi-Su9úuba		with difficulty'

Note that, in the above phrases, there is no definite article **il**. In still other cases, manner adverbs are rendered by a single word:

raaH máshi.	'He went on foot.'
sháalha zitáat.	'He removed it quickly.'
Darábni chidhíi.	'He hit me like this.'

7.7 Further expressions of time

In addition to the time expressions learnt in the units immediately preceding this, the following are highly useful:

mita	'when'
il-yoom	'today'
fin-naháar	'in the daytime'

il-yoom is used to site a particular event at a particular time, for example:

riHt ish-shúghul il-yoom.
'I went to work today.'

fin-naháar (like **bil-layl** 'at night-time') indicates activity over a particular period of time (the part when there is daylight):

9indi shúghul fin-naháar.
'I have work during the daytime.'

'Day shift' in Arabic is in fact **zaam in-naháar.**

Note also: **ams** 'yesterday' and **áwwal ams** 'the day before yesterday'.
Expressions for 'next/last week/month', etc. are formed using the adjectives **jaay** 'coming' and **máaDi** 'past', which agree with the nouns they follow in the normal way:

is-subúu9 il-jaay/il-máaDi	'next/last week'
ish-sháhar il-jaay/il-máaDi	'next/last month'
is-sána l-jáaya/l-máaDya	'next/last year'

The days of the week are as follows:

yoom il-áHad	Sunday
yoom il-ithnáyn	Monday
yoom ith-thaláatha	Tuesday
yoom il-árba9a	Wednesday
yoom il-xamíis	Thursday
yoom il-júm9a	Friday
yoom is-sabt	Saturday

Very frequently, **yoom** is omitted:

9índana máw9id il-árba9a fis-sáa9a sítta u nuSS.
'We've got an appointment on Wednesday at 6.30.'

jaay and **máaDi** (agreeing where necessary) are used for 'next/last Sunday', etc.:

shifnáahum il-áHad il-máaDi.
'We saw them last Sunday.'

zaaróoha il-júm9a l-máaDya.
'They visited her last Friday.'

Note that, when saying what day it is, the phrase is:

il-yoom yoom il-xamíis.
Or **il-yoom il-xamíis.**
'Today is Thursday.'

Dialogue 7.2

 Read aloud and translate the following dialogue into English.

ríHla ila l-kuwáyt (Audio 1; 19)

A   yaa hála yaa hála ábu xalíil! il-Hámdu lilláah 9ala saláamtik!
B   állah yisálmik yaa Hássan.
A   chayf káanat ir-ríHla? riHt biT-Tayyáara, la?
B   ay ná9am. kíllish záyna káanat. wuSált il-kuwáyt fis-sáa9a
    thaláatha il-9áSir u riHt síida min il-maTáar ila s-saalmíyya.
A   hálik saakníin hunáak?
B   ay. ayyáam zamáan kaan 9índahum bayt 9atíij fis-suug bas
    baa9óoh u 'áxadhaw bayt jadíid bil-'ajáar issána l-máaDya. bayt
    Hálu wállah lih Hoosh dáaxili fiih shájar u fiih Hoosh barráani
    kíllah zuhúur.
A   zayn. u riHt mukáan ghayr fil-kuwáyt?
B   ríHna l-Hadáayiq wil-aswáag fin-naháar wil-maTáa9im bil-layl
A   shloon hálik?
B   il-Hámdu lilláah bi xayr. wild 9ámmi wállah maa shíftah min
    zamáan u Saar kíllish 9ood il-Hiin – rayyáal ya9ni. u húwa
    sháaTir bá9ad – Tála9 il-áwwal fil-imtiHaanáat ith-thaanawíyya.

 Exercise 7.4

Translate the following dialogue into Arabic.

A trip to London

- Hello, hello, Hassan! How was your trip?
- Great! We got to London at four in the afternoon and went
  straight from the airport to the hotel. Our room was very big with
  a beautiful view from the window.
- Where did you go in London?
- We visited the museums, the palaces and the restaurants during
  the day and the theatres and cinemas at night. Food is very
  expensive in comparison to Kuwait, but the people are friendly
  and the weather's cool.
- How much did you spend?
- A lot! But never mind! We were happy in London!

Vocabulary

'áala*(aat)	tool	isláam	Islam
ahl (or hal)	family	isláami	Islamic
il-ahráam	the Pyramids	il-ithnáyn	Monday
il-áHad	Sunday	jaa	to come
bil-'ajáar	on a lease; for rent	jaab	to bring
		jaay	coming; next
'ákal	to eat	jaww	weather
amríika	America	jazíira*/jízir	island
amríiki (yyiin)	American	il-júm9a*	Friday
ams	yesterday	káafi	enough
il-'árba9a	Wednesday	kaan	to be
'arz	cedar tree	kasláan(iin)	lazy
áwwal ams	the day before yesterday	kíllish	completely
		law	whether
'áxadh	to take	lubnáan	Lebanon
baag	to steal	lubnáani	Lebanese
báayig/bawáyga	thief	máaDi	past
baa9	to sell	maat	to die
baghdáad	Baghdad	maHDHúuDH (iin)	lucky
bárra	outside (adv.)		
barráani	outer (adj.)	il-manáama	Manama
búTu'	slowness	mánDHar/ manáaDHir	view
chidhíi	like this		
fítaH	to open	maríiD/máraDa	sick; ill
fúnduq/ fanáadiq	hotel	máshi	on foot
		maTáar(aat)	airport
gaal	to say	máT9am/ maTáa9im	restaurant
gaam	to get up; rise		
ghayr	other than	máxzan/ maxáazin	store cupboard; storage place
hádiya/hadáaya	present; gift		
Hadíqa/ Hadáayiq	park; garden	máywa*	fruit
		min	from; of
Hagg	for; to	miskíin	poor; wretched
Il-Hámdu lilláah 9ala salámtik	Welcome back!	míSir	Egypt
		mistáanis(iin)	happy; content
Hoosh/aHwáash	courtyard	naam	to sleep
inn	that (conj.)	naháar	daytime

bin-nísba íla	in relation to; in comparison to	shaal	to remove
il-qáahira*	Cairo	sháaTir(iin)	clever; smart
raaH	to go	shájar	trees (coll.)
ríHla*(aat)	trip; outing	shúrTa*	police
rúxSa*	permission (to leave)	Tála9	to go out; come out of
sá'al	to ask	Táyyib(iin)	pleasant; good (of manner)
is-saalmíyya	Salmiya	ith-thaláatha	Tuesday
is-sabt	Saturday	waqt	time
sáykal	bicycle	min waqt	early
síida	straightaway; straight on	wúSal	to arrive
suhúula*	ease	xaaf	to fear
súr9a*	speed	il-xamíis	Thursday
Saad	to hunt; catch	zaam(aat)	shift (of work)
Saar	to become; happen	zaar	to visit
Sadíiq/aSdiqáa	friend	zahra*/zuhúur	flower
Sáraf	to pay; spend	min zamáan	for a long time (up to the present)
Sayf	summer (n.)	ayyáam zamáan	(in) the old days
Sáyfi	summer (adj.)	zitáat	quickly
Su9úuba*	difficulty	9ajíib	strange; bizarre
shaaf	to look, see	9amm	paternal uncle

 ## Cultural point

The Islamic year

The Islamic calendar has 12 months, but is lunar rather than solar, and so is about 11 days shorter than ours. The sighting of the new moon signals the end of one month and the beginning of the next. This is particularly important with regard to certain religious events, such as determining the end of the fasting month of Ramadan (**ramaDáan**). Islamic dates are reckoned from the migration (**híjra**) of the Prophet Muhammad from Makkah to Medina in 622 AD, so they are roughly 600 years behind Gregorian ones. So, for example, 1 January 2000 was 24 Ramadan 1420. Any given date on the Islamic calendar will occur about 11 days earlier on the Gregorian calendar every year, which means that each Islamic month takes about 30 solar years to rotate to the same point. The Islamic months are as follows:

1	muHárram	7	rájab
2	Sáfar	8	sha9báan
3	rabíi9 al-áwwal	9	ramaDáan
4	rabíi9 ath-tháani	10	shawwáal
5	jumáada al-áwwal	11	dhu l-qá9da
6	jumáada ath-tháani	12	dhu l-Híjja

The Islamic calendar is called **at-taqwíim al-híjri**, 'the Hijri calendar', the adjective **híjri** meaning 'migrational', since its reference point is to the **híjra** 'migration' of the Prophet Muhammad from Makkah to Medina. The Islamic calendar is widely used in the Gulf and Arabia, with the Islamic date often appearing (on official letters, etc.) alongside the Gregorian one, which is called **at-taqwíim al-míilaadi** 'the Christian calendar', the adjective **míilaadi** meaning 'appertaining to the birth (namely of Christ)'. 'Date' is **táariix**, so **at-táariix al-híjri** means 'the Islamic date', and **at-táariix al-míilaadi** 'the Christian ('common era') date'.

There are two major religious festivals in the Islamic calendar. The first is the breaking of the fast at the end of Ramadan, called **9iid al-fiTr** ('the feast of the fast-breaking'). During Ramadan, Muslims fast from sunup to sundown, during which time they must not eat, drink or have sex. The firing of a cannon signals the end of the daily fast, which in the Gulf is traditionally broken by the drinking of water and the eating of dates, before a larger meal is eaten later on. As well as a time for fasting (**aS-Sóom**), Ramadan, as elsewhere in the Muslim World, is a time for prayer, studying the Qur'an and quiet reflection: the pace of life slows and government offices, shops and schools work shorter hours. With the eagerly awaited **9iid** comes an explosion of celebration and a holiday of three days, when each person wishes friends, family and neighbours a 'blessed holiday' (**9iid mubáarak!**) and the children are given new clothes.

9iid al-aD-Ha ('the feast of the sacrifice') comes on the tenth day of **dhu l-Híjja**, the month when those Muslims who have the means and the time make the pilgrimage (**al-Hajj**) to Makkah. The completion of the pilgrimage rituals is marked by the sacrifice of an animal (**dhabiiHa**), usually a sheep, which is then cooked and eaten. The feast lasts three days. The month of **dhu l-Híjja** marks the end of the Islamic year, and the new year begins with the month of **muHárram.**

The month of **muHárram** is particularly significant for the Shi'i communities of the Gulf (in particular Bahrain, where there are large numbers of Shi'a). For several days leading up to the tenth of the month, the Shi'a commemorate the martyrdom of Hussein, son of 'Ali, the Prophet's cousin and brother-in-law, and many members of his family, at Kerbela in Iraq in AD 680, with street processions (known as **9áza** 'mourning') and readings in Shi'i religious centres (known as **mawáatim** or **Husayniyyáat**).

 # Reading Arabic

In this unit, we will practise reading Arabic numbers and Islamic dates.

Here are the names of the Islamic months in Arabic script. They are out of order: match them with the transliterations of their names you met in the Cultural point in this unit.

1	رجب	
2	صفر	
3	جمادى الأول	
4	محرم	
5	شوال	
6	ذو القعدة	
7	ربيع الثاني	
8	رمضان	
9	ذو الحجة	
10	شعبان	
11	ربيع الأول	
12	جمادى الثاني	

Arabic numbers, as we have seen, are normally read from left to right. What are these years?

1	١٩٨٢	4	١٨٣٠	7	١٥٦٧
2	٢٠٠٣	5	١٠٦٦	8	٢٠١٠
3	١٧٦٥	6	١٤٩٢	9	١٦٠٤

Although numbers are read from left to right, dates (day-month-year) are ordered from right to left, in the same direction as Arabic script. So, for example, '17 Ramadan 1429' looks like this:

١٤٢٩	رمضان	١٧

What are the following dates?

١٠٠٨	جمادى الثاني	٢
١٣٤١	ذو القعدة	٢٢
١٢٥٩	محرم	٨
٩٤٦	شوال	١٧
١٤١٠	ربيع الأول	٢٦

We will do further work on reading (Gregorian) dates in Unit 9.

Unit Eight

In this unit you will learn about:

- noun phrases, e.g. 'a woman's face', 'the house-key'
- the elative adjective: how to say 'bigger', 'biggest', etc.
- word order

Language point

8.1 Noun phrases

In Unit One, we saw that expressions of quantity, such as 'a kilo of rice' or 'a bag of cement', were expressed in Arabic by the simple juxtaposition of the two nouns concerned:

káylo 9aysh	'a kilo of rice'	(lit. 'kilo rice')
chiis smiit	'a bag of cement'	(lit. 'bag cement')

In non-quantitative noun phrases, a similar principle applies. Look at the following examples:

miftáaH bayt	'a house-key'	(lit. 'key house')
yad rayyáal	'a man's hand'	(lit. 'hand man')
wajh mára	'a woman's face'	(lit. 'face woman')
lí9bat yiháal	'a children's game'	(lit. 'game children')

Note that the hidden **t** of the feminine noun **lí9ba** 'game' shows up in the last example, just as it does in quantitative expressions such as **gúT9at láHam** 'a piece of meat'.

When such noun phrases are made definite ('*the* house-key', '*the* piece of meat', etc.), the article **il** is prefixed to the second element of the phrase only:

gúT9at il-láHam	'the piece of meat'
miftáaH il-bayt	'the house-key'
lí9bat il-yiháal	'the children's game'
wajh il-mára	'the woman's face'

If an adjective modifies the first element in such a phrase, for example 'the delicious piece of meat' or 'the big house-key', this adjective is nonetheless placed *after* the complete phrase, and agrees grammatically with the noun it modifies, thus:

> **gúT9at il-láHam il-ladhíidha**
> 'the delicious piece of meat'

where **ladhíidha** is feminine since it modifies **gúT9a**, and

> **wajh il-mára l-jamíil**
> 'the woman's beautiful face'

where **jamíil**, which is masculine, agrees with **wajh** although it follows the feminine noun **mára**. If one wishes to say 'the piece of delicious meat' or 'the face of the beautiful woman', the adjective is placed in the same position, but agrees with the second element in the noun phrase:

gúT9at il-láHam il-ladhíidh	**wajh il-mára l-jamíila**
'the piece of delicious meat'	'the face of the beautiful woman'

In noun phrases where more than two nouns are involved, the article **il** must always precede the final noun, if the phrase is definite:

indef.:	**loon wajh mára**	'the colour of a woman's face'
def.:	**loon wajh il-mára**	'the colour of the woman's face'

Exercise 8.1

Translate the following noun phrases into Arabic:

1 the famous company boss

2 the Egyptian headmaster
   (= 'manager of the school')

3 the outside door of the house

4 the fish market

5 the main accounts office   7 the Prime Minister
                                         (= 'head of the ministers')
6 the big boys' school   8 the high prices of materials

Translate into English:

9 wizáarat id-difáa9   13 laytáat ish-shawáari9
10 dáwlat il-kuwáyt   14 wálad mudíir ish-shárika
11 finjáal il-gáhwa   15 bint mudíirat madrása
12 kútub il-máktaba l-waTaníyya   16 daráayish báyti l-9atíij

---

An alternative, and extremely common, way of linking nouns together
into a noun phrase is to use the particle **maal** (f. **maala(t)**), which means
'belonging to'. **maal** is usually used in definite non-quantitative phrases.
Thus, instead of saying

    miftáaH il-bayt   'the house-key'

we may say

    il-miftáaH maal il-bayt

and instead of

    lí9bat il-yiháal   'the children's game'

we may say

    il-lí9ba máalat il-yiháal

Where noun phrases of more than two elements are concerned, the
position of **maal** will depend on the precise meaning one wishes to
convey. Thus instead of

    loon wajh il-mára
    'the colour of the woman's face'

we may say

      il-loon maal wajh il-mára
      'the colour of the woman's face'

or   **loon il-wajh maal il-mára**
      'the woman's face colour'

Possessive pronouns may also be suffixed to **maal/maala**:

il-bayt máali	'my house'
il-byúut máalti	'my houses'
il-bádla z-zárga máaltah	'his blue suit'

Note that **bayt máali** and **bádla zárga máaltah** would mean '*a* house of mine' and '*a* blue suit of his', meaning that 'I' or 'he' had more than one. **maal** is not normally used in quantitative expressions: **chiis is-smiit** means 'the bag of cement', but **il-chiis maal is-smiit** would normally be understood as meaning 'the bag in which cement is put' or 'the cement bag'.

Exercise 8.2

Change the following noun phrases into noun phrases using **maal** that have the same meaning, and translate them into English:

1 madrásat il-banáat	6 jánTatich il-kabíira
2 máktab ir-ra'íis	7 jidráan il-gáSir id-daaxilíyya
3 zaam in-naháar	8 maTáabix máT9am il-'arz
4 qamíiSi l-áHmar	9 SúHuf il-kitáab
5 daráayish il-Híjra l-9óoda	10 firíij il-bagaagíil

Language point

8.2 The elative adjective

The elative adjective, which is used in Arabic in roughly the same way as the comparative and superlative forms of the adjective in English ('bigger', 'biggest'), is formed according to the pattern $aC_1C_2aC_3$, where each 'C' represents a root consonant of the word. Thus, in words where there are no 'weak' consonants in C_3 position:

kabíir	'big'	**ákbar**	'bigger'
jamíil	'beautiful'	**ájmal**	'more beautiful'
zayn	'good'	**ázyan**	'better'

In words where C_3 is 'weak' (**w** or **y**, which in C_3 position are respectively spelt **u** and **i**), the pattern is as follows:

gháni	'rich'	**ághna**	'richer'
Hálu	'sweet; nice'	**áHla**	'sweeter; nicer'

Where C_2 and C_3 are the same, the elative is typically of the form aCaCC:

galíil	'little; few'	**agáll**	'less; fewer'
xafíif	'light (weight)'	**axáff**	'lighter'

When two things are compared, the preposition **min** 'than; from' is used:

sálwa ájmal min fáaTma.
'Salwa is prettier than Faatima.'

il-kuwaytiyyíin ághna min il-baHrayniyyíin.
'The Kuwaitis are richer than the Bahrainis.'

It can be seen from these two examples, in which feminine and plural nouns are being compared, that the elative adjective does not agree with the noun it modifies in number or gender.

There are a few classes of adjectives whose elative adjective cannot be formed according to the above pattern. The elative in these cases is made by using the elative of **kathíir** 'many; a lot' – that is, **ákthar** 'more' – together with the ordinary form of the adjective. Adjectives of the CaCCaan pattern (e.g. **ta9báan** 'tired') and colour adjectives (e.g. **áHmar** 'red') form their elatives in this way. Note that, in cases like these, **ákthar** is not declined, but **ta9báan**, **áHmar**, etc. are:

jáasim ta9báan ákthar min 9áli.
'Jaasim is more tired than Ali.'

fáaTma za9láana ákthar min áHmad.
'Faatima is more upset than Ahmad.'

ir-rayaayíil farHaaníin ákthar min in-niswáan.
'The men are happier than the women.'

il-báHar ázrag ákthar min is-síma.
'The sea is bluer than the sky.'

bádlatik zárga ákthar min bádlati ána.
'Your suit is bluer than mine.'

In order to express the 'superlative', **il** is prefixed to the elative:

sálwa il-áHla **jáasim ta9báan il-ákthar**
'Salwa is the prettiest' 'Jaasim is the tiredest'

máT9am 'il-'arz' il-máT9am il-áHsan fil-imaaráat.
' "The Cedars" restaurant is the best restaurant in the Emirates.'

ish-shárika l-akbar fil-baHráyn shárikat in-nafT il-baHrayníyya.
'The biggest company in Bahrain is the Bahrain Oil Company.'

il-wálad il-kasláan il-ákthar mHámmad.
'The laziest boy is Muhammad.'

The superlative may also be expressed by other turns of phrase involving the elative. Note the following:

1 with a following singular noun:

   9áli áHsan 9áamil fil-qísim.
   'Ali is the best worker in the section.'

   sálwa áshTar bint fiS-Saff.
   'Salwa is the cleverest girl in the class.'

2 with a following definite plural noun:

   9áli áHsan il-9ummáal fil-qísim.
   'Ali is the best worker in the section.'

   sálwa áshTar il-banáat fiS-Saff.
   'Salwa is the cleverest girl in the class.'

3 with a following pronoun:

   kill il-banáat fiS-Saff shaaTríin láakin sálwa áshTarhum.
   'All the girls in the class are clever, but Salwa is the cleverest.'

   káanaw xámsat ixwáan, u 9áli ákbarhum.
   'They were five brothers, and Ali was the eldest (of them).'

Note that, if the pronoun is suffixed to an elative that has a weak final consonant, for example **aġhna** 'richer' or **aġhla** 'dearer; more expensive', the final **-a** is lengthened to **-aa**. Such elative forms as **aġhna** really have a 'hidden' final **-aa**, but this only shows up in suffixed forms:

shift xams sayyaaráat, aghláahum it-tuyúuta.
'I saw five cars, the dearest of them was the Toyota.'

4   with a following **wáaHid** (f. **wáHda**):

kílhum shaaTríin láakin sálwa áshTar wáHda.
'All of them are clever, but Salwa is the cleverest one.'

il-bayt máali ákbar wáaHid fish-sháari9.
'My house is the biggest one in the street.'

 Exercise 8.3

Look at the following example:

sí9ir il-9aysh wáayid gháali.
'The price of rice is very high.'

(láHam)   →   **ay, láakin sí9ir il-láHam ághla bá9ad!**
'Yes, but the price of meat is even higher!'

Transform the following sentences in the same way, using the cue words
in brackets. Translate the sentences.

1   sí9ir il-láHam gháali
    (sámach)   →   _____

2   'ákil il-máT9am zayn
    (bayt)   →   _____

3   banáat míSir Halwíin
    (lubnán)   →   _____

4   sayyáarat il-mudíir kabíira
    (axúuk)   →   _____

5   sikirtíirat il-muHásib kasláana
    (ra'íis)   →   _____

6   dukkán il-xabbáaz wásix
    (baggáal)   →   _____

7   ráatib il-9áamil galíil
    (farráash)   →   _____

8   sámach il-kuwáyt ladhíidh
    (baHráyn)   →   _____

Language point

8.3 Word order

In sentences that contain a verb, the normal word order in Arabic is
verb-subject-object/complement:

fishal 9áli fil-imtiHáan.
'Ali failed in the exam.'

Dárab áHmad axúuh bi shídda.
'Ahmed hit his brother hard.'

In subordinate clauses after **inn**, however, the order is subject-verb:

gaal 9áli inn áHmad raaH il-bayt.
'Ali said that Ahmad had gone home.'

gáalat il-mára inn áHmad maa 9índah fluus wáayid.
'The woman said that Ahmad hadn't got a lot of money.'

In sentences that do not contain verbs – that is, sentences that consist
simply of a subject and non-verbal complement – the subject comes
first:

axúuyi rayyáal zayn.
'My brother is a good man.'

húwwa mudíir ish-shárika.
'He's the boss of the company.'

Sometimes, however, for reasons of emphasis, this order is reversed:

rayyáal zayn, axúuyi!
'My brother's a *really good man*!' (and not a no-good)

mudíir ish-shárika, húwwa!
'He's the company *boss*!' (rather than an ordinary worker).

This reversal of normal order is extremely common when an assertion
is being contradicted. Sometimes, however, it is used without any
deliberate emphasis. For example, the Gulf Arabic equivalent of 'My
friend's job is building' may be either:

shúghul Sadíiqi bannáay
(lit. 'work my friend builder')

or   **Sadíiqi shúghlah bannáay**
     (lit. 'my friend his work builder')

Similarly:

     jinsíyyat abúuyi sa9uudíyya

or   **abúuyi jinsíyyatah sa9uudíyya**
     'My father's nationality is Saudi Arabian.'

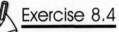

Exercise 8.4

In this exercise, an assertion is made followed by the 'tag question'
muu chidhíi? 'Is that not so?' Contradict the assertion in the manner
exemplified, and translate into English:

               íxit zóojtik ráaHat míSir, muu chidhíi?
(lándan)   **la, zóojti íxitha ráaHat lándan!**

'Your wife's sister went to Egypt, didn't she?'
'No, my wife's sister went to London!'

1 shúghul amíina káatiba, muu chidhíi?
   (mumárriDa) _____

   _____

2 wild 9áli l-ákbar kíllish sháaTir, muu chidhíi?
   (ghábi) _____

   _____

3 il-bayt maal hálik fi firíij il-mukháarga, muu chidhíi?
   (firíij il-Hammáam)_____

   _____

4 jaríimat sálwa ínnaha báagat sitt ímyat diináar, muu chidhíi?
   (gítlat zóojha) _____

   _____

5 il-yoomíyya máalat il-xáadim xámsat danaaníir, muu chidhíi?
   (síttat danaaníir) _____

   _____

6 iT-Táabiq ith-tháani maal il-bank fiih kandíshan, muu chidhíi?
   (maa fiih) _____

   _____

7 bu9d il-baHráyn 9an gíTar xamsíin mayl, muu chidhíi?
   (thalaathíin) _____

   _____

Exercise 8.5 (Audio 1; 20)

This is pronunciation and comprehension practice. Listen to, then read
aloud the following passage and answer the comprehension questions
on it. Consult the Vocabulary where necessary.

il-baHráyn

mamlákat il-baHráyn jazíira Saghíira fil-xalíij il-9árabi. kaan ísimha
fi qadíim iz-zamáan 'dilmúun' u Saar ísimha 'il-baHráyn'
9ógubmaa fitHóoha il-9árab fil-qarn is-sáabi9 bá9ad il-miiláad,
ya9ni 9ógub il-híjra bi shwáy. sammóoha 'il-baHráyn' li'ann fíiha
noo9áyn maay – maay Hálwa u maay báHar.
    káanat ayyáam zamáan il-mukádda l-waHíida máalat
il-baHrayniyyíin il-ghooS ... ya9ni il-ghooS Hagg il-lú'lu'. láakin
fil-arba9iináat wil-xamsiináat Saar is-suug máalah Da9íif shway u
tírkaw il-ghawaawíiS áktharhum il-ghooS u ráaHaw shárikat in-
nifT – ya9ni báapko.
    9ádad is-sukkáan maal il-baHráyn Haalíyyan Hawáali thalaath
ímyat alf áktharhum Táb9an jinsíyyathum baHrayníyya. il-baHráyn
bálad faqíir bin-nísba ila buldáan tháaniya fil-xalíij – máthalan
il-kuwáyt u gíTar – li'ann maa fiih nifT wáayid taHt 'árDha. láakin
il-baHráyn fi rá'yi ána ájmal u áHsan mínhum alf márra. laysh?
li'ánnaha báladi Táb9an! la shakk ínnaha áHsan bálad fil-xalíij!

Now answer the following questions in English:

1 When did the Arabs conquer Bahrain?

2 Why did they name it Bahrain?

3 What happened to the pearl trade in the 1940s and 1950s?

4 Where did the ex-divers find work?

5 What is the population of Bahrain?

6 Why is Bahrain a relatively poor country by Gulf standards?

7 How does the speaker feel about Bahrain in relation to Kuwait
   and Qatar? Why?

Vocabulary

áHsan	better	layt(aat)	light (e.g. of a street, car)
arba9iináat	the (19)40s		
baab/biibáan	door	lí9ba*(aat)	game
bádla*(aat)	suit of clothes	lú'lu'/la'áali	pearl
il-baHráyn	Bahrain	máadda*/	material;
bálad	country; town	mawáadd	substance
bannáay/	builder	maal	belonging to
banáani		mámlaka	kingdom
buldáan	countries	mashhúur	famous
bu9d	distance	máTbax-	kitchen
dáwla*/dúwal	nation-state	maTáabix	
difáa9	defence	máthalan	for example
dukkáan/	shop	miftáaH/	key; opener
dakaakíin		mafaatíiH	
Da9íif(iin)	weak	miiláad	birth
faqíir/fagáara	poor	muHáasib(iin)	accountant
fítaH	to open; conquer	mukádda*	job; way of
galíil(iin)	few; small in number		earning money
		mumárriDa*(aat)	nurse
gítal	to kill	mút9ib	tiring
gúwi/agwiyáa	strong	muu chidhíi?	isn't that so?
ghábi/aghbiyáa	stupid	náadi/nawáadi	club; society
ghawáaS/	pearl-diver	nifT	petroleum
ghawaawíiS		qadíim	ancient times
ghooS	pearl-diving	iz-zamáan	
il-híjra*	The Prophet's flight from Makkah to Medina	qarn/qurúun	century
		rá'y/aráa	opinion
		sáabi9	seventh
		sáakin/sukkáan	inhabitant
Haalíyyan	at the moment	sámma	to name
Hisáab(aat)	(financial) account	sa9úudi(yyiin)	Saudi Arabian
		síma	sky
imáara*(aat)	emirate	sí9ir/as9áar	cost; price
íxit/xawáat	sister	SaHíifa*/SúHuf	page (of a book)
jamíil	beautiful		
jaríima*/jaráa'im	crime	SaHráa	desert
kathíir(iin)	many; numerous	shakk/shkúuk	doubt
		shídda*	strength; intensity

bi shwáy	by a small amount	xamsiináat	the (19)50s
tárak	to leave	yad or iid/ayáadi	hand
Táabiq/ Tawáabiq	storey	yoomíyya*(aat)	day's wages
		zayt	oil
thagíil/thigáal	heavy	ziráa9a*	agriculture
ustáadh/ asáatidha	teacher	zooj/azwáaj	husband
		zóoja*(aat)	wife
waHíid	single; sole	9ádad	number (i.e. total)
wajh/wujúuh	face	9an	from; away from
wazíir/wuzaráa	minister		
xafíif/xifáaf	light (in weight)	9ógub	after (prep.)
il-xalíij	(Arabian) Gulf	9ógubmaa	after (conj.)

Cultural point

Building traditions

We are all familiar with the current fashions in public and private building in the Gulf States: enormous mosques, tall skyscrapers and luxurious modern air-conditioned villas and flats. But it was not always so. Even until as late as the 1950s, the houses of middle-class and even rich Gulf merchant families, where often several generations of the same family would be living, were often built in the traditional style in which the building 'looked inwards' rather than 'outwards' to the hostile natural elements of heat, wind and flying sand. The central element was the **Hoosh**, or open 'courtyard', around which the living and sleeping quarters of the house were arranged. Ventilation, before the days of air-conditioning (**kandíshan** as it was first known), was often by means of a wind tower, known by the Persian term **baadgiir** (or **baakdiir**). The wind tower was built high above roof level and faced the prevailing (northerly) wind, and was constructed in such a way that the wind was deflected downwards by vertical recesses in the plasterwork into the rooms below.

The wind tower is now, of course, a thing of the past, although echoes of it can still be seen in architectural decoration in modern Gulf buildings and shopping malls. Poorer people in the Gulf could not afford buildings made of stone, imported wood and gypsum, and they usually lived in

houses made of various products of the palm tree: dried palm fronds
(**sa9af**) woven into panels and held together by poles and palm rope.
There was a variety of types of construction ranging from the simple
barasti and **9ariish** (pictured below) to the **kabar**, with walls built out
of sea-stone (**fruush**) but with a thatched roof of palm fronds. These
structures were very cool, and often families would move into them for
the summer months when the heat made life in stone-built houses
difficult to endure.

Reading Arabic

In this unit we are going to look at street signs that involve the use of
the noun phrase constructions we met earlier. Look at the sign below.

Can you read the Arabic on this restaurant sign? It says **Sáalat al-
9aa'iláat**. **Sáala** means 'large room' (it's actually a borrowing of Italian
sala). **9aa'iláat** is the plural of **9áa'ila**, meaning 'family'. So the phrase
literally means 'room for families', and is an example of the kind of
phrase we saw in 8.1 above. (Gulf restaurants often have special rooms
of this kind, where women and children can feel more relaxed.)

Here is another restaurant sign involving the same construction, this
time with three nouns strung together, only the last being marked as
definite by having the definite article attached to it.

Can you read it? The script style is a little more difficult. It says
ma'kuuláat máT9am al-afándi, meaning literally 'foods of the
restaurant of the Effendi' – below it there appear pictures of the dishes
served. **ma'kuuláat** is the plural of **ma'kúul**, which means 'food; dish
of food'; the word **máT9am** we have already met; and **al-afándi** means
'the gentleman', a word formerly used in Egypt to refer to middle-class
'gentlemen', which nowadays gives an impression of old-world charm!

So the sign, liberally translated, means 'Dishes served in the Effendi's (or 'Gentleman's') Restaurant'.

Finally, look at this sign for the Qatar Islamic Bank.

Can you read the Arabic? It say **máSraf qáTar al-'isláami**. This is a good example of the placement of the adjective **after the complete noun phrase**, even when the adjective applies to its first element. Thus the noun phrase is **máSraf qáTar**, which means 'Bank of Qatar' or 'Qatar Bank', the word **máSraf** 'bank' being an alternative to the English borrowing *bank*, which we have already met. The adjective **'isláami**, which tells you what kind of bank it is, is placed *after* the whole noun phrase, even though it is the first element of this phrase, 'bank', which it modifies.

Read and translate the following:

1 **dáwli** or **dúwali** means 'international'

مطار الكويت الدولي

2 **siyáaHi** means 'touristic'

شركة "عنتر" السياحية

3 **'ájnabi** means 'foreign'

قسم اللغات الأجنبية

4

بنك البحرين الوطني

5 **Síini** means 'Chinese'

مطعم "الزهرة" الصيني

Unit Nine

In this unit you will learn about:

- past-tense 'doubled' verbs: CaCC
- past-tense 'weak' verbs: CvCa
- time conjunctions, e.g. 'at the time when', 'after', 'before', 'as soon as'
- ordinal numbers: 'first', 'second', etc.
- months, including dates

Language points

9.1 Past-tense verbs: 'doubled' verbs

The first of two further subcategories of the verb is the so-called 'doubled' verb. In 'doubled' verbs, the consonants in second and third position in the consonant skeleton are the same. Thus, we have the root **d-sh-sh** with the basic meaning 'to enter'. By normal rules, the basic form of the verb from this root would be **dashash**; this, however, is an inadmissible verb form in Arabic, and we find **dashsh** 'to enter' instead. In the same way, we find **gaTT** 'to throw' instead of **gaTaT** from the root **g-T-T**. The basic form of the past tense of 'doubled' verbs is always CaCC (where C = consonant), and they are all conjugated according to the following pattern:

shaggáyt	'I tore'	**shaggáyna**	'we tore'
shaggáyt	'you (m.) tore'	**shaggáytaw**	'you (pl.) tore'
shaggáyti	'you (f.) tore'		

shagg	'he tore'	**shággaw**	'they tore'
shággat	'she tore'		

The main difference between the 'doubled' verb conjugation and that of the regular strong verb is that an **-ay-** infix is inserted after the root before consonant-initial endings, that is, before **-t**, **-ti**, **-taw**, **-na**. In Oman, the 2nd and 3rd person feminine plural follow the same pattern, with the normal suffixes, respectively **shaqqáytan** and **sháqqan**, and **sháqqu** with final **-u** for the 3rd masculine plural rather than **-aw** (see Unit Six).

9.2 Past-tense verbs: 'weak' verbs

'Weak' verbs in Gulf Arabic are those that have **y** as final root consonant. This **y** only shows up in those parts of the verb where the ending for person/gender begins with a consonant (see the remarks above on 'doubled' verbs). The basic form of the 'weak' verb is CvCa, for example **mísha** 'to walk', **líga** 'to find; meet', **gára** 'to read' and **dára** 'to know (something)'. The conjugation of these verbs is very similar to that of 'doubled' verbs:

mishávt	'I walked'	**garávt**	'I read'
mishávt	'you (m.) walked'	**garávt**	'you (m.) read'
mishávtí	'you (f.) walked'	**garávti**	'you (f.) read'
mísha	'he walked'	**gára**	'he read'
míshat	'she walked'	**gárat**	'she read'
mishávna	'we walked'	**garávna**	'we read'
mishávtaw	'you (pl.) walked'	**garávtaw**	'you (pl.) read'
míshaw	'they walked'	**gáraw**	'they read'

Again, in Oman, we have 2nd feminine plural **mishávtan**, **qarávtan** as expected; the 3rd person plural, both masculine and feminine, and the 3rd feminine singular retain the **y** of the root consonants, thus **míshyat** 'she walked', **qáryat** 'she read', **míshyu** 'they (m.) walked', **míshyan** 'they (f.) walked', **qáryu** 'they (m.) read' and **qáryan** 'they (f.) read'.

9.3 Time conjunctions

Sequences of past actions can be expressed in Gulf Arabic using a variety of conjunctions:

■ **yoom** 'at the time when'

Examples:

yoom dashsháyt il-bayt, sharábt glaas maay.
'*When* I entered the house, I drank a glass of water.'

Sáarat za9láana yoom sháafat il-ghálaT.
'She got angry *when* she saw the mistake.'

yoom is normally used to link past actions that are more or less simultaneous.

■ **9ógubmaa, xálfmaa, bá9admaa** 'after'

Examples:

9ógubmaa SaaDóohum, Dirbóohum bi shídda.
'*After* they caught them, they beat them severely.'

bídaw sh-shúghul márra tháanya xálfmaa gáamaw min il-gháda.
'They began work again *after* they got up from (their) lunch.'

bá9admaa raaH 9ánni, nisáyt ísmah.
'*After* he went from me, I forgot his name.'

■ **gábilmaa** 'before'

Examples:

maa darayt bih gábilmaa Hicháyt wiyyáak.
'I didn't know about him (what he was like) *before* I spoke to you.'

sakkáyt il-baab gábilmaa wúSlaw.
'I shut the door *before* they arrived.'

■ **layn** 'until; as soon as'

Examples:

dazzáyt iT-Taffáaya layn TáaHat min il-mayz.
'You (m.) pushed the ash-tray *until* it fell off the table.'

**layn wuSált íl-maTáar, riHt il-máktab maal ra'íis shárikat
Tayaráan il-xalíij.**
'*As soon as* I got to the airport, I went to the office of the head of
the Gulf Airways Company.'

Exercise 9.1

A day in the life

In this exercise, you have to translate and connect, using an appropriate
conjunction, sets of sequenced events from an imaginary diary, for
example:

    (as soon as) →   Saw the accident.
                     Telephoned the police.

layn shift il-Háadtha, Dárabt tilifúun lish-shúrTa
'As soon as I saw the accident, I telephoned the police.'

First of all, translate the diary entries into Arabic using the 1st person
singular; then go through the exercise again using the 3rd person 'he'.

Tuesday, 6 April

1 (as soon as) →   Got up.
                    Drank a glass of tea and had breakfast.

2 (after)   →   Finished breakfast.
                    Played with the kids.

3 (before)   →   Read the morning paper.
                    Left the house.

4 (when)   →   Got to the office.
                    Went straight to the factory.

5 (after)   →   Inspected the products.
                    Talked to the foreman.

6 (as soon as) →   Returned to the office.
                    The **farráash** brought me tea.

7 (before)   →   Telephoned my wife.
                    Went to the bank.

8 (when)   →   Finished business at the bank.
                    Walked by the seashore and had lunch.

Language point

9.4 Ordinal numbers

The ordinal numbers from 1 to 10 have masculine and feminine forms, as follows:

Masculine	Feminine	
áwwal	úula	first
tháani	tháanya	second
tháalith	tháaltha	third
ráabi9	ráab9a	fourth
xáamis	xáamsa	fifth
sáadis	sáadsa	sixth
sáabi9	sáab9a	seventh
tháamin	tháamna	eighth
táasi9	táas9a	ninth
9áashir	9áashra	tenth

Unlike other declinable adjectives, the ordinal numbers 1 to 10 may occur before the noun they modify, in which case they are *not* inflected for gender:

tháalith yoom	'the third day'
áwwal wálad	'the first boy'
tháani bint	'the second girl'
sáadis ziyáara	'the sixth visit'

This adjective-noun construction is also used to render the English 'the first one, the second one', etc.:

- ay wáaHid Habbáyt ákthar?
  'Which one did you like more?'

- áwwal wáaHid.
  'The first one.'

If the thing being referred to is feminine by gender:

- ay sayyáara sharáyt?
  'Which car did you buy?'

- tháani wáHda.
  'The second one.'

This ordinal number-noun construction is thus grammatically similar to the elative adjective-noun construction we saw in Unit Eight – **áHsan rayyáal**, although it contains no definite article, means 'the best man'. However, the ordinal numbers can also be placed after the noun they modify, in which case they agree with it in gender, and the definite article **il** must be used:

il-yoom ith-tháalith	'the third day'
il-wálad il-áwwal	'the first boy'
il-bint il-úula	'the first girl'
iz-ziyáara l-xáamsa	'the fifth visit'

When ordinal numbers function grammatically as *nouns* rather than *adjectives*, that is, in noun phrases of the kind described in 8.1, for example 'the fourth of his books' or 'the second of the boys', they do agree in gender with the noun they refer to:

tháani l-awláad	'the second of the boys'
xáamsat il-Hújar	'the fifth of the rooms'
tháalith kútubah	'the third of his books'
sáadsat in-niswáan	'the sixth of the women'

Two exceptions to this are **áwwal** 'first' and **áaxir** 'last', which, when used as nouns, do not decline:

áwwal il-banáat	'the first of the girls'
áwwal is-sána	'the first (part) of the year'
áaxir il-Hicháaya	'the end (part) of the story'

áwwal and **áaxir** are also used in the plural form **awáayil** and **awáaxir** in certain time phrases:

awáayil ish-sháhar	'the first (few days) of the month'
awáaxir ramaDáan	'the last (few days) in Ramadan'

The ordinal numbers from 11 onwards present few problems. They are the same in form as their corresponding cardinals, they do not decline and they always follow their noun:

ish-sháhar il-ithná9shar	'the twelfth month'
il-márra th-thalaathtá9shar	'the thirteenth time'
idh-dhíkra l-xamsíin	'the fiftieth anniversary'

Exercise 9.2

Translate the following phrases and sentences into English:

1 is-safíina l-úula

2 id-dars il-áwwal fi tháalith il-kútub

3 iS-SaHíifa l-9ishríin min it-taqríir il-áaxir

4 áaxir ish-sháhar ir-ráabi9

5 il-bayt is-sittá9shar 9ala l-yamíin

6 xáamis sháari9 9ála l-yasáar

7 áwwal shay, il-fluus maa 9índi u tháani shay maa mish waqt
   káafi.

8 áwwal márra riHt is-sa9uudíyya maa Habbáytha; thaani márra,
   9ijbátni ákthar.

Language point

9.5 Months

In Unit Seven we learnt the names of the months in the Islamic calendar.
The Western calendar is in general use for business and everyday
purposes in the Gulf, but there are alternative names for each month.
The set that is borrowed from European languages is commoner, but
it is good to be able at least to recognise the local names:

European	Local	
yanaayir	kaanúun ith-tháani	January
fabráayir	shubáaT	February
maars	aadháar	March
abríil	niisáan	April
máayo	ayyáar	May
yúunyo	Haziiráan	June
yúulyo	tammúuz	July
awghústos	aab	August
sibtámbar	aylúul	September
uktúubar	tishríin il-áwwal	October
nufámbar	tishríin ith-tháani	November
disámbar	kaanúun il-áwwal	December

Dates are expressed by prefixing the masculine form (where there is one) of the cardinal numbers to the month. No preposition is required to express the English 'on', but sometimes **fi** is used:

wuSált il-kuwáyt (fi) wáaHid Haziiráan min is-sána l-máaDya.
'I arrived in Kuwait on the first of June last year.'

tírkaw s-sa9uudíyya (fi) sába9 disámbar il-máaDi.
'They left Saudi Arabia on the seventh of last December.'

The first of January, New Year's Day, is called **raas is-sána** (lit. 'head of the year').

Dialogue 9.1

 This is a comprehension and translation exercise. Listen to the following dialogue with a man interviewed in the 1970s, and, consulting the Vocabulary and notes below where necessary, answer the comprehension questions. Then translate the dialogue.

il-imaaráat fil-qadíim wil-Hiin (Audio 1; 21)

INTERVIEWER   Saar lik múdda Tawíila fil-xalíij, yaa sáyyid Johnson, muu chidhíi?

JOHNSON   ay wállah, Hawáali saba9tá9shar sána. ána il-Hiin sitt sanawáat fi dubáy, láakin tammáyt iHdá9shar sána fil-baHráyn min gábil.

I   shínhu shúghlak fil-baHráyn, yá9ni?

J   shúghli ya9ni muHáasib ra'íisi fi shárikat tijáara.

I   9áyal laysh jiit il-imaaráat? maa 9íjbatik il-baHráyn?

J   balá, balá,9ijbátni wáayid, láakin iHdá9shar sána múdda Tawíila … yoom min il-ayyáam, gáalat líyyi zóojti ínnaha mállat min il-biláad. gilt líha ínni malláyt min ish-shúghul fi shárikat it-tijáara, ána bá9ad … nzayn, Tarrásht risáala lil-mudíir maal shárikat is-smiit fi dubáy, u Talábt fíiha waDHíifa jadíida. layn ligáyt il-jawáab faráHt li'ánnahum qiblóoni Háalan u 9aTóoni ráatib ákthar min maa 9aTóoni fish-shárika l-baHrayníyya.

I   shrá'yik fil-imaaráat?

J   áwwalmaa jiit il-imaaráat, ya9ni min Hawáali 9ishríin sána, maa kaan fíiha shay – la maay wa la ákil zayn. bi SaráaHa, ya9ni

il-baHráyn áHsan mínha 9ishríin márra láakin shway shway
tagháyyarat il-áshya, Hátta yoom rijá9t, shíftha kíllish ghayr il-
áwwal.
I shloon ghayr, ya9ni?
J fi kill mukáan fii mabáani Dáxma. bunúuk, 9imaaráat, guSúur,
maTáa9im. kill shay mawjúud, maa fii shay náagiS.
I nzayn, wil-imaaráat maal il-Hiin 9íjbatik ákthar min il bálad illi
9aráftah fil-xamsiináat, law bil-9aks?
J su'áal Sá9ab. fil-qadíim, in-naas fagáara, SaHíiH, láakin
glúubhum záyna. il-Hiin la. Sáaraw ághna min áwwal – 9índahum
byúut mafrúusha bi kill shay, u sayyaaráat amriikíyya Dáxma ...
láakin fi rá'yi ána, Sáarat il-anáasa aqáll min maa káanat.
I ya9ni, fi rá'yik záadat il-flúus láakin qállat il-anáasa?
J Sidj ... u záadat il-amráaD bá9ad!

Notes:

Saar lik ... This phrase is commonly used to express the idea of 'have
been here for'. **Saar** is always masculine in form, even when, as here,
its subject **múdda** 'period' is feminine.

• **9áyal** 'well then; so'.
• **9ájab** 'to please someone'.
• **balá** is normally used like the French 'si', that is, to deny a negative
  assertion.
• **ána bá9ad** 'me too'.
• **min maa** 'than what'. **maa** means 'what' in this sense as well as
  'not'.
• **shrá'yik = sh + ra'y + ik** 'what – view – your' 'What's your opinion?'
• **min 9ishríin sána** '20 years ago'. **min** + cardinal number + **sána**
  means 'X years ago'.
• **Illi** is the relative pronoun, and means 'which'.
• **bil-9aks** 'on the contrary; vice versa; the other way round'.

Questions:

1 **Saar lis-sáyyid Johnson cham sána fil-baHráyn?**
2 **shínhu kaan shúghlah hunáak?**
3 **laysh gháyyar** ('changed') **shúghlah?**
4 **shloon HáSSal** ('got') **shúghul jadíid fi dubáy?**
5 **shloon il-imaaráat fil-xamsiináat bin-nísba íla l-baHráyn?**

6 shloon kaanat Haal sukkáan il-imaaráat fil-xamsiináat?
7 fi ra'y is-sáyyid Johnson, ay wáHda áHsan, il-imaaráat
   maal il-qadíim law maal il-Hiin? laysh?

 Vocabulary

aab	August	dhíkra	memory (of something); commemoration
aadháar	March		
áaxir	last; latest	fabráayir	February
abríil	April	fáraH	to be happy; joyful
anáasa*	enjoyment; companionship		
awáaxir	end parts	min gábil	before (adv.)
awáayil	beginning parts	gábilmaa	before (conj.)
		gára	to read
awghústos	August	gaTT	to throw (esp. away)
áwwal	first, previous (adj.); old times (n.); first of all		
		gá9ad	to sit; to get up (in the morning)
áwwalmaa	when first; as soon as (conj.)		
		ghálaT/ aghláaT	mistake
aylúul	September	gháyyar	to change (trans.)
ayyáar	May		
balá	yes, on the contrary	Háadtha*/ Hawáadith	accident
		Háalan	on the spot
bá9admaa	after (conj.)	Habb	to love; like
bída	to begin	HáSSal	to get; obtain
biláad/buldáan	country	Haziiráan	June
dára (bi)	to know (something)	Hícha	to talk
		Hicháaya*	story
dars/druus	lesson	illi	which
dashsh	to enter	kaanúun il-áwwal	December
dazz	to push		
disámbar	December	kaanúun ith-tháani	January
Dárab tilifúun	to telephone	kíshaf (9ála)	to inspect
Dáxim	large; enormous	layn	as soon as; until'

líga	to meet; find	tammúuz	July
maars	March	tijáara*	trade; commerce
máayo	May		
mábna/	building	tindáyl	foreman
mabáani		tishríin il-áwwal	October
mafrúush	furnished	tishríin	November
mall (min)	to get fed up (with)	ith-tháani	
		TaaH	to fall
mantúuj(aat)	product	Taffáaya*(aat)	ashtray
máraD/amráaD	illness	Tálab	to ask for; demand
mísha	to walk		
múdda*	period of time	Tárrash	to send
náagiS	lacking	Tayaráan	aviation
niisáan	April	tháamin	eighth
nísa	to forget	uktúubar	October
nufámbar	November	úula	first (f.)
qíbal	to accept	waDHíifa*/	duty; job; post
qall	to be little, few; become few	waDHáayif	
		xáamis	fifth
ráabi9	fourth	xálfmaa	after (conj.)
raas/ruus	head	yamíin	right-hand side
rayúug	breakfast		
sáadis	sixth	yanáayir	January
safíina*/súfun	ship	yasáar	left-hand side
sakk	to shut	yoom	when (conj.)
sibtámbar	September	yoom min il-ayyáam	one day
siif	seashore		
SaHíiH	true; correct	yúulyo	July
bi SaráaHa*	frankly	yúunyo	June
Sá9ab	difficult	zaad	to increase
shagg	to tear	9áashir	tenth
shubáaT	February	9ájab	to please (someone)
shway shway	slowly; little by little		
		bil-9aks	on the contrary
táasi9	ninth	9áraf	to know (something or someone)
tagháyyar	to change (intrans.)		
		9áTa	to give
tamm	to stay; continue	9áyal	well then; so
		9imáara*(aat)	apartment block

Cultural point

Traditional dress: men

The traditional Gulf everyday male attire is a long white shirt, topped with a headdress and head rope. The long shirt has various regional names within the Gulf, and the way it is cut, and the style of the collar, are also regionally specific. In Kuwait and Oman, the usual word for it is **dishdáasha** (pl. **dashaadíish**), while in Bahrain, Qatar and eastern Saudi Arabia the term is **thoob** (pl. **thiyáab**), which simply means 'dress', and the term can also apply to women's long dresses too. In the UAE there is a third term: **kandúura** (pl. **kanaadíir**). On formal occasions, a lightweight cloak is worn over the long white shirt and is known as a **bisht**. This is of brown or black wool, decorated at the neck, shoulders and front edges with gold thread. A sarong-like loincloth, known as **wizáar** (pl. **wzíra**), is commonly worn by men when they are involved in manual jobs such as building, fishing and agriculture.

The white cotton or (in winter) heavier chequered red and white headdress is known as the **ghútra**, and is worn on top of a plain white skullcap known in Bahrain as the **gaHfíyya**, and elsewhere as the **Taagíyya**. The black head rope that holds the **ghútra** in place is called the **9igáal**. This word literally means 'tethering rope' and it was originally used to hobble camels, a convenient place for storing it when not in use being on the head! In Qatar and the UAE, there is often a long tassel (or two) at the back of the **9igáal** that hangs down to the middle of the wearer's back. In Oman, different headgear is the norm. For the everyday, an embroidered cotton cap is worn, called a **kúmma** (or **kímma**, pl. **kamíim**). There are many designs, but the basic shape is always the same and is unique to Oman. A head wrap may be worn on top of this turban-style, called the **mSarr** – made of cotton for everyday wear and silk for special occasions. In the south of Oman, a tassled version of this is common, known as the **shmaagh**, as in the picture below. The blue, magenta, red and orange silk headdress worn only by the Sultan of Oman and the members of his family is known as **al-9amáama s-sa9iidíyya**, 'the Sa'idi turban', after the name of the Sultan's family, the Āl Bu Sa'id.

The Gulf **ghútra** and   The **shmáagh**, Omani-   The Omani **mSarr**
9igáal   style

Footwear depends on the time of year. In the summer, **ná9al**, sandals
(called **waTíyya** in Oman) are worn. European-style shoes, worn in
winter, are known throughout the Gulf as **júuti** (pl. **jawáati**), an Indian
borrowing.

Reading Arabic

Dates

The names of the months, European and Eastern, written in the Arabic
script, are as follows:

Month	European	Eastern
January	يناير	كانون الثاني
February	فبراير	شباط
March	مارس	آذار
April	ابريل	نيسان
May	مايو	ايار
June	يونيو	حزيران
July	يوليو	تموز
August	اغسطس	آب
September	سبتمبر	ايلول
October	اكتوبر	تشرين الأول
November	نوفمبر	تشرين الثاني
December	ديسمبر	كانون الأول

As with the Islamic dates, dates using these months are read right to left, but the numbers go left to right! Read and translate the following dates:

1	١٩٦٨	نيسان	٢
2	٢٠٠٣	اكتوبر	١٧
3	٢٠٠٨	يناير	٣١
4	١٩٩٥	آب	٤
5	١٩٨٢	تشرين الأول	١٣
6	١٩٧٤	ديسمبر	١٠
7	١٩٦٧	حزيران	٦
8	١٨٤٥	تموز	١٧
9	١٧٠٩	مارس	١٤
10	٢٠٠٦	ايار	٣٠

Note that, when Islamic dates and European or Eastern dates are written together, as they often are in official letters and other documents, the Islamic date is followed by the letter ه for هجري (**hijri**), and the Christian one by م as an abbreviation of ميلادي (**miilaadi**), for example:

ه	١٤٢٩	رجب	١٧
م	٢٠٠٨	يوليو	٢١

Unit Ten

In this unit you will learn about:

- relative clauses, e.g. 'I saw someone who ...'
- demonstrative pronouns: 'this', 'that', these' and 'those'
- demonstrative adjectives, e.g. 'this man' or 'these women'
- the negative in equational sentences, i.e. sentences that don't have a verb or pseudo-verb
- how to say 'somebody' and 'nobody'

Language point

10.1 Relative clauses

■ The relative pronoun as subject of the verb

In the sentence 'I saw the man who broke his leg', the relative pronoun 'who' refers back to the definite noun 'the man', and functions as the subject of the verb 'broke' in the relative clause 'who broke his leg'. This sentence in Arabic is:

shift ir-rayyáal ílli kísar ríilah.

ílli, 'who; which' is used in Arabic relative clauses to refer back to an antecedent noun, whether animate or inanimate, if that noun is definite. It is definite either (as in the above example) by virtue of the definite article **il** or by any pronoun suffix, for example:

shift axúuyi ílli kísar ríilah.
'I saw my brother who broke his leg.'

If the noun that is referred back to (the 'antecedent') is indefinite, **íIli** is not used:

shift rayyáal kísar ríilah.
'I saw a man who broke his leg.'

Wherever an antecedent noun is definite, **íIli** is used to refer back to it in relative clauses; if it is indefinite, **íIli** is not used.

■ The relative pronoun as object of the verb

illi also functions as the object of the verb in the relative clause:

ir-rayyáal illi shíftah fish-sháari9 ...
'The man whom I saw in the street ...'

il-bint illi shíftha fid-dukkáan ...
'The girl whom I saw in the shop ...'

ir-rayyáal íIli gilt lik 9ánnah ...
'The man whom I told you about ...'

in-naas íIli sa'áltik 9ánhum ...
'The people whom I asked you about ...'

il-jaríida íIli 9aTáytik iyyáaha ...
'The newspaper that I gave you ...'

The literal meaning of these phrases is 'The man whom I saw *him* ...', 'The girl whom I saw *her* ...', 'The people whom I asked you about *them*', 'The newspaper that I gave you *it*'. In Arabic, the antecedent noun, if it is the direct or indirect object of the verb is 'echoed' by a pronoun that agrees with it in gender and number. This rule applies regardless of whether the antecedent is definite or indefinite:

rayyáal shíftah fish-sháari9 ...
'A man whom I saw in the street ...'

jaríida 9aTáytik iyyáaha ...
'A newspaper that I gave you ...'

■ 'Verbless' relative clauses

In equational sentences such as:

ir-rayyáal mudárris wil-mára mudárrisa.
'The man is a teacher and the woman is a teacher.'

there is no need for an Arabic equivalent of the English verb 'to be'. When such equational sentences are made into relative clauses in Arabic – 'The man/woman who is a teacher ...' – the following type of construction is used:

ir-rayyáal ílli húwwa mudárris ...
'The man who is a teacher ...'

il-mára ílli híyya mudárrisa ...
'The woman who is a teacher ...'

in-naas ílli húmma fagáara ...
'The people who are poor ...'

Thus, we see that, where the subject of a 'relativised' equational sentence is definite, an independent pronoun that refers back to it is inserted: it is as if one said 'The man who he is a teacher ...', etc.

The Arabic equivalent of 'whose' presents no particular problem:

ir-rayyáal ílli shúghlah mudárris ...
'The man whose job is teaching ...'
(lit. 'The man who his job teacher ...')

il-bint ílli shá9arha áswad ...
'The girl whose hair is black ...'
(lit. 'the girl who her hair black ...')

in-naas ílli awláadhum kaslaaníin ...
'The people whose sons are lazy ...'
(lit. 'the people who their sons lazy ...')

If the antecedent is indefinite, **ílli** is omitted:

bint shá9arha áswad ...
'A girl whose hair is black ...',
'A black-haired girl ...', etc.

Verbless relative clauses expressing possession (using **9ind**) are constructed according to the patterns already illustrated, for example:

– definite antecedent noun:

il-miskíin ílli maa 9índah fluus ...
'The unfortunate who hasn't any money ...'

il-aghniyáa illi 9índhum likúuk ...
'The rich who've got tens of thousands ...'

– indefinite antecedent noun:

>   **miskíin maa 9índah fluus ...**
>   'An unfortunate who hasn't any money ...', etc.

■ The relative pronoun as subject of the main clause

ílli often stands for an unspecified person or thing in the main clause of a sentence, equivalent to the English 'That which ...' 'He who ...':

>   **ílli raaH raaH.**
>   'What's gone is gone.'
>   (i.e. 'Don't cry over spilt milk.')

>   **ílli gilt líyyi 9ánha maa ligáytha.**
>   'I didn't meet the woman you told me about.'
>   (lit. 'She whom you told me about her, I didn't meet her.')

Exercise 10.1

Make as many Arabic sentences as you can from the chart below:

		is the chief accountant
		is a big contractor
	I saw yesterday	is a friend of the ruler
	I wrote a letter to	is an important personality
The man	I sent my report to	is the deputy director
	I told you about	is a famous journalist
	I spoke with	is the deputy Prime Minister
		is the chief engineer

Exercise 10.2

Make as many sensible Arabic sentences as you can from this chart:

The party I went to			famous
The holiday I spent in London			nice
The places I visited	was		expensive
		very	pretty
The hotels I stayed in	were		cheap
The buildings I saw			large
The university I went to			spacious

Exercise 10.3

Make as many questions as you can from this chart:

	ticket	
	letter	I ordered half an hour ago?
	report	I received yesterday?
	newspaper	I gave you?
	file	I wrote?
Where's the	food	I asked for a week ago?
	telegram	I bought this morning?
	pen	I put here 5 minutes ago?
	book	
	parcel	

Language points

10.2 Demonstrative pronouns

The forms are tabulated below, the bracketed elements being optional. As in English, 'this' and 'these' are used to refer to people and objects that are relatively nearer to the speaker in space or time.

	Masculine	*Feminine*
'this'	**háadha**	**háadhi**
'that'	**haadháak**	**haadhíich/haadhíik**
'these'	**(haa)dhayláyn**	
'those'	**(haa) dhayláak/(haa)dhooláak**	

Here are some examples:

háadha zayn.
'This is nice.'
(Or 'This man/boy, etc. is nice.')

háadha bayt 9atíij.
'This is an old house.'

haadháak rayyáal shaghgháal.
'That (one over there) is a hardworking man.'

háadhi fíkra záyna.
'This is a good idea.'

haadhíich bint sháaTra.
'That (one there) is a clever girl.'

haadhayláyn 9ummáal shaghaaghíil.
'These (ones here) are hardworking labourers.'

dhayláyn samaamíich.
'These (men here) are fishermen.'

haadhayláak kaslaaníin.
'Those (people) are lazy.'

dhayláak maa fíihum fáyda.
'Those (people, things) are useless.'
(lit. 'Those not in them use.')

Often in Gulf Arabic, the demonstrative pronoun follows the noun to which it refers. When this happens, the **haa**-element of the form is usually missed off, except in the case of **háadha**, which always retains it. Thus the sentences above could alternatively be expressed as below, with no change in meaning:

zayn, háadha
bayt 9atíij, háadha
rayyáal shaghgháal, dhaak
fíkra záyna, dhi
bint sháaTra, dhiich, etc.

Note the following type of construction, where the person or object referred to by the demonstrative pronoun is definite:

háadha húwwa r-rayyáal.
'*This* is the man.'

háadhi híyya l-bint ílli níjHat fil-imtiHáan.
'*This* is the girl who passed the exam.'

dhayláyn húmma il-kaslaaníin ílli maa ráaHaw sh-shúghul.
'*These* are the lazy (people) who didn't go to work.'

dhooláak húmma illi máa fiihum fáyda.
'*Those* are the ones who are useless.'

A personal pronoun 'he', 'she' ('it'), or 'them' must be inserted between the demonstrative pronoun and its referent in equational sentences of the 'This is the X ...' type.

10.3 Demonstrative adjectives

In order to say 'this man', 'that girl', 'those houses', etc., we prefix the demonstrative pronoun forms that we have just seen to the *defined* form of the noun: it is as if we say 'this the man', 'that the girl', 'those the houses', etc. The forms of the demonstratives that are used in this adjectival function are slightly different:

		'this/these'	*'that/those'*
Singular	m.	**ha(adha) r-rayyáal**	**(haa)dhaak ir-rayyáal**
		'this man'	'that man'
	f.	**ha(adhi) l-mára**	**(haa)dhiich il-mára**
		'this woman'	'that woman'
Plural	m.	**har-rayaayíil**	**(haa)dhayláak ir-rayaayíil**
		'these men'	'those men'
	f.	**han-niswáan**	**(haa)dhayláak in-niswáan**
		'these women'	'those women'

Once again, the bracketed elements are optional. It can be seen that the demonstrative phrases such as 'this X' and 'these Xs' tend to be simply a shortened form of the **haa-** + definite noun, whereas 'that X' and 'those Xs' tend to be the second element of the demonstrative, the part that begins with **dh-** + definite noun, for example:

háadha r-rayyáal zayn.
har-rayyáal zayn.
'This man is good.'

háadhi l-as9áar gháalya.
hal-as9áar gháalya.
'These prices are high.'

haadhíich il-láyla ríHna s-síinama.
dhiich il-láyla ríHna s-síinama.
'That night we went to the cinema.'

haadhayláak il-faraaríish min zaam in-naháar.
dhayláak il-faraaríish min zaam in-naháar.
'Those cleaners are from the day shift.'

An important point to note is that, in all of these examples, omission of the definite **il** would change the sense to 'This is a good man', 'These are high prices', etc. – that is, the demonstrative would function as a pronoun (10.2 above).

Frequently, as with the demonstrative pronoun, the demonstrative adjective is placed *after* the *whole* noun phrase to which it refers. When this happens, the **haa**-element of the form tends to be missed off, except for **haadha**, which is never shortened:

ir-rayyáal háadha zayn.
'This man is good.'

il-as9áar dhi gháalya.
'These prices are high.'

il-faraaríish dhayláak min zaam in-naháar.
'Those cleaners are from the day shift.'

Here are some examples with longer noun phrases:

háadha l-bayt il-9atíij
il-bayt il-9atíij háadha
'this old house'

dhayláak iz-zuwwáar il-miSriyyíin
iz-zuwwáar il-miSriyyíin dhayláak
'those Egyptian visitors'

The shortened forms of 'this' and 'these' in **har-rayyáal** and **hal-mára** are *never* postposed: one does *not* say **ir-rayyáal ha** or **il-mára ha**.

If the demonstrative adjective is postposed, it must be placed after the *complete* noun phrase it refers to. If one wants to say, for example, 'this company director' or 'that Prime Minister', one has to say:

mudíir ish-shárika háadha
ra'íis il-wuzaráa dhaak

mudíir ish-shárika and **ra'íis il-wuzaráa** are the entities that are being referred to, not simply **mudíir** and **ra'íis**, hence the demonstrative follows the complete phrase. Note also that it agrees with the head-noun **mudíir** and **ra'íis**, not **shárika** (f.) or **wuzaráa** (pl.); if we were to say

> **mudíir ish-shárika háadhi**
> **ra'íis il-wuzaráa dhayláak**

these would be understood as 'the director of *this* company' and 'the head of *those* ministers' because **háadhi** can only refer to a feminine noun and **dhayláak** to a plural one. In an example such as

> **miftáaH il-bayt háadha**

the meaning is ambiguous between 'this house key' and 'the key of this house' because both **miftáaH** and **bayt** are masculine nouns. In such cases, the context usually makes the meaning clear; however, there is a tendency to say

> **miftáaH háadha l-bayt**

when one means 'the key of this house' and

> **miftáaH il-bayt háadha**

for 'this (particular) house-key'.

Exercise 10.4

Look at the example below:

| | (bayt) | £500,000 | £300,000 | (gháali) |

→   **hal-bayt ághla min dhaak**
or   →   **háadha l-bayt ághla min haadháak**
or   →   **il-bayt háadha ághla min dhaak**, etc.

Now, using the data below, make similar sentences using these patterns. Try to make several sentences, as illustrated, for each example:

1	(yáahil)	90% correct	60% correct answers	(sháaTir)
2	(sayyáara)	£5,000	£4,500	(gháali)
3	(Híjra)	60 sq. ft.	50 sq. ft.	(wáasi9)

4 (shayb)	80 years old	70 years old	(kabíir)
5 (wálad)	5 ft.	4 ft. 6 in.	(Tawíil)
6 (kútub)	pub. 1902	pub. 1930	(qadíim)
7 (xiyáash)	100 lb	75 lb	(thagíil)
8 (shiqqa)	£500 per month	£700 per month	(raxíiS)
9 (jánTa)	15 lb	20 lb	(xafíif)
10 (shayx)	£10 million	£7 million	(gháni).

Now switch the focus to the second of the things being compared:
instead of

hal-bayt ághla min dhaak, etc.

we could say

haadháak il-bayt árxaS min háadha, etc.

using the opposite of **gháali** 'expensive', which is **raxíiS** 'cheap'. Do
the same for 1–10 above, selecting an appropriate adjective.

Exercise 10.5

Translate into Arabic:

1 This is the clerk who sent the letter.

2 That's the woman who came to your office.

3 These are the unfortunate (people) who have no money.

4 These are the photos I told you about.

5 That is the old man I bumped into yesterday.

6 That is the shop in which I bought these shoes.

7 That's the restaurant I ate in yesterday.

8 This is the suit I bought last week.

9 This is the money I found in the street.

10 These are the labourers who asked for more money.

11 Those are the young men I drank tea with.

12 This is the hotel I stayed in last time I came to Kuwait.

Language points

10.4 The negative in equational sentences

We have noted in previous units that **maa** 'not' is used to negate verbs and 'pseudo-verbs' such as **9ind** and **fii**, for example:

maa baag 9ali flúusik.
'Ali didn't steal your money.'

háadha rayyáal maa shíftah min gábil.
'That's a man I've never seen before.'

maa fii afláam záyna fis-síinama hal-ayyáam.
'There aren't any good films at the cinema these days.'

maa 9índi shay.
'I don't have anything.'

In equational sentences – that is, sentences that do not have a verb or pseudo-verb – **muu** or **mub** is used as the negative particle, for example:

háadha mub zayn.   **il-ákil ihni mub raxíiS.**
'This is no good.'   'The food here isn't cheap.'

ana mub za9láan 9aláyk.   **áHmad muu mawjúud.**
'I'm not angry with you.'   'Ahmed isn't here.'

il-kitáab muu 9ala l-mayz.   **abúuyi muu sammáach.**
'The book isn't on the table.'   'My father isn't a fisherman.'

baghávt 9ali, mub ínta.
'I wanted Ali, not you.'

10.5 'Somebody' and 'nobody'

'Somebody' and 'nobody' are respectively **áHad** and **máHHad**:

     kaan máHHad fil-bayt
or **maa kaan áHad fil-bayt**
     'There was nobody in the house.'

     ligáyt máHHad fish-sháari9
or **maa ligáyt áHad fish-sháari9**
     'I didn't meet anybody in the street.'

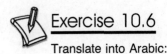

Exercise 10.6

Translate into Arabic:

1 The man I saw wasn't you.
2 When I came back from the office I found no one at home.
3 There's someone outside.
4 This isn't what she wanted.
5 They didn't see anybody and heard nothing.
6 I didn't like the hotel – it wasn't clean and there was a lot of noise.
7 No one came to the airport when I arrived.
8 This milk I bought from you this morning isn't fresh.
9 These spare parts I bought from you aren't any use.
10 Nobody told me you were here.

Dialogue 10.1

(Audio 1; 22)

Listen, then read aloud and translate the following dialogue.

A yaa hála jáasim! shlóonik?
B áhlan áhlan abu xalíil. wállah, ana mub zayn il-yoom.
A laysh? shfíik, ta9báan?
B ay, 9índi zukáam shway … ráasi dáayir.
A maa riHt id-dáxtar?
B bála riHt, bas maa 9aTáani dáwa zayn. wállah, id-daxáatir dhayláak maa fíihum fáyda …
A sh-gaal lik id-dáxtar 9áyal?
B xaraabíiT yá9ni. gaal líyyi bas 'xudh had-dáwa marratáyn kill yoom u xudh ráaHtik fil-bayt'
A u had-dáwa ílli 9aTáak iyyáah, shínhu ya9ni?
B Hbúub báyDa Saghíira bas. layn ríja9t il-bayt akált wáHda mínha láakin idh-dhoog máalha muu zayn – karíih, ya9ni. maa akált mínha bá9ad – gaTTáyt il-báagi.
A ana 9índi fíkra záyna!
B guul!

A hast dáwa áHsan min had-dáwa ílli 9aTáak iyyáah ... u had-dáwa
   mawjúud fith-thalláaja máalti!
B shínhu, ya9ni?
A ghárshat bábsi kíllish báarid!

Vocabulary

áHad	someone	lakk/likúuk	100,000 rupees
báagi	remainder;		(= 10,000 dinars)
	rest	máHHad	no one
bágha	to want	miláffa*(aat)	file; dossier
barqíyya*(aat)	telegram	muu/mub	not
bináaya*(aat)	building	náa'ib/	deputy
dáayir	going round	nuwwáab	
dáwa/adwíya	medicine	naDHíif	clean
Dájja*	noise;	nízal	to stay
	clamour		(in a hotel);
dhoog	taste;		go down
	flavour	ráaHa*	rest
fáyda*	usefulness	riil/ryúul	leg
fíkra*/afkáar	idea;	risáala*/rasáa'il	letter
	thought	Súura/Súwar	picture;
gáDa	to spend		photo
	(time)	sh- (prefix)	what?
gálam/gláama	pen	sháabb/	youth;
gúT9a*/	spare part	shubbáan	juvenile
gúTa9 ghiyáar		shaghgháal/	hardworking
háadha/dhi	this	shaghaaghíil	
haadháak/	that	shaxSíyya*(aat)	personality
dhiich		shayb/shiyáab	old man
haadhayláyn	these	shá9ar	hair (head)
haadhayláak	those	shíqqa*(aat)	apartment
haadhooláak	those	tádhkira*/	ticket
haamm	important	tadháakir	
Habb/Hbúub	pill	Táazij	fresh
Hatt	to put (on, in)	Tard/Truud	parcel
júuti/jawáati	pair of shoes	xárbuTa*/	rubbish;
karíih	horrible	xaraabíiT	nonsense
		zukáam	head cold

Cultural point

Traditional dress: women

Dress is an ever-changing thing and has always been a form of self-presentation and 'image'. This is never more so than in the early twenty-first century Gulf, when there is more of a 'religious' tinge to women's dress code than was true even 20 years ago, and certainly compared with 40. The traditional everyday dress of Gulf women, still seen among the older generation, is quite simple. A pair of loose-fitting light cotton trousers, with narrow, embroidered ankle cuffs, known as the **sirwáal**, is worn, topped with an under-gown consisting of a combined bodice and skirt that reaches to the knee or below. This is called the **darráa9a** (pl. **daraaríi9**). There are several variations in the design: often, in villages, the material is a simple floral-patterned cotton, but for special occasions the **darráa9a** can be much narrower and made of dark (sometimes black) material, with the neck and narrow sleeves heavily decorated with gold embroidery and gilded cord.

Girls up to age of puberty used simply to wear the **sirwáal** and a simple **darráa9a**, with a head covering called a **búxnug** (pl. **baxáanig**), which was a face-revealing hood and waist-length bodice. Adult women, on the other hand, would wear on top of the **darráa9a** an over-dress, or **thoob**, of which there were various types and designations, depending on the material and type of decoration. In Bahrain, for example, a soft silk **thoob** in very bright colours and with extremely elaborate decoration, known as a **thoob in-nashal**, was worn for weddings, **9iid** celebrations and other festivities. Outside the confines of the house, women universally wore a plain black silk cloak, generally without any decoration, known as the **9ába/9abáaya** or **dáffa** (pl. **dfáaf**), usually with a face veil. The black filigree variety of face veil is known as the **milfa9** (pl. **maláaf9a**), but a facemask with eyeholes is also commonly worn in some parts of the Gulf, and is known as the **búrgu9** (pl. **baráagi9**) or **battúula** (pl. **bataatíil**). In some parts of the Gulf (Bahrain, for example), a colourful light cotton cloak is worn by village women, rather than a black silk one, and is known as the **míshmar** (pl. **masháamir**).

'Covering' is known generically as **Hijáab**, and is an expression of the Islamic concept of **Híshma** 'modesty', something that both sexes are enjoined to practise, but especially women. In recent times this has taken the form of a new type of 'Islamic' dress now common in many Arab countries, in which a floor-length, all-encompassing maxi-dress is worn with a headscarf that covers the hair and is wrapped tightly around the face, often in white or black. Women who wear this style are often referred to as **muHajjabáat** 'covered women'.

Young Gulf woman wearing old-fashioned traditional dress, such as might be worn at a wedding or other festive occasion

Reading Arabic

Names and visiting cards

Gulf personal names are generally of the form: given name-father's name-grandfather's name, for example **9áli áHmad muHámmad**, and this applies to both men and women. In some countries, notably Oman and Saudi Arabia, it is quite common to insert **bin** 'son of' between the second and third names (**bint** 'daughter of' between the given name and father's name for women, who do not, incidentally, change their name on marriage). This **bin/bint** is normally inserted in the names of members of Gulf ruling families and other VIPs. A further element is the tribal or clan name, which is put at the end, after either the complete three-part name or after the first two elements. This is optional, but is the norm in some countries, in particular Oman. Thus a typical Omani name might be:

muHámmad bin sayf bin máajid al-balúushi
'Mohammed son of Sayf son of Majid al-Balushi'

The names of ruling families have a different style of tribal reference: they use the word **āl**, meaning 'family' or '(royal) house', and not the same, despite appearances, as the definite article **al-** used in ordinary people's names. So, for example, the name of the current Ruler of Bahrain is:

Hámad bin 9íisa bin salmáan āl xalíifa
'Hamad son of Isa son of Salman of the House of Khalifa'

Names appear most obviously on shop signs and visiting cards. The one below is typical. It is the card of an academic, who precedes his name with the abbreviation د. for دكتور 'Doctor'. Other abbreviations on the card are ص.ب, which stands for **Sandúuq baríid** 'PO box':

What is his name? What is his job? Where is he from? What is his PO box number and location? What other information is given on the card (clue: the word for 'mobile phone' is **jawwáal**)?

Now look at the card below. What is the name on the card, and what other information can you recover from it (clue: he uses a different word for 'mobile' – **mutaHárrik**)?

م / محمد مبارك المري

نائب المدير

ورش المحركات العسكرية

شـركـة الخليــــج لصيانـة الطـائـرات

تليــفـــون : +٩٧١-٢-٥٠٥٧٣١٣	تلكس : ٢٣٢٥٨ جـامكو اي ام
فـــاكس : +٩٧١-٢-٥٧٥٧٢٠٧	ص.ب : ٤٦٤٥٠ أبـوظـبـي
مـتـحـرك : +٩٧١-٥٠-٦٤٢٢٢٧٤	الإمـارات الـعـربيـة المتـحـدة
سـيـتـا : A U H D V G F	
بريدالكتروني : malmurry@gamco. ae	

Review Unit II

Exercise RII.1

Look at the following short dialogue:

- **cham Táabi9 shiráyt?**
- **sítta.**
- **gilt lik sittíin, mub sítta!**

Construct similar dialogues, using the cue words below:

1 money ... take?
    40 dinars
    4 not 40!

2 cartons of cigarettes ... buy?
    12 cartons
    2 not 12!

3 days holiday ... take?
    15 days
    5 not 15!

4 bags of rice ... buy?
    16
    6 not 16!

5 spoonfuls of medicine ... take?
    2 spoonfuls
    4 not 2!

Exercise RII.2

Look at the following dialogue:

- **limán Tarrásht it-taqríir?**
- **lil-muHáasib ir-ra'íisi.**
- **gilt lik il-muhándis ir-ra'íisi, mub il-muHáasib!**

Construct similar dialogues, using the cue words:

1 give the money to?
    the **farráash**
    the clerk, not the **farráash**!

2 sell the fridge to?
   the Egyptian woman
   the Lebanese, not the Egyptian!

3 give the news to?
   the deputy director
   the director, not his deputy!

4 send the telegram to?
   your brother in America
   my brother in England, not the one in America!

5 send the invitation to?
   the head of the trading company
   the head of the travel agency, not the trading company!

Exercise RII.3

Look at the following dialogue:

- **shiráyt lih jánTa min jild.**
- **háadhi mub il-hádiya ílli bagháaha, Tálab míHfaDHa jadíida.**
- **bas húwwa maa gaal líyyi chidhíi!**

Reconstruct the dialogue using the cue words below:

Presents for him	Presents for her
1 a shirt – a tie	1 a dress – a pair of shoes
2 a watch – a suit	2 a skirt – a blouse
3 a book – a CD	3 a camera – a ring
4 a mobile phone – a radio	4 a computer – a bicycle
5 a jacket – a pair of trousers	5 a calculator – a pen

Exercise RII.4

Look at the dialogue below:

- **háadhi Hadíiqa jamíila**
- **ay, láakin hast ájmal min háadhi fil-baHrayn**
- **wállah? 9úmri maa shíftha!**

Make similar dialogues using the following phrases:

1 big school – in the city centre

2 poor quarter – near the bridge

3 beautiful mosque – opposite the old palace

4 old building – near the post office

5 dirty restaurant – next to the Antar cinema

6 beautiful beach – five miles from here

7 tall minaret – near the Arab Bank

8 modern airport – in Sharja

 Dialogue RII.1

 Listen to and read the following dialogue aloud and answer the questions on it, then translate it.

At the restaurant (Audio 1; 23)

MUBARAK   zayn, shínhu 9índakum zayn, yá9ni? mub wáayid
           yuwáa9a íHna.

WAITER   kill shay 9índana. fii máthalan diyáay máshwi, u fii 9aysh
           u símich … fii 9índana láHam xarúuf bi róoba, u fii bá9ad
           shuwárma.

MUBARAK   la la yaa sáyyidi, iT-Tabxáat dhi kíllaha maal il-xalíij.
           shway thagíila ya9ni. maa fii 9índakum HúmmuS bi
           TaHíina u baylinjáan máHshi u mujáddara … akláat
           xafíifa lubnaaníyya yá9ni? mub yuwáa9a li hal-gadd,
           yá9ni.

WAITER   balá fii ákil lubnáani 9ala káyfik!

MUBARAK   nzayn, jiib lína SáHnat mujáddara kabíira u HúmmuS u
           … mázza káamla, yá9ni.

WAITER   insháallah.

JASIM   wayn il-gaarsóon?

MUBARAK   káhu yaay!

WAITER   zayn, háadhi SaHnatáyn diyáay u háadha hu l-9aysh u
           s-símich illi Talabtóoh.

JASIM   la la háadha xáTa' yaa xúuyi. hal-ákil mub Hággna Hna!
Hagg naas ghayr, láazim. iHna Talábna mázza káamla,
mub hal-áshya ílli jíbtha!

WAITER   la la háadha ílli jíbtah 9ádil! Talabáatkum maktúuba 9ala
hal-wáraga! shúufu!
'SaHnatáyn diyáay ...'.

MUBARAK   iT-Táwla háadhi shu r-ráqam máalah?

WAITER   sittá9shar.

MUBARAK   nzayn, shu r-ráqam illi kitábtah 9ala hal-wáraga?

WAITER   maktúub 'sítta'. Ohóo, 9áfwan yaa jimáa9a, ána
ghalTáan, hal-ákil muu máalkum, SaHíiH, maal dhayláak
is-sa9uudiyyíin il-gaa9idíin minnáak! wil-mázza máalkum
9aTáythum iyyáaha!

Questions:

1 **shínhu T-Tabxáat illi Tilbóoha jáasim u mbáarak fil-máT9am?**

2 **laysh Tílbaw akil xafíif?**

3 **shínhu jaab líhum il-gaarsóon?**

4 **limán 9áTa il-mázza máalhum?**

Vocabulary

áala*(aat) Háasiba	calculator	**gadd**	extent
		gáfsha*(aat)	spoon
áalat*(aat) taSwíir	camera	**ghálab**	to overcome; beat
bantalóon	pair of trousers	**ghalTáan(iin)**	mistaken
il-baríid il-jáwwi	airmail	**Hadíith**	modern
baylinjáan	aubergine	**HúmmuS bi TaHíina**	chickpeas with sesame oil (Lebanese)
bluus(aat)	blouse		
búga	to remain		
búghsha*(aat)	envelope	**jakáyt(aat)**	jacket
dá9wa*(aat)	invitation	**jawwáal**	mobile phone
faríiq/fúruq	team; group (of musicians)	**jild**	leather; skin
		jimáa9a*(aat)	community; group of people
gaarsóon	waiter		
gáa9id	sitting	**jísir/jusúur**	bridge; causeway

ka + indep. pron.	Here's ...!
káhrab	electricity
kambyúutar (aat)	computer
9ála kayf + suffix pron.	as ... like(s); as ... want(s)
kíllah wáaHid	it's all the same; it makes no difference
kraafáat(aat)	necktie
má'dhana*/ ma'áadhin	minaret
máHshi	stuffed
máktab il-baríid	post office
man	who
mandúub(iin)	delegate
máshwi	roast
mázza*	(Lebanese) hors d'oeuvres
mujáddara*	dish of lentils
nafnúuf/ nafaaníif	dress
ráqam/arqáam	number
raSíid	receipt
ráydo(waat)	radio
róoba*	yogurt
sáaHil/ sawáaHil	shore
siidii(aat)	CD
SáaHi	sober; awake
Sádir	chest (anat.)

SáHan(a*)/ SuHúun	plate
shíkil maa	like; just as (conj.)
shíra	to buy
shuuf/i/u!	look! (imp.)
shuwárma	('doner') kebab
tannúura*(aat)	skirt
tí9ab	to get tired
Táabi9/ Tawáabi9	postage stamp
Tábxa*(aat)	cooked dish
Táwla*(aat)	table
Tuul/aTwáal	length; along (prep.)
wakáala*(aat)	agency
wakáalat is-safariyyáat	travel agency
wáraga*/ awráag	piece of paper
wasT/awsáaT	centre; middle
wúja9/awjáa9	pain
xáatam/ xawáatim	ring (for the finger)
xarúuf/xirfáan	lamb; mutton; sheep
xáTa'/axTáa'	mistake
9áadi	ordinary
9ádil	correct; just
9áfwan	sorry; pardon
9úmri + maa + past-tense verb	I've never ... in my life

Unit Eleven

In this unit you will learn about:

- the imperfect verb: basic forms
- the imperfect verb: different stem types, e.g. 'hollow', 'weak' and 'doubled'
- the verb forms we have met so far, to review your knowledge
- the uses of the imperfect: habitual action, ability, current or future actions and 'used to'

Language points

11.1 The imperfect verb: basic forms

The verb forms we have encountered thus far, such as **shárab**, **gaal** and **búga**, are used to describe completed actions that took place in the past – hence the conventional translations 'he drank', 'he said' and 'he remained'. We come now to the 'imperfect' verb, which is used to describe incomplete actions taking place at the moment of speech ('he is eating'), to describe habitual, or 'timeless', actions ('he eats breakfast at 7.00 a.m. every day', 'he eats a lot'), and to describe future actions or intentions to act ('he'll eat with us tonight'). For all these various English tense forms, Arabic uses the imperfect verb. The full imperfect conjugations of the strong verbs **shárab** 'to drink' and **kítab** 'to write' are given below:

'... writing/write/will write'		'... drinking/drink/will drink'	
áktib	'I am ...'	áshrab	'I am ...'
táktib	'you (m.) ...'	tíshrab	'you (m.) ...'
taktibíin	'you (f.) ...'	tishrabíin	'you (f.) ...'
yáktib	'he/it ...'	yíshrab	'he ...'
táktib	'she/it ...'	tíshrab	'she ...'
náktib	'we ...'	níshrab	'we ...'
taktibúun	'you (pl.) ...'	tishrabúun	'you (pl.) ...'
yaktibúun	'they ...'	yishrabúun	'they ...'

It can be seen from this that the consonant skeletons, **sh-r-b** and **k-t-b**, remain unchanged, as they do in the perfect tense. The imperfect verb, however, basically consists of a *stem* to which prefixes and suffixes are added. In strong verbs such as **shárab** and **kítab**, this stem is of the -CCvC- form: **-shrab-** and **-ktib-**. The vowel in the imperfect stem of strong verbs can be **a**, **i** or (more rarely) **u**: thus from **dáxal** 'to enter' the stem is **-dxal-**, from **tíras** 'to fill' **-tris-** and from **Dárab** 'to hit' **-Drub-**. Make a point of learning the stem vowel of each verb as you meet it, since there are no general rules that allow you to predict what it will be. The stem vowels given in this book, like the rest of the grammatical forms given, are those that appear to be in the widest circulation among educated speakers in all Gulf States, but there is nonetheless considerable local variation. The imperfect stems of all verbs so far encountered in the text are given for practice in 11.3 below.

Turning now to the prefixes, we see that **a-** is used for 'I', **t-** for all forms of 'you' and 'she', **n-** for 'we' and **y-** for 'he' and 'they'. The vowel of the prefix in Gulf dialects is determined by the following rule of thumb:

if the stem vowel is **a** the prefix vowel is **i**
if the stem vowel is **i** or **u** the prefix vowel is **a**.

This rule of 'vowel dissimilation', as it is called, is a noticeable feature of speech in most areas of the Gulf.

As far as the imperfect suffixes are concerned, it can be seen that **-iin** denotes feminine in the 2nd person (e.g. **táDrub** 'you (m.) hit', **taDrubíin** 'you (f.) hit'), while **-uun** denotes plurality (e.g. **yísma9** 'he hears', **yisma9úun** 'they hear').

The dependent personal pronouns are suffixed directly to the imperfect verb, as they are to the past-tense verb:

yaDrúbni	'he hits me'
asmá9ha	'I hear her'
yis'alúunich	'they're asking you (f.)'

However, in verb forms such as **taktibíin, taktibúun, yishrabúun**, etc. (whether suffixed or not), in which a long stressed syllable is preceded by a short unstressed one, there is a strong tendency in Gulf Arabic, especially in uneducated or casual speech, to 'rearrange' the syllables to give alternatives such as **takitbíin, takitbúun, yishirbúun, yisi'lúunich**, etc. When this happens, the vowel of the prefix is often also very much weakened, or dropped altogether: one hears **tkitbíin, yshirbúun**, etc. Exactly the same process of syllable rearrangement takes place when dependent personal pronouns beginning with a vowel are suffixed to forms of the verb that do not have a final long syllable. Thus one often hears: **yishírbah** or **yshírbah** instead of **yíshrabah** (**yíshrab + ah**) 'he drinks it', and **tiDírbich** or **tDírbich** instead of **táDrubich** (**táDrub + ich**) 'she hits you (f.)'. When this 'syllable rearrangement' occurs, the stem vowel in the resulting form is almost always **i**.

A note needs to be added here on Omani verb forms. The forms given above are not dissimilar to those found in areas of Oman where 'Bedouin' dialects are spoken (the deserts of the south, west and north of Oman near the UAE border), except that they have a gender distinction in the 2nd and 3rd persons plural that is little used in the rest of the Gulf. But the 'settled' Omani dialects of the Capital Area, the mountainous interior of the north and most of the Batina coast are different, in that do not have the **-n** ending of the 2nd feminine singular and the 2nd and 3rd masculine plural forms. So, for example, the equivalent Omani 'settled' dialect forms of the imperfect strong verb typically look like this:

'... writing/write/will write'

áktib	'I am ...'	**niktib**	'we ...'
tíktib	'you (m.) ...'	**tikitbu**	'you (m. pl.) ...'
tikítbi	'you (f.) ...'	**tikítban**	'you (f. pl) ...'
yíktib	'he/it ...'	**yikítbu**	'they (m.)...'
tiktib	'she/it ...'	**yikitban**	'they (f.) ...'

11.2 The imperfect verb: different stem types

We noted such different types as 'hollow', 'weak' and other kinds of verb when considering the past tense. Corresponding distinctions are also made in the imperfect tense, which we now consider.

■ 'Hollow' verbs

These are verbs in which the middle consonant of the consonant skeleton is **w** or **y**, and consequently fails to show up in the past-tense verb, for example **gaal** 'he said' (< **gawal**), **shaal** 'he removed' (< **shayal**). The imperfect stem of hollow verbs is always of the -CvvC-type, to which the normal prefixes and suffixes are added. The long vowel of the stem may be **uu**, **ii** or (more rarely) **aa**. The correct stem vowelling for hollow verbs, as in the case of strong verbs, has to be learnt by heart. The prefix vowel is always **i**. Conjugations for **gaal** 'to say', **shaal** 'to remove' and **naam** 'to sleep' are given below. As already noted, there is a strong tendency for the unstressed **i** of the prefix vowel to be dropped:

agúul	ashíil	anáam	'I ...'
tigúul	tishíil	tináam	'you (m.) ...'
tiguulíin	tishiilíin	tinaamíin	'you (f.) ...'
yigúul	yishíil	yináam	'he ...'
tigúul	tishíil	tináam	'she ...'
nigúul	nishíil	nináam	'we ...'
tiguulúun	tishiilúun	tinaamúun	'you (pl.) ...'
yiguulúun	yishiilúun	yinaamúun	'they ...'

Again, Omani 'settled' dialects lack the final **-n** (**tiqúuli, tiqúulu, yiqúulu**, etc.) in their equivalents to the above forms, and have separate 2nd and 3rd feminine plural forms, which have the **-an** suffix (**tiqúulan, yiqúulan**, etc.).

■ 'Weak' verbs

'Weak' verbs have **w** or **y** as final consonant in their skeletons. One verb, **ja(a)** (often **ya(a)**) 'to come', is 'doubly weak', having **y** as both second and third consonant. In its past-tense form it behaves like a hollow verb, but in its imperfect more like a weak verb. There are two types of weak imperfect stem: -CCa- and -CCi-. In both cases the vowel of the stem is dropped when the **-iin** and **-uun** suffixes are attached.

Unit 11

159

The prefix vowel is **i**. Examples are **mísha** 'to walk' and **líga** 'to find; receive; meet':

ámshi	nímshi	álga	nílga
tímshi	timshúun	tílga	tilgúun
timshíin		tilgíin	
yímshi	yimshúun	yílga	yilgúun
tímshi		tílga	

The imperfect of **ya(a)/ja(a)** 'to come' is as follows:

ayíi / ajíi	nyíi / nijíi
tyíi / tijíi	
tyíin / tijíin	tyúun / tijúun
iyíi/ ijíi	
tyíi / tijíi	iyúun / ijúun

Omani 'settled' verb forms lack the final **-n**, as usual, in those forms in the above tables that have it, but they have the usual 2nd and 3rd feminine plural forms with the **-an** suffix. A further special feature of Oman is that the **y** of the consonantal skeleton is retained in the 2nd feminine singular and all of the 2nd and 3rd plural forms. So the Omani equivalent paradigms to the above are:

ámshi	nímshi	álqa	nílqa
tímshi	timíshyu	tílqa	tiláqyu
tmíshyi	timíshyan	tiláqyi	tiláqyan
yímshi	yimísyhu	yílqa	yiláqyu
tímshi	yimíshyan	tílqa	yiláqyan

When dependent personal pronouns are suffixed to forms ending in **-a** or **-i**, this vowel is lengthened and becomes stressed:

a9Tii	'I give'	a9Tíik	'I give you'
ábghi/ábbi	'I want'	abghíihum/abbíihum	'I want them'
yígra	'he reads'	yigráaha	'he reads it'
tínsa	'you forget'	tinsáana	'you forget us'

■ 'Doubled' verbs

'Doubled' verbs are those in which the second and third consonants of the skeleton are the same. The imperfect stem is always of the -CvCC-

type. The stem vowel is usually **i** or **u**. The prefix vowel is always **i**.
Examples are the verbs **Habb** 'to like; love' and **DHann** 'to think':

aHíbb	nihíbb	aDHúnn	niDHúnn
tiHíbb	tiHibbúun	tiDHúnn	tiDHunnúun
tiHibbíin		tiDHunníin	
yiHíbb	yiHibbúun	yiDHúnn	yiDHunnúun
tiHíbb		tiDHúnn	

In 'settled' Oman, as usual, the forms above that have it lack the final
-n, and the 2nd and 3rd feminine plural forms have the **-an** ending, so:
tiHíbban, **yiHíbban**, etc.

■ Verbs with a glottal stop as C₁

The most important verbs in this group are **'ákal** 'to eat' and **'áxadh**
'to take'. In the imperfect, the initial **'** is dropped and the prefix vowel
is lengthened. The imperfect of **'ákal** is thus:

áakil	náakil
táakil	taaklúun
taaklíin	
yáakil	yaaklúun
táakil	

Just as the unstressed **i** is elided when followed by **-iin** or **-uun**, so it
is when vowel-initial dependent personal pronouns are suffixed to
áakil, **táakil**, etc.: **áaklah** 'I eat it', **yáaklah** 'he eats it'.
    Oman has **táakli**, **táaklu** and **yáaklu** as expected, as well as feminine
plural forms **táaklan** and **yáaklan**. However, this verb, and others that
have a glottal stop as C₁ are also heard in Oman with **oo** rather than
aa as stem vowel, for example **óokil**, **tóokil**, **tóokli**, etc.

■ Verbs with a 'guttural' consonant as C₁

'Guttural' consonants are those pronounced from the back of the throat,
namely **x**, **gh**, **9**, **H** and **h**. Verbs that have one of these consonants
in C₁ position may be conjugated with a normal 'strong' imperfect
stem (-CCvC-) but often, in Gulf dialects, they have a -CaCiC- or
-CaCC- stem. The verb **ghásal**, for example, which means 'to wash',
may have either a **-ghsil-** or **-ghasil-** stem; **9áraf** 'to know' may have
a **-9ruf-** or (much more commonly) a **-9arf-** stem.

Compare:

ághsil	or	aghásil	á9ruf	or	a9árf
tághsil		tghásil	tá9ruf		t9árf
taghsilíin		tghaslíin	ta9rufíin		t9arfíin
yághsil		yghásil	yá9ruf		y9árf
tághsil		tghásil	tá9ruf		t9árf
nághsil		nghásil	ná9ruf		n9árf
taghsilúun		tghaslúun	ta9rufúun		t9arfúun
yaghsilúun		yghaslúun	ya9rufúun		y9arfúun

Unstressed **i** is elided where a vowel-initial dependent pronoun is suffixed: **yghásil** 'he washes', **ygháslah** 'he washes it'.

In Oman, these verbs are generally treated like ordinary strong verbs (see the Omani conjugation of 'to write', above).

■ Verbs with **w** as C$_1$

There are a number of common verbs, such as **wúgaf** 'to stop; stand' and **wuSal** 'to reach; arrive', that typically have an **-oo-** element in the prefix (compare the **-aa** of **yáakil**). Instead of **áwSil** 'I arrive', we get **óoSil** – **aw** becoming **oo** as it does often in Gulf Arabic. The full paradigm is:

óoSil	nóoSil
tóoSil	tooSlúun
tooSlíin	
yóoSil	yooSlúun
tóoSil	

In Oman, there are the expected forms, for example **tóoSli** 'you (f.) arrive', **tóoSlu** 'you (m. pl.) arrive', **tóoSlan** 'you (f. pl.) arrive', etc.

11.3 Review of verb forms

Listed below, according to imperfect stem type and stem vowel, are all the verbs that we have met in this book so far. Try conjugating a few verbs from each category aloud, according to the models given in this unit. Check that you remember the meaning of every verb listed.

■ Strong verbs

Stem -CCvC-, base form yvCCvC

stem vowel a: dáxal gá9ad kúbar níjaH ríja9 síma9 fítaH sí'al
                  shárab Tála9 fáraH qíbal tí9ab

stem vowel i: físhal kísar kítab rígad síkar tíras gítal tárak
                  kíshaf nízal

stem vowel u: Dárab Sáraf Tálab

Stem -CCvC- or -CaCiC, base form yaCCvC or yCaCiC ('gutturals')

ghásal Hámal xáraj 9ájab 9áraf ghálab

Stem -aaCiC-, base form yaaCiC (' as C₁)

'ákal 'áxadh

Stem -ooCvC-, base form yooCvC (w as C₁)

stem vowel i: wúSal
stem vowel u: wúgaf

■ Hollow verbs

Stem -CvvC-, base form yiCvvC

stem vowel aa: naam xaaf
stem vowel ii: baa9 jaab shaal Saad Saar TaaH zaad
stem vowel uu: baag gaal gaam kaan maat raaH shaaf zaar

■ Weak verbs

Stem -CCv-, base form yiCCv

stem vowel a: líga bída gára nísa
stem vowel i: ja mísha dára Hícha 9áTa bágha gáDa shíra

■ Doubled verbs

Stem -CvCC-, base form yiCvCC

stem vowel i: dashsh dazz Habb sakk shagg tamm
stem vowel u: gaTT HaTT DHann

From this point on, new verbs listed in the Vocabulary will be given
with their imperfect base form.

11.4 The uses of the imperfect

■ Habitual action

The imperfect is typically used to describe what *usually happens*, that is, it is used like the present simple in English. The following examples are taken from a description of Gulf marriage customs:

yirúuH Hagg abúuha, yigúul lih ána ábghi bíntik ...
'He goes to her father and says to him "I want your daughter" ...'

yídfa9 mahárha gadd maa yáTlub abúuha ...
'He pays her dowry according to what her father demands ...'

íji wíyya zóojtah, yidaxlúun fi Híjra u ysikkúun 9aláyhum il-baab.
'He comes with his wife, they enter a room and they shut the door on them.'

Further examples:

fi waqt il-faráagh níl9ab il-kúura iT-Táa'ira.
'In (our) free time we play volleyball.'

táskin fi firíij il-Húura, muu chidhíi?
'You live in al-Houra quarter, don't you?'

maa yísma9 Háchi n-naas.
'He never listens to people's gossip.'

■ Ability

The imperfect is used in Arabic in many cases where English uses 'can/can't' or 'know how to':

ásma9 sh-ygúul láakin maa áfhamah.
'I can hear what he's saying but I can't understand him.'

maa asúug sayyáara.
'I can't drive a car.'

maa y9árf il-lúgha l-faarsíyya.
'He doesn't know Persian.'

■ Contemporary action

Actions (or states) that are taking place (existing) at the moment when
the speaker is speaking are expressed by the use of the imperfect:

níbni bayt jadíid hal-Házza.
'We're building a new house at the moment.'

yífraH li-ánnah níjaH fil-imtiHáan.
'He's happy because he passed the exam.'

- **guul líyyi wayn ligáythum.**
- **háadha ána agúul lik, la!**
- 'Tell me where you found them.'
- 'I'm just telling you that, aren't I!'

■ Future action/intention

The future particle **b-** is prefixed to the imperfect verb to give it a future
meaning, or to express an intention to do something:

barúuH lándan u bádris áwwal sána 9ála Hsáabi.
'I'll go to London and study for the first year at my own expense.'

bagúul lik shay wáaHid ...
'I'll tell you *one* thing ...'

maa ba9Tíik il-fluus.
'I'm not going to give you the money.'

gábil la nrúuH bina9Tíikum 9unwáanna l-jadíid.
'Before we go, we'll give you our new address.'

bitíg9ad lo bitímshi?
'Do you intend staying or going?'

Note that **b-** becomes **bi-** before verb forms that begin with a prefix **n-**
or **t-**.

■ 'Used to'

If the relevant person of the past tense of **kaan** 'to be' is used with an
imperfect verb, the meaning is of habitual action in the past – 'used to':

yoom ana Saghíir, kint ál9ab fil-firíij wíyya l-awláad.
'When I was small I used to play in the neighbourhood with the
boys.'

ayyáam zamáan káanaw ybii9úun it-támar bil-jílla.
'In the old days they used to sell dates in 56lb baskets.'

maa kínna niHíbb il-mádrasa li'ánn il-mudíir kaan yaDrúbna.
'We usedn't to like school because the headmaster used to beat us.'

maa kaan yisíkk baab il-Hamáam bá9ad maa yiTla9 mínnah.
'He never used to close the bathroom door after he came out of it.'

Drills

Below are eight substitution drills to help you manipulate present-tense verb forms. A model dialogue is given, and against each number that follows is written a word or words. Repeat the dialogue, substituting the Arabic equivalent of the word(s) given in the appropriate place in the dialogue. This 'new' dialogue is then changed by the next substitution to a slightly different dialogue, and so on.

Exercise 11.1

- **cham ráatib ta9Tíih?**
- **a9Tíih xamsíin diináar kill sháhar**
- 'How much salary do you give him?'
- 'I give him 50 dinars a month.'

1	them	4	week	7	seventy-five
2	sixty	5	us	8	fortnight
3	her	6	me		

Exercise 11.2

- **shu l-ákil illi tiHíbb il-ákthar?**
- **aHíbb il-mázza l-lubnaaníyya**
- 'What food d'you like most?
- 'I like Lebanese mazza.'

1	he likes	4	English food	7	they
2	rice and fish	5	you (f.)	8	stuffed aubergines
3	you (pl.) like	6	roast chicken		

Exercise 11.3

- **wayn bitrúuH fiS-Sayf?**
- **barúuH lándan azúur háli.**
- 'Where're you going in the summer?'
- 'I'm going to London to visit my family.'

1 going to Egypt to see the pyramids
2 going to Syria to study Arabic
3 you (pl.)
4 they
5 going to sea to fish
6 he
7 going to the mountains to have a rest

Exercise 11.4

- **sáa9a cham bityúun?**
- **binyíi sáa9a sítta u nuSS**
- 'What time are you coming?'
- 'We'll come at 6.30.'

1 3.30	4 4.45	7 she
2 they	5 you (f.)	8 3.20
3 he	6 12.00	

Exercise 11.5

- **tíshrab bábsi?**
- **la, máa ashrab.**
- 'Do you drink Pepsi?'
- 'No, I don't.'

1 tea	4 he	7 you (f.)
2 coffee	5 cold drink	8 they
3 you (pl.)	6 fruit juice	

Exercise 11.6

- **shiráytaw bayt jadíid?**
- **la, maa shiráyna bá9ad. biníshri ish-sháhar il-jaay.**
- 'Have you bought a new house?'
- 'No, we haven't yet. We'll buy next month.'

1	car	4	piece of land	7	fridge
2	they	5	next week	8	you (f.)
3	you (m.)	6	she		

Exercise 11.7

- **maa tá9jibich il-kuwáyt, muu chidhíi?**
- **la, múu maa ta9jíbni l-kuwáyt! ta9jíbni wáayid!**
- 'You don't like Kuwait, isn't that so?'
- 'No, it isn't that I don't like Kuwait! I certainly do like it!'

1	Bahrain	4	he	7	the Saudis
2	you (pl.)	5	the Kuwaitis	8	you (f.)
3	Saudi Arabia	6	she		

Exercise 11.8

kint ál9ab kúurat il-qádam yoom ana Saghíir
'I used to play football when I was small'

1	volley ball	4	they	7	go fishing
2	marbles	5	stay at home	8	he
3	she	6	old		

Dialogue 11.1

Listen to and translate the following dialogue.

---

fil-garaaj **'At the garage'** (Audio 1; 24)

A is-saláam 9aláykum.
B u 9aláyk is-saláam … HáaDir.

A sayyáarati háadhi maa tímshi zayn. maa adri waysh fíiha ...
yúmkin fiih shay fil-blaagáat lo fil-karbráytir ...

B zayn, shiil il-bánid nshúuf dáaxil shwáy ... la, il-blaagáat
maa fíiha shay ... nshúuf il-plaatíin ... háadha shwáy wásix,
yábbi lih tanDHíif, láakin muu háadha s-sábab ... wállah,
múshkila háadha ...! míta yá9ni áaxir márra HaTTáyt fíiha
zayt?

A maa adri biDH-DHabT ... gábil iji shahráyn thaláatha ...

B ohóo! mub zayn háadha yaa xúuyi! láazim tiHúTT kill sháhar
fi haT-Taqs il-Háarr. nshúuf il-mustáwa máalah ... shuuf!
mustawáah kíllish náazil! nífdat illa shwáyya! baHúTT lik
9ulbatáyn u bitshúuf sayyáartak tímshi 9ádil ... láakin la, Hátta
9ulbatáyn muu káafya ...! nzíid 9úlba bá9ad ... háadha zayn
chidhíi ... xaláaS! haay diinaaráyn u nuSS min fáDlik.

A haay flúusik ... u shúkran.

B laysh maa táaxidh 9úlba bá9ad? yumkin yifíidik fiT-Taríig!

A Sidj ... 9áTni 9úlba 9óoda baHúTTha fiS-Sandúug.

Dialogue 11.2

Read the following telephone conversation and, after reading it, try to
answer the questions that follow.

ila l-liqáa 'See you soon!'

A allÓ?

B allÓ?

A allÓ? jáasim?

B la, háadha ábu jáasim, mínhu yíHchi?

A ána áHmad mbáarak, Sadíig wíldik.

B ha! állah yisálmik, yaa áHmad! gaal líyyi jáasim ínnik bitóoSil
il-yoom, muu chidhíi?

A ay ná9am. bitrúuH iT-Tayyáara min il-kuwáyt is sáa9a ithná9shar
u rub9. ídhan bóoSil is-sáa9a thintáyn taqríiban ... insháallah
maa bykúun fii ta'xíir.

B insháallah. zayn, ana bashúufik is-sáa9a thintáyn fil-maTáar.

A shloon? jáasim maa biyíi?

B 9áfwan, nisáyt agúul lik inn jáasim maríiD shway ... rí9aj min
  ish-shúghul ta9báan ams, u gaal lih id-dáxtar yitímm yoomáyn
  fil-bayt layn yiSíir áHsan ... mub shay xaTíir wíla shay, bas yíbghi
  lih shway ráaHa ... ana bayíik fil-maTáar.
A háadha min Tíibik! 9ása jáasim yíshfa bi súr9a.
B wila yihímmik! láakin chayf ba9árfik fil-maTáar? sh-bitílbas?
A bálbas bádla Sáfra u qamíiS ázrag.
B zayn! nshúufik is-sáa9a thintáyn, insháallah.
A insháallah. fi amáan illáh.
B fi amáan il-karíim, u íla l-liqáa!

Questions:

1 Who answers the phone?
2 What time does the plane leave Kuwait?
3 What time does it arrive?
4 Who is going to meet Ahmad at the airport?
5 Why can't Jasim meet him?
6 How will Jasim's father know Ahmad?

Vocabulary

bánid	bonnet (car)	Házza*	moment; time
bína/yíbni	to build	9ala Hsáab + pron.	at (someone's) expense
blaag(aat)	spark plug		
dáras/yádris	to study	ídhan	so; therefore
biDH-DHabT	exactly	ijíi (or iyíi)	approximately
DHann/ yiDHúnn	to think	jílla*(aat)	56lb basket of dates
faad/yifíid	to be of use	karbráytir	carburettor
fáarsi	Persian	9ála kíllin	anyway; however that may be
fáham/yífham	to understand		
hamm/yihímm	to concern; be important (to someone)	kúura*	ball
		kúurat il-qádam	football
wila yihímmik!	Don't worry about it!	il-kúura iT-Táa'ira	volleyball
		láazim	incumbent; necessary
HáaDir	at your service		
Háchi/Hacháawi	talk; gossip	líbas/tílbas	to dress; wear

ila l-liqáa	see you soon!	tanDHíif	cleaning
máhar	bride price	taqríiban	approximately
mustáwa(yaat)	level; standard	tíila	marbles
náazil	low (level)		(game)
nífad/yínfad	to run out	Taríig/Túrug	road
plaatíin	breaker points	Tiib	goodness
	(car)	xaláaS	finished; over
ríkab/yárkub	to get on, in	xaTíir	grave;
	(vehicle)		dangerous
saag/yisúug	to drive	zaal/yizáal	to cease
sábab/asbáab	reason; cause	maa zaal	to still be ...
síkan/yáskin	to live (in a	9ása +	hopefully ...
	place)	noun/pron.	
Sandúug	boot (car)	9aSíir	pressed fruit
shífa/yíshfa	to get better;		juice
	be cured	9unwáan/	address
ta'xíir	delay	9anaawíin	

Cultural point

Marriage: traditional and modern

A famous Bahraini colloquial poet, Abdurrahman Rafii', wrote a poem in the 1970s ironically entitled **il-9irs il-9ádil**, meaning 'Marriage as it should be' or 'Proper marriage'. In it, the poet laments the difficulties involved in finding a local bride – the large sum of money required for the dowry, the expensive presents and the celebrations to which family, friends, workmates and neighbours all have to be invited, and the economies that have to be made before the marriage to pay for it. For a brief moment, the poet considers resorting to India to find a cheaper marriage partner (as many Gulf Arabs did in the past), but rejects it because he wants 'the real thing'. Although written many years ago, the problems that this poem humorously rehearses are still there today. But it was not always so. In the pre-oil Gulf, getting married for ordinary people was a straightforward affair. Many girls were promised (some as soon as they were born) to their cousin on their father's side (**ibn il-9amm**), and the marriage would be made when they were not much more than fourteen years old, with only a token dowry (**máhar**). Here is an account of marriage in Bahrain as it was in the 1940s and 1950s, in the words of a middle-aged woman:

'The custom was to go and ask for the girl in marriage through the father, the boy's father, who would present himself to the girl's father. He would go and ask for her, and if they agreed, we brought her the trousseau and the presents that they used to give, and the clothes ... We took them and delivered them, and the dowry money, and we made the marriage contract (**mílcha**), the boy's father and the girl's father went and made the contract with the religious sheikh ... Then came the henna night (**láylat il-Hánna**), when they beat drums, and brought musical instruments, and beat drums. They did their drum beating and singing and henna-ed the bride, and then it was the wedding night, and they drummed some more, they slaughtered animals, they cooked, and they pushed her in [to the wedding chamber], or they delivered her in this rug ... The custom of the real old days was not to wash her at all, or clean her up, they just presented her in the clothes she stood up in, they just took her and shoved her in with her husband ... Anyway, in the morning, they would take her and wash her, clean her up, garland her with sweet basil and gold ... and that was it.'

Typically, a few days after the **láylat id-dáxla** or **láylat id-dáshsha** 'the night of the entering', when the marriage was consummated in a special decorated bedchamber called the **fársha**, the young bride would move from her father's house to that of her new husband's family, where she would join the wives of her new husband's brothers in a large, extended family house. These young wives were collectively known as **chanáayin** (sing. **channa**), 'daughters-in-law' and their contribution to the work of the communal household was determined by their all-powerful mother-in-law, who to many was a figure of fear. One woman described her life thus:

áwwal mischíina, mitghárbila ... wila líha jaah, chínnha sabíyya, tighásil, tixúmm, tiráwwi u tíTbax, wi r-ráyil bass kíllah fi shoor úmmah ... il-9ayáayiz kíllahum chláab áwwal.

'In the old days, [the young wife] was wretched, at her wit's end ... she had no status, she was like a prisoner ... she would wash, sweep, fetch water and cook, and her husband was totally under his mother's control ... the mothers-in-law were all dogs in the old days.'

Nowadays, all this has changed. Marriage is no longer automatically to the girl's paternal cousin (though this is still not uncommon) and generally occurs when the girl is much older – typically in her twenties. Before the marriage, the fiancé now gives an engagement (**xuTúuba**) present of expensive jewellery known as the **shábka** and an engagement ring (**díbla**) as in the West, a custom that used not to exist. The wedding celebrations are often in five-star Western-style hotels, and the bride's apparel also often owes something to its Western equivalent, although traditional, elaborate wedding gowns with much gold and old-fashioned jewellery are also popular. Many couples go away on honeymoon (**shahr il-9ásal**) just like Westerners. And often, when they return, the young couple will live on their own in their own apartment or small house, rather than with their in-laws.

The sums of money given as dowries became very large in the 1970s and 1980s. In 1998, the UAE passed a law restricting the size of the dowry and the opulence of the wedding celebrations, and the governments of a number of Gulf States, such as Kuwait, now give grants to bridegrooms to help them meet the cost if they get married to a local girl. One peculiarity of weddings Gulf-style is the popularity of 'mass weddings', in which several hundred couples get married at the same time. This is popular as an economy measure, and is supported by Gulf governments, who see locally contracted marriages as the cement that holds Gulf societies together.

 ## Reading Arabic

In this unit we are going to look at some more difficult signs. Look at the one below, from Dubai airport.

You can see from the translation what this airport sign means; but can you work out the exact wording of the Arabic, and relate it to the grammar we have covered so far? The first word is **Sáala**, which we

met in the Reading Arabic section of Unit Eight, meaning 'saloon, lounge'. Next we have **dáraja**, a word we have already met in the sense of 'degree', but whose meaning here is 'class'. The next word is **rijáal** 'men', the plural of **rájul** 'man'. This is the Modern Standard Arabic form of this word – we have already seen that, in the Gulf, 'man' is usually **rajjáal** or **rayyáal** (pl. **rajaajíil** or **rayaayíil**), although, in the Cultural point, in the quotation from the old Bahraini lady, the word **ráyil** (also pronounced **rájil**) occurred, meaning 'man' in the sense of 'husband'. Finally, we have the word **al-'a9máal**, the plural of **9ámal**, whose basic meaning is 'job; work'. The phrase **rijáal al-'a9máal**, literally 'men of works', is the Arabic equivalent of 'businessmen', so the sign says, literally, 'the lounge (of) the class (of) businessmen' or 'Business Class Lounge'.

Can you work out the meaning of the sign above, which appears over a traditional Omani door in the town of Nizwa? (Clues: **wáHda** means 'unit'; **wizáara** 'ministry'; **naql** 'transport' and **ittiSaaláat** 'communications'.)

Unit Twelve

In this unit you will learn about:

- verb strings, i.e. two or more verbs that follow each other, e.g. 'he wants to go'
- the imperative: strong verbs, e.g. 'Drink!' or 'Write it!'
- the imperative: other types of verb, e.g. 'Stop!' or 'Eat!'
- the negative imperative, e.g. 'Don't go!' or 'Don't drink it!'

Language point

12.1 Verb strings

A verb string is two or more verbs that follow each other without an intervening particle such as **'inn** 'that'. For example, an English expression such as 'he wants to go' is translated into Arabic by a verb string that means literally 'he wants he goes'; 'he couldn't do it' is literally 'he couldn't he does it'. The first verb in such strings is usually called an auxiliary verb. In this unit we will look at some of the more important verb strings involving the imperfect tense.

■ **bágha** + verb: 'to want to do something'

bágha may be in the past or imperfect tense, but the verb following in the verb string is imperfect:

> **áHmad yábbi yishúufik báachir.**
> 'Ahmad wants to see you tomorrow.'

maa ábghi a9Tíik hal-gadd fluus.
'I don't want to give you that much money.'

bagháyt amúrr 9aláyk il-báarHa, láakin maa gídart.
'I wanted to call in on you yesterday, but I couldn't.'

With a suffixed pronoun, **bágha** + verb is used to mean 'to want someone to do something'. In this case, the *pronoun* and the *following verb* must agree with each other (i.e. the sentence immediately below means literally 'You want me I come with you?'):

tabghíini ayíi wiyyáak?
'Do you want me to come with you?'

abbíich tiguulíin líyyi bi Saráaha ...
'I want you to tell me frankly ...'

maa bagháaha tít9ab.
'He didn't want her to get tired.'

bágha is also used in an idiomatic sense with following **li** + pronoun + noun to mean 'to need':

iz-zawáaj yábghi lih fluus.
'Marriage requires money.'
(lit. 'The marriage wants for itself money.')

has-sayyáara tábbi líha tanDHíif
'This car needs cleaning.'
(lit. 'wants for itself ...')

hal-wásix yábghi lih shayaláan.
'This dirt needs removing.'

Exercise 12.1

Translate:

1 He wanted me to go home.
2 I want you (m.) to tell me something.
3 She wants him to wash the car.
4 We want you (pl.) to eat this food with us.
5 Do you (f.) want me to tell you the truth?

6 They wanted to study in Cairo.

7 You (f.) wanted to buy those shoes, didn't you?

8 This room needs cleaning.

9 That door needs repairing.

10 She needs money.

■ **gídar** + verb: 'to be able to do something'

The construction is similar to that of **bágha** + verb, for example:

maa ágdar agúul lik cham yábbi.
'I can't tell you how much he wants.'

maa gídar yishíil il-janaTáat ith-thagíila.
'He couldn't lift the heavy cases.'

tígdar tárkuD ásra9 min hal-wálad?
'Can you run faster than this boy?'

maa gídraw yiHillúun il-múshkila.
'They couldn't solve the problem.'

■ **gaam** + verb: 'to begin to do something'

gaam has the literal meaning 'to get up; stand up'. When used as the first element in a verb string it means 'to begin to do something' – similar to the English expression 'to up and do something':

layn síma9 il-xábar, gaam yíbchi.
'When he heard the news, he began to weep.'

gumt a9ídd il-asáami fis-síjill.
'I began to count the names on the register.'

gaam + verb can also denote the beginning of a habitual action:

layn wúSlat lándan, gáamat tílbas azyáa gharbíyya.
'As soon as she got to London, she started wearing Western fashions.'

bá9ad maa hadd shúghlah fish-shárika, gaam yiSíid sámach kill yoom.

'After he gave up his work at the company, he took to going fishing every day.'

■ **DHall/tamm** + verb: 'to keep on doing something'

Both the verbs **DHall** and **tamm** mean 'to stay; continue' and can be used as verbs on their own:

DHalláyt fil-jaysh sanatáyn.
'I stayed in the army for two years.'

il-jaww tamm ráTib.
'The weather continued humid.'

When followed by an imperfect verb, they mean 'to continue doing something' or 'to do something constantly':

físhlaw fil-imtiHáan, láakin DHállaw ydirsúun fi maa bá9ad.
'They failed in the exam, but they kept on studying afterwards.'

DHállat tábghi tzúur faránsa.
'She continued to want to visit France.'

támmaw yaaklúun athnáa l-muHáaDra.
'They continued eating during the lecture.'

tamm yigúul lihum 'la' min Tílbaw mínnah shay.
'He kept on saying no when(ever) they asked him for anything.'

■ **maa zaal** + verb: 'to still do something'

The verb **zaal** is not much used in its positive form (meaning 'to come to an end'), but with **maa** it is commonly used in the sense of 'not cease to do/be something', 'to still do/be something', when followed by an imperfect verb. **zaal** is a hollow verb conjugated like **gaal**:

maa zilt aHíbb dhiich il-bint.
'I still love that girl.'
(lit. 'I have not ceased I love that girl.')

yáddati wáayid 9óoda, láakin maa záalat tádhkir il-qíSaS maal awwal.
'My grandmother is very old, but she still remembers stories from the old days.'

Like **tamm**, **maa zaal** can also be used with a following adjective or noun, as well as an imperfect verb, for example:

maa zilt Táalib.   **maa záalaw za9laaníin.**
'I'm still a student.'   'They're still upset.'

Exercise 12.2

Translate:

1 I couldn't close the door.

2 They can't reach here before nine o'clock.

3 Were you able to read his writing?

4 When he saw the mistake, he began to laugh.

5 When I was 20 I started to smoke.

6 After an hour, the aeroplane began to descend.

7 I continued to live in Riyaad for two more years.

8 She kept on walking for three hours.

9 They continued to telephone me every day.

10 You still live near the post office, don't you?

11 He still drives a Ford.

12 I still remember that day.

■ **gáa9id** + verb: 'to be in the process of doing something'

gáa9id (f. **gáa9da**, pl. **gaa9díin**) is the active participle of the verb **gá9ad** 'to sit', but is used with a following imperfect verb to describe actions that are going on continuously at the time of speaking. It has, when used in this way, no overtones of the original meaning 'sitting':

– **wayn jáasim?**
– **gáa9id yíl9ab bárra wíyya l-awláad.**
– 'Where's Jaasim?'
– 'He's outside playing with the boys.'

yoom yiit, kínna gaa9díin níTbax il-gháda.
'When you came, we were in the middle of cooking lunch.'

■ láazim + verb: 'to have to do something'

Like **gáa9id**, **láazim** is an active participle, but, unlike it, it does not agree in gender/number with the imperfect verb that follows it. It signifies obligation to do something:

láazim truuH il-mustáshfa.
'You must go to the hospital.'

láazim yitímm fi hash-shúghul.
'He has to continue in this job.'

láazim tíshrab had-dáwa.
'She must take this medicine.'

Sentences containing **láazim** used like this can be negated in two ways, which carry different meanings. If **láazim** itself is negated (using **muu** or **mub**), the sentence expresses *lack of obligation*:

mub láazim truuH il-mustáshfa.
'You don't have to go to the hospital.'

mub láazim tíshrab had-dáwa.
'She's not obliged to take this medicine.'

or 'It's not necessary for her to take this medicine.'

But if the verb following **láazim** is negated (using **maa**), the sentence denotes *negative obligation*:

láazim maa truuH il-mustáshfa.
'You mustn't go to the hospital.'

láazim maa yitímm fi hash-shúghul.
'He mustn't continue in this job.'

láazim maa tíshrab had-dáwa.
'She mustn't take this medicine.'

In contrast to the above usage of **láazim** with the imperfect verb, it is worth noting that, when used with a following *past tense*, it means 'must have', for example:

láazim ráaHat.
'She must have gone.'

láazim nisáytah fil-fúnduq.
'You must have left it in the hotel.'

■ **yúmkin** + verb: 'to be possible to do something/
that something happens'

yúmkin means literally 'it is possible; it may be', and is used with a
following imperfect to denote a possible future happening:

yúmkin áaxidh máw9id wiyyáah.
'Maybe I'll make an appointment with him.'

yúmkin ya9Túunkum iyyáaha baláash.
'Perhaps they'll give you it free of charge.'

yúmkin kítab háadha, maa ádri wállah.
'Maybe he wrote this, I don't know.'

Exercise 12.3

Translate:

1 I'm in the middle of writing a letter.

2 Amina's in the middle of reading a magazine.

3 She's just this minute sweeping the floor.

4 You mustn't read this rubbish.

5 He doesn't have to return tomorrow, does he?

6 You mustn't be afraid of that man.

7 You don't have to go immediately.

8 Maybe he wants to go.

9 Maybe they can't read.

10 Maybe he'll be happy when he sees it, I don't know.

■ **gaal** + verb: 'to tell someone to do something'

We saw in Unit Seven that **gaal** + **inn** means 'to say that ...'. When
gaal is used without **inn**, and with a following imperfect verb, the sense
is 'to tell someone to do something':

gaal lihum iyiibúun il-milafáat.
'He told them to bring the files.'

gilt liha tárgid Háalan.
'I told her to go bed immediately.'

gáalaw líyyi a9Tíihum il-fluus.
'They told me to give them the money.'

Note that the dependent pronoun and the following verb agree: it is as if one says 'He said to them they bring the files', 'I said to her she ...', etc.

■ **raaH** + verb: 'to go and do something'
Examples:

muu láazim yirúuH yishúufha.
'He doesn't have to go and see her.'

riHt ásbaH fil-báHar.
'I went for a swim in the sea.'
(lit. 'I went I swim in the sea.')

■ **jaa** + verb: 'to come and do something; come doing something'

There are two types of sentence in which an imperfect verb is used with **jaa**. The first specifies the mode of coming, for example:

jáana yírkuD.
'He came running to us.'

yaw yimshúun (or **yaw máshi**).
'They came on foot.'
(lit. 'They came walking.')

The second usage is similar to **raaH** + verb:

kill sána iyúun il-yiháal yiTilbúun baxshíish Hagg il-9iid.
'Every year the children come and ask for a gratuity for the Eid.'

yiit tis'álni 9an il-mashrúu9 il-jadíid, muu chidhíi?
'You've come to ask me about the new plan, haven't you?'

Drills

Below are a number of drills aimed at giving you practice in manipulating the verb strings introduced in this unit.

Exercise 12.4

Look at the following dialogue:

- **yoom húwwa 9úmrah sittá9shar sána, kaan yíl9ab kúura.**
- **Sidj, u maa zaal yíl9ab!**
- 'When he was *16, he used to play football.*'
- 'That's true, and *he still does!*'

Using this dialogue as a model, make appropriate substitutions in those parts of the translated dialogue above that are italicised:

		Age	Activity
1	he	10	play volleyball
2		15	love that girl
3		20	go to the cinema twice a day
4		21	drive a Cadillac
5	she	12	cook well
6		19	wear Western fashions
7		6	read for two hours every day
8		14	write stories

Exercise 12.5

Make appropriate substitutions in the following dialogue as indicated:

- **sh-yigúul il-mudíir?**
- **yabghíik trúuH máktab il-baríid.**
- 'What does the boss say?'
- 'He wants you to *go to the post office.*'

1 bring him a coffee
2 wash his car
3 go to the market

4 remove the rubbish from this room

5 come tomorrow at 4.00 p.m.

Now substitute in the drill **mudíira** (female boss, headmistress) and use the feminine singular form of 'you':

6 play with her children

7 bring her a glass of water

8 telephone the police

9 shut the outside door

10 call in at the bank and give a letter to the manager

Exercise 12.6

Make the appropriate substitutions in the italicised part of the translation:

layn raaH lándan gaam yílbas maláabis gharbíyya.
'When *he went to London, he began wearing Western clothes.*'

1 went to Kuwait – wear a dishdasha

2 read the article – laugh

3 got in the bus – talk in a loud voice

4 saw the mistake – weep

Instead of 'he', use 'I':

5 arrived in the Gulf – drink a lot of coffee

6 was in Oman – walk in the mountains

7 bought a television – stay at home a lot

8 went to Cairo – go out to parties a lot

Exercise 12.7

Make appropriate substitutions in the italicised parts of the translation:

– **láazim tíTla9 il-Hiin!**
– **la, mub láazim il-Hiin ... báTla9 bá9ad shway.**
– 'You must *go out* now!'
– 'No, I don't have to now ... I'll *go out* in a little while.'

1 go to the bank	6 take this medicine
2 go to the market	7 write that reply
3 wash the dishes	8 go and get the stamps
4 read this book	9 give him a call
5 cook lunch	10 drop in on her

Now use the feminine form of 'you' in the same dialogue; then go through it again using the plural form of 'you'.

Exercise 12.8

Make appropriate substitutions in the italicised parts of the translation:

- **mit'ássif li'ánni maa gidárt ayíik is-subúu9 il-máaDi.**
- **maa 9alayh ... haadha ínta yiit il-Hiin!**
- 'Sorry that I couldn't *come and see you last week*.'
- 'Never mind ... *you've come* now!'

1 give him the letter last week
2 give you the news yesterday
3 invite you to the party before
4 give him the contract last month
5 read the article before
6 give you your salary yesterday
7 read her report before

Exercise 12.9

Make appropriate substitutions in the italicised parts of the translation:

gilt lih yigúum min in-noom láakin tamm yináam.
'I told him to *get up* but he went on *sleeping*.'

1 sit down – standing
2 read the book – listening to the radio
3 wear a dishdasha – wearing trousers
4 keep quiet – talking loudly
5 stay in bed – getting up
6 eat lunch – playing in the street
7 listen to me – reading his newspaper

8 stop – driving
9 run – walking slowly
10 take a rest – studying

Exercise 12.10

Make appropriate substitutions in the italicised parts of the translation:

- **guul li jásim iyíi íhni Háalan!**
- **maa yígdar. hu gáa9id yítbax il-gháda.**
- 'Tell Jaasim to *come here* immediately!'
- 'He can't. He's in the middle of *cooking the lunch*.'

1 wash the car – talking with the boss
2 come and look at this – taking photographs
3 sweep the floor – painting the door
4 go to the bank – writing an important report
5 go to the post office – studying for the examinations

Language points

12.2 The imperative: strong verbs

The imperative form of the verb consists of the *imperfect stem* of the verb to which suffixes denoting person are added. The strong verbs **shárab** 'to drink' (imperfect stem **-shrab-**) and **kítab** 'to write' (stem **-ktib-**) have the following imperative forms:

Masculine	Feminine	Plural	
íshrab	íshrabi	íshrabu	'Drink!'
íktib	íktibi	íktibu	'Write!'

We saw that, in the imperfect, forms like **tíshrabah** 'you (m.) drink it' (< **tishrab + ah**) tend to undergo a rearrangement of syllables to become **tishírbah**; the same thing tends to happen with the feminine and plural of the imperative. Thus **íshrabi** (< **ishrab + i**) is often heard as **shírbi**, and **íshrabu** (< **ishrab + u**) as **shírbu**. One also hears **kítbi** instead of **iktibi**, etc.

The final **-i** and **-u** of the feminine and plural forms are lengthened when a vowel-initial dependent pronoun is added (as we have seen in

other cases of verb, noun and particle forms that end with a vowel).
For example, if **-ah** 'him; it' is suffixed to the imperatives of **shárab**
and **kítab**, we get:

Masculine	Feminine	Plural	
íshrabah	shirbíih	shirbúuh	'Drink it!'
íktibah	kitbíih	kitbúuh	'Write it!'

The masculine forms **íshrab** and **íktib** obviously do not end in a vowel,
but the suffixing of **-ah** gives rise to a form – **íshrabah**, **íktibah** – which
is liable to undergo syllabic rearrangement in the way we have already
described: just as **yíshrabah** tends to become **yshírbah**, so **íshrabah**
tends to become **shírbah**, **íktibah** becomes **kítbah**, etc.

When a consonant-initial pronoun is suffixed, we typically get the
following forms in the strong verb:

Masculine	Feminine	Plural	
íshrabha	shirbíiha	shirbúuha	'Drink it!'
íktibha	kitbíiha	kitbúuha	'Write it!'

12.3 The imperative: other types of verb

The imperative of other types of verb is formed in the same way as in
the strong verb – by adding **-i** and **-u** to the stem to form the feminine
and plural forms. Note, however, that the feminine form in weak verbs
normally ends in **-ay** rather than **-i**. Here are some sample forms:

	Masculine	Feminine	Plural	
Hollow verbs	guul	gúuli	gúulu	'Say!'
	naam	náami	náamu	'Sleep!'
	shiil	shíili	shíilu	'Remove!'
Doubled verbs	sikk	síkki	síkku	'Shut!'

	Masculine	Feminine	Plural	
Weak verbs	ígra	ígray	ígru	'Read!'
	íbni	íbnay	íbnu	'Build!'
Initial '	íkil	íkli	íklu	'Eat!'
Initial **w**	óoguf	óogfi	óogfu	'Stop!'

The final vowels of forms that end with a vowel are lengthened when pronominal forms are suffixed, in the way we have already exemplified. It should be noted that the imperative forms of the verb **9aTa** 'to give' are as below:

9aT	9áTi	9áTu	'Give!'

The verb **yaa/jaa** 'to come' does not have imperative forms that are derived from its stem. Instead, the following forms are universally employed:

ta9áal	ta9áali	ta9áalu	'Come!'

12.4 The negative imperative

The negating word in negative commands is always **la**. The verb forms are the same as the imperatives except that the appropriate prefix, **ta-**, **ti-** (often simply **t-**) or **taa-** must be used. Here are some examples of different verb types:

	Imperative		Negative imperative	
	ruuH!	'Go!' (m.)	la trúuH!	'Don't go!' (m.)
	ísma9!	'Listen!' (m.)	la tísma9!	'Don't listen!' (m.)
	íktibi!	'Write!' (f.)	la táktibi!	'Don't write!' (f.)
or	kítbi!		la tikítbi!	
	ímshu!	'Walk!' (pl.)	la tímshu!	'Don't walk!' (pl.)
	íkil!	'Eat!' (m.)	la táakil!	'Don't eat!' (m.)
	shirbúuh!	'Drink it!' (pl.)	la tshirbúuh!	'Don't drink it!' (pl.)
	óoguf íhni!	'Stop here!' (m.)	la tóoguf íhni!	'Don't stop here!' (m.)

The negative imperative of **jaa** is formed regularly:

ta9áal!	'Come!' (m.)	la tyíi!	'Don't come!' (m.)
ta9áal!	(f.)	la tyíi!	(f.)
ta9áalu!	(pl.)	la tyúu!	(pl.)

Note that fem. and pl. forms are also heard with the final **-n** retained, e.g. **la taktibíin** 'don't write!' and **la tshirbúunah** 'don't drink it!'.

Exercise 12.11

Translate into English the short imperative sentences below. Go through the sentences three times practising (1) the masculine form (2) the feminine form and (3) the plural.

1 Don't stop!	12 Stop near the bank!
2 Go home!	13 Don't put it (f.) there!
3 Don't tell me that!	14 Bring them to me!
4 Take this away!	15 Say something!
5 Give it (m.) to me!	16 Have a rest!
6 Shut the door!	17 Don't fall!
7 Go outside!	18 Turn left here!
8 Come here!	19 Don't turn right!
9 Don't drink!	20 Sit down next to me!
10 Don't forget her!	21 Write it (f.) quickly!
11 Eat them all!	22 Throw them away!

 Dialogue 12.1

Listen to, read aloud and translate the following dialogue.

fit-tíksi **'In the taxi'** (Audio 1; 25)

A ábbi arúuH il-bank il-9árabi. cham táaxidh?
B nuSS diinár.
A la, yaa xúuyi, nuSS diinár maa yiSíir. xudh thaláth ímyat fils!
B árba9 ímya.
A zayn.
B il-bank il-9árabi fi wayn yá9ni biDH-DHabt?
A fi shári9 ish-shaykh salmán ... Tuuf id-dawwáar háadha ... zayn
   ... u xudh áwwal sháari9 ila l-yamíin ... liff yasáar 9ind máT9am
   il-kaazíino ... u ruuH síida – la! la! gilt lik tilíff yasár mub yamíin!
   shfiik?
B 9áfwan. haadha ána asúug táksi thaláathat ayyáam bas.
   la tíz9al!
A maa yihímm ... óoguf íhni min fáDlak ... haay flúusik ... shúkran.

Now translate the parallel dialogue below into Arabic:

A I want to go to the Foreign Ministry.
B Where is that?
A Don't you know? In Maghrib Street, near the Kuwait Bank.
B One dinar.
A Take 750 fils.
B OK.
A Go round the island ... OK ... now turn left ... take the second
  street on your right ... no! ... don't go straight on! I said to take
  the second on the right!
B Sorry, I don't know this area.

Exercise 12.12 (Audio 1; 26)

Listen to, read and translate the set of instructions (to a woman) below.

Tabx iS-Saalúuna 'Cooking a stew'

1 áwwal shay, xúdhi shwáyyat 9aysh u Súbbi 9aláyh maay.
2 HúTTi l-jídir 9ála D-Daww u la tinsáyn tiDHíifi nítfat milH.
3 gáSgiSi ('cut up') il-láHam Sigháar bi sichchíin Háadd u Hamríiha
  ('brown it') bi shwáyyat díhin.
4 DHíifi l-bhaaráat 9ala káyfich wíyya nítfat TiHíin.
5 Súbbi 9ala l-láHam maay Haarr u xuuríiha 9ala D-Daww layn
  yíghli.
6 gháTTi ('cover') l-jídir u xallíih ('leave it') yíghli 9ishríin dagíiga
  layn yábriz.
7 shíili l-9aysh min iD-Daww layn yínDHaj u shaxlíih Hátta yánshif.

Now translate the parallel set of instructions (to a woman) below into
Arabic:

1 Take a little rice and wash it in cold water.
2 Cover it with cold water and put the pot on to the heat.
3 Add a little salt.
4 Cut up the chicken into small pieces and brown it.
5 Add a little flour and stir for two minutes.
6 Pour hot water on to the chicken pieces and stir with a spoon
  until it boils.

7 Cover the pot and reduce (**xáfDi**) the heat.
8 When the rice is ready, take it off the heat and sieve it. Do not let the rice boil for more than 15 minutes.

Note that a number of verbs used in these exercises (e.g. **xáffaD, Hámmar, xálla, gáSgaS**) are of a type not yet introduced, and have been translated in the text. These will be dealt with in the next and subsequent units.

Vocabulary

aDHáaf/yiDHíif	to add	**hadd/yihídd**	to leave; abandon
arDíyya*	floor	**háwa**	weather; air
athnáa	during	**Haadd**	sharp
baláash	free of charge	**Hall/yiHíll**	to solve
báraz/yábriz	to be ready	**Hámmar/ yiHámmir**	to brown; roast
baxshíish	gratuity; tip	**jadd** (or **yadd**)	grandfather
fi maa bá9ad	afterwards	**jádda*** (or **yádda***)	grandmother
bháar(aat)	spices	**jaysh/juyúush**	army
bícha/yíbchi	to weep	**kínas/yáknis**	to sweep
DáHak/yíD-Hak	to laugh	**laff/yilíff**	to turn
Daww	fire; light	**maqáal(aat)**	article (newspaper)
dhíkar/yádhkir	to remember; mention	**marr/yimúrr 9ala**	to call in on someone
DHall/yiDHíll	to remain	**mashrúu9/ mashaaríi9**	plan; project
faráash(aat)	bed	**mínTaqa*/ manáaTiq**	area
faránsa	France	**muHáaDra*(aat)**	lecture
gáa9id (+ verb)	to be in the middle of	**mujálla*(aat)**	magazine
gáSgaS/ yigáSgiS	to chop up into bits	**mustáshfa(yaat)**	hospital
gídar/yígdar	to be able	**niDHaj/yínDHaj**	to ripen; be ready; be cooked
ghála/yíghli	to boil (intrans.)		
gharb	west	**níshaf/yánshif**	to become dry
ghárbi	western	**qíSSa*/qíSaS**	story
gháTTa/ yigháTTi	to cover		
haay (short for **haadha**)	this		

ráTib	humid	TiHíin	flour
ríkaD/yárkuD	to run	xaar/yixúur	to stir
síbaH/yísbaH	to swim	xáffaD/yixáffiD	to decrease;
sichchíin/	knife		lower
sachaachíin			something
síjill(aat)	register	xálla/yixálli	to let; allow
síkat/yáskit	to be quiet	xaTT	handwriting
Sabb/yiSúbb	to pour	yíbas/yíybas	to become
Síbagh/yíSbagh	to paint		dry
Sidq	truth	yúmkin	maybe
Soot/aSwaat	voice; noise	zawáaj	marriage
sháxal/yíshxal	to sieve	zayy/azyáa	fashion
shayaláan	removal	zí9al/yíz9al	to get upset
tíksi(yaat)	taxi	9áali	high; loud
Taaf/yiTúuf	to go round	9add/yi9ídd	to count;
	something		enumerate
Tíbax/yíTbax	to cook	9ázam/yi9ázim	to invite

Cultural point

Driving

The Gulf vocabulary of the car owes much to English, whose speakers introduced it to the region. Rather than the MSA word **sayyáara**, the original word for any kind of 'car' was **móotir** (pl. **mawáatir**), a word still used by a few old-timers, and the make of a vehicle sometimes became the generic name for the type to which it belonged. In the early days of the Gulf oil companies, for example, trucks made by the General Motor Corporation (GMC) were used to transport the workers, and the pick-up truck as a vehicle, whatever its make, became known as a **jims** from the GMC logo on its hood. In later years, the ubiquitous Toyota pick-up truck became known as a **wanáyt** (pl. **wanaytáat**), from its '1.8' engine capacity. In eastern Saudi Arabia, the general name for a truck was **dooj** (pl. **adwáaj**) from the make emblazoned on its nose – 'Dodge'. 'Estate cars', or 'shooting brakes' as they were known in the 1950s, were called **sayyáarat buks**, 'box-car' from English 'box', presumably because of the box-like, square shape of the back. The trend to borrow from English continues: nowadays we have the **forwíil** 'four-wheel drive'.

Car parts also are commonly known by their English rather than their 'official' names, for example **bánid** 'bonnet; hood', **layt** 'headlight', **tayr** 'tyre', **blaag** 'spark plug', **plaatíin** 'breaker points' (from 'platinum'), **giir** 'gear', **agzúuz** 'exhaust', **bámbar** 'bumper' and **mídgaar** 'mud-guard', these last two now sounding rather old-fashioned. The terminology of driving also contains many English terms, for example **ráywis** 'reverse', as in the command **imshi ráywis!** 'Reverse!', **bánchar** 'puncture' and some novelties such as the Bahraini expression **rángsayd** from 'wrong side', as in the policeman's **inta truuH rángsayd!** 'You're going the wrong way (down a one-way street)!' The Gulf word for 'driver' itself is a corruption of the English term – **dráywil** (pl. **draywilíyya**), although now this is increasingly replaced by the 'correct' Arabic word **saa'iq.**

Motoring through the ages, Gulf style
(Left) A Delaunay Belleville, 1928, one of only four cars in Oman at the time. It belonged to the British Political Agent, Muscat. From W.D. Peyton, *Old Oman*, published by Stacey International © 1983. (Right) Formula One racing at the Sakhir Circuit, Bahrain, 2008. © Getty Images

 Reading Arabic

Traffic signs in the Gulf are usually – but not always – in both Arabic and English, but it is as well to be able to recognise and understand the Arabic of some of the common ones. The shapes of the signs are similar to those found in Europe, as are the instructions that they give. And here is an opportunity to see some imperatives in action! Traffic signs are written in the standard form of the language, so there are some differences between what you have learnt as spoken Gulf Arabic imperatives, and what you will see on some traffic signs, but many are quite similar. Take the following sign from Sharja, which is the equivalent of the UK 'Give way' sign when joining a major road.

What is the Arabic word for 'Give way!'? It is the imperative **ífsaH** from the verb **fásaH** 'to make room; create space'. Look at the notes on the imperative of strong verbs (12.2) and you will see that **ífsaH** is similar in form to **íshrab** 'Drink!'. There is a word added – **aT-Tariiq** 'the road' – so this sign literally means 'Make the road clear!' or 'Cede the way (for traffic already on the main road)'. This sign is exactly like its French equivalent 'Cédez le passage.'

Now look at the temporary traffic sign on the right.

Can you read what it says at the top? It says **ílzam al-yamíin**, which means 'Keep right'. The imperative **ílzam** means 'to stick to; keep to', and **al-yamíin** is 'the right (hand side)'. Can you read the words at the bottom of the sign? They say **as-sayr bi ttijaaháyn**. The word **sayr** basically means 'movement' or here 'traffic', and **bi ttijaaháyn** 'in two directions'; **ittijaah** means 'direction' and the **-ayn** suffix, as you already know, is the dual, meaning 'two'. So this part of the sign means 'Two-way traffic', and the whole thing: 'Keep right. Two-way traffic.'

Finally, look at last sign on the right. This is the familiar 'stop' sign that sometimes is bilingual, sometimes not. The Arabic word for the imperative 'Stop!' is **qif!**, which is different from the Gulf Arabic for 'Stop!', which we saw above

in this unit: **óoguf!** But the difference is not in fact that great. First of all, we have standard Arabic **q** instead of Gulf **g**, and then the long vowel **oo** of the Gulf Arabic word is missing from the standard Arabic imperative. If you remove this **oo** from the Gulf word, it looks quite like the standard Arabic equivalent. This is part of general rule: Gulf Arabic treats verbs such as **wugaf** 'to stop', which have **w** as their initial consonant, exactly like ordinary strong verbs, retaining the **w** (although it is converted to an **oo** here by regular rule), whereas standard Arabic drops this **w** altogether in the imperfect and the imperative.

Some signs contain no words at all. The one below uses the familiar 'countdown' 3-2-1 stripes before a turn-off or other traffic management device. Can you interpret what it means? It means '200 metres to a traffic roundabout (**dawwáar**)', the م standing for متر 'metres' with Arabic digits from '200' to its right. The sign for the roundabout tells you what can be expected after these 200 metres.

Unit Thirteen

In this unit you will learn about:

- the active participle, used to imply that an event of the past is still having consequences now
- the passive participle, e.g. 'broken' or 'stolen'

Language point

13.1 The active participle

In addition to the past-tense verb, which, we have seen, is used to describe completed past action, and the imperfect tense, which has a variety of present and future uses, Arabic has another tense that is roughly analogous with the English perfect tense. This kind of meaning is expressed in Arabic by what is grammatically a kind of adjective called the active participle. As with the English perfect tense in sentences such as 'I've broken my leg', the use of the active participle in Arabic often implies that an event that took place in the past (my breaking my leg) is still having consequences at the time of speaking (I can't play football this afternoon). Just as, in English, 'I broke my leg' (no particular implication for what's happening now) contrasts with 'I've broken my leg', so:

kisárt ríili (past tense)   'I broke my leg'

contrasts with:

káasir ríili (active participle)   'I've broken my leg'

Thus **káasir ríili** might be given in a telephone conversation as an excuse in reply to an invitation to play football, go climbing or go to a discotheque, without further explanation. **kisárt ríili** simply states that the accident happened in the past – maybe five or ten years ago – and has no implications for one's ability to play football, etc. at the time of speaking.

Look at the example sentences below. In each case there is an implication that is unstated. What this implication is depends on the context:

mínhu sháayil il-awráag?
'Who's taken away the papers?'
(implied – they aren't here now)

wayn HaaTT id-dabbáasa?
'Where have you put the stapler?'
(implied – I can't see/find it).

The same sentences with a past verb:

mínhu shaal il-awráag?
wayn HaTTáyt id-dabbáasa?

are simply questions about something that happened in the past; in the first case the speaker might be conducting an enquiry into who took away some papers that are now back on his desk, or that he knows the exact whereabouts of at the time of speaking; in the second case, someone may have put away the stapler in a place where it could not be found by anyone else, and the person who put it away is now observed to be using it – the enquiry is into the matter of its past (and temporary) disappearance. Here are some more examples:

il-yáahil máakil ghadáah.
'The child has eaten his lunch.'
(implied – he doesn't want/need the food you're offering now)

mínhu láabis thiyáabi?
'Who's been wearing my clothes?'
(implied – they look crumpled or dirty)

shínhu Táabix lil-9ásha?
'What've you cooked for dinner?'
(implied – what's ready?)

In other cases, particularly with verbs of motion and durative verbs
such as 'to stand' or 'to sleep', the Arabic active participle is more
accurately translated into English by a present tense:

wayn ráayiH?
'Where are you going?'

inta jaay lil-muHáaDra il-yoom?
'Are you coming to the lecture today?'

il-yáahil náayim foog.
'The child is sleeping (asleep) upstairs.'

laysh wáagif 9ind il-baab?
'Why are you standing at the door?'

From the grammatical point of view, active participles behave partly
like adjectives and partly like verbs. Like adjectives, they have the **-a**
and **-iin** endings when their subject is feminine and plural respectively;
like adjectives, they are negated by **muu** or **mub**. However, they are
like verbs in that dependent object pronouns can be suffixed to them.
The basic form of the active participle in the simple strong verb is
$C_1aaC_2iC_3$, where the numbers represent the three consonants in the
verb skeleton. The feminine form is CaaCiCa and the plural CaaCiCiin
(often CaaCCa and CaaCCiin through the loss of unstressed **i**). Here
are some sample forms:

shírab 'to drink':	**sháarib/sháarba/shaarbíin** 'having drunk; drinking'
'ákal 'to eat':	**máakil/máakla/maaklíin** 'having eaten; eating'
wúgaf 'to stand; stop':	**wáagif/wáagfa/waagfíin** 'having stood; standing'
HaTT 'to put':	**HaaTT/HáaTTa/HaaTTíin** 'having put; putting'
gaal 'to say':	**gáayil/gáayla/gaaylíin** 'having said; saying'
nisa 'to forget':	**náasi/náasya/naasyíin** 'having forgotten; forgetting'

Note that:

1 The active participle in verbs beginning with ' (mainly **'ákal** and **'áxadh**) is normally **máakil, máaxidh,** etc. rather than **'áakil, 'áaxidh,** although the latter forms are sometimes encountered.

2 Doubled verbs such as **HaTT** have CaaCC rather than CaaCiC in the masculine form.

3 Hollow verbs always have **y** as their 'missing' middle consonant.

When used as an adjective, the meaning of the active participle depends on the type of verb it is used with, and the context of use. For example:

il-yáahil il-máakil ghadáah
(lit. 'the child the eater (of) his lunch')

may mean 'the child who is eating his lunch' or 'the child who has eaten his lunch', while

ir-rukkáab ir-raayHíin il-kuwáyt
(lit. 'the passengers the goers (to) Kuwait')

may indicate 'the passengers who are going to Kuwait (and haven't yet left)' or 'the passengers who have set out for Kuwait (and haven't yet arrived)'. Only the context can indicate exactly what is intended.

In other cases, with verbs describing habits or states of being, no particular time is or can be indicated. In these cases, the active participle functions exactly like an adjective:

rayyáal cháadhib (from **chídhab** 'to lie; cheat')
'a dishonest man' (lit. 'a man lie-teller')

han-niswáan iS-Saadgíin (from **Sádag** 'to tell the truth')
'these honest women' (lit. 'these women the truth-tellers')

maay jáari (from **jára** 'to run')
'running water'

Tabxáat báarda (from **bárad** 'to be cold')
'cold dishes'

The active participle is negated by **muu** or **mub**, like other adjectives:

muu sáami9 il-xábar?
'Haven't you heard the news?'

dhayláak mub maaklíin shay.
'Those people haven't eaten anything.'

inti mub yáaya wiyyáana?
'Aren't you (f.) coming with us?'

In definite noun phrases involving a negative adjective, **illi** 'which' is used rather than **il**. Thus one says:

il-yáahil ílli muu máakil ghadáah
'The child who hasn't eaten his lunch'

and *not*:

il-yáahil il-muu máakil ghadáah

The active participle may, like a verb, have dependent object pronouns suffixed directly to it. Study the following examples, in which both vowel-initial (**-ah**, **-ik**), and consonant-initial (**-ha**, **-na**) pronouns are suffixed to the active participle forms of **Darab** 'to hit':

Dáarib	+	ah	→	Dáarbah	'having hit, hitting him'
	+	ik	→	Dáarbik	'... ..., ... you (m.)'
	+	ha	→	Daaríbha	'... ..., ... her'
	+	na	→	Daaríbna	'... ..., ... us'
Dáarba	+	ah	→	Daarbáttah	'... ..., ... him'
	+	ik	→	Daarbáttik	'... ..., ... you (m.)'
	+	ha	→	Daarbátha	'... ..., ... her'
	+	na	→	Daarbátna	'... ..., ... us'
Daarbíin	+	ah	→	Daarbíinah	'... ..., ... him'
	+	ik	→	Daarbíinik	'... ..., ... you (m.)'
	+	ha	→	Daarbíinha	'... ..., ... her'
	+	na	→	Daarbíinna	'... ..., ... us'

The feminine form **Dáarba** contains the 'hidden' final **t** that we have noted in other feminine adjective and noun forms, and that only appears on suffixation. However, it is a characteristic feature of Gulf Arabic that, when a vowel-initial pronoun such as **-ah** or **-ik** is suffixed to feminine forms such as **Dáarba**, the 'hidden' **t** is doubled. It is worth mentioning also that, in some parts of the Gulf region (notably the villages of Bahrain, parts of the UAE and Oman), alternative forms for the suffixed masculine and feminine active participle forms are found. These alternatives involve the insertion of an **-in-** or **-inn-** element between the participle and the suffixed pronoun. Thus:

instead of		one hears	
	Dáarbah		**Daarbínnah**
	Daarbáttah		**Daarbatínnah**
	Daaríbha		**Daarbínha**
	Daarbátha		**Daarbatínha**

Such forms are widely regarded as 'uneducated', though extensively used nonetheless. It is as well to be able to recognise them (though not imitate them).

Two common constructions in which the active participle is often used involve the use of **bá9ad** + pronoun and **taw(w)** + pronoun. **bá9ad** + pronoun is used with a following negative verb (very often the active participle) to signify 'not to have done something' or 'to still not have done something':

bá9adni muu ráayiH lándan.
'I haven't been to London yet.'

bá9adhum muu naajHíin.
'They haven't succeeded yet.'

bá9adha mub gaaryáttah.
'She hasn't read it yet.'

The same meaning can be rendered by using the independent pronouns and placing **bá9ad** at the end of the sentence, thus:

ána muu ráayiH lándan bá9ad.
húmma muu naajHíin bá9ad.
híyya mub gaaryáttah bá9ad.

However, the first type of sentence with **bá9ad** + dependent pronoun is very typical of Gulf speech.

taw(w) on the other hand, can only be used with suffixed pronouns. It means 'to have just done something':

táwni yaay il-xalíij.
'I've just (recently) come to the Gulf.'

il-yiháal táwhum naaymíin.
'The kids have just gone to bed.'

táwwah ráasim har-rásim.
'He's just drawn this picture.'

taw is often used by itself in answer to questions:

- **ínta gáa9id íhni múdda Tawíila, muu chidhíi?**
- **la, táwni.**
- 'You've been sitting here a long time, haven't you?'
- 'No, I've just arrived.'

Exercise 13.1

Translate the following dialogue pairs into English:

1 – wayn iD-DáabiT il-káatib hat-taqríir?
  – máa ádri, muu sháayfah il-yoom.

2 – inta ráayiH míSir?
  – la, bá9adni. barúuH is-sána l-jáaya insháallah.

3 – ígra áwwal fáqara fiS-SáfHa l-xáamsa min FáDlik.
  – ismáH lii, ustáadh, rifíiji l-gháayib máaxidh kitáabi!

4 – diir báalik mínnah, háadha rayyáal cháadhib lin-niháaya!
  – muu bas cháadhib, báayig ba9ad! miHfáDHti baayígha!

5 – la tíz9al yaa Habíibi!
  – shloon maa áz9al? Daarbíinni bi 9áSa dhayláak il-loofaríyya!

Exercise 13.2

Translate the following dialogues into Arabic:

1 – Where have you put my notebook? I can't find it.
  – In the right-hand drawer of the desk.

2 – Where's your new suit?
  – I haven't picked it up from the tailor's yet.

3 – Give them a glass of tea!
  – No, they don't want any. They've already drunk two cups each.

4 – Where has that man come from?
  – I bumped into him in the street.

5 – How come you haven't taken away that table?
  – I can't lift it, it's too heavy.

Exercise 13.3

Look at the following dialogue:

- **sháayif il-fílim il-jadíid lo bá9ad?**
- **la, muu sháayfah bá9ad.**
- 'Have you seen the new film yet or not?'
- 'No, I haven't seen it yet.'

Make similar answers, and translate the dialogues:

1 – máaxidh ish-shaháada th-thaanawíyya lo bá9ad?
   – _____

2 – fáahìm il-lúgha l-9arabíyya lo bá9ad?
   – _____

3 – máaxidh ir-rayúug lo bá9ad?
   – _____

4 – gáari il-fáqara dhiich lo bá9ad?
   – _____

5 – wáaSil niháayat il-qíSSa lo bá9ad?
   – _____

6 – laagyíin il-fluus illi faqadtóoh lo bá9ad?
   – _____

7 – Saaydíin il-báayig lo bá9ad?
   – _____

8 – jaaybíin iT-Ta9áam illi Tilabtóoh lo bá9ad?
   – _____

9 – raaj9íin min ir-ríHla lo bá9ad?
   – _____

10 – raayHíin il-másyid lo bá9ad?
   – _____

Exercise 13.4

Look at the dialogue below:

- **9abáali yiit il-baHráyn gábil xams sanawáat.**
- **la, la, táwni yaay!**
- 'I thought you came to Bahrain five years ago.'
- 'No, no, I've only just come!'

Make similar appropriate responses to each cue, and then translate:

1 – 9abáali shiráyt hal-bádla min zamáan.
  – _____

2 – 9abáali ríj9at amíina min súuriya áwwal ams.
  – _____

3 – 9abáali dáshshaw l-Híjra gábil thaláath saa9áat.
  – _____

4 – 9abáali raaH id-dáxtar gábil yoomáyn.
  – _____

5 – 9abáali shift il-ghálaT gábli.
  – _____

6 – 9abáali níshraw l-kitáab is-sána l-máaDya.
  – _____

7 – 9abáali 'akáltaw l-9ásha bá9ad rujúu9kum bi shway.
  – _____

8 – 9abáali ghíslat il-mawaa9íin gábil maa Tíl9at.
  – _____

Language point

13.2 The passive participle

The Arabic passive participle corresponds roughly in meaning to the English past participle, for example 'broken', 'chosen', 'beaten', 'eaten', etc. In Arabic the passive participle mainly functions as an adjective, and when it does so it agrees with the noun to which it refers in accordance with the principles described earlier. The passive participle is of the basic form maCCuuC, feminine maCCuuCa and plural maCCuuCiin. It only occurs in transitive verbs. Some examples follow.

■ Equational sentences

il-baab maftúuH.   (from **fítaH** 'to open')
'The door is open(ed).'

id-daríisha maskúuka.   (from **sakk** 'to close')
'The window is closed.'

ir-rayaayíil mashghuulíin. (from **shághal** 'to busy; occupy')
'The men are busy.'

■ Noun-adjective phrases

il-yáahil il-mad9úum   (from **dá9am** 'to knock down (car)')
'the knocked-down child'

il-ghársha l-matrúusa   (from **tíras** 'to fill')
'the full (filled) bottle'

il-ashyáa l-mabyúuga   (from **baag** 'to steal')
'the stolen things'

iD-DubbáaT il-majruuHíin (from **járaH** 'to wound')
'the wounded officers'.

A summary of forms for the different verb types encountered so far is given below:

tíras 'to fill'
    matrúus/matrúusa/matruusíin   'filled'

wújad 'to find'
mawjúud/mawjúuda/mawjuudíin   'found; existent'

'ákal 'to eat'
    ma'kúul/ma'kúula/ma'kuulíin   'eaten'

gaTT 'to throw away'
    magTúuT/magTúuTa/magTuuTíin   'thrown away'

shaal 'to remove; lift'
    mashyúul/mashyúula/mashyuulíin   'removed; lifted'

nísa 'to forget'
    mánsi/mansíya/mansiyíin   'forgotten'

Some Arabic verbs, such as **símaH li** 'to excuse (someone)' or **Hákam 9ála** 'to sentence (someone to a punishment)', govern their object by means of a preposition, for example:

    símaH lil-bint trúuH il-bayt.
    'He allowed the girl to go home.'
    (lit. 'He allowed to the girl she goes home.')

Híkmaw 9ála r-rayaayíil bi sanatáyn síjin.
'They sentenced the men to two years jail.'
(lit. 'They sentenced on the men with two years jail.')

When the objects in such sentences are made into passivised subjects ('the girl allowed to go home', 'the men sentenced to two years jail'), the passive participle does **not** agree with its referent, but a pronoun referring back to it, agreeing with it in gender and number, is suffixed to the prepositional part of the verb:

il-bint il-masmúuH líha ...
'The girl allowed to ...'

ir-rayaayíil il-maHkúum 9aláyhum ...
'The men sentenced to ...'

Whenever complex verb-phrases such as **símaH li** + noun, **Hákam 9ála** + noun are passivised, the passive participle remains in the simple (masculine singular) form, whatever the gender/number of the referent. Here are some more examples:

il-mujrimíin il-maHkúum 9aláyhum bil-moot
'the criminals sentenced to death'
< **Híkmaw 9ála l-mujrimíin bil-moot**

in-natáa'ij il-marghúub fíiha
'the desired results'
< **ríghbaw fin-natáa'ij**

The passive participle may refer not only to an action that has already affected its referent, but to an action that may *potentially* affect it. In the phrases:

kútub manshúura fi urúbba
'books published in Europe'

il-9aadáat il-majyúuba min il-xáarij
'customs imported from outside'

the passive participles refer to books that may not yet have been published, and customs that may not yet have been actually imported, as is clear from the sentences:

9índi mashrúu9 ayíib kútub manshúura fi urúbba.
'I have a plan to bring in books published in Europe.'

gáalaw ínnahum maa byigbalúun il-9aadáat il-majyúuba
min il-xáarij.
'They said that they won't accept customs imported from
outside.'

The passive participle is never used in Gulf Arabic with an agent. To
translate 'agentless' sentences such as 'The bag was stolen', one may
say

il-jánTa mabyúuga

or one may turn the sentence into an active one with an unspecified
subject: 'They stole the bag':

báagaw l-jánTa

or

il-jánTa baagóoha

But if one wishes to say 'The bag was stolen by that man', only the
sentence types with active verbs are permissible:

ir-rayyáal dhaak baag il-jánTa

or

il-jánTa báagha dhaak ir-rayyáal

The passive participle may also, by extension, function as a noun. For
example, from the verbs:

sá'al	'to ask'	→	mas'úul	'one who is asked' = 'responsible person'
kítab	'to write'	→	maktúub	'something written' = 'letter'
fáham	'to understand'	→	mafhúum	'something understood' = 'concept'
HáSal	'to get'	→	maHSúul	'something got' = 'crop; profit'
nádab	'to entrust'	→	mandúub	'one entrusted' = 'delegate'

Exercise 13.5

Translate the following sentences into English:

1 háadhi bint ma9rúufa fil-firíij.
2 muu máaxdha t-tannúura min il-xayyáaT li'ánn il-Háashya maalátha mashgúuga.
3 il-mághsala dhi matrúusa bi maay li'ánn il-bayb máalha masdúud bi awsáax.
4 sháayif hal-achyáas il-blaastíik il-magTúuTa 9ala s-sáaHil? láazim tishíilha l-Hukúuma.
5 bagháyt áHchi wiyyáak ams bit-tilifúun, láakin il-xaTT kaan kíllah mashghúul.
6 ligáyt il-fluus il-mafqúuda? la, mub laagíiha bá9ad.
7 sh-tábbi táakil? ábbi wállah bayD mághli wíyya nítfat láHam máshwi!
8 mínhu mas'úul 9an hal-xárbuTa háadhi? mub íHna, yaa ustáadh, dhayláak húmma l-mas'uulíin!
9 yoom kínna Sigháar, lí9bat it-tíila wáayid maHbúuba 9índana.
10 sáami9 il-xábar? wazíir id-difáa9 magtúul!
11 il-marHúum ish-shayx salmáan kaan Háakim mashhúur.
12 il-buldáan il-9arabíyya maftúuHa li kill wáaHid – kill in-naas masmúuH líhum id-duxúul.

Exercise 13.6 (Audio 1; 27)

Throughout the Arab world, jokes are told about a mythical Arab called **júHa**. These jokes are extremely popular, and most Arabs can usually produce several. Read the following joke, and see if you can understand it; a translation is provided in the 'Answer key'.

júHa yoom wáaHid náashir thóobah foog is-sáTaH. nízal ba9adáyn, mixallíih yánshif foog. gaam júHa yiSíiH. yísma9ah jáarah u yíTla9 bárra. ila yigúul lih 'sh-fíik júHa?' yigúul lih 'thóobi TáaH min foog is-sáTaH lil-arD!' yigúul lih jáarah 'shu Saar?' ila yigúul lih Júha 'lo ána fith-thoob chaan mitt!'

Notes:
- **níshar** (here) 'to spread'; **sáTaH** 'roof'.
- **mixallíih** 'having left it'; **níshaf** 'to dry'; and **SaaH** 'to cry out'.
- **íla** particle is used to lend immediacy to a narrative: **íla yigúul lih** 'and so he says to him ...'.
- **shu Saar** 'So what?' (lit. 'what happened?').
- **lo** 'if'.
- **chaan** particle introduces a hypothetical event: 'would have'.

Proverbs

9aT il-xabbáaz xúbzik lo baag núSSah.
'Give the baker your bread even if he steals half of it.'
(i.e. 'If you want a job doing well give it to an expert even if it costs a lot.')

lo yádri 9ammáar shagg jáybah.
'If Ammaar knew, he'd tear the front of his shirt.'
(i.e. 'What the eye doesn't see the heart doesn't grieve over.')

midd ríilik 9ala gadd liHáafik.
'Stretch out your leg according to the size of your sheet.'
(i.e. 'Don't be overambitious, make do with what you have.'/
'Cut your coat according to your cloth.')

Vocabulary

bayb(aat)	pipe		**fáqad/yáfqid**	to lose
blaastíik	plastic		**fáqara*(aat)**	paragraph
cháadhib	dishonest		**gábil** + noun	... ago
chídhab/ yáchdhib	to lie; cheat		**gáDa 9ála**	to sentence; condemn
dabbáasa*(aat)	stapler		**gíbal/yígbal**	to accept
dara bi	to know about		**ghaab/yighíib**	to be absent
dá9am/yíd9am	to collide (car)		**Háashya*(aat)**	hem
diir báalik!	Be careful!		**Habíib**	dear; darling
durj/adráaj	drawer		**Hákam 9ála**	to sentence
duxúul	entry		**Hukúuma*(aat)**	government
DáabiT/ DubbáaT	officer		**jaar/jiiráan**	neighbour
			jára/yájri	to run; flow

járaH/yíjraH	to wound; injure	rifíij/rifgáan	friend
kíllah	always	rísam/yársim	to draw; paint
mafhúum/	concept	rujúu9	return
mafaahíim		sadd/yisídd	to block
mághsala*/	sink	sáTaH/suTúuH	roof
magháasil		síjin/sujúun	prison
maHSúul	crop; profit	símaH/yísmaH li	to allow
majnúun/	mad; crazy		someone
majaaníin		súuriya	Syria
marHúum	late (i.e. dead)	SaaH/yiSíiH	to cry out;
mas'úul	responsible		shout
mashghúul(iin)	busy; engaged	Sádag/yáSdig	to tell the truth
ma9lúum	known (fact)	shághal/	to busy; occupy
moot/amwáat	death	yíshghal	
mújrim(iin)	criminal	taw + pron.	to have just ...
natíija*/natáa'ij	result	9an Taríig	via; by way of
niháaya*	end; conclusion	Ta9áam	food
lin-niháaya	extremely	urúbba	Europe
níshaf/yánshif	to become dry	wújad	to find
níshar/yánshir	to publish	xáarij	outside
ráakib/rukkáab	passenger	xaTT/xuTúuT	telephone line
raghab/	to desire	xayyáaT(iin)	tailor
yirghab fi		9áada(aat)	custom; tradition
rásim/rusúum	drawing; painting	9abáal + pron.	I thought ...
		9áSa	stick

Cultural point

In the market

The Middle East is famed for the bargaining (**musáawama**) that is supposed to accompany the buying of almost anything in the market. But this is no longer really true, and certainly not in the Gulf. The modern Gulf shopping mall with its designer clothes has fixed prices, as in the West. It is in the 'traditional' markets in the older, downtown areas of Gulf cities where negotiation over price is possible, especially where we are talking about larger items such as rugs, carpets and second-hand traditional goods such as coffee pots and women's heavy jewellery. This will usually be done over a cup of traditional sweet red tea (**istikáanat chaay**) or two. But fruit and vegetable prices tend to be fixed, and gold, which is everywhere and a very popular purchase with Gulf women, is sold according to its carat rating and weight.

In former times, the traditional Gulf market was divided into separate streets and areas according to what was sold there. So there would be a special area for coppersmiths (**Saffáara**, sing. **Saffáar**) who made cooking pots and trays; ironmongers (**Haddáada**, sing. **Haddáad**) who made household goods such as kettles, hooks and nails; potters (**fuxxaariyyíin**, sing. **fuxxáari**) who made water pots and other items made from clay; greengrocers (**bagáagiil**, sing. **baggáal**) in the special vegetable market (**suug il-xuDáar**); butchers (**gaSáaSiib**, sing. **gaSSáab**) in the meat market (**suug il-láHam**); fishmongers (**jazaazíif**, sing. **jazzáaf**) who sold the produce they bought from the fishermen (**samaamíich**, sing. **sammáach**) in the fish market (**suug is-sámach**); and traditional pharmacists/perfumiers (**Hawaawíij**, sing. **Hawwáaj**) who sold remedies for common ailments.

Mutrah market, Oman

There were also some special markets that were held on certain days and named after them (e.g. Bahrain's **suug al-árba9a** 'Wednesday market') that specialised in certain commodities. One such, which is still being held, is the livestock market held in the centre of Nizwa, Oman every Friday morning.

Some Gulf markets have been 'theme-parked' and become part of the burgeoning 'heritage industry' of the Gulf. An example is the **suug wáagif** or 'standing market' in Doha, Qatar, which used to be the main market of the city. It still functions as a market, although it is more of a tourist attraction nowadays, complete with policemen who dress in the style of Qatari policemen of the 1950s and 1960s! Below is a photograph of the **suug wáagif** as it was in March 1970, taken from the balcony of the Bismillah Hotel, which stands at one end of it. Below it is the same, now pedestrianised, street photographed in March 2007.

Reading Arabic

Look at the market price tags for the fruit and vegetables below. Can you read them, and the prices per kilo on each? The words (in no particular order) are: **mooz** 'bananas', **tufáaH** 'apples', **shuwándar** 'beetroot', **burtuqáal** 'oranges', **jázar** 'carrots' and **malfúuf** 'cabbage'. Notice that, in these handwritten texts, the double dots over the letter ت are written as a single long stroke, and the three dots in the ش of **shuwándar** are written as an upturned 'v'. These are typical of the kinds of abbreviation that occur in handwritten Arabic, such as you will see on price tags in markets.

Here is another set for different meats: **kabáab** 'kebab', **láHam xarúuf** 'mutton', **dajáaj** 'chicken' and **láHam bágar** 'beef'. Can you match these transliterations to the Arabic tags, and say how much per kilo each is? Notice that the word **láHam** 'meat' is often put before the word for 'cow' and 'sheep' to distinguish the meat from the animal, so one literally says 'cow meat' and 'sheep meat' for 'beef' and 'mutton'. Notice also how the word **láHam** is written; in printed Arabic, it would be لحم but in handwritten Arabic the letters look as if they have been piled one on top of the other.

Unit Fourteen

In this unit you will learn about:

- the derived themes of the verb (1): CaCCac, CaaCaC, tiCaCCac and tiCaaCaC

Language point

14.1 The derived themes of the verb (1): CaCCaC, CaaCaC, tiCaCCaC, tiCaaCaC

As we have seen, the simple verb consists of a three-consonant skeleton C_1-C_2-C_3 on to which various vowel patterns are superimposed to denote tense, person and gender. In this unit, we begin the study of verbs that are derived from this simple skeleton by the addition of various consonants, or by the lengthening of vowels. These verbs are called 'derived themes'.

■ CaCCaC

These are verbs in which C_2 is doubled (and hence pronounced twice as long as the single consonant). Here are some examples:

Root	Past	Imperfect	
x-l-S	xállaS	yixálliS	'to finish (something)'
b-n-d	bánnad	yibánnid	'to close (something)'
b-T-l	báTTal	yibáTTil	'to open (something)'

Root	Past	Imperfect	
ch-y-k	cháyyak	yicháyyik	'to check; verify'
H-w-l	Háwwal	yiHáwwil	'to get down, off, out of'
s-w-y	sáwwa	yisáwwi	'to do; make'
gh-n-y	ghánna	yighánni	'to sing'

These verbs are conjugated as follows:

Strong		Hollow		Weak	
xalláSt	axálliS	chayyákt	acháyyik	sawwáyt	asáwwi
xalláSt	tixálliS	chayyákt	ticháyyik	sawwáyt	tisáwwi
xalláSti	tixalSíin	chayyákti	tichaykíin	sawwáyti	tisawwíin
xállaS	yixálliS	chayyák	yicháyyik	sáwwa	yisáwwi
xállaSat	tixálliS	cháyyakat	ticháyyik	sáwwat	tisáwwi
xálláSna	nixálliS	chayyákna	nicháyyik	sawwáyna	nisáwwi
xalláStaw	tixalSúun	chayyáktaw	tichaykúun	sawwáytaw	tisawwúun
xállaSaw	yixalSúun	cháyyakaw	yichaykúun	sáwwaw	yisawwúun

Omani verbs have, as expected, the **-tan** and **-an** endings in the 2nd and 3rd feminine plural of the perfect, for example **xalláStan** and **xállaSan**, and the predictable forms for the corresponding forms in imperfect, for example **tixálliSan** and **yixálliSan**. In Omani verbs that have **y** as the final radical, the **y** is retained in all the same forms as we saw for the simple verb, so, for example, the perfect tense is: **sáwyat** 'she made', **sáwyu** 'they (m.) made', **sáwyan** 'they (f.) made'; and the imperfect tense: **tisáwyi** 'you (f.) make', **tisáwyu** 'you (m. pl.) make', **tisáwyan** 'you (f. pl.) make', **yisáwyu** 'they (m.) make' and **yisáwyan** 'they (f.) make'.

Note that:

1 From the point of view of form, CaCCaC verbs in the past tense behave exactly like the simple verbs we have already studied: both strong and hollow verbs simply add the endings for person and gender, while CaCCaC verbs that are weak (i.e. have C_3 = **y**) behave exactly like simple weak verbs (compare **nisáyt**, **ligáyt**, etc.).

2 In the imperfect, the stem vowel pattern is -CaCCiC-. The vowel of the prefix is always **i**.

3 Whenever an ending beginning with a vowel is suffixed to the stem
(e.g. **-iin**, **-uun** or **-i**, **-u**, in the imperative) the **i** of the stem is dropped
and the doubled consonant is made single (except in weak verbs):

yixálliS	**+ uun**	→	**yixalSúun**
'he finishes'	'pl.'		'they finish'
tixálliS	**+ iin**	→	**tixalSíin**
'you finish'	'f.'		'you (f.) finish'
xálliS!	**+ i**	→	**xálSi!**
'Finish!'	'f.'		'Finish (f.)!'

The same process of i-dropping and consonant reduction occurs when
object pronouns that begin with a vowel are suffixed to the stem:

yixálliS	**+ ah**	→	**yixálSah**
'he finishes'	'it'		'he finishes it'

Weak CaCCac verbs behave, in this context, just like simple weak
verbs, lengthening their final vowel whether the suffix begins with a
vowel or not:

nisáwwi	**+ ah**	→	**nisawwíih**
'we do'	'it'		'we do it'
yighánni	**+ ha**	→	**yighanníiha**
'he sings'	'it'		'he sings it'

The imperative of CaCCaC verbs is typically:

Masculine	*Feminine*	*Plural*	
báTTil!	**báTli!**	**báTlu!**	'Open!'

Weak verbs:

Masculine	*Feminine*	*Plural*	
saww!	**sáwwi!**	**sáwwu!**	'Do!'

In the negative imperative, the masculine of weak verbs exceptionally
preserves the final **-i** of the imperfect:

Masculine	*Feminine*	*Plural*	
la tisáwwi!	**la tisáwwi!**	**la tisáwwu!**	'Don't do!'

CaCCaC verbs in general often have a causative or factitive meaning, that is, they denote *making* someone or something be or do something. For example, the simple verb **9álam** (root **9-l-m**) is one of the verbs meaning 'to know'; **9állam** means 'to make someone know; to teach; instruct'; the hollow simple verb **Daa9** (root **D-y-9**) means 'to get or be lost; go missing', while its corresponding CaCCaC verb **Dáyya9** means 'to waste; squander':

> **jánTati Dáa9at.**
> 'My bag's disappeared.'

> **la tiDáyyi9 flúusik!**
> 'Don't waste your money!'

The word **ghayr** means 'different; other than':

> **9aadáatkum ghayr 9aadáatna.**
> 'Your customs are different from ours.'

The corresponding CaCCaC verb **gháyyar** means 'to alter; make different':

> **ghayyárt il-barnáamaj.**
> 'I changed the programme.'

> **gháyyaraw afkáarhum.**
> 'They changed their minds.'

Not every CaCCaC verb has causative or factitive meaning, however, and some verbs that have a causative meaning are sometimes used as intransitive verbs. An example of the first type is **Háwwal** 'to get down, off, out of' and of the second **bánnad** 'to close (something)', which can also be used like this:

> **id-dukkáan yibánnid is-sáa9a sáb9a.**
> 'The shop closes at seven o'clock.'

The extremely common CaCCaC verb **xálla** 'to let; leave' is used with a suffixed pronoun and following verb to mean 'to allow someone to do something':

> **xalláytah yisúug sayyáarti.**
>   ↑_____↑
> 'I allowed him to drive my car.'

xalláani ayíi mubákkir.

'He allowed me to come early.'

maa biyxallíich taaxdhíin hal-gadd yoom 9úTla.

'He won't let you (f.) take that many days' holiday.'

◼ CaaCaC

These are verbs in which the first vowel is lengthened to twice the length of a short vowel:

Root	Past	Imperfect	
s-9-d	sáa9ad	yisáa9id	'to help'
w-f-g	wáafag	yiwáafig	'to agree on something'
g-b-l	gáabal	yigáabil	'to meet someone (by appointment)'
j-w-b	jáawab	yijáawib	'to answer'
s-w-m	sáawam	yisáawim	'to bargain; haggle'
l-g-y	láaga	yiláagi	'to meet someone (by chance)'

Conjugations are as follows:

Strong		Hollow		Weak	
saa9ádt	asáa9id	jaawábt	ajáawib	laagáyt	aláagi
saa9ádt	tisáa9id	jaawábt	tijáawib	laagáyt	tiláagi
saa9ádti	tisaa9díin	jaawábti	tijaawbíin	laagáyti	tilaagíin
sáa9ad	yisáa9id	jáawab	yijáawib	láaga	yiláagi
sáa9adat	tisáa9id	jáawabat	tijáawib	láagat	tiláagi
saa9ádna	nisáa9id	jaawábna	nijáawib	laagáyna	niláagi
saa9ádtaw	tisaa9dúun	jaawábtaw	tijaawbúun	laagáytaw	tilaagúun
sáa9adaw	yisaa9dúun	jáawabaw	yijaawbúun	láagaw	yilaagúun

Imperatives are as follows:

Masculine	Feminine	Plural	
sáa9id!	sáa9di!	sáa9du!	'Help!'
jáawib!	jáawbi!	jáawbu!	'Answer!'
laag!	láagi!	láagu!	'Meet!'

It can be clearly seen from this that CaaCaC verbs behave in all respects like CaCCaC verbs (e.g. in the dropping of the **i** in the stem -CaaCiC- when certain suffixes are added, in the masculine imperative of the weak verb). Omani CaaCaC verbs differ from those of the rest of the Gulf in the same ways as we have already noted above for the CaCCaC group.

CaaCaC verbs usually denote actions taking place between two parties, often on a reciprocal basis (e.g. 'to agree on', 'to haggle'). Some examples of use are:

> **wáafagaw 9ala daf9 il-máblagh il-maTlúub.**
> 'They agreed to pay the sum demanded.'
> (lit. 'They agreed on the paying of the sum demanded.')

> **la tsáawim wiyyáah! yiDáyyi9 wáqtik!**
> 'Don't bargain with him! He'll waste your time!'

> **xaabaróoni bit-tilifúun ínnik yiit!**
> 'They informed me by telephone that you had come!'

> **laagaynáahum biS-Súdfa fis-suug.**
> 'We met them by chance in the market.'

Exercise 14.1

Using the CaCCaC and CaaCaC verbs introduced so far, and also those listed below, translate the following commands:

1 Don't send that boy!
2 Repair the fridge!
3 Don't stop the car!
4 Take me home please!
5 Think before you do anything!

6 Put it (f.) in the post!
7 Show me your (pl.) photos!
8 Lend me 50 dinars please!
9 Don't speak to them!
10 Don't try to go!

CaCCaC

rákkab	'to fix; insert; attach'	**fánnash**	'to fire; sack'
9áddal	'to adjust; put right'	**Tárrash**	'to send'
SállaH	'to repair'	**wáSSal**	'to take someone to somewhere'
xáffaD	'to lower; decrease'	**sállaf**	'to lend'
wággaf	'to stop (something)'	**9álla**	'to raise; increase'

fákkar	'to think'	wádda	'to put; send'
dárras	'to teach'	ráwwa	'to show'

CaaCaC

sáafar	'to travel'	Háacha	'to address someone'
Háawal	'to try'		

Translate into English:

11 ja rákkab ir-rásim á9waj láakin 9áddalah ba9adáyn.

12 la trákkib it-tayr dhaak – fiih bánchar.

13 nádHDHif il-jaamáat min fáDlik u SálliH il-baab iT-TáyiH.

14 9áTni t-taqrír u bafákkir fil-mawDúu9.

15 waddóoni l-mádrasa yoom ana 9úmri xams siníin.

16 sáafaraw l-hind u búgaw hináak múdda Tawíila.

17 la tiHaachíini bil-láhja dhi! xáffiD Sóotik!

18 layn fannashóoh min shúghlah fish-shárika, gaam yisálliH sayyaaráat xarbáana.

19 bá9admaa rawwáytah il-hádiya ílli 9aTóoni iyyáaha, DHall yifákkir Sáamit.

20 bamúrr 9aláych báachir awáSlich bayt 9ámmich.

21 maa asím9ik! 9all Sóotik!

22 xaffáDna l-as9áar bi xams u 9ishríin bil-míya.

23 darrást sanatáyn fi mádrasa Hukuumíyya.

24 la twáddi s-saamáan minnáak! wáddah minníi!

■ **tiCaCCaC and tiCaaCaC**

Two more derived themes are formed by prefixing **ti-** (or **ta-**) to CaCCaC and CaaCaC verbs. The first of these, tiCaCCaC, often indicates a reflexive or sometimes passive sense of the corresponding CaCCaC verb:

Root	CaCCaC	tiCaCCaC
gh-y-r	gháyyar	tigháyyar
	'to change (something)'	'to be changed; to change (intrans.)'
b-n-d	bánnad	tibánnad
	'to close (something)'	'to be closed; to close (intrans.); to be closable'

Root	CaCCaC	tiCaCCaC
z-w-j	**záwwaj** 'to marry (someone to someone)'	**tizáwwaj** 'to get married'
9-l-m	**9állam** 'to teach'	**ti9állam** 'to learn'
dh-k-r	**dhákkar** 'to remind'	**tidhákkar** 'to remember'
gh-d-y	**ghádda** 'to give lunch (to someone)'	**tighádda** 'to eat lunch'
9-w-d	**9áwwad** 'to accustom (someone to something)'	**ti9áwwad** 'to get used to'

tiCaaCaC verbs indicate, more clearly than CaaCaC verbs, the *reciprocal* nature of an activity, and are often equivalent to English verbs involving the use of 'each other' or 'one another':

Root	CaaCaC		tiCaaCaC	
w-f-g	**wáafag**	'to agree'	**tiwáafag**	'to agree with each other'
g-b-l	**gáabal**	'to meet'	**tigáabal**	'to meet one another'
s-9-d	**sáa9ad**	'to help'	**tisáa9ad**	'to help each other'
H-ch-y	**Háacha**	'to address someone'	**tiHáacha**	'to talk to each other; converse'

Examples of these verbs are conjugated as below:

tiCaCCaC:

Strong and hollow		Weak	
ti9allámt	**at9állam**	**tighaddáyt**	**atghádda**
ti9allámt	**tit9állam**	**tighaddáyt**	**titghádda**
ti9allámti	**tit9allamíin**	**tighaddáyti**	**titghaddíin**
ti9állam	**yit9állam**	**tighádda**	**yitghádda**
ti9államat	**tit9állam**	**tigháddat**	**titghádda**
ti9allámna	**nit9állam**	**tighaddáyna**	**nitghádda**
ti9allámtaw	**tit9allamúun**	**tighaddáytaw**	**titghaddúun**
ti9államaw	**yit9allamúun**	**tigháddaw**	**yitghaddúun**

Imperative forms:

Masculine	Feminine	Plural	
ti9állam!	ti9állami!	ti9államu!	'Learn!'
tighádd!	tigháddi!	tigháddu!	'Have lunch!'

Thus the perfect stem is tiCaCCaC- and the imperfect stem -tCaCCaC (weak verbs tiCaCCa- and -tCaCC-). As previously noted for CaCCaC and CaaCaC verbs, the negative imperative of weak verbs has a final vowel in the masculine form, which in this case is **-a**, not **-i**:

Masculine	Feminine	Plural	
la titghádda!	la titgháddi!	la titgháddu!	'Don't eat lunch!'

tiCaaCaC:

Strong and hollow		Weak	
tisaa9ádt	atsáa9ad	tiHaachávt	atHáacha
tisaa9ádt	titsáa9ad	tiHaacháyt	titHáacha
tisaa9ádti	titsaa9adíin	tiHaachávti	titHaachíin
tisáa9ad	yitsáa9ad	tiHáacha	yitHáacha
tisáa9adat	titsáa9ad	tiHáachat	titHáacha
tisaa9ádna	nitsáa9ad	tiHaacháyna	nitHáacha
tisaa9ádtaw	titsaa9adúun	tiHaacháytaw	titHaachúun
tisáa9adaw	yitsaa9adúun	tiHáachaw	yitHaachúun

Imperative forms:

Masculine	Feminine	Plural	
tisáa9ad!	tisáa9adi!	tisáa9adu!	'Help each other!'
tiHáach!	tiHáachi!	tiHáachu	'Talk to each other!'

Obviously, the notion of reciprocity that is contained in many tiCaaCaC verbs makes it unlikely that any singular imperative forms will be encountered. The only tiCaaCaC imperative in common use in the singular, for example, is one that does not have a 'reciprocal' meaning: **ta9áal!** 'Come!'

The vowelling of the prefixes of tiCaCCaC and tiCaaCaC verbs is one of the many points of variability in the subdialects that go to make up what we have been calling 'Gulf Arabic'. Some of these subdialects have a **ta-** and some a **ti-** prefix in the past tense of these verbs, and some a **yit-** type and some a **yti-** type prefix in the imperfect. A certain amount of variability in these and other forms has been deliberately introduced into this book in order to accustom you to the non-standardisation of Gulf speech (another example is **lii** and **líyyi** 'to me'). The differences are usually relatively slight, but it is as well to be aware of common variants that have the same meaning.

Some examples of the use of tiCaCCaC and tiCaaCaC verbs are given below. Notice that the meaning of the imperfect of these verbs can express the potentiality to do something: **yitbáTTal** may mean 'opens', 'is opened' or 'can be opened'.

il-kuwáyt tigháyyarat.
'Kuwait has changed.'

hal-makaatíib tiTárrashat min zamáan.
'Those letters were sent a long time ago.'

tiwáafagaw 9ala ínnahum maa yitHaarabúun bá9ad.
'They agreed not to fight each other any more.'

háadha mawDúu9 taHaacháyna fiih múdda Tawíila.
'This is a subject we discussed for a long time.'

háadha S-Sandúug maa yitbánnad.
'This box won't close.'

hal-gúuTi maa yitbáTTal.
'This can won't open.'

yitráawa líyyi ínnik láazim titxállaS min dhaak ir-rayyáal.
'It seems to me that you ought to get rid of that man.'

laysh maa titsaa9adúun?
'Why don't you help each other?'

káanaw yisiknúun fi firíij il-jáami9, 9ala maa atdhákkar.
'They used to live in the quarter where the main mosque is, as far as I remember.'

il-jaww maal il-xalíij maa tit9áwwad 9aláyh bi súr9a.
'You can't get used to the Gulf climate quickly.'

Exercise 14.2

Using the verbs **tiráyyag** 'to have breakfast', **taghádda** 'to have lunch' and **ta9áshsha** 'to have dinner', translate the following:

1 She has breakfast every day at six.

2 I often have lunch in this restaurant.

3 What time are we dining tonight?

4 Why don't you (pl.) have lunch with us tomorrow?

5 Have breakfast with me tomorrow!

Using the verbs **tibánnad** 'to close', **tibáTTal** 'to open', **tiwádda** 'to be sent, delivered, deposited', **tirákkab** 'to be fixed, inserted' and **taSállaH** 'to be repaired', translate the following:

6 This tyre can't be fitted on this car.

7 The storeroom door won't open.

8 Letters are always delivered by hand.

9 This market never closes.

10 The broken plate can't be repaired.

The construction **xall** ('let!') + pronoun + verb means 'Let us/them ...!', for example:

> **xállna nitsáawam!**   'Let's bargain!'

Using the verbs **taHáacha** 'to talk to one another', **tifáaham** 'to understand each other', **tisáa9ad** 'to help each other', **tigáabal** 'to meet each other' and **tiSáalaH** 'to make peace', translate:

11 Let's talk a little about this problem!

12 Let's understand each other on this point!

13 Let them help each other in this matter!

14 Let's meet again the day after tomorrow!

15 Let them make peace with each other!

Using the verbs **taHáchcha** 'to talk', **tizáwwaj** 'to get married', **ta9állam** 'to learn', **ta9áwwad** 'to get used to', **tiwáafag** 'to agree with each other' and **tisáa9ad** 'to help each other', translate:

16 Why don't they talk?

17 Why doesn't he get married?

18 Why don't you learn English?

19 Why don't we agree with each other on this?

20 Why don't you (pl.) help each other more?

21 Why can't you (f.) get used to the food?

The present and passive participles of the verb types we have studied in this unit are all formed with a **mi-** prefix. They are all formed according to simple and regular principles that are outlined below.

■ CaCCaC and CaaCaC verbs

Active participle of the form miCaCCiC and miCaaCiC, for example:

	mirákkib	'fixing; having fixed'	**(rákkab)**
	mi9áaqib	'punishing; having punished'	**(9áaqab)**
(weak verbs)	**misámmi**	'naming; having named'	**(sámma)**
	midáari	'taking care of; having taken care of'	**(dáara)**

Passive participle of the form miCaCCaC and miCaaCaC, for example:

mirákkab	'fixed; having been fixed'
mi9áaqab	'punished; having been punished'
misámma	'named; having been named'
midáara	'taken care of; having been taken care of'

■ tiCaCCaC and tiCaaCaC verbs

Active participle of the form mitCaCCiC and mitCaaCiC, for example:

	mitgháyyir	'changing; having changed'	**(tigháyyar)**
	mitsáa9id	'helping each other; having helped each other'	**(tisáa9ad)**
(weak verbs)	**mit9áshshi**	'dining; having dined'	**(ta9áshsha)**
	mitláagi	'meeting each other; having met each other')	**(tiláaga)**

Passive participles are of the form mitCaCCaC and mitCaaCac, but occur very rarely because tiCaCCaC and tiCaaCaC are normally intransitive in meaning.

The feminine and plural forms (used with animate nouns) are obtained in the normal way, namely by suffixing **-a** and **-iin** respectively. Weak verbs, as usual, have **-ya** and **-yiin**, for example **misámmya**, **misammyíin** 'naming'. However, the feminine form of the *passive* participle of weak verbs is the same as the masculine form. When object pronouns are suffixed to the active participle of weak verbs, the **-i** is lengthened and stressed, and all feminine active participles have the 'hidden' **t** that shows up on suffixation. Thus we find the masculine form **misámmi** 'naming' becoming **misammíih** when **-ah** 'it' is suffixed, and the feminine form **misámmya** becoming **misámmyatah**; when the feminine pronoun **-ha** is suffixed, the corresponding forms, as would be expected from our study of simple verb participles (13.1), are **misammíiha** and **misammyátta**, the **h** of the **-ha** suffix being assimilated to the **t** of the participle. Some examples of participial usage are:

in-naas dhayláak íHna msammíinhum 'bastakíya'.
'We call those people "Bastakis".'

had-díira misámmya báni-jámra.
'This village is called Bani-Jamra.'

ána táwni mitgháddi, maa ábbi áakil bá9ad.
'I've just had lunch, I don't want to eat any more.'

il-qaraaráat illi mitwaafgíin 9aláyha maa titgháyyar.
'The decisions that have been mutually agreed on cannot be changed.'

ir-rayyáal ílli mHáachyatah abúuha.
'The man who she's talking to is her father.'

il-úghniya ílli mghanníiha mub Hálwa.
'The song he's singing isn't nice.'

har-rusúum illi msawwyátta wáayid 9aajbátni.
'These designs she's done have really impressed me.'

Note from the above examples that the **i** of the **mi-** prefix is, as an unstressed vowel, frequently dropped, especially if **mi-** is preceded by a word ending in a vowel.

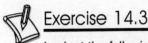

Exercise 14.3

Look at the following two-line dialogue:

- **xallást ish-shúghul il-báarHa, muu chidhíi?**
- **la, mub mixálSah bá9ad!**
- You finished the work yesterday, didn't you?
- No, I haven't finished it yet!

Now translate the following similar dialogues into Arabic:

1 – You spoke to the boss yesterday, didn't you?
 – No I haven't spoken to him yet!

2 – You repaired the machine yesterday, didn't you?
 – No I haven't repaired it yet!

3 – You cleaned the bedroom this morning, didn't you?
 – No I haven't cleaned it yet!

4 – You sent the letter the day before yesterday, didn't you?
 – No I haven't sent it yet!

5 – You agreed to the plan last month, didn't you?
 – No I haven't agreed to it yet!

6 – You inspected the factory last week, didn't you?
 – No I haven't inspected it yet!

7 – You tested out that new restaurant yesterday, didn't you?
 – No I haven't tested it out yet!

8 – You sacked those workers last week, didn't you?
 – No I haven't sacked them yet!

9 – You checked the oil level half an hour ago, didn't you?
 – No I haven't checked it yet!

10 – You changed the tyres last week didn't you?
 – No I haven't changed them yet!

Now translate these dialogues again using first the you (f.) form, and then the you (pl.) form (replying using 'we').

Exercise 14.4 (Audio 1; 28)

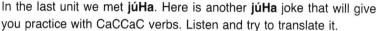

In the last unit we met **júHa**. Here is another **júHa** joke that will give
you practice with CaCCaC verbs. Listen and try to translate it.

> júHa raaH ir-ráydo máalah u shághghalah. illi yighánni yigúul
> '9aTsháan yaa Habíibi!' gaam júHa u HáTTah fi bríij il-maay u
> Tálla9ah. tamm yighánni '9aTsháan yaa Habíibi!' radd HáTTah
> fil-maay u Tálla9ah … il-Hiin byishághlah maa ishtághal. gaal lih
> 'mínta il-Hiin tishtághil? yoom ínta 9aTsháan 9aTáytik, u l-Hiin
> wugáft?'

Notes:
- **briij** 'pot for water'.
- **ishtághal/yishtághil** 'to work'. (We will meet this type of verb form
  in Unit Sixteen.)

Proverbs and sayings

maa yíswa fils fi waqt il-ghíla.
'He isn't worth a fils (even) at a time of high prices.'
(i.e. 'He is a completely worthless person.')

tays bawwáal
'a pissing he-goat'
(said of an extremely uncouth man)

illi maa y9árf iS-Ságar yishwíih.
'He who does not know what a falcon is will roast it.'
(Said of a person who is ignorant of the true value of what he or
she possesses, and misuses it.)

Vocabulary

áwwal il-layl	afternoon (shift)	**barnáamaj/ baráamij**	programme
á9waj, (f.) **9óoja**	crooked; bent	**báTTal/yibáTTil**	to open
báddal/yibáddil	to change (e.g. clothes, tyres)	**briij/burgáan**	water pot
		cháyyak/ yicháyyik	to check
bánchar(aat)	puncture	**dáara/yidáari**	to take care of
bánnad/yibánnid	to close	**daf9**	payment

dárras/yidárris	to teach	sáafar/yisáafir	to travel
Dayya9/yiDáyyi9	to waste; squander	saamáan	stuff; gear
dhákkar/yidhákkir	to remind	sáawam/ yisáawim	to bargain
fákkar/yifákkir	to think	sáa9ad/yisáa9id	to help
fánnash/yifánnish	to sack; fire	sállaf/yisállif	to lend
fáttash/yifáttish	to inspect	sáwwa/yisáwwi	to make; do
gáabal/yigáabil	to meet; be opposite to, across from'	síwa/yíswa	to be worth, equal to
ghánna/yighánni	to sing	Sáamit	silent(ly)
Háacha/yiHáachi	to address (someone)	SállaH/yiSálliH	to repair; correct
Háawal/yiHáawil	to try; attempt	biS-Súdfa	by chance
Háwwal/yiHáwwil	to get down, out of	shághghal/ yishághghil	to operate (a machine, etc.)
Hukúumi	governmental	taHáarab/ yitHáarab	to fight each other
ishtághal/ yishtághil	to work	taHáchcha/ yitHáchcha	to talk
jáami9	main (Friday) mosque	taxállaS/ yitxállaS min	to get rid of; be free of
jáawab/yijáawib	to answer	tayr(aat)	tyre
járrab/yijárrib	to test out; try	ta9áshsha/ yit9áshsha	to dine
láaga/yiláagi	to meet (by chance)	tibánnad/ yitbánnad	to close (intrans.); be closeable
láhja*(aat)	tone of voice; accent; dialect	tibáTTal/ yitbáTTal	to open; be openable
mawDúu9/ mawaaDíi9	subject; topic	tidhákkar- yitdhákkar	to remember
míthil	for example	tifáaham/ yitfáaham	to understand each other
mubákkir	early	tigáabal/yitgáabal	to meet each other
náDHDHaf/ yináDHDHif	to clean	tighádda/ yitghádda	to have lunch
núqTa*/núqaT	point at issue	tiHáacha/ yitHáacha	to converse
radd + verb	to do something again	tirákkab/ yitrákkab	to be fixed, installed
rákkab/yirákkib	to attach; install		
ráwwa/yiráwwi	to show		

tiráyyag/ yitráyyag	to breakfast	wáafag/ yiwáafig (9ála)	to agree to (something)
tisáa9ad/ yitsáa9ad	to help each other	wádda/yiwáddi	to put; send
tiSáalaH/ yitSáalaH	to make peace; call a truce	wággaf/yiwággif	to stop (something)
tiTárrash/ yiTTárrash	to be sent	wáSSal-yiwáSSil	to take (someone somewhere); give a lift to (someone)
tiwáafag/ yitwáafag	to mutually agree		
tizáwwaj/ yitzáwwaj	to get married	xáabar/yixáabir	to inform (someone about something)
ti9állam/ yit9állam	to learn		
ti9áwwad/ yit9áwwad (9ála)	to get used to	xaráab	broken down; useless
TáayiH	broken; dilapidated	9áaqab/yi9áaqib	to punish
Tálla9/yiTálli9	to take (something) out of (something)	9áddal/yi9áddil	to straighten; put right
		9álla/yi9álli	to raise
Tárrash/yiTárrish	to send	9állam/yi9állim	to teach; instruct

Cultural point

Football

There is no doubt that football is the Gulf's most popular sport. From small beginnings in the 1950s, Gulf teams have participated in the final stages of the World Cup, beginning with Kuwait in the 1982 tournament in Spain. Since then, Saudi Arabia has participated in four World Cups, and the UAE one. The local Arabian Gulf tournament, the Gulf Cup, was launched in 1970, the first tournament being held in the small stadium in Isa Town, Bahrain. Since then, the Cup has been held approximately every two years, on the last occasion in the UAE in January 2007, when the host nation defeated Oman 1–0 in front of 60,000 people and took the Cup for the first time. Kuwait has dominated the competition over the years, having won it nine times, with Saudi Arabia winning three times, Iraq three, Qatar two and the UAE now once. Oman and Bahrain have never won it, nor has Yemen, which is, for this purpose, counted as a Gulf country. There is a great deal of money lavished on football in the Gulf: the opening ceremony of the 2007 Gulf Cup alone cost 33 million UAE dirhams, and famous foreign managers have often been hired. Don Revie resigned from the job of England manager to coach the UAE national team in 1977, and in Kuwait there have been several high-profile Brazilian coaches. Among the legendary Gulf players are several from the all-conquering Kuwaiti team of the early 1970s, which won the Gulf Cup for five of the first six times it was held, and performed excellently at the 1982 World Cup finals, drawing with Czechoslovakia and narrowly losing to England and France. The centre forward of that team, Jasim Ya'goub, was known as the 'black pearl', and the goalkeeper, Ahmed al-Tarabulsi, an exceptional player by any standard, was a Palestinian by birth who was (exceptionally) granted Kuwaiti citizenship so that he could play for Kuwait.

The terminology of Gulf football owes quite a lot to English, even though there are 'official' Arabic terms for every aspect of the game. 'Goal' is usually **gool**, as in **jaab gooláyn** 'he scored (lit. 'brought') two goals', although 'goalkeeper' is usually translated using the 'official' Arabic term **Háaris il-márma**, (lit. 'guardian of the goal'). 'To shoot' is

From small beginnings: a football match in the 1950s at the Kuwait Oil Company's sports ground in Ahmadi

A scene from the first Gulf Cup tournament in 1970 in Bahrain

sháwwaT, as in **sháwwaT il-kúura** 'he shot the ball'. 'Pass' is **baas**, as in **9aT baas!** 'Pass it!' (lit. 'give pass!'). A 'penalty' is **bílanti**, and a 'corner' is **kúrnar**. When the ball goes out of play, the TV commentators are apt to say things such as **tíTla9 il-kúura bárra … awt** 'the ball goes out of play', adding **awt**, an Arabicisation of English 'out', even though they have already said this by using the Arabic word **bárra**.

Reading Arabic

We have been studying imperatives in the last few units, and in the reading section of thus unit and the next, we are going to look at how commands on signs may be made more (or less) 'polite'.

First, look at this sign (on the right), which was taped to the door of a mosque in the small Omani town of al-Hamra.

(اقطع اتصالك
بالدنيا لأجل
الأخره)

"الرجاء غلق
الهاتف النقال قبل
دخول المسجد"

The command in brackets at the top puts things in a direct and religious way:

íqTa9 ittiSáalik bid-dunya li 'ajl il-áaxira!
'Cut off your communication with this world for the sake of the next!'

(**íqTa9** 'cut' is in form the imperative of a simple verb similar to the one we met on traffic signs: **ífsaH** 'give way'.)

This is, in fact, an instruction to worshippers to perform a simple operation, as is made clear in the polite and less cryptic version immediately below it! This says:

ar-rajáa' ghalq al-háatif an-naqqáal qabla duxúul al-másjid.
'Please turn off (your) mobile phone before entering the mosque.'

The phrase **ar-rajáa'** is a polite form of words in MSA roughly equivalent to 'please', and it is usually followed by a verbal noun, here **ghalq** 'closing; turning off'. When the request is to not do something, this is usually politely done by using the verbal noun **9ádam** 'lack, absence' … followed by another verbal noun describing the activity being discouraged, for example:

الرجاء عدم التدخين
ar-rajáa' 9ádam at-tadxíin
No smoking please
(lit. 'please absence of smoking')

Look at the following polite signs, with requests positive and negative. What do they mean?

1 الرجاء عدم الدخول
2 الرجاء غلق الباب
3 الرجاء عدم قطف الزهور
4 الرجاء لزوم اليمين
5 الرجاء عدم الوقوف
6 الرجاء عدم الخروج
7 الرجاء عدم الإزعاج

(Words you may not know: **wuqúuf** 'parking'; **'iz9áaj** 'disturbance'; **qaTf** 'picking'; **luzúum** 'keeping to'.)

Unit Fifteen

In this unit you will learn about:

- the verbal noun, e.g. 'doing' or 'deed'
- coordinated negatives, e.g. 'only', 'neither … nor' or 'couldn't do this or that'
- compound adjectives, e.g. 'much of wealth' for 'rich', or 'long of tongue' for 'impudent'
- 'self' as in 'myself' or 'themselves'

Language point

15.1 The verbal noun

Verbal nouns in English are formed by the addition of **-ing** to the verb stem, for example 'doing', 'acting' or 'dying', by other types of suffix, for example -ion in 'action', or by changes in vowelling, for example 'deed' and 'death'. In Gulf Arabic there are a number of fixed patterns used to form the verbal noun in simple verbs, and a single pattern for each of the derived themes. There are five common patterns used in the simple verb, and the particular pattern that any given verb takes is more or less fixed. As with 'broken' plurals, it is a good idea to learn the form of the verbal noun of each verb as you meet it, and from this point on the verbal noun of each new simple verb will be listed as it occurs in the Vocabulary.

By far the commonest simple verbal noun pattern is CvCC, which becomes CooC or CayC where hollow verbs are concerned, and CaCi for weak verbs, for example:

Strong	Hollow	Weak	Doubled
Tabx 'cooking'	**gool** 'saying'	**máshi** 'walking'	**Hall** 'solution'
dhikr 'remembering'	**TayH** 'falling'	**Háchi** 'talk'	**Hubb** 'love'

In many cases, it is possible to add the feminine ending **-a** (with 'hidden' **t**) to these verbal nouns in order to form an 'instance' noun: for example, **Tábxa** means 'a dish' (i.e. an instance of cooking), **Dárba** means 'a blow' (compare **Darb** 'beating') and **Táyha** means 'a fall'. In some cases, the verbal noun with **-a** signifies the way of doing something, for example **máashi** 'walking' and **máshya** 'gait'.

The next most common pattern is CvCaaC(a):

Hadáag	'fishing'	**Tawáaf**	'going round'
sagáay	'irrigating'	**kitáaba**	'writing'
ziyáara	'visit'	**giráaya**	'reading'
gaTáaT	'throwing away'	**faráara**	'fleeing'

Other patterns are: CuCuuC, which occurs only in strong and doubled verbs, for example **rujúu9** 'return' (from **ríja9**) and **murúuur** (from **marr**), which literally means 'passing', but has acquired the meaning 'traffic' or 'traffic police' (short for **shúrTat il-murúur**); CaCaC, which is similarly only found in strong and doubled verb stems (**fáraH** 'happiness', **málal** 'boredom'); and CiCCaan/CaCaCaan, which occur mainly with weak and hollow verbs (e.g. **nisyáan** 'forgetting' from **nísa**, **shayaláan** 'removal' from **shaal**, **xawaráan** 'stirring' from **xaar**).

The verbal nouns of the derived themes are almost wholly predictable. CaCCaC verbs have the verbal noun pattern taCCiiC (taC-Ciya for weak verbs):

SállaH	'to repair'	**taSlíiH**	'repair'
xáTTaT	'to plan'	**taxTíiT**	'planning' (e.g. in **wizáarat it-taxTíiT**)
9áyyan	'to appoint'	**ta9yíin**	'appointment'
rábba	'to bring up'	**tárbiya**	'upbringing'

A very small number of weak verbs, some of them important, have the pattern tiCCaa (with 'hidden' **t**):

sáwwa	'to do; make'	tiswáa	'doing; deed'
bádda	'to begin'	tibdáa	'beginning'
Hálla	'to decorate'	tiHláa	'decoration'

CaaCaC verbs have the verbal noun pattern muCaaCaCa (with 'hidden' **t**):

sáa9ad	'to help'	musáa9ada	'help'
Háajaj	'to argue'	muHáajaja	'argument'
Háawal	'to try'	muHáawala	'attempt'
láaga	'to meet'	muláaga	'meeting (by chance)'

There are odd instances of an alternative form of verbal noun, CiCaaC, but this tends to occur only in set phrases, usually borrowed from Literary Arabic, for example **sibáaq il-khayl** 'horse-racing' (from **sáabaq** 'to race; compete') and **wizáarat id-difáa9** 'Ministry of Defence' (from **dáafa9** 'to defend').

tiCaCCaC verbs have tiCaCCuC verbal nouns:

ta9ájjab	'to be surprised'	ta9ajjub	'surprise; amazement'
taxáSSaS	'to specialise'	taxáSSuS	'specialism'
taHáchcha	'to talk'	taHáchchi	'talk'

In some cases, such as **taHáchcha**, the verbal noun **taHáchchi** is not much used, the verbal noun of the simple verb **Háchi** being used instead. Another example is **taHámmal bi** 'to take care of (someone)', where the simple verbal noun **Hamáala** is used rather than **taHámmul**.

tiCaaCaC verbs have tiCaaCuC verbal nouns:

tiwáafag	'to mutually agree'	tiwáafug	'mutual agreement'
ta9áawan	'to cooperate'	ta9áawun	'cooperation'
taHáacha	'to converse'	taHáachi	'conversation'

The verbal noun has a number of uses in Arabic, most of which are paralleled in English.

Verbal nouns can denote an **activity in general**:

il-Hadáag mamnüu9 íhni.
'Fishing is prohibited here.'

it-tilmíidh dhaak wáayid Da9íif fil-giráaya.
'That pupil is very poor at reading.'

When used in sentences of this type, Arabic, unlike English, requires the definite article **il**.

Verbal nouns can denote **the doing of something to something else**, and in such cases the verbal noun often replaces a clause. In the examples below, the pairs of sentences are parallel in meaning:

tiswáatik muu záyna.
'Your deed was not good.'
ílli sawwáytah muu zayn.
'What you did was not good.'

wáafag 9ála daf9 il-máblagh il-maTlúub.
'He agreed payment of the sum demanded.'
wáfag 9ála 'an yídfa9 il-máblagh il-maTlúub.
'He agreed to pay the sum demanded.'
('**an** 'that' functions in a similar way to '**inn**.)

dhikr maa gaal lii yizá99ilni.
'The remembrance of what he said to me upsets me.'
layn ádhkur maa gaal lii, áz9al.
'When I remember what he said to me, I get upset.'

mujárrad shóofatah tixáwwifni.
'The mere sight of him frightens me.'
mujárrad ashúufah, axáaf.
'I only have to see him and I'm afraid.'

taSlíiH sayyaaráat, háadha shúghli.
'Repairing cars, that's my job.'
aSálliH sayyaaráat, háadha shúghli.
'I repair cars, that's my job.'

Verbal nouns can in some cases denote *what is (or needs to be) done*:

hal-jaamáat tábbi liha tanDHíif.
'These window panes need cleaning/to be cleaned.'

hal-chaay yábbi lih xawaráan.
'This tea needs stirring/to be stirred.'

Some other typical uses of the verbal noun are given below. One that strikes the English speaker as somewhat strange is the use of the verbal noun as a kind of 'echo' of the verb from which it is derived. It is, however, quite common in casual speech:

fírHaw li áaxir fáraH.
'They were really happy.'
(lit. 'They were happy to the last happiness.')

taHammált bih Hamáalatin záyna.
'I took really good care of him.'
(lit. 'I took care of him a good taking-care-of.')
(The **-in** suffix on **Hamáala** is a feature of uneducated speech.)

The two following examples involve the verbal nouns of intransitive verbs in noun phrases:

maa yáDrub iz-zar9 min gíllat il-máTar.
'The crops don't take because of the lack of rain.'

zood il-Harr mut9íbni wáayid.
'The increased heat has tired me a lot.'
(lit. 'The increase of the heat …')

Note also the useful phrases **9ála gooláthum** or **9ala góolat il-gáayil**, which are equivalent to the English 'as they say':

haay tays bawwáal, 9ala góolat il-gáayil.
'He's a very uncouth man, as they say.'
(lit. 'This is a pissing he-goat, as the sayer says.')

In more educated speech, in which matters of more than immediate interest are discussed, phrases involving verbal nouns borrowed from Literary Arabic may occur, for example:

wizáarat	**id-difáa9**	'Ministry of Defence'
	it-taxTíiT	of Planning'
	it-tárbiya wit-ta9líim	of Education'
	il-9ámal	of Labour'
	it-taTwíir il-iqtiSáadi	of Economic Development'

Exercise 15.1

Translate the following sentences into English, and then change them into sentences that have the same meaning, but in which you use a verbal noun. The parts of the sentences that can be replaced by a verbal noun are underlined.

1 maa wáafag 9ála 'an yisáa9id in-náadi.

2 mamnúu9 tidáxxin fi ghúrfal in-noom.

3 illi sawwóoh maa byifíidna ábadan.

4 mínhu símaH lich tidxalíin?

5 mujárrad ashúuf il-wijh máalah áz9al.

6 il-mufáttish 'ámar ish-shúrTi bi 'an yiwággif il-baaS.

7 yibíi9 u yíshri shiqqáat, haay shúghlah.

8 kássar il-jaam bidúun maa yáqSud.

Translate the following sentences into Arabic, using verbal nouns where possible:

9 These books need to be thrown away.

10 No car-parking here!

11 He doesn't know how to swim.

12 What he said needs to be confirmed.

13 Checking these accounts is a tiring business.

14 Don't pay any attention to what people say!

15 We're buying less than before because of the increased prices.

16 What's your speciality? Teaching languages.

 # Language point

15.2 Coordinated negatives

The Arabic equivalent of 'only' in sentences such as 'He gave me only two dinars' and 'I said only a few words' is **maa ... ílla** 'not ... except', similar in usage to the French 'ne ... que':

> **maa 9aTáani ílla diinaaráyn.**
> 'He gave me only two dinars.'

> **maa gilt ílla cham min kalimáat.**
> 'I said only a few words.'

> **maa mish ílla háadha.**
> 'This is all there is.' (lit. 'There isn't except this.')

Below we look at some other examples of 'coordinated negatives'.

■ maa ... wa la ...

This construction is used for negating two verbs with the same subject, and is like the English 'neither ... nor':

maa shíftah wa la Haacháytah.
'I neither saw him nor spoke to him.'

il-mislimíin maa yaaklúun láHam xanzíir wa la yishrabúun xámar.
'Muslims neither eat pork nor drink alcohol.'

With 'pseudo-verbs' **hast/fii/mish** and **9ind-**:

maa fii ákil wa la maay.
'There's neither food nor water.'

maa 9ind il-mudíir máani9 wa la 9índi bá9ad.
'The boss has no objection and nor do I.'

The construction can also be used where **maa** negates the verb and **la** a noun:

maa y9árf il-giráaya wa la l-kitáaba.
'He can't read or write.'
(lit. 'He doesn't know reading and not writing.')

■ la ... la

This construction is usually used in negating nouns, pronouns and adjectives (not usually verbs):

la 9ayb wa la Haráam!
'Neither a disgrace nor a shame!'

la ínta wa la ána ágdar asáwwi háadha.
'Neither you nor I can do that.'

ílli gumt bih la zayn wa la shayn.
'What you undertook was neither good nor bad.'

Where statements are being strongly contradicted, **la ... la** may be used with verbs:

ráaHaw l-mádrasa u ta9államaw l-kitáaba.
la ráaHaw mukáan wa la ta9államaw shay!
'They went to school and learnt to write.'
'They didn't go anywhere and they didn't learn anything!'

Exercise 15.2

Translate into Arabic, using coordinated negatives:

1 He only heard a little of what was said.
2 Neither the car lights nor the battery has been repaired.
3 He gave us no encouragement and no help.
4 You can't cook and you don't want to learn: I'm going to sack you!
5 You'll improve by frequent practice.
6 I don't like bargaining, either in the market or with taxi drivers.
7 She couldn't eat or sleep because of her worries.
8 They've got neither manners nor morals!
9 We haven't received or sent any letters this week.
10 Neither you nor anyone else can help me in this.
11 I looked, but couldn't find apples or oranges.
12 He's a good man: he doesn't come to work late or leave early.

Language points

15.3 Compound adjectives

One of the more colourful ways Arabic forms adjectives is through adjective + definite noun constructions, for example **kathíir il-maal** 'rich' ('much of wealth') and **qalíil il-ádab** 'rude' ('little of manners'). Some of the adjectives formed in this way have meanings rather difficult to guess at from their component parts, for example **Tawíil il-lisáan** 'impudent' ('long of tongue'), **xafíif id-damm** 'charming' ('light of blood') and **thagíil id-damm** 'boring; dull' ('heavy of blood').

These adjectives behave in the same way as the adjectives we have met so far, agreeing with the nouns they describe in gender and number. When annexed to a definite noun, the adjectival element of the compound becomes definite too:

> **rayyáal kathíir il-maal**   **ir-rayyáal il-kathíir il-maal**
> 'a rich man'   'the rich man'

The feminine form shows its 'hidden' **t**:

hal-bint xafíifat id-damm.
'This girl is charming.'

Plural forms may be either 'broken' (where they exist) or 'strong':

hal-banáat il-xifáaf id-damm   **ískitu yaa qaliilíin il-ádab!**
'these charming girls'   'Be quiet, you rude people!'

15.4 'Self'

In the sense of 'by my- his- its-, etc. self', the Gulf expression is **bruuH** + pronoun (**ruuH** means 'soul; spirit; self'):

sawwáyt háadha brúuHi.
'I did this by myself.'

Saar il-yáahil yímshi brúuHah.
'The child has started to walk by himself.'

il-makíina wáagfa brúuHha, máHHad waggáfha.
'The machine has stopped by itself, nobody stopped it.'

bruuH is often idiomatically used to mean 'separately':

zará9t il-báSal mínni brúuHah, wiT-TamáaT mínni brúuHah.
'I planted the onions and tomatoes separately: onions over here and tomatoes over here.'

In the reflexive sense, 'self' is often not overtly expressed, but is part of the meaning of certain tiCaCCaC verbs, for example:

id-daríisha tibánnadat.
'The window closed itself.' (e.g. the wind blew it shut)

il-awláad tizábbaraw Hagg il-9iid.
'The boys spruced themselves up for the Eid.'

However, **ruuH** + pronoun is commonly used as the reflexive object pronoun:

járaH rúuHah 9an qaSd.
'He wounded himself deliberately.'

fállat rúuHah min foog is-sáTaH.
'He threw himself off the roof.'

ni9áTlik u ni9áTTil rúuHna.
'We're stopping you from working and stopping ourselves.'

An alternative to **ruuH** in its reflexive sense is **nafs**, which is used in exactly the same way:

yiDáyyij náfsah ákthar min maa yiDáyyijni.
'He's annoying himself more than he's annoying me.'

However, **nafs** is also commonly used to mean 'the (very) same ...', for example **nafs ish-shay** 'the same thing':

háadhi nafs il-ghúrfa~lli nizált fiiha gábil iHdá9shar sána!
'This is the same room I stayed in eleven years ago!'

mushkílti nafs mushkíltik.
My problem is the same as yours.'

Exercise 15.3

Translate into Arabic:

1 Do it by yourself, I'm not going to help you!
2 They didn't want to travel by themselves.
3 *He* won't help you; help yourself!
4 She asked me the same question – I gave her the same answer.
5 Your business is the same as mine.
6 I didn't put the stuff all in the same place: I put the nails separately in a box and the hooks separately in a bag.
7 I didn't open the window – it opened by itself.
8 This is the exact same house the old woman went into.
9 The stolen wallet is the same as this one.
10 You mustn't go to that area by yourselves – it's very dangerous!

Exercise 15.4

In the passage below, a Gulf Arab describes what he sees as the usefulness of fasting – **fáydat iS-Soom**. During the month of Ramadan, Muslims of all nations are not supposed to eat or drink from sunup to sundown. Translate the passage into English. You will see that a large number of verbal nouns occur: try and specify which verbs they come from.

fáydat iS-Soom

iS-Soom, fáydatah áwwal shay wállah min jíhat il-jísim ... il-jísim ya9ni míthil il-áala maal sayyáara. ídha fi kill síttat áshhur aw kill sána maa twaddíiha Hagg il-xídma, Hagg it-tachyíik, Hagg it-tanDHíif Hagg it-ta9díil, Hatta lo tikúun sittíin alf aw xamsíin alf, fi xiláal sanatáyn thaláath sanawáat tí9dam 9aláyk. wis-sayyáara bil-9aks alf diináar idha fi kill sittat shuhúur ticháyyikha wil-mikaaníik yífHaS 9aláyha u yishúufha ídha hi záyna, SáalHa, maa tátlif wil-jísim shíkil is-sayyáara – yábghi lih ráaHa wi ta9díil aHyáanan. fil-waqt il-HáaDir záadat il-amráaD ... laysh? min il-ákil iz-záayid ...

Exercise 15.5 (Audio 1; 29)

Another Juha joke for translation!

júHa yirúuH id-dáxtar

yoom min il-ayyáam, júHa raaH id-dáxtar. 9aTáah dáwa fi ghársha. gaal lih id-dáxtar 'layn bitíshrab had-dáwa, xuDD il-ghársha.' il-Hiin júHa raaH il-báyt u shárab id-dáwa bidúun maa yixúDDah. yoom tidhákkar maa gaal lih id-dáxtar, íla yigúul 'ohoo!' u gaam yitrámmaz chidhíi. gaalóo lih il-yiiráan 'waysh fiik júHa?' ila yigúul 'nisáyt axúDD il-ghársha gábil la áshrab id-dáwa – háadha ana axúDDah fi báTni!'

Proverbs and sayings

xáshmak mínnak wa lo kaan á9waj.
'Your nose is part of you even if it's crooked.'
(i.e. 'Your family is your family, however badly behaved members of it may be.'/'Blood is thicker than water.')

shóofat il-aHíbbaa xayr min alf julúus fid-dunya.
'The sight of loved ones is worth more than a thousand social gatherings in this world.'
(lit. '... better than a thousand sittings in this world.')

ílli faat maat.
'What's past is dead.'
(i.e. 'Let bygones be bygones.')

Vocabulary

ádab/aadáab	manners	Haráam	prohibited (by Islam)
aHyáanan	occasionally	Harr	heat
'ámar/yá'mur/ 'amr	to order someone to do something	iqtiSáad	economy
		iqtiSáadi	economic(al)
axláaq (pl.)	morals	jálas/yájlis/julúus	to sit
bádda/yibáddi (v. n. tibdáa*)	to begin	jálsa*	sitting; session
		min jíhat + noun	from the point of view of ...
bidúun maa + verb	without ...ing	kálima*(aat)	word; utterance
bítri(yaat)	battery		
chilláab/ chilaalíib	hook	kássar/yikássir	to smash
		káthra*	abundance; large amount
dáafa9/yidáafi9 (9an)	to defend	lisáan/alsína*	tongue; language
damm	blood		
dáxxan/yidáxxin	to smoke	máaras/yimáaris	to practise (a skill)
Dárab/yíDrub/ Darb	to hit; take (crops)	mall/yimill/málal	to get bored
Dáyyaj/yiDáyyij	to irritate; annoy	mamnúu9	prohibited
		máshya*	gait; style of walking
faat/yifúut/foot	to pass		
fáttash/yifáttish	to inspect	máTar/amTáar	rain
fállat/yifállit	to fling; throw	mismáar/ masaamíir	nail
farr/yifírr/faráara	to flee	mujárrad + noun/verb	the mere ...
gaam (bi)/ yigúum/goom	to undertake		
gílla*	lack; scarcity	murúur	traffic; traffic police
hamm/humúum	cares; worries	nafs + noun/pron.	the same ...
Háajaj/yiHáajij	to argue with (someone)	qáSad/yáqSud/ qaSd	to intend
Habíib/aHíbbaa	darling; loved one	rábba/yirábbi	to bring up; raise (children, animals, etc.)
Hádag/yiHádig/ Hadáag	to fish (with a line)		
Hálla/yiHálli (v. n. tiHláa*)	to decorate	ruuH: bruuH + pron.	by ... self
Háqqaq/yiHáqqiq	to confirm; verify	sáayig/suwwáag	driver
		sibáaHa*	swimming

sibáaq	race (sport)	**xaDD/yixúDD/ xaDD**	to shake (something)
SáaliH	proper; valid; in good order	**xámar**	alcohol
		xanzíir/xanaazíir	pig
Sáam/yiSúum/ Soom	to fast	**xáshim**	nose
		xáTar/axTáar	danger
shájja9/yishájji9	to encourage (someone) to (**9ála**) do something	**xáTTaT/yixáTTiT**	to draw lines; make plans
		xáwwaf/yixáwwif	to frighten
shayn	bad; evil	**xayl** (pl.)	horses
taHámmal/ yitHámmal (bi) (v. n. **Hamáala**)	to take care of; look after	**xayr (min)**	better (than)
		xídma*(aat)	service
		fi xiláal	in the space of (time)
taTwíir	development (economic, etc.)	**zára9/yízra9/zar9** or **ziráa9a**	to plant; sow
taxáSSaS/ yitxáSSaS (fi)	to specialise (in)	**zá99al/yizá99il**	to annoy; upset
ta9áawan/ yit9áawan	to cooperate	**9ajúuz/9ajáayiz**	old woman
		9ámal/a9máal	work; job; employment
ta9ájjab/yit9ájjab	to be surprised, amazed	**9áTTal/yi9áTTil**	to put out of action; make redundant; stop someone (from working)
tilaf/yátlif/tálaf	to spoil; go bad		
tirámmaz/ yitrammaz	to jump up and down	**9ayb/9uyúub**	shame; disgrace
tizábbar/yitzábbar	to dress up smartly	**9áyyan/yi9áyyin**	to appoint (someone)
tufáaH	apples	**9ídam/yí9dam**	to be ruined, spoilt
il-waqt il-HáaDir	the present time		

Cultural point

History (3): the Indians

The links between the Gulf and India are of extremely long standing. The third Caliph, 'Uthman ibn 'Affan (d. 656 AD), who began the process of collecting the Quran into a canonical written text, which up until that time was preserved only in the memories of oral reciters, is supposed to have rejected as authorities Quranic reciters from Arab tribes living on the eastern seaboard of Gulf because their Arabic was deemed to be 'unreliable' (**ghayr mawthuuq biha**) in its purity. This was supposedly due, even at this early date, to their long-term mixing with Persians, Indians and other non-Arab traders and incomers. In fact, Gulf trade with India goes back much further than this (to 2000 BC) to the Indus valley civilisation of Mohenjo-Daro in what is now Pakistan. The old Gulf term for Indians, **baanyáan**, is a corruption of the Gujerati word **vaaniya**, meaning a man of trading caste, which itself derives from the Sanskrit **vanij** 'merchant'. This linguistic evidence is perhaps the best indication of what has always been the main dynamic for contact between the Gulf and India – trade, either as a destination for goods, or as an entrepôt for them. India was historically the source of many luxury items, from carpets to gold jewellery, and trade links with India became even stronger from the establishment of the British East India Company, and then the British Raj. More recently, as already noted in the section on marriage in the Gulf, India has been looked to as a source of brides for Gulf men, especially because of the rise in the size of the dowries demanded by Gulf brides.

The gradual increase in British influence in the Gulf countries from the late nineteenth century onwards strengthened the India connection, since the development of a basic infrastructure – a civil service, a post office, a health service and so on – required manpower with a level of literacy and with technical skills that were then unavailable in the Gulf but in plentiful (and cheap) supply in India. Even after the Gulf States started to become politically independent in the late 1960s and early 1970s, there were still many Indian clerks and technical staff employed in Gulf public concerns and private enterprises – the word for 'clerk' in Gulf Arabic, **kráani**, is an Indian word, as is the word for 'note; memorandum', **chitti** (whence also the British English 'chitty'). All this began to change with the development of indigenous education, and the gradual replacement of Indians with locally trained manpower. After the oil price rises of the 1970s, the explosion of development in large civil engineering projects that occurred from the early 1980s – from the construction of airports, to tanker terminals, to road systems to universities – produced a new wave of more temporary immigrants from south Asia, though this time they were manual labourers rather than the clerks and technicians of previous generations. As anyone who has visited the region cannot have failed to notice, large parts of the local economy in countries such as the UAE, Oman and Qatar depend on a south Asian workforce, and the popular areas of Gulf cities can sound and look more like Indian or Pakistani ones, with plentiful Indian restaurants and bazaars where one can hear half a dozen different Indian languages spoken by shopkeepers and customers alike. Cricket in the UAE is probably a more popular sport than football!

Boys at an Indian cricket camp in Dubai. Photo © Preston Merchant

Reading Arabic

We saw in Unit Fourteen that polite prohibitions on signs can be made with the phrase ... عدم الرجاء (**ar-rajáa' 9ádam** ...). But it's possible to be more direct with the word ممنوع 'prohibited; forbidden'. Look at the sign below, placed near a place in a village in Oman where women wash clothes:

Can you read the Arabic? The top line says **háadhihi l-amáakin xáaSSa bin-nisáa'** 'These places (**amáakin**) are reserved (**xáaSSa**) for women (**nisáa'**).'

The second line says:

ممنوع مرور الرجال فيها

= **mamnúu9 murúur ar-rijáal fíihaa**, which means 'men are prohibited from passing through them'. The word **mamnúu9** 'prohibited' precedes the verbal noun that specifies what is prohibited, here **murúur ar-rijáal fíihaa** 'the passing of men through them (i.e. these places)'. Look at the following signs and translate them:

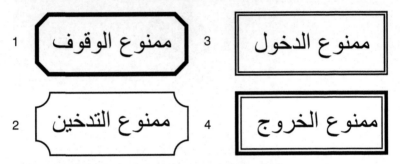

Prohibitions on signs can also, as in spoken Arabic, be accomplished by negative imperatives. Look at this next Omani sign:

The top line says: **áxii al-muwáaTin … áxii az-z-záa'ir** 'My brother citizen … my brother visitor'. The next line says: **ínna miyáah al-'afláaj ní9ma min alláah lánaa** 'Verily, the waters of the falajes are a bounty from God to us.' (The **fálaj** (pl. **afláaj**) is an irrigation channel for bringing water to crops, widely used in the Omani countryside.)

The next line contains the prohibition:

فلا تلوثها بغسل الملابس و الأواني

meaning 'so do not pollute them by washing (**ghasl**) clothes (**al-maláabis**) and kitchenware (**al-'awáanii**) in them'. The negative

prohibition is لا تلوثها (**laa tulawwíthhaa**) 'don't pollute them' from the
verb **láwwath** 'to pollute', a verb of the type CaCCaC that we saw in
Unit Fourteen with a doubled middle root consonant. The final line
completes the things that are prohibited: **wa 'ilqáa' al-faDaláat fíihaa**
'or by throwing litter into them'.

What are the following prohibitions? Can you read the Arabic aloud?

1	لا تدخن
2	لا تقطف الزهور
3	لا تدخل من هذا الباب
4	لا تلوث الفلج
5	لا تقف هنا
6	لا تخرج من هنا
7	لا تلوث الحديقة

A backstreet in Al-Hamra, Oman

Review Unit III

Read aloud and translate the telephone dialogue below.

TELEPHONIST	alló?
ENQUIRER	alló, SabáaH il-xayr!
T	SabáaH in-nuur!
E	haay <u>shárikat il-xalíij liT-Tayaráan</u>? (a)
T	ná9am.
E	múmkin aHáachi l-mudíir il-9aam min fáDlich? ána ísmi Johnson, ana <u>mudíir wakáalat is-safariyyáat '9áalam jadíid'</u>. (b)
T	láHDHa, il-xaTT máalah mashghúul ... (pause) ... mit'assifa, ya sáyyid Johnson, sikirtíirtah tigúul ínnah muu mawjúud il-Hiin. Tíla9 gábil xams dagáayig tigúul ...
E	<u>míta byírja9</u> yá9ni? (c)
T	láHDHa, ás'al sikirtíirtah ... tigúul maa tádri ...
E	ágdar aHuTT lih xábar 9índaha?
T	tafáDDal.
E	abbíiha tigúul lih ínnana <u>mwaafgíin 9ala sh-shurúuT íIli waddáaha 9aláyna bin-nísba lil-9aqd</u> (d)
T	nzayn, ba9Tíiha l-xábar u híyya bitxáabrah layn yírja9.
E	mashkúur.
T	il-9áfu.

Exercise RIII.1

In the dialogue above there are four underlined sections. In (a) the enquirer asks whether he has been connected with the organisation he wanted; in (b) he announces who he is; in (c) he asks for further information; in (d) he leaves a message. In the following exercise, you have to substitute alternative sentences at points (a) to (d) using the words supplied.

(a) Note that the structure of the phrase **sharikat il-xalíij liT-Tayaráan** (lit. 'company of the Gulf for aviation') is

    Noun + Noun + Preposition + Noun

where the first two nouns are linked together in the kind of relationship we saw in 8.1, and the preposition + Noun phrase that follows this Noun + Noun phrase merely adds some further information – that the company is concerned with aviation rather than, say, exports. Make similar phrases from the words below, substituting them in the sentence **haay …?** as in the dialogue.

Noun	*Noun*	*Noun*
		nifT (oil)
		smiit (cement)
shárika	**xalíij**	**bináa** (construction)
		taTwíir iqtiSáadi (economic development)
		mantuujáat ziraa9íyya (agricultural products)

Now try other substitutions: **mu'ássasa** 'establishment; foundation' for **shárika** and **kuwáyt, baHráyn**, etc. for **xalíij**.

Another common structure for complex noun phrases is exemplified by **is-shárika l-kuwaytíyya lil-bináa**, where the structure is

    Noun + Adjective + Preposition + Noun

As in the previous example, the Preposition + Noun phrase defines the function of the Noun + Adjective phrase. Make phrases of this type using the words below, and fit them into the question **haay …?**

Noun	Noun	Noun
		taSdíir in-nifT (export of oil)
		taSdíir il-asmáak (export of fish)
mu'ássasa	**wáTani**	**taswíiq il-láHam** (marketing of meat)
		taSlíiH is-súfun (repair of ships)
		San9 il-aaláat iS-Sinaa9íyya (manufacture of industrial tools)

(b) In (b), where the caller announces his identity:

ana mudíir wakáalat is-safariyyáat '9álam jadíid'

the structure is

Noun + Noun + Noun + Proper name.

Make similar phrases from the chart below, substituting them in the sentence beginning **ana** ... .

Noun	Noun	Noun	Proper name
		smiit	**'9ántar'**
	shárika	**bináa**	**'ziyáad'**
mudíir		**anbáa**	**'ay bii sii'**
	wakáala	**9ámal**	**'fayrúuz'**

(c) **míta byírja9?** is a request for further information. Here are some others for you to translate into Arabic:

1 Where's he gone?
2 Has he any appointments this afternoon?
3 Is he free tomorrow?
4 Is he busy all day?
5 Can he meet me later?
6 Has he read my report?
7 Has he talked to my colleague?
8 Has he written to us yet?
9 Has he signed the contract or not?
10 Has he received my letter?

(d) In (d) the speaker leaves a message. Using the introduction **abbíiha tigúul lih ínnana** ..., leave the following messages:

1 We've thought about his offer and will give our answer next week.

2 We've thought about his offer but have rejected the conditions he's imposing on us.

3 We do not agree to his offer in its present form.

4 We do not agree to the changes he's demanding.

5 We've accepted his conditions and will reply officially in a few days.

Exercise RIII.2 (Audio 1; 30)

Here is a short account of marriage customs as they were only a few decades ago in the Gulf, as told by an old woman. You have already read a rough English translation of some of it in the Cultural point of Unit Eleven. Read aloud and translate, using the notes below where necessary:

iz-zawáaj il-qadíim

abu l-wálad yitqáddam Hagg abu l-bint u yixTúbha. ídha yá9ni tiwáafagaw, waddáyna hal-hadáaya máalat il-áwwal with-thiyáab, u waddáyna líhum bayzáat u maláchna 9ind ish-shayx. Saar 9aad láylat il-Hánna. yiTablúun Tubúul, u yisawwúun Tagg u agháani, u yiHannúunha, u ba9adáyn yidhibHúun dhibáaH u yiTabxúun. 9ógub, yaaxdhúunha, il-9arúus ya9ni, u yiHuTTúunha fi zuulíyya, u yidizzúunha 9ala ráyilha.

Notes:

– **maal(at) il-áwwal** 'belonging to the old times, old fashioned'.

– **shayx** refers here to a religious elder, not to the ruling family.

– **9aad** 'then; so'. This word is frequently untranslatable. It is often used with imperatives to increase their force: **iskit 9aad!** '*Do* be quiet!

– **Hánna** 'henna'. **láylat il-Hánna** was the night before the wedding when the bride's body was decorated with henna.

– **Tagg** 'beating', means here a kind of hand clapping.

– **yidhibHúun dhibáaH** 'they slaughtered a slaughtering', means that an animal was killed in celebration. This use of the verbal noun as the object of the verb from which it is derived is very common. Other examples are **Taggáytah Tagg** ('I hit him a hitting') = 'I gave him a good beating' and **fírHaw li áxir fáraH** ('They were happy to the last happiness') = 'They were really happy' (see 15.1).

– **zuulíyya** 'rug'. Brides were traditionally wrapped in these before being presented to their husbands.

Vocabulary

alló	hello (telephone)	**Sináa9i**	industrial
bináa	construction	**shákil/ashkáal**	form; shape; type
dhíbaH/yídhbaH/ dhibáaH	to slaughter (animal)	**sharT/shurúuT**	condition; stipulation
Hánna/yiHánni/ Hanna*	to paint with henna	**taswíiq**	marketing
ídha	if	**taSdíir**	exporting
jawáab/ajwíba*	answer; reply	**tìlágga/yitlágga**	to get; receive
láHDHa*(aat)	moment	**tiqáddam/ yitqáddam**	to proceed; present oneself
málach/yámlich/ mílcha*	to betroth	**Tábbal/yiTábbil**	to drum
mashkúur	thanks; grateful	**Tábil/Tubúul**	drum (n.)
mu'ássasa*(aat)	establishment	**Tagg/yiTígg/ Tagg**	to beat; hit
múmkin	possible; maybe	**wáqqa9/ yiwáqqi9**	to sign
nába'/anbáa	piece of news		
qáadim	next	**xáTab/yíxTub/ xúTba**	to betroth
ráfaD/yárfuD/ rafD	to refuse; reject	**zamíil/zumaláa**	colleague
ráyil (or **rájil**)/ **rijáal**	man; husband (alternative to **rayyáal/ rayaayíil**)	**ziráa9i**	agricultural
		zuulíyya*/ zawáali	rug
safaríyya*(aat)	journey; travel	**9aad**	so; then
sámak/asmáak	fish (more formal equivalent of **simich**)	**9áalam**	world
		9aam (adj.)	general
SabáaH	morning	**il-9áfu**	Don't mention it! (reply to 'thanks')
SabáaH il-xayr	Good morning!		
SabáaH in-nuur	Good morning! (reply)	**9aqd/9uqúud**	contract
Sána9/yíSna9/ San9	to manufacture	**9arD/9urúuD**	offer; proposal
		9arúus (f.)/ **9aráayis**	bride

Unit Sixteen

In this unit you will learn about:

- the derived themes of the verb (2): aCCaC, inCaCaC, iCtaCaC and istaCCaC
- conditional sentences: 'possible' and 'hypothetical' conditions, and the use of 'unless' and 'even if'

Language point

16.1 The derived themes of the verb (2): aCCaC, inCaCaC, iCtaCaC and istaCCaC

In this unit we complete our survey of the three-consonant Arabic verb.

■ aCCaC verbs

These verbs, which are relatively rare in spoken Gulf Arabic, form their past tense by the prefixing of **a-** to the root consonants:

Root type	Example		
Strong	**á9lan**	'to announce'	(9-l-n)
Doubled	**aSárr**	'to insist'	(S-r-r)
Weak	**álgha**	'to cancel'	(l-gh-w)
Hollow	**adáar**	'to manage; run (e.g. a business)'	(d-w-r)

In the past tense, aCCaC verbs are conjugated like simple strong, doubled, weak and hollow verbs, namely:

a9lánt	'I announced'		**sharábt**	'I drank'
aSarráyt	'I insisted'	compare	**shaggáyt**	'I tore'
algháyt	'I cancelled'		**ligáyt**	'I found'
adírt	'I managed'		**gilt**	'I said'

In the imperfect, they are conjugated with an **i** stem vowel, which is long in hollow verbs. Note that the 1st person prefix is **u-**, not **a-**:

ú9lin	**uSírr**	**úlghi**	**udíir**
tí9lin	**tiSírr**	**tílghi**	**tidíir**
ti9liníin	**tiSirríin**	**tilghíin**	**tidiiríin**
yí9lin	**yiSírr**	**yílghi**	**yidíir**
tí9lin	**tiSírr**	**tílghi**	**tidíir**
ní9lin	**niSírr**	**nílghi**	**nidíir**
ti9linúun	**tiSirrúun**	**tilghúun**	**tidiirúun**
yi9linúun	**yiSirrúun**	**yilghúun**	**yidiirúun**

Imperatives are formed in the normal way:

i9lin/i/u!   **Sirr/i/u!**   **ílghi** (m./f.)**/u!**   **diir/i/u!**

The active and passive participles are formed according to the same principles described for the other derived themes (see Unit Fourteen), except that the prefix in aCCaC participles is usually **mu-** rather than **mi-**. Thus one finds:

mú9lin	'announcing; an announcer'
mú9lan	'announced; something announced'
múlghi	'cancelling; someone/something that cancels'
múlgha	'cancelled', etc.

Many common nouns are in fact participles of this kind, for example **mudíir** 'manager' is derived from **adáar** 'to manage; run'.

The verbal noun of aCCaC verbs is formed according to the pattern iCCaaC, for example **i9láan** 'announcement', **iSrár** 'insistence' and **ilgháa** 'cancellation'. Hollow verbs add a final **-a**, for example **idáara** 'management; administration'.

Here are some examples of aCCaC verbs in use:

il-Hukúuma á9lanat ínnaha tiSírr 9ala daf9 il-máblagh il-maTlúub

or, using the verbal noun:

il-Hukúuma á9lanat iSráarha 9ala daf9 il-máblagh il-maTlúub
'The government has announced that it is insisting on the payment of the sum demanded.'

mínhu l-mas'úul 9an il-idára fi dhiich ish-shárika?
'Who is responsible for administration in that company?'

Tárrashaw lina i9láan ilgháa kill il-9uqúud il-mitwáafag 9aláayha.
'They sent us an announcement of the cancellation of all the contracts agreed on.'

■ inCaCaC verbs

inCaCaC verbs are very commonly used and may be freely formed from simple transitive verbs by the prefixing of **in-**. This prefix passivises the meaning of the simple verb:

Root type	Example		
Strong	**in9áraf**	'to be known, knowable'	(**9áraf** 'to know')
Doubled	**inHáll**	'to be solved, solvable'	(**Hall** 'to solve')
Weak	**ingára**	'to be read, legible'	(**gára** 'to read')
Hollow	**insháal**	'to be removed, removable'	(**shaal** 'to remove')

The past tense of these verbs is conjugated according to the patterns for simple strong, doubled, etc. verbs (**in9aráft** 'I was known', **in9írfat** 'she was known' (compare **9aráft** 'I knew', **9írfat** 'she knew'), **inshílt** 'I was taken away', **insháalaw** 'they were taken away' (compare **shilt** 'I took away', **sháalaw** 'they took away')). Imperfects are formed as below:

an9írif	**anHáll**	**angára**	**ansháal**
tin9írif	**tinHáll**	**tingára**	**tinsháal**
tin9irfíin	**tinHallíin**	**tingaríin**	**tinshaalíin**
yin9írif	**yinHáll**	**yingára**	**yinsháal**
etc.	etc.	etc.	etc.

It can be seen from this that, except for the strong verb, the stem vowelling in the imperfect is the same as in the past. In the strong verb, it is usually **i-i** in the imperfect (though some Gulf dialects have **i-a** or **a-a**). The imperative is rarely used in inCaCaC verbs, for obvious reasons. Where it occurs, it follows the normal pattern, for example the verb **inchább** 'to go away; leave (vulgar)', which is the passive of **chabb** 'to knock over; spill' is **inchább/i/u!** 'Go away!'

Participial forms of inCaCaC are rare. It is normal to use the passive participle of the simple verb rather than that of the inCaCaC verb, for example **ma9rúuf** 'known' (not **min9áraf**), **maHlúul** 'solved' (not **minHáll**) and **mashyúul** 'removed' (not **minsháal**).

The verbal noun of inCaCaC verbs is of the pattern inCiCaac, though this is relatively rare in everyday speech, being restricted to words and phrases borrowed from Literary Arabic, for example **insiHáab il-jaysh** 'the withdrawal of the army' and **inqiláab il-hukúuma** 'the overthrow of the government'. The verbal noun of the simple verb is routinely used instead of inCiCaaC, thus **shayalán il-awsáax** 'the removing/ removal of the rubbish' (not **inshiyáal** ...) and **Hall il-múshkila** 'the solving of/solution to the problem' (not **inHiláal** ...).

Here are some examples of the use of inCaCaC verbs:

> **il-xaTT máalah maa yingára.**
> 'His hand-writing is illegible.'

> **dhayláyn yin9írif áSilhum bi mujárrad lahjáthum.**
> 'Their origin is obvious simply from their accent.'
> (lit. 'Them is-known their origin by merely their accent.')

> **haay múshkila maa bitinHáll bi suhúula.**
> 'This is a problem which will not be solved easily.'

> **maa tinghílib ínta!**
> 'You can't be bested, you!'
> (Said of someone wily or skilful, e.g. in haggling.)

> **inDammáyt fin-náadi gábil sitt siníin.**
> 'I joined the club six years ago.'

■ iCtaCaC verbs

These occur very commonly in Gulf Arabic. Generally speaking, they are intransitive or passive in meaning (like tiCaCCaC verbs).

Root type			
Strong	**ishtághal**	'to work'	**(sh-gh-l)**
Doubled	**ihtámm**	'to be interested, concerned (in something)'	**(h-m-m)**
Weak	**ishtáka**	'to complain'	**(sh-k-w)**
Hollow	**iHtáaj**	'to need'	**(H-w-j)**

Past tenses are formed as per the usual pattern, for example **ishtaghált**, **ishtághalat** 'I/she worked'; **ihtammáyti, ihtámmaw** 'You (f.)/they were interested'; **ishtakáytaw, ishtákaw** 'You (pl.)/they complained'; and **iHtíjt, iHtáajat** 'I/she needed'. Forms on the pattern **iHtaajáyt** 'I needed' are also heard, but these are considered very colloquial. Imperfect patterns are detailed below:

ashtághil	**ahtámm**	**ashtáki**	**aHtáaj**
tishtághil	**tihtámm**	**tishtáki**	**tiHtáaj**
tishtaghlíin	**tihtammíin**	**tishtakíin**	**tiHtaajíin**
yishtághil	**yihtámm**	**yishtáki**	**yiHtáaj**
etc.	etc.	etc.	etc.

The imperfect stem vowel pattern is thus **a-i** in strong and weak roots, while doubled and hollow roots behave like inCaCaC verbs, retaining **a** or **aa**: compare **yihtámm/yinHáll** and **yiHtáaj/yinsháal**.

Imperatives:

ishtághil/i/u!	'Work!'	**ihtámm/i/u!**	'Be interested!'
ishták/i/u!	'Complain!'	**iHtáaj/i/u!**	'Need!'

Note the lack of a final vowel in the masculine imperative of weak verbs, which we also noted for all other derived themes (see Unit Fourteen).

Participles:

Active:	**mishtághil**	**mihtámm**	**mishtáki**	**miHtáaj**
Passive:	**mishtághal**	**mihtámm**	**mishtáka**	**miHtáaj**

Verbal noun on the pattern iCtiCaaC:

ishtigháal	**ihtimáam**	**ishtikáa**	**iHtiyáaj**

Again, the verbal noun of the corresponding simple verb is often used instead of iCtiCaaC, for example **shughl** 'work', **shákwa** 'complaint' and **Háaja** 'need'.

There are a few special cases of iCtaCaC verbs – those that have **w**, **y** or **'** initial root consonant. The initial root consonant in these verbs is assimilated to the -t- infix, thus **ittájah** 'to go; direct oneself' instead of **iwtájah** (root **w-j-h**) and **ittáxadh** 'take for oneself' instead of **i'táxadh** (root **'-x-dh**).

Another small group of verbs, those that have an 'emphatic' consonant (**S**, **T**, **D**, **DH**) in C₁ position, cause the alteration of the infix -t- to -T-. Thus one finds **iDTárr** 'to force, oblige' (root **D-r-r**) instead of **iDtárr**. In all other ways, these two special groups of iCtaCaC verbs behave normally.

Here are some examples of the use of iCtaCaC verbs:

- **shínhu shúghlik?**
- **ashtághil dráywil fi shárikat taSdíir in-nifT.**
- 'What's your job?'
- 'I work as a driver for the Oil-exporting Company.'

maa 9índi ihtimáam bi hal-áshya.
'I've no interest in these things.'

ir-rayyáal illi iHna miHtaajíin lih muu mawjúud.
'The man we need isn't here.'

háadhi hiyya l-mishtáka 9aláyha.
'This is the woman who's been complained about.'

xudh iT-Taríig il-mittíjih min il-jinúub íla sh-shimáal.
'Take the road that leads from south to north.'

■ istaCCaC verbs

These verbs, in which an **ista-** prefix is added to the root consonants, are of frequent occurrence in Gulf Arabic, for example:

Root type

Strong	ista9mált/istá9malat	'I/she used'	(9-m-l)
Doubled	istaHaqqáyt/istaHáqqat	'I/she deserved'	(H-q-q)
Weak	istaghnáyt/istághnat	'I/she did without'	(gh-n-y)
Hollow	istafádt/istafáadat	'I/she benefited'	(f-y-d)

An alternative to **istafádt** is **istafaadáyt**.

Imperfect forms:

astá9mil	**astaHíqq**	**astághni**	**astafíid**
tistá9mil	**tistaHíqq**	**tistághni**	**tistafíid**
tista9milíin	**tistaHiqqíin**	**tistaghníin**	**tistafiidíin**
yistá9mil	**yistaHíqq**	**yistághni**	**yistafíid**
etc.	etc.	etc.	etc.

Note that the strong and weak root types form their imperfects in exactly the same way as iCtaCaC verbs, namely with an **a-i** stem vowel pattern. The doubled and hollow verbs behave in the same way as aCCaC verbs – they have an **i** or **ii** stem vowel.

Participles:

Active:	**mistá9mil**	**mistaHíqq**	**mistághni**	**mistafíid**
Passive:	**mistá9mal**	**mistaHáqq**	**mistághna**	**mistafáad**

Imperatives:

istá9mil/i/u!	'Use!'
istaHíqq/i/u!'	'Deserve!'
istághni (m./f.)/u!	'Do without!'
istafíid/i/u!	'Benefit!'

The verbal noun is of the form istiCCaaC (istiCaaCa for hollow verbs; compare the final **-a** of the verbal noun of hollow aCCaC verbs):

isti9máal	**istiHqáaq**	**istighnáa**	**istifáada**

Here are some examples of use:

kínna na9Tíihum bayzáat yistafiidúun mínha.
'We used to give them money, which they found useful.'

fii áshya niHtáaj líha maa nígdar nistághni 9ánha.
'There are things we need that we can't do without.'

Note that, in all the verb types described in this chapter, the Omani forms follow exactly the same principles as for the other Omani verbs illustrated in earlier units, namely the lack of a final **-n** in the 2nd feminine singular and 2nd and 3rd masculine plural forms, and the existence of feminine plural forms in the 2nd and 3rd persons that end in **-an**.

Exercise 16.1

Look at the two examples below, in which active verbs are passivised in different ways: through the use of the **ti-** prefix if they are CaCCaC verbs, and through the use of the **in-** prefix if they are simple CvCaC verbs:

- ígra illi maktúub 9ála hal-wáraga!
→ - illi maktúub maa yingára!
- 'Read what's written on this paper!'
- 'What's written is illegible!'

- baTTált id-daríisha?
→ - la, had-daríisha maa yitbáTTal!
- 'Have you opened the window?'
- 'No, this window can't be opened!'

Make similar replies to the commands and questions in the exercise below, choosing the correct passive form:

1   – kisárt il-glaasáat, muu chidhíi?
→ – la, _____

2   – rakkábt it-tayráat il-jadíida?
→ – la, _____

3   – shiil dhiich il-Hijáara!
→ – _____

4   – waddáyt it-taqríir fi hal-búghsha, muu chidhíi?
→ – la, _____

5   – xáfDu as9áarkum shway, arjúukum!
→ – la, _____

6   – sh-rá'yik fil-ákil il-inglíizi?
→ – _____

7   – bándi l-baab min fáDlich!
→ – _____

8   – haay maay shurb, muu chidhíi?
→ – la, _____

9   – gidárt tismá9hum min ba9íid?
→ – la, _____

10 – gháyyaraw 9aadáathum 9ála máda z-zamáan, muu chidhíi?
→ – la, _____

Now translate the sentences into English.

Exercise 16.2

In the example below, a verb phrase (underlined) has been replaced by an equivalent expression that uses a verbal noun:

daráyt *bi'ánnahum ihtámmaw* **bil-lugháat.**
→ **daráyt bi ihtimáamhum bil-lugháat.**
'I knew that they were interested in languages.'
→ 'I knew about their interest in languages.'

In the sentences below, transform the underlined verb phrases into verbal nouns, making any other changes in the sentences that may be necessary:

1 aSárr 9ála 'an yiqáabil il-wazíir shaxSíyyan.

→ _____

2 yiHíbb yílqi l-muHaaDráat bil-lúgha l-9arabíyya.

→ _____

3 maa símHaw lii astá9mil il-aaláat maaláthum.

→ _____

4 illi iqtáraH muu ma9gúul fi rá'yi ána.

→ _____

5 láazim ticháyyik il-makíina gábil la tirákkib il-blaagát.

→ _____

Now translate the sentences into English.

Exercise 16.3

In the example below, direct speech has been put into its reported form:

'ta9allámt il-Hisáab min kint fil-mádrasa.'
→ **gáalat 'ínnaha ta9államat il-Hisáab min káanat fil-mádrasa.**
'I learnt arithmetic when I was at school.'
→ 'She said that she learnt arithmetic when she was at school.'

Put the following statements into reported form, and translate them:

1 'istafádt wáayid min had-dóora.'
→ gaal _____

2 'iHtíjna ila musáa9ada ázyad láakin maa HaSSalnáaha.'
→ gáalaw _____

3   'maa ágdar astághni 9an háadha l-kitáab.'
     → gáalat _____

4   'yoom íHna Sgháar, ihtammáyna wáayid bi jam9 iT-Tawáabi9.'
     → gáalaw _____

5   'tammáyt a9íish hash-shákil Tuul Hayáati.'
     → gaal _____

 Language point

16.2 Conditional sentences

■ 'Possible' conditions

'Possible' conditions are those where there is some real possibility of the stated condition being met, either in the present or future.

The conditional clause may be introduced by any of the particles **idha**, **lo**, **in chaan** or **ila** ('if'), and the verbs in both the conditional and resultative clauses are put in the appropriate tense:

idha yábbi iyíi wiyyáana, guul lih yixáabirni min gábil.
'If he wants to come with us, tell him to inform me beforehand.'

in chaan yiHaachíini bil-lúgha l-ingliizíyya, maa áfham sh-yigúul.
'If he speaks to me in English, I don't understand what he says.'

ila yóoSil gábil is-sáa9a sítta, barúuH alaagíih fil-maTáar.
'If he arrives before six o'clock, I'll go and meet him at the airport.'

lo mTársha l-xaTT, la tigúul líha l-xábar.
'If she has sent the letter, don't tell her the news.'

ila timtini9 min it-tadxíin shway, bitshúuf SiHHatik titHássan.
'If you give up smoking for a bit, you'll see your health will improve.'

■ 'Hypothetical' conditions

What is meant here is the kind of condition in English sentences of the type 'If I were in your position (but I'm not), I'd …', that is, conditions that *could* be fulfilled, but are unlikely to be. In the Arabic equivalent of sentences of this type, past-tense verbs are used in both the conditional and resultative clauses:

lo sháafat maa sawwáyt, zí9lat.
'If she saw what you've done, she'd be angry.'

ídha 9índi thalaathíin alf dooláar, ishtaráyt sayyáara jadíida.
'If I had 30,000 dollars, I'd buy a new car.'

in chaan Haacháani bi hal-láhja, Taggáytah Tagg.
'If he spoke to me in that tone of voice, I'd give him a beating.'

■ 'Hypothetical' conditions in the past

We are dealing here with the Arabic equivalent of the English 'If I had seen him, I would have ...', that is, conditions that it is truly impossible to fulfil because they refer to a hypothetical past. In Gulf Arabic, past tenses are again used, but the particle **chaan** is inserted before the resultative clause:

ídha yiit fil-waqt il-mináasib, chaan shift shay yi9íjbik.
'If you'd come at the appropriate time, you'd have seen something that would've pleased you.'

Note that, in this example, only the *main* verb of the resultative clause is in the past tense, while the verb in the relative clause stays in the imperfect.

lo káanat 9indi fíkra bi hal-mawDúu9, chaan gilt lich.
'If I'd had an idea about that topic, I'd have told you (f.).'

in chaan ishtákaw 9aláyh 9ind ish-shúrTa, chaan qibDaw 9aláyh.
'If they'd complained about him to the police, they'd have arrested him.'

ila gidárt óoSil gáblik, chaan HaDDárt lik Háfla.
'If I'd been able to arrive before you, I'd have prepared a party for you.'

■ 'Unless'

The Arabic equivalent is **ílla ídha** ('except if'):

batímm ashtághil ílla ídha tifanníshni.
'I'll carry on working unless you sack me.'

■ 'Even if'

The phrase **Hátta lo** is used:

Hátta lo tifanníshni, batímm ashtághil.
'Even if you sack me, I'll carry on working.'

Exercise 16.4

Translate into Arabic the resultative clause in the following conditional
sentences:

lo káanat 9índi I-fúrSa, chaan ...
If I'd had the chance, I'd've ...

1 ... visited Cairo.

2 ... learnt to drive.

3 ... worked as a teacher.

4 ... bought a restaurant.

5 ... got married at 20.

6 ... learnt to swim.

ídha yaak il-Hiin ...
If he came to you now, ...

7 ... would you tell him the truth?

8 ... would you lend him what he asked for?

9 ... would you teach him to read Arabic?

10 ... would you introduce him to the boss?

11 ... would you give him a job?

12 ... would you help him in his studies?

Translate into Arabic the conditional clause in these sentences:

... ya9Tíik iyyáah.
... he'll give it to you.

13 If you ask him for it ...

14 If you inform him now ...

15 If you use it correctly ...

16 If you accept his conditions ...

17 If you send him the money …
18 If you give up smoking …

Dialogue 16.1

(Audio 1; 31)

Translate the two short conversations below, in which two young
women describe their jobs.

A kínti tishtaghlíin áwwal fil-maTáar?
B ay. Saar li ya9ni sána káamla fil-maTáar … u fil-bank sána u
 cham min sháhar. 9aad kint áwwal ashtághil maashíin obráytir u
 ba9adáyn taghayyárt Hagg il-kambyúutar, u bá9ad il-kambyúutar
 Hagg il-kawnts táHat … yá9ni Hagg dhayláyn illi yifatHúun
 Hisaabáat u illi yidaxlúun chaykáat fi Hsaabáathum … hal-loon,
 háadhi shúghlati ána.[†]

[†] Note that technical English words such as 'computer', 'machine operator' or
'accounts' are freely borrowed into everyday Gulf speech.

A yi9íjbich il-má9had ihni?
B wállah kint ábbi arúuH il-jáami9a ádris Huqúuq …
A laysh maa ríHti?
B káanat iDH-DHurúuf Sá9ba shwáyya áwwal … iDTurráyt
 ashtághil, u ishtaghált fi mustáshfa l-irsaalíyya l-amriikíyya …
 ishtaghált wállah sanatáyn bas …
A Ishtaghálti shínhu?
B káatiba … ishtaghált ihnáak sanatáyn u maa ádri kaan it-taym
 iS-SubH u bá9ad iDH-DHúhur, fa gáalat úmmi yá9ni záHma tyiin
 iS-SubH u bá9ad iDH-DHúhur, fa adáwwir lii shúghla tháanya.
 bas híyya aSárrat 9ála 'an ádxal il-má9had Hátta aSíir mudárrisa.[†]

[†] Note that **taym** (English 'time') means 'office hours'; more formally, **dawáam**.

Proverbs and sayings

il-qird fi 9ayn úmmah ghazáal.
'The monkey is a gazelle in the eye of his mother.'
(i.e. 'Beauty is in the eye of the beholder.')

wild il-chalb chalb míthlah.
'The son of a dog is a dog like him.'
(i.e. 'Like father like son.')

il-fluus tyíib il-9arúus.
'Money brings the bride.'
(i.e. 'Money talks.')

 Vocabulary

adáar	to run; manage	**imtána9/**	to abstain
álgha/yílghi	to cancel	**yimtíni9 (min)**	(from)
álqa/yílqi	to give	**inchább/**	to go away
muHáaDra*	(a lecture)	**yinchább**	(vulg.)
arjúu + pron.	I ask; I beg …	**inDámm/**	to join;
aSárr/yiSírr	to insist	**yinDámm (íla)**	be joined (to)
áSil/uSúul	origin; principle	**iqtáraH/yiqtáriH**	to suggest
á9lan/yí9lin	to announce	**irsaalíyya***	mission
chalb/chiláab	dog	**istafáad/**	to benefit (from)
dáwwar/	to look for	**yistafíid (min)**	
yidáwwir		**istághna/**	to do without
diráasa*(aat)	study (v. n.)	**yistághni (9an)**	
dooláar(aat)	dollar	**istaHáqq/**	to deserve
dóora*(aat)	course	**yistaHiqq**	
	(e.g. of training)	**istaqáam/**	to live on
fa	then; so	**yistaqíim (9ála)**	(e.g. a type of
fúrSa*(aat)	opportunity		food)
ghazáal	gazelle	**istá9mal/**	to use
Háaja*(aat)	need	**yistá9mil**	
HáDDar/	to make ready	**ishtáka/yishtáki**	to complain
yiHáDDir	(something)	**ishtára/yishtíri**	to buy
Hájar/Hijáara*	stone	**ittájah/yittájih**	to direct
Haqq/Huqúuq	right; law		oneself
Hayáa*	life	**ittáxadh/**	to take for
iDTúrr/yiDTárr	to be obliged,	**yittáxidh**	oneself
	forced	**jíma9/yíjma9/**	to collect
ihtámm/	to be interested	**jam9**	
yihtámm (bi)	(in)	**jinúub**	south
iHtáaj/	to need	**kaláam**	speech; talk
yiHtáaj (íla)		**kamáa yájib**	correctly, as it
			should be

máda in **9ála** **máda z-zamáan**	with the passage of time	**shimáal**	north
makíina*/ **makáayin**	machine; engine	**shimáali**	northern; left (side)
ma9gúul	reasonable	**taym**	office; shift hours
má9had/ **ma9áahid**	institute; college	**tiHássan/** **yitHássan**	to improve
mináasib	appropriate; convenient	**wájab/yájib/** **wujúub**	to be incumbent
mína9/yímna9/ **man9**	to prevent	**záHma***	chaos; bother; trouble
muqtáraH(aat)	suggestion	**9aash/yi9íish/** **9aysh**	to live
qábad/yíqbaD/ **qabD**	to arrest; get hold of	**9árraf/yi9árrif**	to acquaint someone with (**9ála**) someone; introduce someone to someone
qird/qurúud	monkey		
siyáaqa*	driving		
SíHHa*	health		
shákwa/ **shakáawi**	complaint	**9ayn** (f.)/**9uyúun**	eye

Cultural point

Tribes

One of the most important forms of social organisation in the Gulf States and Saudi Arabia is the **gabíila** (pl. **gabáayil**) or 'tribe'. This is a large, sometimes enormous, set of related male descent lines. Generally, the tribe is known by the term **Bani X**, where **Bani** means 'the sons of …' and the individual named as 'X' is the so-called **jadd**, literally 'progenitor' (the word also means 'grandfather') of the tribe, a figure who often reaches far back into the mists of (a sometimes mythical) history. Other technical terms in use are **bayt**, literally 'tent' or 'house', and **faxdh**, literally 'thigh', both used to designate a single descent group smaller than the **gabíila** and forming one part of it. The ruling families of the Gulf have generally adopted the term **aal** 'family', (written Āl in their transliterated names) to refer to themselves, as in the Āl Thani of Qatar, the Āl Khalifa of Bahrain, the Āl Nahayan of Abu Dhabi and the Āl Maktoum of Dubai, the latter two families ultimately descending from the same large south Arabian tribe the Bani Yas. The Āl Sabah of

Kuwait and the Āl Khalifa of Bahrain are also distantly related, both ultimately being offshoots of the central Najdi tribe, the Bani 9utub.

The head of a tribe, or of one of its descent groups, was originally an elected senior member of it, and termed **shayx** (pl. **shuyuux**), which means simply 'old man'. There was originally no assumption that the eldest son, or indeed any of the sons, of a tribal **shayx** would succeed automatically to his position on his death, since it was an elected one based on fitness for the job. This is still (at least theoretically) the case, although among Gulf ruling families it would be unheard of for the new ruler to be from outside one of the main royal descent lines. Nowadays, the term **shayx** itself has become an honorific routinely applied to any member of a ruling family who attains a certain age and holds any kind of public office, as well a title conferred on almost any senior member of any tribe.

Tribes are often thought of as a form of Bedouin social organisation, but this is by no means the case. They often contain descent lines that consider themselves 'Bedouin' and others that have long been 'sedentary' in lifestyle. An example is the large Duru9 tribe of north-western Oman. Bedouin tribes traditionally controlled a **díira** or tribal territory, within which they owned the wells and pasturelands and were in principle responsible for the safety of any visitor from outside the tribe. All of this has, of course, now disappeared with the establishment of central governments, but tribal politics can still be a highly sensitive issue in rural areas, and everywhere in the Gulf genealogy is a powerful element in social cohesion. In the burgeoning Gulf cities, people may still cling on, in the form of their names at least, to a tribal affiliation, but the tendency now is towards increasing intermarriage and the formation of nuclear families outside tribal descent lines, if not (as we will see in Unit Seventeen) across sectarian ones.

 Reading Arabic

Part of the dawn call to prayer is the statement, in Classical Arabic:

aS-Saláatu xáyrun min an-nawm
'Prayer is better than sleep'

which, in written form is:

الصلاة خير من النوم

Statements and adages of this kind are frequently encountered on signs
on roadsides, public buildings such as schools and hospitals, and in
public parks. A common one to encourage people not to drop litter in
public parks is:

النظافة من الايمان

Can you read it? It is the equivalent to the English saying 'Cleanliness
is next to godliness' and literally says 'cleanliness (**niDHáafa**) is of
(religious) faith (**iimáan**)'. Notice how, in this adage as well as in the
quotation from the dawn call to prayer, the nouns in such general
statements always have the definite article **al-** 'the' prefixed to them;
one says 'the prayer is better than the sleep', etc. Here is another,
from a banner hung outside a health centre:

الوقاية خير من الشفاء

The structure of this is identical with the call to prayer: 'X is better than
Y'. Can you read it? It says: **al-wiqáaya xáyrun min ash-shifáa'** or
'prevention is better than cure'. Now have a look at the road sign below,
and see if you can work out the words of wisdom! The first word is **at-
ta'áxxur**, which means 'lateness'.

Unit Seventeen

In this unit you will learn about:

- quadriliteral verbs, i.e. verbs that have four instead of three root consonants
- how to say 'to wish/want' and 'to prefer'
- verbs with double objects, e.g. 'Give it to me!' or 'He gave me it'

Language point

17.1 **Quadriliteral verbs**

'Quadriliteral' means quite simply 'having four (as opposed to three) root consonants', and with these verbs we bring to a close our study of the Arabic verb system. Quadriliteral verbs are of the CaCCaC pattern, but are different from the CaCCaC verbs we studied in Unit Fourteen by virtue of the fact that the middle two consonants are not identical. Typical 'strong' quadriliterals are **tárjam** 'to translate', **xárbaT** 'to mix up; disarrange', **ghárbal** 'to confuse (someone)' and **kánsal** 'to cancel; abolish something'. From the point of view of the patterning of vowels and consonants, these verbs are exactly the same – CaCCaC – as verbs such as **rákkab** 'to fix' and **cháyyak** 'to check', in which there is a doubled consonant in the middle of the verb. Quadriliterals in fact behave exactly like **rákkab**, **cháyyak**, etc. in all respects:

Past tense		Imperfect	
tarjámt	'I translated'	atárjim	'I translate'
tarjámt	'You translated'	titárjim	'You translate'
tarjámti	'You (f.) translated'	titarjimíin	'You (f.) translate'
etc.		etc.	

Imperatives and participles are also formed as for 'ordinary' CaCCaC verbs, for example:

tárjim/i/u!   'Translate!'

mutárjim   'translator'   mutárjam   'translated'

Compare these forms with those from the 'ordinary' CaCCaC verb wállad 'to generate':

muwállid   'generator'   muwállad   'generated'

Verbal noun patterns, however, are a little more varied in the quadriliteral verb than in ordinary CaCCaC verbs. They are usually of the type CaCCvCa, for example **tárjama** 'translation' and **xárbuTa** 'mix-up; confusion', but other types occur, for example **ghirbáal** 'confusion'. Where the verbal noun denotes the object produced by the action rather than the action itself, verbal noun plurals are possible, usually on the pattern CaCaaCiC or CaCaaCiiC: **taráajim** 'translations' and **xaraabíiT** 'nonsense; foul-ups'. As in the ordinary CaCCaC verb, hollow and weak verb stems occur. Hollow verbs have **w** or **y** as second consonant, for example **sáyTar** 'to control; dominate' and **sóolaf** 'to chat' (note that, in this last example, **oo** is written instead of **aw** since **oo** reflects more nearly the usual pronunciation). An example of a weak quadriliteral is **gáhwa** 'to give someone coffee', as in:

gahwóona u 9aTóona gadúu9 zayn.
'They gave us coffee and a nice morning snack.'

yaa 9áli, xudh haadhooláak u gahwíihum!
'Ali, take those people and give them coffee!'

One other kind of quadriliteral verb is the so-called reduplicative, in which the two syllables in the CaCCaC pattern are the same, for example **gáSgaS** 'to chop up into bits' and **gámgam** 'to nibble'. All of these verbs are conjugated in the same way as their equivalent 'ordinary' CaCCaC verbs.

Quadriliterals may be passivised or reflexivised by the prefixing of
ti-, as for other CaCCaC verbs, for example **xárbaT** 'to mix up', **tixárbaT**
'to get mixed up', **gáhwa** 'to give someone coffee' and **tigáhwa** 'to
take coffee (oneself)'. Some simple sentences illustrating quadriliterals
in use are given below:

tárjamaw il-maqáal min 9árabi íla inglíizi.
'They translated the article from Arabic into English.'

tarjámtah muhub SaHíiHa.
'His translation is incorrect.'
(Or, 'The translation of it is incorrect.')

gharbálna ghirbáal ams.
'He really got on our nerves yesterday.'

la tixallíih yishtághil brúuHah fil-wársha – akíid byitxárbaT.
'Don't let him work on his own in the workshop – he'll really get
himself into a mess.'

nitgáhwa kill yoom bá9ad maa yintíhi sh-shúghul.
'We have coffee every day after work is over.'

tammáyna nisóolif ila nuSS il-layl.
'We carried on chatting until midnight.'

giTá9tah li múddat árba9 siníin u istáwat 9índi HárHasha.
'I gave it up (smoking) for four years, and I got a hoarse cough.'
(From **HárHash** 'to cough hoarsely'.)

na9Tíih lil-Hayaawíin yigamgimúun fiih.
'We give it (hay) to the animals for them to nibble on.'

il-láHam háadha maa yitgáSgaS.
'This meat can't be chopped into small pieces.'

 ## Exercise 17.1

Model Arabic sentences are given below. After each, cue words are
given that are to be substituted in the appropriate place in the sentence,
and that require other changes to be made. Look at the example:

atgáhwa kill yoom gábil la arúuH ish-shúghul.
'I have coffee every day before I go to work.' (Cue: you (m.).)
→ **titgáhwa kill yoom gábil la truuH ish-shúghul.**

1 she	5 you (pl.)
2 we	6 the labourers
3 Ali	7 the boss
4 they	8 my mother

idha tixallíih yisáwwi háadha brúuHah, byitghárbal.
'If you let him do this by himself, he'll get confused.'

9 them	13 your secretary (f.)
10 her	14 the mechanic
11 faaTma	15 these children
12 the driver	16 us

Hátta lo 9aTáani qaamúus, chaan maa gidárt atárjim hal-maqáal.
'Even if he had given me a dictionary, I wouldn't have been able to translate this article.'

17 you (f.)	21 the girl
18 us	22 my colleague
19 the students	23 the clerk
20 you (pl.)	24 you (m.)

Exercise 17.2

Look at the sentence below:

idha tisóolif wiyyáah yistáanis li'ánnah yiHibb is-sawáalif.
'If you *chat* with him he'll be happy because he likes *chatting*.'
(**sawáalif** is the plural of the verbal noun **sáalfa** from **sóolaf** 'to chat')

Substitute in this sentence appropriate verbs and verbal nouns using the following cues:

1 play – playing	5 talk – talking
2 joke – joking (**nákkat** 'to joke')	6 gamble – gambling
3 stroll – strolling	(**qáamar** 'to gamble')
4 fish – fishing	7 sing – singing

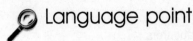 Language point

17.2 'To wish/want' and 'to prefer'

We have seen that the verb **bágha** 'to want' can be used to translate the English 'I want to ...' as well as 'I want you/him/her, etc. to ...'. There are a number of other ways of expressing wishes and wants:

■ **Habb** + verb

This construction is similar to the one involving **bágha** + verb:

> **aHíbb arúuH is-síinama.**
> 'I like going to the cinema.'
> Or 'I would like to go to the cinema.'

With object pronoun:

> **aHíbbik trúuH is-síinama.**
> 'I would like you to go to the cinema.'

■ **9ájab** + pronoun + verb

Here, the verb **9ájab** 'to please' is used as an impersonal verb to form phrases meaning literally 'It pleases me/you/him, etc. to ...':

> **yi9jíbni arúuH is-síinama.**
> 'I like going to the cinema' or 'I would like ....'

> **yi9jíbni trúuH is-síinama.**
> 'I would like *you* to go to the cinema.'

■ **widd** + possessive adj. + verb

In this third type of construction, **widd**, which is a noun meaning 'wish; desire', has a possessive adjective suffixed to it: 'my/your/his, etc. desire (is) ...':

> **wíddi arúuH is-síinama.**
> 'I would like to go to the cinema.'

> **wíddik arúuH is-síinama?**
> 'Would you like *me* to ...?' (lit. 'Is it your wish I go ...?')

The construction involving **widd** is always interpreted as a specific statement of 'desire' rather than a general statement of 'like' – it means

'I/you, etc. would like to …' rather than 'I/you, etc. like …', in contrast to the constructions involving **Habb** and **9ájab**, which can mean either, depending on context. Preference can be conveyed by any of these expressions when used with **áHsan** 'better' or **ákthar** 'more':

aHíbb arúuH is-síinama áHsan min il-mubáara.
'I'd rather go to the cinema than the match.'

maa tiHíbbah yirúuH is-síinama áHsan min il-mubáara?
'Wouldn't you rather he went to the cinema than to the match?'

wíddik ysaafrúun áHsan min yitimmúun fil-bayt?
'Would you prefer them to travel than to stay at home?'

yi9jíbni áTbax ákthar min anáDHDHif il-bayt.
'I prefer cooking to cleaning the house.'

Another way of expressing preference involves the use of the verb **fáDDal … min**:

afáDDil áTbax min 'an anáDHDHif il-bayt.
'I prefer cooking to cleaning the house.'

Or

afáDDil iT-Tabx min tanDHíif il-bayt.

It is also possible to use this construction with object pronouns:

nifáDDilkum tyiibúun janaTáatkum ihni min tixallúunha fil-fúnduq.
'We prefer you to bring your bags here than leave them in the hotel.'

Exercise 17.3

Taking the sentence

ána wíddi arúuH il-jáami9a u ádris Huqúuq
'I'd like to go to university and study law'

substitute the cue words below into the sentence making any necessary changes. This is a 'progressive substitution' drill: use the sentence that results from the first substitution as the input to the second, and so on, so progressively changing the sentence. Be careful – in this exercise the cue words are sometimes nouns, sometimes verbs, sometimes pronouns!

1 híyya	5 húwwa	9 9ájab
2 húmma	6 hándisa	10 ínta
3 íHna	7 riyaaDiyáat	
4 Habb	8 il-lúgha l-9arabíyya	

The next case involves a dialogue:

- **yi9íjbik tishtághil fil-imaaráat?**
- **la, maa yi9jíbni. afáDDil ashtághil fil-kuwáyt.**
- 'Would you like to work in the Emirates?'
- 'No, I wouldn't. I'd rather work in Kuwait.'

Make appropriate substitutions and changes in this dialogue:

| 11 he | 13 they | 15 your father |
| 12 you (pl.) | 14 she | |

Now, for 'work in the Emirates – work in Kuwait' substitute:

16 work as a driver – work as a messenger

17 visit the Emirates – stay at home

18 eat in a restaurant – do without food

19 get up early – get up late

20 learn to ride a bike – learn to drive a car

 Language point

17.3 Verbs with double objects

The English sentences 'He gave me it', 'You showed it him' contain two object pronouns: 'me' and 'it' in the first case, 'it' and 'him' in the second. In both sentences 'it' is the direct object of the verb – it refers to the thing that undergoes the action of the verb. The pronouns 'me' and 'him' in these sentences, on the other hand, are the so-called 'indirect objects', that is, the beneficiaries of the action. In Arabic there are a number of verbs that can have both direct and indirect objects. The commonest of these, which we have already met, is **9áTa** 'to give'. Study the examples below:

9áTni iyyáaha!   **9aTóoch iyyáahum.**
'Give it to me!'   'They gave them to you (f.).'

Notice that, in Arabic, it is the *indirect* object pronoun that is suffixed
to the verb, while the direct object pronoun is suffixed to a 'carrier'
preposition **iyya-**, whose sole function is to 'carry' that pronoun. Quite
a large number of verbs can be used in constructions of this type. Here
are some examples:

haay hum iS-Súwar illi rawwáytich iyyáahum min gábil.
'These are the pictures that I showed you (f.) before.'

lo ish-sharíiTa ma9áay sammá9tik iyyáaha.
'If I had the tape with me I'd let you hear it.'

waysh sawwáyt fi has-sayyáara? xarrábtha iyyáana!
'What have you done to this car? You've ruined it for us!'

**iT-Tiráaz háadha, káanaw yilabsúunhum iyyáah ayyáam
zamáan.**
'This type of dress here, they used to dress them in it in the old
days.'

Exercise 17.4

háadhi hi S-Súura íli rawwáytna iyyáaha is-subúu9 il-máaDi?
'Is this the *picture* that *you showed us* last week?

Substitute and change as necessary:

1 Is this the *book* _____ ?
2 _____ *they* _____ ?
3 _____ *tape* _____ ?
4 _____ *gave her* _____ ?
5 _____ *made her listen to* _____ ?
6 _____ *you* _____ ?

Exercise 17.5

Translate into Arabic:

1 Don't give it (f.) to her!   4 Don't let her hear her!
2 Don't show them to us!   5 Don't give them to him!
3 Don't ruin it (m.) for me!   6 Don't show me it (m.)!

Dialogue 17.1

Below is a short dialogue on the effects on children of watching TV.
Translate into English, and then answer the comprehension questions
in Arabic.

The effects of TV on children (Audio 1; 32)

A yiguulúun yáahil fállat rúuHah min is-sáTaH lil-arD yiqállid rayyáal
  gúwi sháafah fit-tilifizyúun.
B ay, muqállid istiif, hu.†
A laysh yisawwúun chidhíi l-yiháal?
B iT-Tífil maa yífham. maa tshuuf Sbay ílla yitáabi9 hal-musálsal.
  ba9ad hu yi9tábir náfsah stiif u yinúTT min bayt li bayt u yiTíiH ...
A sh-áHsan barnáamij bin-nísba lich il-Hiin?
B a'áyyid il-baráamij il-9ilmíyya máthalan. il-Hiin yixallúun kil subúu9
  'is-sána l-úula if Hayáat iT-Tífil' háadha yá9ni kíllish zayn.
  mistafíid ya9ni. tiTáali9 afláam fit-tilivizyúun?
A la. fiih afláam fit-tilifizyúun fíiha manáaDHir xalláa9a maa tíSlaH.
  bint bas fíiha Sadríyya u haaf ya9ni shay Haráam fil-isláam.
  tháani shay idha ish-shabáab shaaf hash-shay yá9ni láazim hu
  byisáwwi múnkar.

Questions:
1 Sáarat Háaditha axíiran. shínhu Saar?
2 shínhu sábab hal-Háaditha?
3 shloon il-baráamij illi ti'áyyidha il-muHádditha B.?
4 shloon ti'áththir manáaDHir xalláa9a fi sh-shabáab, fi ra'y
  il-muHáddith A?

---

† Note that stiif is a reference to Steve Austin, the 'Bionic Man'.

Proverbs and sayings

márratin Hálwa márratin murr.
'One time sweet, one time bitter.'
(i.e. 'You have to take the rough with the smooth.')

SáaHib il-Háaja á9ma la yiríid ílla qaDáaha.
'He who needs something is blind to all else until he has his need
fulfilled.' (Self-explanatory!)

Vocabulary

áamin	safe; secure	**i9tábar/yi9tábir**	to consider
akíid	certain; sure	**jabáan/jubanáa**	coward
aráad/yiríid	to want	**lábbas/yilábbis**	to dress
'áththar/	to have an		(someone)
yi'áththir (fi)	effect (on)	**maal/amwáal**	goods; money
axíiran	recently	**múnkar(aat)**	atrocity; bad act
'áyyad/yi'áyyid	to support;	**musálsal**	serial (TV, radio,
	favour		etc.)
dall/yidíll/daláal	to indicate;	**mutárjim(iin)**	translator
	show	**muwállid**	generator
fáDDal/yifáDDil	to prefer		(electric)
gadúu9	morning snack	**nákkat/yinákkit**	to joke
gáhwa (v.)/	to give someone	**naTT/yinúTT**	to jump
yigáhwi	coffee	**qáamar/yiqáamir**	to gamble
gámgam/	to nibble	**qaamúus/**	dictionary
yigámgim		**qawaamíis**	
ghárbal/	to confuse;	**qaDáa**	execution;
yighárbil/	upset		termination
ghirbáal		**qállad/yiqállid**	to imitate; copy
haaf	shorts	**riDa/yírDa/ríDa**	to agree;
hándisa*	engineering;		consent
	geometry	**riyaaDiyáat**	mathematics
Háarab/yiHáarib	to fight; make	**sáalfa*/sawáalif**	conversation;
	war		chat
Hajj/yiHíjj/Hajj	to go on the	**sámma9/**	to make
	pilgrimage	**yisámmi9**	(someone) hear
Hayawáan/	animal	**sáyTar/yisáyTir/**	to dominate;
Hayaawíin		**sáyTara* (9ala)**	control
HárHash/	to cough	**sóolaf/yisóolif**	to chat
yiHárHish	hoarsely	**SáaHib/aSHáab**	owner;
Húkum	power;		possessor
	judgement	**Sadríyya***	bra
intáha/yintíhi	to come to an	**Sbay(aan)**	lad; boy
	end	**SílaH/yíSlaH/**	to be proper,
istáanas/	to be happy,	**SaláaH**	right
yistáanis	content	**shabáab**	youth
istáslam/	to surrender		(in general)
yistáslim		**sharíiTa*/**	tape recording
istáwa/yistáwi	to happen;	**sharáa'iT**	
	become		

shijáa9a*	bravery	**Táala9/yiTáali9**	to watch; look at
táaba9/yitáabi9	to follow		
tárjam/yitárjim	to translate	**Tiráaz**	type; style; fashion
tárjama*/ taráajim	translation		
tigáhwa/ yitgáhwa	to have coffee	**wársha*(aat)**	workshop
		widd + poss. adj.	to want
tighárbal/ yitghárbal	to get confused, mixed up	**xaan/yixúun/ xiyáana***	to betray
timáshsha/ yitmáshsha	to stroll	**xalláa9**	shameless; depraved
tináazal/ titnáazal (9an)	to abdicate; relinquish control of	**xárbaT/yixárbiT**	to confuse; mix up (something)
tiwáffa/yitwáffa	to pass away; die	**xárrab/yixárrib**	to ruin
tixárbaT/ yitxárbaT	to get mixed up	**9áadil**	just; fair
		9ílmi	scientific

 Cultural point

Religion, sect and ethnicity

We saw in Unit Sixteen that tribal affiliation is an important element in the make-up of many Gulf Arabs. Just as important, and perhaps more sensitive, is religious affiliation and ethnic origin. Probably more than 99 per cent of Gulf Arabs are Muslims. But, within Islam, as within Christianity and Judaism, there are sects. The majority of Gulf Arabs, like the majority of Arabs in general, are orthodox Muslims, knows as Sunnis (the word is derived from the **sunna** of the Prophet Muhammad, which means his 'practice' or 'custom' and 'Sunni' means a person who follows it). But the largest non-orthodox sects, the so-called Shi'a, are also quite numerous in many regions of the Gulf, in Bahrain and eastern Saudi Arabia in particular. The Arabic word **shii9a** means 'party' and is short for **shii9at 9ali** 'the party of 'Ali'. 'Ali was the fourth Caliph (that is, 'leader of the Muslim community'), who was also the cousin and brother-in-law of the Prophet. The Shi'a are so-called because they believe that the Caliphate should, after 'Ali, have passed down through his family line; but Sunnis do not accept this. One of the sons of 'Ali, Hussein, was killed (the Shi'a would say 'martyred') at Kerbela, Iraq in AD 680, and has become the central figure in Shi'ite hagiography as a paragon of saintly virtue. Every year in the Muslim month of Muharram, in Bahrain and Iraq, and in a smaller way in some parts of the Lower Gulf where there are also Shi'a communities, Hussein's death is commemorated in street processions that re-enact, with much chanting and breast-beating, the events of 14 centuries ago. There has always been a political edge to these public manifestations of religious fervour, because the Shi'a consider themselves to have been historically discriminated against, and the Muharram processions provide an annual opportunity for a public demonstration of group solidarity in the face of governments and ruling families that are exclusively Sunni.

   The Shi'a are a religious sect, but sect in the Gulf partly coincides with and partly crosscuts other elements of identity. It is sometimes claimed that the Gulf Shi'a are all ultimately of Iranian origin, neighbouring Iran having been, for the last 500 years or so, overwhelmingly Shi'a. But this is very far from the truth. While there are certainly groups of Shi'a in the Arabian Gulf States who are historically migrants from the other side of the Gulf (and known to Gulf Arabs as **9ájam** 'Persians'), the majority of the Shi'a on the Arab side of the Gulf are ethnically and linguistically Arabs. They are generically known (to themselves and to others) as **baHáarna**, the plural of **baHráani**, which, confusingly enough, originally meant 'Bahraini', even though communities of indigenous **baHáarna**, who are all Shi'a, and all speak Arabic as their first language, can be found in Kuwait, Qatar, eastern Saudi Arabia and the UAE as well as in Bahrain itself. The term is an ethno-historical one: the **baHáarna** consider themselves to have been the 'original' inhabitants of the coastal regions of the Arabian Gulf, and among the very earliest converts to Shi'ism, but, unlike the elements in the population that are descended from Bedouin stock and originally came from central Arabia (known locally, and equally confusingly, as **9árab** 'Arabs'), they are not tribalised, and have traditionally led an agriculture-based, non-belligerent lifestyle in small villages.

   In Saudi Arabia, the doctrine of Wahhabism holds sway – in essence a puristic form of Sunni Islam that regards the Qur'an and the Sunna of the Prophet as the only basis for the constitution of the state. The Muharram processions of the Shi'a (of whom there are large numbers in Saudi Arabia's eastern province) in particular are an anathema and are banned. In Oman, the majority of the populations are of the Ibadi sect, again traditionally a simple, somewhat Calvinistic, ascetic form of Islam.

From this kaleidoscopic mix of tribal, religious and ethnic affiliations radiate the underlying 'fault lines' of Arab Gulf society, although this may not be initially apparent to the visitor. The particular nature of the mix differs from one Gulf country to another, as does the sensitivity of the issue. The Iranian Revolution of 1978, in which the credo of the new Iranian leaders was unabashedly religious and Shi'ite, came as a seismic shock to the Arab side, where there were significant Shi'ite minorities whose loyalty fell under suspicion. Part of the problem is a surprising degree of mutual ignorance on the part of these different religious and ethnic communities. Unsurprisingly, one of the main concerns of the governments of Arab Gulf States since that time has been to foster a greater degree of social and political inclusion, and a unified national, as opposed to a fragmented religious or ethnic consciousness.

 Reading Arabic

Script styles

Just as in English, in Arabic there is a wide variety of writing styles. Calligraphy is a valued art throughout the Arab World and, as you walk around the streets of any Gulf city, you will see evidence of this. Of course, these days, one does not have to be a trained artist to produce beautifully written Arabic: the font menus of Arabic word-processing software, just as in English, offer a huge variety of traditional and new styles to everyone. In this unit, we will look at the main traditional ones, and in the Reading Arabic sections of the remaining units of the book there will be further exemplification and reading practice in them.

In this unit, we will look at five of the main writing styles (there are others!) and how they render the phrase **bism illáahi r-raHmáan ir-raHíim** 'in the name of God the beneficent, the merciful', with which each chapter (**súura**) of the Qur'an begins, and which is often uttered (or written) by Muslims at the beginning of any job or activity (including such mundane matters as eating).

1 The style called **rúq9a** (رقعة) is the style that used to be taught as the standard 'copybook' hand in schools in the eastern part of the Arab World (though apparently no longer). It looks like this:

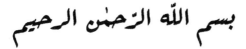

2 The **thúluth** (ثلث) style is mainly used in headings rather than for complete texts, and is strongly associated with religious writing. It looks like this:

3 The **násxi** (نسخي) style is the one most commonly encountered in ordinary printed Arabic texts of all kinds:

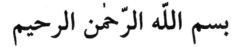

4 The **diiwáani** (ديواني) ('courtly') style was originally a Turkish invention, but has been adopted by the Arabs and is commonly seen on commemorative stones, plaques and in other contexts where a 'grand' effect is aimed at:

5 The **kúufi** (كوفي) ('Kufic', from the town of Kufa in Iraq) is the oldest style, and is characteristically square and chunky looking:

Unit Eighteen

In this unit you will learn about:

- diminutives, e.g. 'little boy', 'very small'
- uses of **ábu** and **umm**, 'father' and 'mother', to denote special characteristics and nicknames
- how to exclaim 'How big!', etc.
- 'so-and-so', i.e. 'a certain person'
- forms of personal address
- exhortations, e.g. 'God give you strength!', 'May your life be a long one!'

Language points

18.1 Diminutives

The word for 'a dog' in Arabic is **chalb**; 'a little dog' is **chuláyb**. This example illustrates that diminutives in Arabic are often formed not by adding an adjective meaning 'small', as in English, but by changing the internal vowel pattern of the word. The basic pattern of vowels and consonants for most diminutives is CuCayC(a). Thus:

wálad	'boy'	(w-l-d)	**wuláyd**	'little boy'
kuut	'fort'	(k-w-t)	**kuwáyt**	'little fort; Kuwait'
gál9a	'castle'	(g-l-9)	**guláy9a**	'little castle'

Nouns and adjectives having a long vowel in their basic form, for example **Saghíir** 'small', **jáasim** 'Jasim' (name), **kitáab** 'book' and also nouns having an **m** prefix, have a CuCayyiC or CuCayCiC diminutive form:

jáasim	'Jasim'	(j-s-m)	juwáisim	'little Jasim'
záayid	'Zayd'	(z-y-d)	zuwáyyid	'little Zayd'
Saghíir	'small'	(S-gh-r)	Sugháyyir	'very small'
kitáab	'book'	(k-t-b)	kutáyyib	'booklet'
márgad	'bed'	(r-g-d)	muráygid	'little bed'

Note that, with CaaCiC basic forms, **w** is the second consonant in the CuCayCiC diminutive. Plurals of all these diminutive forms are formed by suffixing **-aat**, for example **wulaydáat** 'little boys' and **kutaybáat** 'booklets'.

18.2 Uses of ábu and umm

ábu 'father' and **umm** 'mother' are used in Gulf Arabic to denote the possession of a special quality or characteristic. Thus, one can describe a man with a beard as **ábu líHya** 'father of a beard' or, more idiomatically in English, 'beardy'. A two-door (as opposed to a four-door) car can be called **sayyáara ábu daxlatáyn** 'father of two entrances'. Phrases with **ábu** are useful in distinguishing similar people or things:

- mínhu tá9ni, ir-rayyáal dhi?
- la, haadháak, ábu gáshma.
- 'Who d'you mean, this man?'
- 'No, that one, wearing glasses.'
(lit. 'father of spectacles')

umm is used in a similar way:

musájjila umm mikrufúun tháabit
'a tape recorder with a fixed microphone'.

It is a strange fact of grammar that **ábu** is normally used where the noun that *follows* it is grammatically feminine, and **umm** where it is masculine, without regard for whether the *possessor* is masculine or feminine. For example, some years ago there was a Kuwaiti pop song entitled **ábu 9uyúun fattáana** 'the one with the seductive eyes', regardless of the fact that the possessor of the eyes, to judge from the rest of the song, was clearly feminine! The reason for the use of **ábu** rather than **umm** is that **9ayn** 'eye' is grammatically feminine.

ábu and umm are also widely used in the Gulf to form names that are alternative modes of address to given names. A man who has a son called 9áli may be called ábu 9áli, and his mother umm 9áli. However, conventional nicknames formed with ábu are commonly used to denote anyone (whether or not he or she has children) with a certain name. The use of the nickname indicates a fairly informal, friendly style of address. Some of the commonest nicknames are:

Given name	Conventional nickname	Given name	Conventional nickname
mHámmad	ábu jáasim	ibraahíim	ábu xalíil
9íisa	ábu 9abdállah	9álawi	ábu háashim
yúusif	ábu ya9qúub	áHmad	ábu yúusif
9áli	ábu Husáyn	9ábdurraHmáan	ábu ráashid
Hásan or Husáyn	ábu 9áli		

18.3 'How big!', etc.

The Arabic equivalent of exclamations such as 'How big!' and 'How nice!' is formed by a prefix meaning 'what' – sh- or waysh – and the appropriate noun, 'bigness', 'beauty', etc. Such phrases are also an idiomatic way of saying 'a really big/nice ...'. Here are some examples:

bint sh-Haláawatha!
'What a pretty girl!' (Or, 'a really pretty girl')

maa yaaklúun ílla wájba wáHda u kil wáaHid dábbatah waysh kúburha!
'They only eat one meal a day and each one has got a really big belly!'

shuuf il-awáadim sh-kíthirhum yaw!
'Look at how many people have come!'

18.4 'So-and-so'

The Arabic for 'a certain person', 'Mr/Mrs So-and-so' is flaan(a):

yitHachchúun 9aláyna: 'flaan sáwwa chidhíi u fláana sáwwat chidháak'.

'They're gossiping about us: "Mr So-and-so did this and Mrs So-and-so did that".'

The phrase **flaan áadmi** (**áadmi** 'human') is similarly used:

ídha iyíik flaan áadmi u yigúul lik ...'
'If some fellow comes up to you and says ...'.

18.5 Forms of personal address

Gulf Arabic is very rich in address forms that show the speaker's status vis-à-vis the person addressed. These forms are freely used in everyday conversation, and it is as well for learners to be at least aware of their 'social' meaning, even if it would be inappropriate for them to use them themselves. The system described below is that used in Bahrain. The same or a similar one is used in all Gulf States.

When addressing a person judged to be of equal age and social rank, a speaker may frequently insert the phrase **yaa xuuy** 'O my brother' (to a man) and **yaa xti** 'O my sister' (to a woman) into what the speaker says. This is familiar without being disrespectful.

When addressing his or her immediate family, a speaker will use **yaa buuy** 'O my father', **yaa mmi** 'O my mother', **yaa 9ammi** 'O my (paternal) uncle', etc. and will get the reply **yaa wildi** 'O my son', **yaa binti** 'O my daughter', etc. However, there is a common convention of address that is often used instead of the above, which strikes the Westerner as strange. A man addressing an equal will often say to him **yaa xuuk** 'O your brother' or **yaa xwáyyik** 'O your little brother', to which the equal will reply with the same form of address; a woman will say to another of the same age **yaa xtich** 'O your sister' or **yaa xwáytich** 'O your little sister'. These forms cannot be translated literally – they are simply a convention of address. Note that the pronoun suffix always reflects the sex of the addressee, and the noun reflects the relationship (literal or metaphoric) of the speaker to him or her. Thus:

kamáa gilt lik min gábil, yaa xwáyyik, ána mub mwáfıg 9ála háadha.
'As I told you before, I don't agree to this.'
(male to male of equal age/status)

laysh sawwáyti chidhíi, yaa xúuch?
'Why have you done this?' (male to female of equal age/status)

A father or mother addressing a child will use the following forms:

yaa búuk   (father to son)   **yaa búuch**   (father to daughter)
yaa mmik   (mother to son)   **yaa mmich**   (mother to daughter)

Alternatively, the father may simply use the abbreviated form **yúbba**, and the mother **yúmma** to children of either sex. The reply from the child is **yaa búuy** 'O my father' or **yaa mmi** 'O my mother'.

Similar forms to the **yaa búuk**-type exist for other kinds of relationship, for example **yaa 9ámmik** 'O your uncle' (uncle to nephew) and **yaa 9ámmich** (uncle to niece). **yúbba**, **yúmma** and **yaa 9ámmik**, and to some extent **yaa búuk**, **yaa mmik**, etc., are used by extension as a means of address by any older to a younger person, especially when cajoling or 'pulling rank':

> **9aad la tsáwwi chidhíi, yúbba!**
> 'Now don't do that, will you!'
> (male to junior male)

> **9aTíini illi fı yádich, yaa 9ámmich!**
> 'Give me what's in your hand, now!'
> (male to junior female)

When a large group of people need to be greeted (for example on entering a room that is filled), the word **jimáa9a** 'community; group' is used:

> **is-saláam 9aláykum yaa jimáa9a!**
> 'Hello, everyone!'

> **yaa jimáa9a, ána ísmi …**
> 'My name, everyone, is …'
> (from the beginning of a radio play).

18.6 Exhortations

Normal Arabic conversation is liberally laced with exhortations of various kinds, which sound slightly odd when literally translated into English. These usages reflect a part of the cultural and religious framework within which the language exists, and with which it is essential to be at least passively familiar. Many set phrases involve invocations of **állah**, and are often part of a conventional exhortation–response formula. Here are some examples:

- **gúwwa!**
  (said to someone engaged in a hard physical or mental effort)
- **állah yigawwíik!**
- 'Strength!'
- 'God give *you* strength!'
- **il-Hámdu lilláah 9ala saláamtik!**
  (said to one returning safely from a voyage, or who has
  recovered from illness)
- **állah yisálmik!**
- 'Thanks be to God for your safety!'
- 'God save *you*!'
- **na9íiman!**
  (said to someone who has just had a bath, haircut, etc.)
- **állah yín9im 9aláyk!**
- 'May it be comfortable!'
- 'God bestow his comfort on *you*!'

There are many other phrases used on different occasions that are not
part of formulaic exhortation–response routines, some of which are
exemplified here. Note that the verb may be a past or imperfect verb,
but the meaning is always a future wish:

jaazáak állah xayr!
'May God reward you!'
(said to someone who has done one a favour, or any 'good
works')

aghnáak állah!
'May God make you rich!'
(said to someone engaged in any venture intended to increase
their material prosperity)

állah yhadáak/állah yihaddíik!
'May God guide you!'
(said to someone who is doing or thinking something the speaker
thinks is misguided)

állah yíHfaDHik!
'May God preserve you!'
(said as a general greeting to anyone, especially if not seen for
some time)

állah yighárbilik!
'May God confuse you!'
(a mild curse)

kárram állah wajh is-sáami9!
'May God honour the listener's face!'
(said after the mention of anything considered **9ayb** 'shame' or
Haráam 'prohibited', e.g. drinking alcohol, eating pork, loose
morals, certain parts of the body)

báyyaD állah wájhik!
'May God brighten your face!'
(said to the bringer of good news, or to someone who has done
the speaker a favour)

The oath **walláhi l-9aDHíim!** 'By the great God!' is also commonly
used in conversation. Some other useful phrases that do not involve
the use of **állah** are given below:

tíkram!
'Be honoured!'
(used in the same circumstances as **kárram állah wajh is-
sáami9**)

9úmrik ábqa!
'May your life be longer!'
(said after mention of someone's death, e.g. **háadha min sána
twáffat záynab – 9úmrik ábqa!** 'That was the year Zaynab died
– may your life be longer!')

Taal 9úmrik!
'May your life be a long one!'
(a general conversation-filler, often used when hesitating during
the telling of a story, e.g. **ána fi dhaak iz-záman, Taal 9úmrik,
yúmkin asáwwi sab9 sníin** 'At that time I'd be about – er –
maybe seven years old')

ál9an abúuh ha ... (noun)! or **ha ...** (noun) **ál9an abúuh!**
'I curse the father of this ...!'
(a phrase of exasperation, e.g. **hash-shúghul, ál9an abúuh!
maa niHáSSil min waráah fáyda!** 'We get no bloody benefit
from this job!' (lit. 'This work, I curse its father! We get no benefit
from behind it!'))

During the **9iid** 'feast', which follows the end of Ramadan – **9iid il-fiTr** – and that which follows the end of the rites of the pilgrimage – **9iid il-áD-Ha** – Arabs greet each other with the phrase **9iid mubáarak!** 'Blessed feast!', to which the reply is **kill 9aam wa íntum bi xayr!** 'May you be well with every passing year!' On any occasion of success, for example the passing of an examination or the buying of a new house, the greeting to the lucky person is **mabrúuk!** 'May it be blessed', to which the reply is **állah yibáarik fiik!**

Exercise 18.1

Below is an extract from the beginning of a radio programme in the series **9ála Taríiq il-fann** 'In the way of art', in which the comedian Jasim il-Khalaf tells the story of his early life. He is talking to an interviewer (whom he addresses **yaa xwayyik**) but addressing his radio audience through him. Read aloud and translate.

A Bahraini childhood

wállah, bidáyt Hayáati ána, yaa xwáyyik, fil-arba9iináat. kint Tífil Saghíir u 9úmri 9ála maa atdhákkar xams aw sitt isníin, alláahu á9lam. wállah, u kint mistáanis u ál9ab fil-faríig wíyya l-wulaydáat, wíyya xwáanna yá9ni, mistáanis u la 9índi bid-dínya bá9ad. maa shift yoom wáaHid ílla abúuy axádhni u waddáani l-mu9állim. il-mu9állim ílli waddáani yisammúunah bin Humúud. wa ittakált 9ála llah u riHt il-mu9állim ... wállah, tammáyt maa ádri, sána u nuSS lo sanatáyn. wállah xatámt il-qur'áan yá9ni. kaan 9índi aSdiqáa wáajid – naas ráaHaw, naas maa a9árfhum il-Hiin yá9ni. wállah, istaanást fil-mu9állim íji sanatáyn háadhi, u táali gaam abúuy u gaal binwaddíik il-mádrasa ... u shaalóoni min il-mu9állim u waddóoni l-mádrasa, il-mádrasa l-gharbíyya, Haalíyyan híyya mádrasat ábu bakr. u ga9ádt fil-mádrasa – Hattóoni áwwal shay fi áwwal Hadíiqa ... ay, wállah ... bá9ad múdda támmaw ysawwúun riwaayáat u masraHiyyáat fil-mádrasa, wállah ... u ba9D il-asáatidha yixallúunna yá9ni fit-tamthiilíyya ... wállah u Sírna iyyáahum. u 9ála maa atdhákkar yáHDur ir-riwaayáat il-marHúum ish-shayx A. bin I., wazíir il-ma9áarif ... u yáHDur il-ustáadh A. il-9. háadhi r-riwaayáat. wi nimáththil adwáar záyna, wil-ustáadh A. il-9., 9ógub maa nxálliS, ya9Tíina hadáaya ... atdhákkar min ba9D il-hadáaya ya9Tíina aghráash burtugáal, u ya9Tíina háadha maal hándisa ... maa ádri, nisáyt,

raaH 9ala báali, maa á9ruf waysh ísmah u dafáatir maal rásim uu
búghsha fíiha 9áshra rubbiyáat u júuti – tíkram – ábyaD maal
riyáaDa u haaf ázrag fiih shaxT ábyaD, ya9Tíina.

Notes:

- **alláahu á9lam** 'God knows' (lit. 'God knows better').
- **xwáanna** 'our brothers'. Here, as elsewhere, the speaker refers to himself in the plural.
- **la 9índì bid-dínya** ... 'I had nothing else in the world'.
- **maa shift ílla abuuy** ... 'I hardly knew what had happened before my father ... '.
- **mu9állìm** is a Qur'anic school teacher. An ordinary teacher is a **mudárris.**
- **ittákal** 'to put one's trust in' (root **w-k-l**, verb type iCtaCaC).
- **iyyáahum** is an alternative to **wiyyáahum.**
- **ba9D** 'some of' (see Unit Nineteen).
- **raaH 9ála báali** 'It's gone out of my mind.'

Exercise 18.2 (Audio 1; 33)

See if you can understand (and translate) the joke below. Note that
the phrase **fiik duud** 'You've a worm in you' is used to describe people
who can't keep still, who are forever running around.

kaan fii wáaHid báayig raaH yá9ni u gaam ríkab foog jidáar
yábghi yinuTT dáaxil. bas húwwa TaaH min foog ila táHat u
kássar kíllish jísmah. waddóoh il-mustáshfa. kíshaf 9alayh
id-dáxtar u kítab lih Hubúub bas, yá9ni maa HaTT lih dáwa
Hagg ryúulah. nzayn, gáalaw lih bas 'ruuH iS-Saydalíyya u xudh
had-dáwa.' 9aad raaH iS-Saydalíyya u 9aTóoh bas Hubúub.
gaal lihum 'waysh maktúub? hal-Hubúub maal shínhu?' gáalaw
lih 'maal duud!' gaal líhum 'háadhi Hubúub maal duud?! chayf
Hubúub maal duud?' gáalaw lih 'waysh darráana? ruuH ís'al
id-dáxtar.' gaam raaH iT-Tabíib yigúul lih 'il-Hiin jismi mitjárraH u
ta9Tíini Habb maal duud, maal báTin?' gaam id-dáxtar yigúul lih
'ay wállah! lo maa fiik duud chaan maa ríkábt foog!'

Notes:

- **ryúul** (or **rjúul**) pl. of **riil** (or **rijl**) 'foot; leg'. Like all parts of the body that come in pairs, **riil** is feminine gender. **rajáayil** is an alternative plural.

- **waysh darráana**? 'How should we know?' (lit. 'What has made us know?')
- **Tabíib** is the more 'formal' word for 'doctor' instead of the dialectal **dáxtar.**

Proverbs and sayings

biT-Tiib wíla bil-gháSub!
'By kindness or by force!'
(i.e. 'By hook or by crook!')

9árrha u guul márHala!
'Put a handle on it and call it a basket!'
(said disparagingly of a slipshod piece of work. **márHala** is a kind of large basket with handles made of palm branches. The verb **9árra** is derived from **9úrwa** 'handle')

Vocabulary

áadmi/awáadim	someone; a human being; (pl.) people	**fann/funúun**	art
		fattáan	seductive; mischievous
ághna/yíghni	to make (someone) rich	**flaan(a)**	So-and-so (i.e. unknown name)
án9am/yín9im (9ála)	to bestow favours (on)	**gál9a*(aat)**	castle; fort
báarak/yibáarik	to bless	**gáshma*(aat)**	spectacles
báTin/buTúun	stomach; guts	**gáwwa/yigáwwi**	to give (someone) strength
báyyaD/yibáyyiD	to brighten; lighten		
ba9D	some of	**gúwwa**	strength
chidháak	like that	**gháSub**	compulsion; coercion
dábba*(aat)	belly		
dárra/yidárri	to make (someone) know	**háda/yiháda**	to give (someone) guidance
dáxla*(aat)	opening; entrance	**HáDar/yáHDur/ HuDúur**	to attend; be present
id-dínya	the world (and its works)	**Hadíiqa***	kindergarten; park
door/adwáar	role; turn	**Haláawa***	sweetness; prettiness
duud	worms		

HífaDH/yíHfaDH/ HafáaDH	to keep; preserve	riwáaya*(aat)	drama
ittákal/yittákil (9ála)	to put one's trust (in)	riyáaDa*	sport
jáaza/yijáazi	to reward	rubbíya*(aat) or rabáabi	rupee (old currency = 100 fils)
jísim/ajsáam	body	Saydalíyya*(aat)	chemist's
kárram/yikárrim	to honour	shaxT/shuxúuT	stripe
kíthir	number; amount	táali	next; then; after
kúbur	size; age	tamthiiliyya* (aat)	play; drama
kuut	fort; castle	tijárraH/yitjárraH	to be hurt, injured
lá9an/ yíl9an/la9n	to curse	Taal/yiTúul/Tuul	to be long
líHya*/líHa	beard	Tabíib/aTibbáa	medical doctor
mabrúuk	blessed	tháabit	fixed; immovable
márgad/ maráagid	bed; sleeping place	wájba*(aat)	meal; repast
márHala*/ maráaHil	type of basket; phase (e.g. of a plan)	xátam/yáxtim/ xatm	to read the Qur'an from cover to cover
masraHíyya*(aat)	play	yúbba	address form: father to child
máththal/ yimáththil	to act; represent	yúmma	address form: mother to child
mikrufúun(aat)	microphone	záman	period; point in time
mubáarak	blessed	9aDHíim	great; enormous
musájjila*(aat)	tape recorder	9álam/yá9lam/ 9ilm	to know
mu9állim(iin)	Qur'an teacher	9amm/a9máam	paternal uncle
na9íiman	greeting for someone who has just had a bath, haircut, etc.	9árra/yi9árri	to put a handle on something
il-qur'áan	the Qur'an		

Cultural point

Pearls

The Gulf has been producing pearls for at least 4,000 years. The first mention of a parcel of 'fish eyes' from Dilmun, the old name for Bahrain, appears in an Assyrian inscription of c.2000 BCE, and the industry of pearl-diving seems to have continued without a break until the late 1950s. Theophrastus (d. 287 BCE), the Greek philosopher and polymath, mentions Gulf pearls, and they crop up regularly in the works of mediaeval Arab geographers and travellers, such as the Moroccan Ibn Battuta, who gives a detailed eye-witness account of how Gulf pearls were fished in the mid-fourteenth century CE, which could pass for a description of the same activity 500 years later, so little had the methods changed. The pearling industry was the mainstay of the Gulf economy until the advent of oil in the mid-1930s, and from that point onwards the traditional pearl trade went into a steep and terminal decline, brought about by three factors: the discovery in Japan of a method for cultivating pearls artificially and cheaply in controlled conditions; the recession of the late 1920s and early 1930s, which depressed world demand for expensive natural pearls; and the Gulf oil industry, which offered abundant employment opportunities with a regular weekly wage, and was far less strenuous and dangerous than the seasonal (May–September) adventure of pearl-diving.

Today, the pearl has a special place in Gulf social history and popular culture. Re-creations of the 'heroic' days of the divers, the skul-duggery of the boat captains, the dangers of deep diving and dramatic shipwrecks at sea are a staple of Gulf TV and radio soap operas and plays. Pearl-diving is also often the subject of nostalgic popular poetry and song, and the pearl-diving 'houses', that is, the family concerns that ran the boats, are now the places where what is left of the last generation of divers meet together and sing the pearling songs of their youth. The boats that were used for pearling are now preserved as museum pieces, and the age-old practice of wooden boat-building

On board a Gulf pearling dhow in the 1930s

Source: William Facey and Gillian Grant, *Kuwait by the First Photographers*, The London Centre of Arab Studies, 1998, p. 94

survives only as a 'heritage' rather than a real working industry (as in the boatyard at Sur, Oman), or as a subject for theme parks.

 Reading Arabic

In Unit Seventeen, we looked at five of the main script styles used in Arabic. But there are many other 'variations' on these themes that computer-generated graphics enable the easy production of. Here are a couple of examples:

This sign is on the wall of the coffee shop inside Nizwa fort, in Oman. It is in a stylised version of Kufic, and reads, in normal typescript, مقهى maqhaa (in Gulf pronunciation usually mágha) 'coffee house' or 'coffee shop'.

Now here is one from the streets of Doha. It's a bilingual sign advertising a 'Big sale'. But can you read the Arabic?

The sign is in a 'chunky' script style often used in newspaper headlines, and says التنزيلات الكبرى or **at-tanziiláat al-kúbraa**, literally 'very large reductions', or, as in the English translation, 'big sale'. **tanziiláat** is the plural of **tanziil**, which is the verbal noun from the verb **názzal** 'to reduce, bring down'. The word **kúbraa** is the feminine form, on the pattern CuCCaa, of the elative adjective **ákbar** 'bigger, biggest' (see Unit Eight), and is feminine to agree with the feminine noun **tanziiláat**. This pattern, CuCCaa, is not used much in the Gulf dialect, but it is common in the written language. It is seen on road signs in the Capital Area of Muscat and Matrah, Oman in the form مطرح الكبرى 'Greater Matrah'. The aCCaC/f. CuCCaa pattern also has an intensive 'very ...', 'most ...' sense, as it does in the 'big sale' sign, and, in its masculine form, in the opening of the call to prayer: **alláahu ákbar!** 'God is most great!'

Unit Nineteen

In this unit you will learn about:

- verb strings involving **kaan/yikúun**, e.g. 'used to do', 'had been doing', 'will be doing', 'will have done'
- more conjunctions, e.g. 'whoever', 'in whatever way', 'as long as'
- how to say 'as if'
- expressions meaning 'I think'
- how to say 'some' and 'each other'
- adverbs in **-an**, e.g. 'usually', 'by chance', 'instead of'

Language point

19.1 **Verb strings involving** kaan/yikúun

In this section we look at the Arabic equivalent of certain of the English 'compound' and other non-simple tenses. They all involve use of the past or imperfect of the verb **kaan** 'to be; become'.

kaan + imperfect: 'used to do'

The past tense of **kaan** and the imperfect tense of a verb (both verbs in the appropriate person) expresses the sense of the English 'used to' – that is, habitual action in the past:

   kint ársim tamáam yoom kint fil-madrása.
   'I used to draw excellently when I was at school.'

kaan yishtághil naaTúur áwwal.
'He used to work as a watchman before.'

kaan + active participle: 'had done/been doing'

Typically, this construction links together two past actions (or states), one of which had already begun/(or even been completed) when the second interrupted it:

il-mubáara káanat báadya min wuSálna.
'The match had begun when we arrived.'

min xaabártha káanat mitgháddiya.
'When I phoned her she had (already) had lunch.' (i.e. she was in the state of having had lunch.)

simá9t kint mimáshshi sayyáartah.
'I heard you'd been driving his car.'

With certain so-called 'durative' verbs – that is, verbs denoting non-episodic actions or states (e.g. 'to hold', 'to carry', 'to think', 'to believe', etc.) – the sense is often similar to the English 'was doing ... when ...':

kaan mijáwwid jánTat jild áHmar layn shifnáah.
'He was holding a red leather case when we saw him.'

kaan is also used with **láazim** 'necessary' to express a number of past-tense senses involving need and obligation. We noted in Unit Twelve that **láazim yirúuH** 'He must/ought to go' can be negated in two ways:

mub láazim yirúuH.
'He needn't go.' (lit. 'It's not necessary he goes.')

Or

láazim maa yirúuH.
'He mustn't/oughtn't to go.' (lit. 'It's necessary he doesn't go.')

All of these sentences can be put into the past tense by prefixing them with **kaan**:

kaan láazim yirúuH.
'He had to go/ought to have gone.'

kaan mub láazim yirúuH.
'He needn't have gone/didn't have to go.'

kaan láazim maa yirúuH.
'He oughtn't to have gone.'

An important point here is that, unlike the other constructions involving **kaan** + active participle (for that is what **láazim** is, grammatically speaking), neither **kaan** nor **láazim** agree in gender/number with the subject of the main clause when used in the sense of 'It's necessary':

kaan láazim maa truuHíin.
'You (f.) shouldn't have gone.' ('It was necessary ....')

kaan láazim tishtári líha hádiya.
'You (m.) ought to have bought her a present.'

■ **yikúun** + imperfect: 'will be doing'

The imperfect of **kaan** is used with a following imperfect in a predictive sense:

la timúrr 9aláyhum il-Hiin, yikuunúun yit9ashshúun.
'Don't call in on them now, they'll be having dinner.'

íktib líha risáala, tikúun tifakkiríin nisáytha.
'Write her a letter, she'll be thinking you've forgotten her.'

■ **yikúun** + active participle/past tense: 'will have done'

yikúun followed by either an active participle or a past-tense verb has the sense of anticipating the completion of action in the future:

	HaSSált	
min tishúufni s-sána l-jáaya, akúun		**9ala sh-shaháada**
	miHáSSil	

'When you see me next year, I will have got the diploma.'

Note that, in all the constructions above involving it, **yikúun** agrees in gender/number with the following verb or participle.

Exercise 19.1

Translate into Arabic:

min tírja9 ...
'By the time you come back I will have ... '

1 got a driving licence   5 gone to Saudi Arabia
2 got married   6 washed up
3 repaired your car   7 got a new job
4 passed the exam   8 had lunch

Look at the following exchange:

- **dagg il-mismáar fil-HáayiT.**
- **kaan láazim yidíggah fil-baab!**
- 'He knocked the nail into the wall.'
- 'He ought to have knocked it into the door!'

Now translate the parallel exchanges below:

 9 – He took the number 15 bus.
     – He ought to have taken the number 50!
10 – He gave me the large hammer.
     – He ought to have given you the small one!
11 – They did two hours' overtime yesterday.
     – They ought to have done three!
12 – I hired a two-door car.
     – You ought to have hired a pick-up truck!
13 – I told the foreman to be here at 8.30.
     – You ought to have told him to be here at 7.00!

In the following sentences, practise the use of the compound tenses.
Translate:

14 By the time we got there, the film had started.

15 We saw they had finished removing the furniture.

16 She had been wearing a green skirt when she got on the plane.

17 When I got in touch with him, he had changed his mind.

18 When the Minister's car arrived, the police had gained control of
the situation.

19 I used to be interested in cameras and take lots of photos.

20 I used to work as a carpenter when I first came to the Gulf.

21 What used Kuwaitis to eat in the old days?

The following dialogues give practice in the use of **láazim** in expressing probabilities, needs and obligations. Translate:

22 – Where's Ali?
   – Not here. He must have gone home.
   – He should have stayed two hours more!

23 – Can you lend me ten dinars?
   – Sorry, I've spent all my salary.
   – You shouldn't have spent it *all*!

24 – Where are the dirty dishes?
   – I've just washed them up.
   – You needn't have done that!

25 – How long did you stay at your parents?
   – Only two days. We had to meet you.
   – You needn't have been in such a hurry!

26 – Where's the foreman?
   – He must have gone to the warehouse.
   – He shouldn't have left these men on their own!

 Language point

19.2 More conjunctions

In Unit Nine we met time conjunctions such as 'before', 'after' and 'as soon as'. We now look at some other words that link clauses together. The first group exemplified below perform functions similar to those of English conjunctions ending in '-ever', such as 'whoever', 'whatever', etc.:

kíllmin: 'whoever; everyone who …':

   kíllmin iyi, magbúul.
   'Whoever comes will be accepted.'

   kíllmin raaH il-Harb ingítal.
   'Everyone who went to the war was killed.'

kíllmaa: 'whenever; whatever':

   kíllmaa taHáchcha 9an wíldah il-máyyit, gaam yíbchi.
   'Whenever he spoke about his dead son, he began to cry.'

kíllmaa miHtáaja lih, Tílbatah min 9ind abúuha.
'Whatever she needed, she asked for it from her father.'

(Note that this sentence is ambiguous; it could be understood: 'Whenever she needed it, she asked for it from her father.')

cháyfmaa: 'however; in whatever way':

cháyfmaa Saar, láazim dáxal u baag is-saamáan.
'However it happened, he must have got in and stolen the stuff.'

wáynmaa: 'wherever; in whatever place':

wáynmaa dáwwar, maa líga lih áHad yígdar yiHíll mushkíltah.
'Wherever he looked, he couldn't find anyone who could solve his problem.'

shkíthirmaa and shgáddmaa: 'however much':

shkíthirmaa tídfa9, maa tiHáSSil 9ála maa tábbi.
'However much you pay, you won't get what you want.'

shwáqtma: 'at whatever time':

shwáqtmaa tábbi tiHaachíini, ittáSil fíini bit-tilifúun.
'Whenever you want to talk to me, contact me by phone.'

Note that **shwáqtmaa** is an alternative to **kíllmaa** in sentences of this type only.

We look now at a number of other commonly used conjunctions:

míthilmaa: 'as; just as; in the same way as':

míthilmaa tádri, ílli yábbi yiSíir muqáawil, maa yigúum nóoba wáHda.
'As you know, someone who wants to be a contractor doesn't become one overnight.' (lit. '... does not rise up in one go.')

maa Sáarat il-muqáabla míthilmaa tiwaqqá9na.
'The meeting didn't happen as we expected it would.'

áwwalmaa: 'the first time that ...':

áwwalmaa báyyan, 9írfat ínnah rayyáal karíim.
'From the moment he appeared, she knew he was a generous man.'

yóommaa: 'as soon as':

yóommaa jáwwad it-túfga, Saar míthil maynúun.
'As soon as he got hold of the gun, he became like a madman.'

maadáam: 'as long as ...':

maadáam ríilik ti9áwrik la tigúum min il-faráash.
'As long as your leg hurts don't get out of bed.'

Exercise 19.2

Translate into Arabic:

1 Whatever you want we can get.

2 Whenever you need anything, call in on me.

3 As long as I'm here, I'll keep trying to get in touch with him.

4 As you know, I shall have sent the letter by the time he returns.

5 Wherever you go, don't forget to leave your address with me.

6 Everyone who enters the museum has to pay 250 fils.

7 However hungry you were, you shouldn't have eaten that.

8 However much you spend, don't waste your money on worthless things.

 Language points

19.3 'As if'

The conjunction **chinn-/kinn-**, to which pronouns are suffixed, means 'as if' or 'like'. It can also introduce a sentence with the sense 'It's as if ...':

wájhik chínnah gúuTi muxáffaS!
'Your face is like a crushed can!' ('Your face as if it ....')

báSal sh-kúbrah chínnah tufféaH!
'An onion so big it's like an apple!'

chínnak maa tírDa yitzáwwaj ...'
'It's as if you don't want him to get married ...'

gáamaw yifatshúun 9ála z-zar9 kínnhum xubaráa.
'They began inspecting the crops as if they were experts.'

19.4 Expressions meaning 'I think'

We have already met the expression **fi rá'yi** 'in my opinion'. Several
other expressions are also in common use that perform the same
modifying function. **9ála báali** (or **9abáali**) 'to my mind' or 'as I thought'
is used when one wishes to say what one (often mistakenly) thought
to be the case:

- **cham Saar lik fil-bank?**
- **sanatáyn.**
- **wállah? 9abáali ákthar min háadha.**
- 'How long have you been at the bank?'
- 'Two years.'
- 'Really? I thought it was more than that.'

baal can of course have other pronouns suffixed to it:

9abáalik bint Hálwa, muu chidhíi?
'You think (or thought) she's a pretty girl, don't you?'

The expression **9ála DHánni** (or **9aDHánni**) is used in an exactly similar
way:

9aDHánnhum mub láazim yikamlúun diráasathum has-sána.
'They think they don't have to complete their studies this year.'

- **il-Háfla chayf káanat?**
- **9aDHánni mub shay.**
- 'How was the party?'
- 'Not much good, I thought.'

19.5 'Some' and 'each other'

The word **ba9D**, which basically means 'some of', has a number of
important uses in Gulf Arabic. With a following defined noun it signifies
'some of' or 'part of':

ba9D in-naas yi9taqidúun inn it-tilivizyúun Haráam.
'Some people believe that TV is forbidden (by Islam).'

yibáyyin maaxdhíin ba9D il-xiyáash u mxallíin bá9Dha.
'It appears they've taken some of the sacks and left some
of them.'

mustáwa l-maay náazil – bá9Dah láazim inshárab.
'The level of the water's gone down – some of it must have
been drunk.'

ráasi yi9awwírni fi ba9D il-aHyáan.
'My head gives me pain now and again.' ('… in some of the
times.')

The construction ba9D + pronoun … (il-) ba9D is used to mean 'each
other':

yikrahúun bá9Dhum ba9D.
'They hate each other.' ('Some of them hate some.')

Dírbaw bá9Dhum il-ba9D.
'They had a fight.' ('Some of them hit some.')

In some cases the verb requires a preposition:

9árraf il-muwaDHDHafíin bá9Dhum 9ála ba9D.
'He introduced the officials to each other.'
('… some of them to some.')

19.6 Adverbs in -an

A great many of the adverbs that describe how or when an action is
done are formed in all dialects of Arabic (and Gulf Arabic is no exception)
by suffixing -an to nouns or adjectives: we have already met, for
example, shaxSíyyan 'personally', derived from sháxSi 'personal'
(which itself is derived from shaxS/ashxáaS 'person') and máthalan
'for example', derived from máthal/amtháal 'example'. We look here
at the use of some of the commonest of these adverbs in everyday
speech:

9áadatan: 'usually':

9áadatan maa tizíid yoomíyyat il-9áamil 9ála sitt
danaaníir.
'A labourer's daily wage isn't usually more than six dinars.'

Táb9an: 'naturally':

> **... u Táb9an il yáahil maa yidíir báalah min háadha l-xáTar ...**
> '... and naturally, the child pays no attention to this danger ...'

taqríiban: 'approximately; more or less':

> **... fi dhiich is-sáa9a, 9úmri taqríiban thalaathtá9shar sána ...**
> '... at that time, I was about 13 years old ...'

Súdfatan: 'by chance':

> **ligáytah Súdfatan fish-sháari9.**
> 'I met him by chance in the street.'

ghá Sban 9ála + pronoun: 'unwillingly':

> **inDammáyt fil-jaysh ghá Sban 9alíyyi.**
> 'I joined the army against my will.'

ábadan: 'never; not at all':

> – **mistá9mil hal-áala min gábil?**
> – **ábadan.**
> – 'Have you used this tool before?'
> – 'Never.'

aHyáanan: 'sometimes' (syn. **ba9D il-aHyáan**):

> **maa nshúufhum wáayid, bas aHyáanan yá9ni.**
> 'We don't see them a lot, only occasionally.'

rá'san: 'directly' (syn. **síida**):

> **waSSílni rá'san il-bayt, lo simáHt**
> 'Take me straight home, would you?'

i9tibáaran min: 'with effect from':

> **i9tibáaran min báachir, il-mudíir maa yísmaH líkum tiTla9úun fi faráaghkum.**
> 'As from tomorrow, the headmaster will not allow you to go out during your free periods.'

An alternative to **i9tibáaran min** ... is **min** ... **ráayiH**, for example **min báachir ráayiH** 'from tomorrow on' and **min is-sána l-jáaya ráayiH** 'from next year on'.

bádalan min: 'instead of':

baTárrish wáaHid bádalan min arúuH il-ijtimáa9 náfsi.
'I'll send someone instead of going to the meeting myself.'

This, of course, is not an adverb but a conjunction, but is derived from a noun (**bádal** 'alternative') by the addition of **-an** in the same way as the adverbs.

Dialogue 19.1

Listen and translate the following dialogue into English.

Getting a driving licence (Audio 1; 34)

A ídha tábbi tiHáSSil 9ála rúxSat is-siyáaqa ... láysan, yá9ni ...
   sh-láazim tsáwwi?

B áwwal trúuH sh-yisammúunah – il-gál9a – u yisajjilúunik u
   yifHaSúun 9ala n-náDHar. 9ógub yoomáyn taqríiban ya9Túunik
   in-natíija: ídha sítta fi sítta, zayn, u idha Da9íif yiguulúun lik 'jiib
   in-naDHDHáara, ílbas naDHDHáara' ... haay illi yiguulúun, ána
   xub maa riHt ...

A u ba9adáyn, táaxidh it-tist?

B ay, it-tist. tidíshsh wíyya D-DáabiT u ídha sháafik tamáam nijáHt,
   sháafik mu tamáam raddáyt.

A wis-sayyáara láazim tikúun maal is-sáayiq náfsah?

B la, 9áadatan maal il-mu9állim. táaxidhha sáa9a, tidíshsh wiyya
   D-DáabiT u ta9Tíih íjra. ídha nijáHt ta9Tíih ikraamíyya ya9ni
   chidhíi hádiya bi munaasábat in-najáaH, ya9ni.

Vocabulary

aatháath	furniture	**baal**	mind
ábadan	never; not at all	**9ála baal** + pron.	I/you, etc. think
awirtáym	overtime	**gháyyar il-baal**	to change one's mind
áwwalmaa	when first; from the first time that ...	**bádalan min**	instead of
		báyyan/yibáyyin	to appear

cháyfmaa	however; in whatever way	máthal/amtháal	example; proverb
chinn-/kinn-	as if; like	máwqif/ mawáaqif	situation; position
dagg/yidígg/ dagg	to knock; hit	máyyit	dead
9ála DHann + pron.	I/you, etc. think	míTraga*/ maTáarig	hammer
farg	difference; gap	míthilmaa	just as
ghásban 9ála + pron.	unwillingly	bi munaasábat + noun	on the occasion of
Harb (f.)/Hurúub	war	muqáabla*(aat)	meeting
Hiin/aHyáan	time; period	muwáDHDHaf (iin)	official; employee
Hurríyya*	freedom		
íjra	fee	mu9táqad(aat)	belief
ikraamíyya*	bonus; honorarium	naaTúur/ nawaaTíir	watchman
istáajar/yistáajir	to rent; hire	nádHar	sense of sight
istá9jal/yistá9jil	to hurry	naDHDHáara* (aat)	eyeglasses
ittáSal/yittáSil (fi)	to get in touch with	najáaH	success
ixtálaf/yixtálif	to differ	natíija*/natáayij	result
i9táqad/yi9táqid	to believe	nóoba wáHda	in one go; all at once
i9tibáaran min	with effect from		
jáwwad/ yijáwwid	to grasp; hold on to	qárya*/qúra	village
		rá'san	directly
kámmal/ yikámmil	to complete	ráayiH: min ... ráayiH	from ... onwards
kárah/yíkrah/ kárah	to hate	radd/yiridd/ radáad	to repeat; do again
		rúxSat siyáaqa*	driving licence
karíim/kiráam	generous; kind	sájjal/yisájjil	to record; register
kíllmaa	whatever; whenever		
kíllmin	whoever	Súdfatan	by chance
láysan	driving licence	shgáddmaa	however much
maadáam	as long as	shkíthirmaa	however much
majáal	room; scope	shwáqtmaa	at whatever time
máshsha/ yimáshshi	to progress (a project); to drive (e.g. a car)	tamáam	excellent; perfect
		taqríiban	approximately
		tilifúun(aat)	telephone
		tist(aat)	driving test

tiwáqqa9/	to expect;	xabíir/xubaráa	expert
yitwáqqa9	anticipate	xáffaS/yixáffiS	to crush; squash
ti9áTTal/	to break down;	xub	intensifying
yit9áTTal	be unemployed		particle meaning
túfga*/tífag	gun		'heck!;really!'
waalidáyn	parents	yóommaa	as soon as
waalidáy + pron.	my/your, etc.	9áadatan	usually
	parents	9ádam	lack; dearth
wanáyt(aat)	pick-up truck	9áwwar/	to cause pain;
wáynmaa	wherever	yi9áwwir	hurt

 ## Cultural point

Arabiizi

One of the consequences of the enormous rise in disposable income in the Gulf States over recent decades has been investment in the education of the upcoming generations. Forty years ago, there was only one university in the Gulf – Kuwait University, which opened its doors in 1966. Now there are tens of universities, some government funded, some privately owned, together with offshoot campuses of American and British institutions of higher education. In practically all of these, there are certain subjects in which the language of instruction is English, notably commerce, business studies and the applied and pure sciences. These tertiary-level institutions are fed by the graduates of a burgeoning English-medium private school sector. One of the consequences of this educational expansion, and of other phenomena such as the influx of multinational companies (there are over a 1,000 with offices in Dubai alone), the massive increase in travel to the West, and exposure to Western media, has been an explosion in the number of Gulf Arabs who are now fully proficient in English. For many Gulf Arabs working in the increasingly globalised economy, English has become the language of work. Of course, among themselves, and certainly within their own families, they speak Gulf Arabic, but in many situations constant exposure to English, the international language of business, has led to a mixing of the two languages. We have all heard of 'Spanglish' and 'Franglais'... now we are seeing the birth of what is known as **9arabíizi**, a portmanteau cross between **9árabi** 'Arabic' and **inglíizi** 'English'.

A humorous film charting this interpenetration of Arabic and English was made in 2006 called, simply, **Arabiizi**. The phenomenon is not confined to the Gulf, although in the Gulf you find perhaps more speakers of Arabiizi than anywhere else. But there are Jordanian and Egyptian speakers of it too, and the film investigates their linguistic behaviour and the changing attitudes towards English and Arabic among its habitual users. Mostly, Arabiizi involves the embedding of phrases from one language into the other, but often wholesale switching between the two languages from sentence to sentence, a process that the speakers themselves are often hardly even aware of. Of course, the borrowing of English technical and work-related terms into everyday Gulf speech has been going on for a long time, as we noted earlier in Unit Four. Here is an actual example of a quite ordinary Bahraini, employed at the oil refinery, describing his job. This man didn't know much English, but still his description is peppered with Arabised English words of a technical nature. The underlined words are English words borrowed into Arabic:

> al-Hiin náaxidh fi <u>tónki</u>, yá9ni <u>kruud</u> maxlúuT <u>áayil</u> u <u>díizal</u>, u haay kull shay maxlúuT … yá9ni náaxdhah min il-<u>bambáat</u> u ndáxlah fi <u>ikstínjah</u>, mithil shay Tawíil ya9ni, fiih <u>tyuubáat</u> … ba9déen nxallíih, ndáxlah dáaxil <u>híitar</u>.

Translation:

> 'Now we take into the <u>tank</u>, the <u>crude</u> (oil), a mixture of <u>oil</u> and <u>diesel</u>, all completely mixed up … we take it from the <u>pumps</u> and pass it into the (heat) <u>exchanger</u> – that's like a long thing in which there's <u>tubes</u> … then we make it- … we pass it into a <u>heater</u>.'

But this kind of mixing isn't Arabiizi, as it is limited to word-level insertions in work contexts. The real thing is much more like the following, taken from the film *Arabiizi*. In it, a 24-year-old Kuwaiti woman, casually dressed in a Barcelona football shirt and jeans, describes who she is and what she does for a living:

> ísmi 9áysha xáalidi, mawlúuda wa 9áysha bil-kweet, <u>and I also lived in Egypt when I was younger</u> u 9isht árba9 sníin fi amríika fil-jáam9a. <u>I'm the sports editor of the Daily Star. I really love that</u>

job, it's amazing. I was a journalist major, so it worked out for me.
9úmri árba9 u 9ishríin sána u ana ataHáchcha 9arabíizi.

Translation:

'My name is Aysha Khalidi, I was born and live in Kuwait, and I
also lived in Egypt when I was younger, and I lived in America for
four years at university. I'm the sports editor of the Daily Star. I
really love that job, it's amazing. I was a journalist major, so it
worked out for me. I'm 24 years old and I speak Arabiizi.'

There is unease in some quarters in the Gulf about such language
behaviour, and some people have concluded that the Arabic language
is under threat. Be that as it may, it seems Arabiizi, the product of a
globalised economy and education system, is here to stay.

Reading Arabic

Mistranslations

English translations – and not always felicitous ones – accompany many
Arabic shop signs you will see in the Gulf. Take a look at this one,
from Qatar:

The feminine noun **thárwa** does indeed mean 'abundance' or 'wealth'
in Literary Arabic, and the adjective that follows it, **samakíyya**, also
feminine to agree with it, comes from **sámak** 'fish'. The word **idáara**
means 'management', so the whole is literally 'management of fishy
wealth'. What it actually refers to is a government department concerned
with maintaining fish stocks and preventing overfishing. In English we
would perhaps express this more normally as 'Department of Fish
Resources', but this kind of mistranslation is very common on shop
and office signs. Another extremely common one appears in this:

Mustafawi is the name of the shop owner; but what are we to make of 'exhibition'? Is this a museum, or an art gallery? The answer lies in the mistranslation of the word **má9riD**, just above and to the right of the shop owner's name in the Arabic. It does indeed mean, in the right context, 'exhibition', but not in this commercial one, where we would normally say 'showroom' or simply 'store' in English. Nonetheless, one sees 'exhibition' used when what is really meant is 'shop'/'showroom', all over the Gulf. A Gulf 'car exhibition' (معرض للسيارات) is much more likely to be a place you go to buy a new car than admire a vintage one! Another frequent translation oddity involves the word مكتبة (**máktaba**). This word basically means 'library', but it is very commonly used in shop signs as a name for 'bookshop' or even 'stationery store'. Such mistranslations are not confined to shop signs. In 2005, at the entrance to Wadi Dayqa in Oman, the author noticed a sign (below) warning visitors about the dangers of flash flooding. Cases of drowning, it noted, were very 'popular', a mistranslation of كثيرة **kathíira**, which means 'many; numerous'.

Unit Twenty

In this unit you will learn about:

- how to put everything you have learnt together, in order to understand and translate some colloquial texts

Texts

In this concluding unit, some abridged extracts from a recent 'black comedy' broadcast by a Gulf radio station are presented for comprehension and translation. These extracts are highly colloquial in style, being aimed at a local audience, and will give good practice in coping with the 'real thing'. Read through each extract with the help of the notes that follow, and answer the comprehension questions. When you have worked through each extract in this way, try to write an idiomatic translation of the whole thing. The play is entitled **id-dínya maSáaliH**, which means roughly 'The world is business'. In the first extract the main character, Muhammad bin Rashid, introduces himself to the audience:

Exercise 20.1 (Audio 1; 35)

yaa jimáa9a, ána ísmi mHámmad bin ráashid. mitzáwwij min jaríib
– tisa9tá9shar sána bas, wíla 9índi 9iyáal … tammáyt múdda
Tawíila adáwwir shúghul, shúghul yirayyíHni … ashgháal wáayid,
bas maa tinaasíbni … ábbi shúghul maa fiih kaláafa – yirayyíHni u
aHáSSil mínnah fluus, yilást ayyáam Tawíila u ána afákkir fish-
shúghul … afákkir u afákkir u táali yátni fíkra: laysh maa ashtághil
dáxtar? u bil-fi9l, ishtaghált dáxtar li'ann, ayyáam iz-zamáan kaan
yáarna híndi – dáxtar híndi – u min hash-shákil ta9allámt shloon

yidaawúun in-naas ... láakin, yaa jimáa9a, 9índi Sadíiq 9azíiz min
ayyáam il-muTáwwa9, bas hu yishtághil Haffáar gubúur u ana dáxtar.
haS-Sadíiq sáwwa fíini nágla 9óoda, u min hal-Hálqa wil-Halaqáat
il-yáaya, abbíikum tisim9úun qíSSati ma9áah u má9a zóojti ...

Notes:
- **min jaríib** 'recently'. **jaríib** is one of those words in which some
  speakers have **j** instead of **g**: **garíib** 'near; close'.
- **9iyáal** 'family dependants'. In the context, he means 'children'.
- **muTáwwa9** 'Qur'an school teacher'. In Bahrain, this is the Sunni
  term; the Shi'a use the word **mu9állim**.
- **nágla 9óoda** 'a great burden', that is, 'a lot of trouble'.
- **Hálqa*/Halaqáat** 'episode' in a radio or TV serial.

Questions:
1 **How long has Muhammad been married?**
2 **What does Muhammad want from any job he takes?**
3 **What job did he settle on in the end?**
4 **How did he first come into contact with this profession?**
5 **What does his friend do for a living?**
6 **How long has Muhammad known him?**

Dialogue 20.1

(Audio 1; 36)

In this extract, Muhammad, who is about to hang himself because he
can stand life with his wife no longer, is interrupted by his friend Khalid.

K ána ákrah ínnik tintíHir ... 9ayb, wállah 9ayb, Hátta lo ínta rifíiji,
   lo a'ákkil 9iyáali min waráak xámsat ayyáam ... háadhi waDHíifti,
   shasáwwi yaa xuuk?
M 9aad ínta wíddik antíHir Hátta tistánfi9 min waráay? láakin maana
   bi mintíHir!
K la tintíHir! ígTa9 rízji! xall 9iyáali yimuutúun min il-yuu9!
M yaa, wállah míshkil! yoom maa antíHir 9iyáalik yimuutúun min
   il-yuu9?
K ay, ínta is-sábab fi hal-Háala illi íHna fíih! áwwal, il-wáaHid
   yímraD, yoom, yoomáyn, thaláatha, il-yoom ir-ráabi9 yiwáddi9, u
   nistánfi9 min waráah.

M yaa! sh-hal-kaláam yaa xáalid?

K yiit il-Hiin, wil-maríiD illi byimúut ta9Tíih duwa tixallíih yi9íish! u
   min 9ala Hsáabah? 9ala Hsáabi ána! laysh inta 9aníid? laysh inta
   anáani? laysh?

M yaa yúbba, haay shúghlati, sh-asáwwi?

K laysh maa tixallíina nisáwwi hídna li múddat sána wáHda bas,
   binistafíid mínha ána u ínta!

M yaa! shínhi hal-hídna?

K sállimk állah, kill maríiD iyíik íhni, dhíbHah aw 9áTah dúwa bil-
   ghálaT u a9Tíik nuSS il-máblagh illi aHáSlah min ghasáalah!

M áwwal shay, ána yaa xúuyi mub gaSSáab … tháani shay maa
   ágdar axúun ir-risáala illi HaTTóoh 9ala chátfi.

K yaa, wállah, illi yisím9ik yigúul haay maa fóogah foog, muul!

M ána bá9ad 9índi DHamíir u 9indi iHsáas …

K zayn, 9índik DHamíir u 9índik iHsáas, zayn maa 9aláyh … kill
   maríiD iyíik íhni tigúul lih maa fiik máraD layn yistíHi u yimúut
   bas!

M arjúuk, yaa xúuyi, maa ágdar!

K yaa! ínta la tinTábax wila tinshíwi!

Notes:

− **intáHar** 'to commit suicide'.
− **'ákkal** 'to feed'.
− **min waráak** 'because of you' (lit. 'from behind you').
− **waDHíifti = shúghlati**.
− **máana bi mintíHir** 'I'm not going to commit suicide.' The construction
   maa + independent pronoun (+ **bi**) + noun/adjective is a way of
   negating **ána mintíHir** 'I'm going to commit suicide' that can be used
   instead of **ána mub mintíHir**. Instead of saying **ána mub ráayiH**,
   one can say **máana bráayiH**; instead of **hum mub maaklíin**, **maa
   hum bi maaklíin**, etc.
− **la tintíHir!** 'Don't kill yourself then!' ('See if I care!').
− **yiwáddi9** 'he bids farewell', that is, he dies.
− **min 9ála Hsáabah?** 'At whose expense?' (lit. 'who at his expense?').
   This type of interrogative phrase is common. Other examples are:
   min Hággah sawwáyt háadha? 'Who did you do that for?' (lit. 'who
   for him did you …'); **sh-mínnah maSnúu9?** 'Made from what?' (lit.
   'What from it made?'). In each case the suffixed pronoun refers back
   to the question word.

- **sállimk állah** 'God save you!' = **yisallímk állah** or **állah yisálmik.**
- **ghasáal** means here specifically the washing of the corpse.
- **muul** 'completely' – used like **kíllish.**
- **la tinTábax wila tinshíwi!** 'You can't be cooked and you can't be roasted', meaning that Khalid can't convince him to do what he wants no matter what proposal he makes.

Questions:
7 **How has Muhammad affected Khalid's livelihood?**
8 **What deal does Khalid suggest to Muhammad?**
9 **What is Muhammad's reaction? What reasons does he give?**

Dialogue 20.2

(Audio 1; 37)

Muhammad and Khalid make a deal.

M yaa 9azíizi ána mwáafig a9Tíik illi Tilábtah! alf! alf!
K ta9Tíini iyyáahum? 9áshra xúDur?
M ay ná9am, nooT yínTaH nooT! 9áshra xúDur!
K xúDur xúDur! 9áshra xúDur, ya9ni 9áshra?
M ay ná9am, yúbba!
K bismilláah ir-raHmáan ... (faints).
M ohóo! radd TaaH márra tháanya! guum, yúbba, guum!
K ána wayn? mHámmad? yáwwidni! sáa9idni!
M guum yúbba, Siir rayyáal u ísma9 kaláami u xall 9ánnik iT-TayHáat bas. 9aad malláyna.
K arjúuk yaa xuuk laa tifáawil 9alíyyi! xállni áwwal aHáSSil alf xúDur, xállni aHáSSilhum!
M bitiHáSSilhum ... bas ána míthilmaa git lik –
K ána yaa xuuk astáahil mínnik, ána ábghi –
M Saaj, Saaj, u ba9Tíik alf ... bas lii sharT ...
K íshruT! sharT wáaHid bas?
M sharT wáaHid Sugháyyir ...
K wállah, lo tabghíini áglub il-báHar Hílu! lo tabghíini aHáwwil lik nyúum is-sími! lo tabghíini –
M abghíik, yaa xúuyi tídhbaH zóojti!

Notes:
- **xúDur** 'green ones', that is, Bahraini ten-dinar notes. Each dinar is worth ten rupees, hence 100 dinars = 1,000 rupees.
- **nooT/niiTáan** 'banknotes' (from English 'note').
- **yínTaH** 'butts', that is, one note packed against another, 'oodles of cash'.
- **bismilláah** etc. The full phrase is **bismilláah ir-raHmáan ir-raHíim** 'In the name of God the Compassionate, the Merciful.' This phrase is used at the inception of any project, activity or action.
- **xall 9ánnik iT-TayHáat** 'Stop falling down!' ('Keep from you the falls!')
- **malláyna** 'We've got bored with it!' Note that 'we' here refers to the (singular) speaker only.
- **tifáawil** is from the verb **fáawal** 'to diddle; cheat' (from the English football term 'foul').
- **git lik** = **gilt lik**. The l is often dropped in this phrase.
- **Saaj** 'You're right'; f. **Sáaja**, pl. **Saadgíin**.
- **nyúum** 'stars' and **sími** 'sky'. These words in more educated speech would be **nujúum** (sing. **nájim**) and **simáa**.

Questions:
10 How much does Muhammad offer Khalid?
11 What does Khalid offer to do for the money, if Muhammad were to ask him?
12 What does Muhammad ask Khalid to do in fact?

Now try to translate the whole of the text into idiomatic English.

Vocabulary

'ákkal/yi'ákkil	to feed	**gabr/gubúur**	grave; tomb
anáani	selfish	**gálab/yíglub/**	to turn over
chatf/chtúuf	shoulder	**galb**	(something);
dáawa/yidáawi	to treat; give medicine to		turn something into something
DHamíir	conscience	**min garíib**	recently
fáawal/yifáawil (9ála)	to cheat; dupe	**hídna***	truce
bil-fi9l	indeed; in fact	**híndi/hunúud**	Indian
		Haffáar(iin)	digger

Hálqa*/Halaqáat	episode	náTaH/yínTaH/ náTaH	to butt
iHsáas	sensitivity		
intáHar/yintíHir	to commit suicide	ráyyaH/yiráyyiH	to relieve; give rest
istáahal/ yistáahil	to deserve; merit	risáala*	vocation; mission
istáHa/yistáHi	to be shamefaced	rizg (or rizj)	sustenance; food (fig.)
istánfa9/ yistanfi9(min)	to profit; benefit (from)	Saaj/Saadgíin	truth-telling
kaláafa*	bother; trouble	shúghla*	job
máraD/yímraD/ máraD	to be ill; fall ill	TáyHa*(aat)	fall, swoon
		wádda9/ yiwáddi9	to bid farewell
máSlaHa*/ maSáaliH	interest; benefit; business		
muul	completely; absolutely	yuu9	hunger
		9aníid	stubborn
náasab/yináasib	to suit; match	9azíiz	dear; cherished
nágla*	burden	9iyáal	family dependants; children
nájim/nujúum	star		

Cultural point

Colloquial poetry

The art that is prized above all others in the Arab world is poetry. It is the oldest form of wordsmithery, with an unbroken tradition that goes back at least 14 centuries. All the most famous Arab poets, ancient or modern, write in the Classical, or Literary form of the language. But alongside this great literary tradition, there is one of poetic composition that is just as old in the spoken, dialectal language. In the Gulf, this tradition has various names, but the most common is **as-shi9r an-nábaTi**, the so-called 'Nabati poetry'. This poetry, Bedouin in origin, is composed by all social classes, from the rulers of the Gulf States (a modern example is Sheikh Mohammed bin Rashid al-Maktoum, ruler of Dubai) down to nightwatchmen. As one of the true local arts of the Gulf, this poetry has recently become very high profile, at a time when there is a fear in some quarters that the Gulf is losing touch with its ancient roots. One of the most popular programmes on Abu Dhabi TV in the early 2000s features this poetry. Young poets, male or female, send in short oral poems in their dialect, and the best are invited to perform them before a panel of judges and a studio audience; viewers at home can text their judgement of which was the best poem. The programme is called **sháa9ir il-milyóon** 'The Million (Dirham) Poet', so called because the winner wins one million UAE Dirhams, and the format seems to have been cloned from the Saturday evening ballroom-dancing and pop-singing contests so beloved of the main UK TV channels. Arabic oral poetry is often a commentary on something: local social or political issues, or even international ones. It often has an 'edge' – critical, satirical or humorous. A well-known oral poet is the Bahraini Abdurrahman Rafi'. Rafi' worked for many years as a school teacher, and he is an acute observer of Gulf life, with poems on everything from the unruliness of his own pupils, to the high prices in the market, to the difficulties in getting together enough money to get married. Here is an extract from one of his poems (with a (liberal) rhyming translation) concerned with how Bahrain society has changed, supposedly for the better (although the poet makes it clear he has doubts). The refrain is about how what was once a cheap kind of fish – **shí9ri** – has now become expensive. This poem dates from the late 1960s:

alláah yijaazíik, yaa zamáan!	God punish you o time!
maa lik amáan	To trust in you's a crime!
ish-shí9ri ib thamáan	Four pounds of shi9ri's eight
alláah yijaazíik yaa zamáan!	rupees – God punish you o time!
gaalóo li: maa fi bláadna	They told me: 'In this land of ours,
hal-ayyáam fagíir	These days, there's none who lack.
ish-shirb báylar	The water's sweet as nectar, and
wi s-sawáaHli Saar Haríir	Our clothes are silk not sack.
u aHsan dyaay	The choicest type of tasty fowl
ráayiH u yaay	Is there for all to eat;
w ahl il-barastíyya ightanaw	The palm-hut folk are rich now: look!
fríshaw naháali	Carpets beneath their feet!
u Hrígaw dhaak il-HaSíir	They've burnt that tattered ancient mat ...

id-dínya ghayr	The world has changed a lot,
wi n-naas fi xayr	See everyone's in clover now; of worries not a jot!'
gilt: yímkin in-naas yiSadgúun	'If that's what people think,' I said,
háadhi yihúun	'That's easy, that's just fine;
kíllah yihúun	No problem with that thought, but hey!
bas illi mub fi múxxi dáashsh	What never crossed my mind:
ish-shí9ri, laysh ish-shí9ri ib thamáan	Four pounds of shi9ri eight rupees?!
alláah yijaazíik yaa zamáan!	God punish you o time!
alláah yijaazíik yaa zamáan!	God punish you o time!'

There are one or two words here that are new: **amáan** means trustworthiness or reliability; **báylar** from English 'boiler' means sweet water brought by tanker; **sawáaHli** is a cheap clothing material; **Haríir** is silk; **barastíyya**, singular **barasti**, were palm-huts in which many Bahrainis once lived; **naháali** is a rug or carpet; and **háadhi yihúun** means 'that's of no consequence'.

The poem continues in a similar vein, with faint praise being lavished on the 'improvements' to everyday life brought about by modernisation, but concluding with the thought that the times change and we all must change with them.

Reading Arabic

In this course, the Reading Arabic sections have concentrated on acquainting you with the kinds of short texts in Modern Standard (that is, Literary) Arabic (MSA), which it is useful for you to be able to read and understand even if your main aim is simply be able to speak and understand Gulf Arabic: business cards, street signs, menus, bank-notes, stamps and so on. With these kinds of text, you rarely have to know much about the grammar of MSA to be able to understand them. If, however, you want to go on and learn the written form of Arabic, so as to tackle more complicated running texts, you will need to learn MSA grammar. The differences between that and what you have learnt in this book at first seem considerable, but they should not be exaggerated, as basically Arabic is one language, despite its regional variants, as you come to realise the more you study it.

One of the main difficulties you will face with running texts is the absence of vocalisation: that is, the short vowels that are normally part of the word as written on the page, with the exception of the Qur'an, which is always vocalised to ensure correct pronunciation, and some children's school books. So for example, the word

يكسر

is simply, on paper, four consonants **yksr**, and out of any context could be read in several different ways. It could be, for example, **yaksir** 'he/it breaks', **yuksar** 'he/it is broken', **yukassir** 'he/it smashes' or **yukassar** 'he/it is smashed', depending on what the short vowels are and whether or not the **s** is doubled or single. Only a real context (a sentence) will tell you which of these possible readings it actually is. These readings are all, of course, MSA ones, some of which, like the passives **yuksar** and **yukassar**, do not occur in relaxed spoken Gulf Arabic, where the inCaCaC form (Unit Sixteen) would be used instead: **yinkisir** 'it is broken, smashed'. Learning to read longer texts in Arabic thus involves learning the grammar of MSA in order to be able to distinguish between the many possible ways a word could be read. In practice, context reduces the readings in most cases to a single one; and where the writer of the text thinks there may be the possibility of confusion, he or she will indicate by putting in a vowel, or the **shadda** mark that indicates a doubled consonant, in order to disambiguate. Thus:

يكسَر

indicates that the vowel following the **s** is **a**, which indicates that the verb is passive, not active,that is, either **yuksar** or **yukassar**. But by no means all writers give this kind of help consistently; basically, you have to know a lot of MSA grammar before you can read an unvowelled text correctly.

Have a look at this text:

الحجر يكسر المقص ، المقص يقطع الورق ، الورق يغطي الحجر

Transliterated as it stands, without vowels, this is:

al-Hjr yksr al-mqS, al-mqS yqT9 al-wrq, al-wrq yghTy al-Hjr.

Without knowing what the vowels on the 3rd person imperfect verbs are (all begin with **y-**), or even knowing what the nouns are (which all begin with **al-** 'the'), one can still see that the structure is:

'The X ...s the Y, the Y ...s the Z, the Z ...s the X'

where '...s' stands for the imperfect verb. In fact, if you can spot the fact that the root consonants of the verbs are **ksr** 'to break', **qT9** 'to cut' and **ghTy** 'to cover', you can probably guess it means 'stone breaks scissors, scissors cut paper, paper covers stone'. Or, with short vowels and doubled consonants:

> **al-Hajar yaksir al-miqaSS, al-miqaSS yaqTa9 al-waraq,**
> **al-waraq yughaTTiy al-Hajar.**

And even then, the vowelling isn't complete, as we've left out the case vowels on the end of the nouns, and the mood vowels on the end of the verbs ... welcome to Modern Standard Arabic!

Modern Doha, Qatar

Answer key

Unit 1

Exercise 1.1
1 nuSS káylo láHam 2 búTil Halíib 3 dárzan bayD 4 káylo sámach
5 nuSS dárzan burtugáal 6 sandawíich jíbin

Exercise 1.2
1 Ahmad, make me a glass of tea please. 2 Layla, give me a bit of
fish please. 3 Muhammad, go and fetch me a packet of cigarettes
please. 4 Abdallah, give me a cup of coffee please. 5 Salwa, go and
fetch me a dozen oranges please.

Exercise 1.3
1 jiib lii nuSS káylo láHam min fáDlak. 2 9áTni nítfat jíbin min fáDlak.
3 ruuH saww lii sandawíich jíbin min fáDlak. 4 sawwi lii finjáal gáhwa
min fáDlich. 5 rúuHi jíibi lii glaas Halíib min fáDlich. 6 rúuHi jíibi lii dárzan
bayD min fáDlich.

Exercise 1.4

Male shopkeeper	Female shopkeeper
1 9áTni gúuTi chibríit min fáDlak.	8 9aTíini chiis putáyta min fáDlich.
2 gúuTi milH	9 káylo báSal
3 búTil díhin	10 gúuTi Saabúun
4 shwáyyat/nitfat xast	11 rub9 káylo shákkar
5 nuSS káylo 9aysh	12 káylo támar
6 gúuTi zíbid	13 gúT9at láHam
7 rub9 káylo TamáaT	14 glaas maay

Exercise 1.5

1 Kuwait 2 Riyadh 3 Doha 4 Bahrain 5 The Emirates

Exercise 1.6

1 Dubai 2 Muscat 3 Dammam 4 Qatar 5 Abu Dhabi

Unit 2

Exercise 2.1

1 il-mudíir 2 il-farráash 3 ir-rayyáal 4 il-poolíis 5 is-sikirtíir 6 is-sammáach 7 il-gaSSáab 8 il-mudárris 9 il-9áamil 10 ish-shárika

Exercise 2.2

1 sharikatáyn 2 darzanáyn 3 guT9atáyn 4 baHrayniyyáyn 5 guuTiyyáyn 6 jigaaratáyn 7 glaasáyn 8 is-sikirtiiráyn 9 il-muhandisáyn 10 is-smichatáyn 11 il-mukaanáyn 12 il-finjaaláyn 13 il-mikaanikiyyáyn 14 il-baytáyn

Exercise 2.3

1 Bring me the notebook! 2 Go to the office please! 3 Make me two cheese sandwiches please! 4 Give me a pen! 5 Take the car and go! 6 Go to the baker's and bring me two loaves! 7 Take the money! 8 Make me a cup of coffee, Ahmad! 9 Give me the cups! 10 Go to the butcher's and bring me two kilos of meat! 11 Go home! 12 Go to the headmaster (chief) please and bring me the books!

Exercise 2.4

1 xudh ish-shákkar! 2 ruuH il-muHássin! 3 jiib lii shwáyyat maay! 4 xudh is-sandawiicháat! 5 ruuH is-suug min fáDlak! 6 jiib lii d-dafáatir! 7 xudh buTláyn Halíib! 8 ruuH il-ingliiziyyáyn! 9 jíibi l-agláam min fáDlich! 10 xúdhi guuTiyyáyn jigáara! 11 rúuHi d-dáxtar! 12 xúdhi nítfat 9aysh! 13 jíibi l-akwáab! 14 jíibi l-kitaabáyn min fáDlich! 15 rúuHi l-mudarrisáat!

Exercise 2.5

Channel 5 = CNN. Channel 6 = Euro News. Channel 11 = MBC. Channel 13 = LBC. Channel 15 = Rotana Cinema. Channel 22 = Super Movie. Channel 23 = Movie Time. Channel 24 = Star. Channel 25 = Dream.

328

Answer key

Unit 3

Exercise 3.1

1 – cham dáftar hast/fii? – maa hast/fii/mish dafáatir bil-márra. 2 – cham shúrTi hast/fii? – maa hast/fii/mish bil-márra. 3 – cham láHam hast/fii? – maa hast/fii/mish láHam. 4 – cham mára hast/fii? – maa hast/fii/mish niswáan. 5 – cham búTil hast/fii? – maa hast/fii/mish b Táala bil-márra.

In all these answers, you can also say **máaku dafáatir**, etc., and **maa shay dafáatir**, etc. (Kuwaiti and Omani forms).

Exercise 3.2

1 – hast/fii xúbuz? – ay, hast/fii. 2 – hast/fii báSal? – la, maa fii/hast/mish il-yoom. 3 – hast/fii naas íhni? – la, maa hast/fii/mish ihni il-yoom. 4 – hast/fii mudarrisíin hunáak? – ay, hast/fii. 5 – hast/fii daxáatir íhni? – la, maa hast/fii/mish.

Exercise 3.3

1 bi cham dárzan bayD? 2 bi cham búTil díhin? 3 bi cham káylo burtugáal 4 bi cham gúuTi jigáara? 5 bi cham chiis áalu? 6 bi cham gúuTi chibríit? 7 bi cham xáyshat 9aysh? 8 bi cham ghárshat bábsi? 9 bi cham glaas chaay? 10 bi cham káylo rubyáan?

Dialogue 3.1

A How many clerks are there in the company?
B Nine.
A And how many secretaries?
B There're six.
A OK, are there messengers as well?
B Yes, there are two.
A And drivers … how many are there?
B There are no drivers at the moment.
A Right … are there any labourers?
B Yes.
A How many?
B Ten.

Exercise 3.4

1 – cham wálad fii fiS-Saff? – tís9a. 2 – cham yoom fii fil-usbúu9? – sáb9a. 3 – cham Híjra fii fil-bayt? – xams Híjar u Hammaamáyn. 4 – cham muhándis fii fish-shárika? – maa fii. 5 – cham fluus fii fil-míHfaDHa? – sáb9a danaaníir.

Dialogue 3.2

C Peace be upon you.
B And peace be upon you.
C Is there any beef today?
B Yes there is.
C How much is it per kilo?
B Two and a half dinars.
C Fine, give me half a kilo please.
B All right ... is there anything else (you want)?
C Is there any chicken?
B No, there's no chicken today. Tomorrow, God willing.
C OK. Good-bye.
B Good-bye.

Exercise 3.5

1 (a) il-yoom fii báSal? (b) il-chiis bi cham? (c) 9áTni chiis (d) u hast áalu? 2 (a) il-yoom fii tufáaH? (b) il-káylo bi cham? (c) 9áTni nuSS káylo (d) u fii burtugáal? 3 (a) il-yoom fii bayD? (b) id-dárzan bi-cham? (c) 9áTni darzanáyn (d) u hast 9ínab? 4 (a) il-yoom hast Halíib? (b) il-búTil bi cham? (c) 9áTni thaláatha bTáala (d) u fii jíbin? 5 (a) il-yoom fii 9aysh? (b) il-xáysha bi cham? (c) 9áTni árba9 xiyáash (d) u hast shákkar?

Note that, if the vendor is female, the correct imperative form is **9aTíini.**

Reading Arabic

Arabic	Transliteration	Translation
الرميلة	ar-rumayla	Al-Rumeila
مستشفى	mustashfa	hospital
حمد	Hamad	(name)

Unit 4

Exercise 4.1

1 il-ghúuri 9atíij. 2 il-karáasi jadíida/jíddad. 3 il-buyúut kabíira/kibáar. 4 il-yiháal farHaaníin. 5 il-Híjar Saghíira/Sigháar. 6 il-axáyn Tiwáal. 7 il-mára samíina. 8 il-gáhwa záyna. 9 il-Halíib raxíiS. 10 il-baaSáat xáalya. 11 il-míHfaDHa gháalya. 12 ir-rayyaaláyn ta9baaníin.

Exercise 4.2

1 il-Híjra jadíida.	The room is new.
il-buyúut jadíida/jiddad.	The houses are new.
il-mudarrisáat jiddad.	The female teachers are new.
il-farráash jadíid.	The messenger is new.
2 is-sayyáara gháalya.	The car is expensive.
il-kútub gháalya.	The books are expensive.
il-jíbin gháali.	The cheese is expensive.
il-chaay gháali.	The tea is expensive.
3 il-mudíir gháni.	The boss is rich.
il-bintáyn aghniyáa.	The two girls are rich.
il-málika ghaníyya.	The queen is rich.
il-waladáyn aghniyáa.	The two boys are rich.

Exercise 4.3

1 The tall boys 2 The fast aeroplane 3 An empty bus 4 The sun is hot 5 Old houses 6 The big (old) girls 7 Rich merchants 8 Give me the two big glasses please! 9 There are no cheap books here. 10 There are five new departments in the company.

Exercise 4.4

1 mikáaniki zayn 2 il-mudíir mit'áxxir 3 il-yoom báarid 4 il-máktab il-jadíid 5 il-mára ghaníyya 6 sáa9a raxíiSa 7 il-ákil ladhíidh 8 il-gáSir il-9atíij 9 sikirtíir jadíid 10 il-múshkila l-kabíira

Exercise 4.5

The old palace is a very large building. It has two outer doors and four inner doors. Its walls are white and its windows are of yellow and blue glass.

Exercise 4.6

wállah yaa 9áli, ána wáayid 9aTsháan ... jiib lii báarid min fáDlak.
'By God, Ali, I am very thirsty ... bring me a cold drink, please.'

   ... jiib lii glaas chaay min fáDlak.
   '... bring me a glass of tea, please.'
   ... jiib lii kuub maay min fáDlak.
   '... bring me a cup of water, please.'
   ... jiib lii gúuTi bábsi min fáDlak.
   '... bring me a bottle of Pepsi, please.'

wállah yaa 9áli, ána shway yuu9áan ... jiib lii rúuti jíbin.
'By God, Ali, I am a little hungry ... bring me a cheese roll.'

   ... jiib lii sandawíich láHam.
'... bring me a meat sandwich.'
   ... jiib lii 9aysh uu símich.
'... bring me some rice and fish.'

Exercise 4.7

– How are you Ahmad?
– God save you. How are you?
– I'm really tired today ...
– Why?
– Because there's a lot of work (to do).

– ána il-yoom za9láan – li'ann is-sayyáara xarbáana
– ána il-yoom za9láan – it-tilivizyúun xarbáan
– ána il-yoom za9láan – ith-thalláaja xarbáana
– ána il-yoom za9láan – il-ghassáala xarbáana
– ána il-yoom farháan – li'ann maa fii shúghul
– ána il-yoom farháan – li'ann maa fii mádrasa
– ána il-yoom farháan – li'ann il-yoom fii 9úTla
– ána il-yoom farháan – li'ann il-jaww báarid

Exercise 4.8

1 ana bardáan uu yuu9áan ... fii ákil? 2 fáaTma uu áHmad ta9baaníin li'ánn fii shúghul wáayid il-yoom. 3 il-makíina xarbáana ... hast mikáaniki íhni? 4 il-mudíir laysh za9láan? 5 il-bayt ábyaD uu lih sagf áxDar. 6 9áTni l-qamíiS il-áHmar wil-júuti l-ábyaD. 7 wizáarat id-daaxilíyya binyáan ábyaD 9ood. 8 is-sifáara l-briiTaaníyya fil-faríij il-9atíij. 9 il-bank il-wáTani binyáan Saghíir lih baab áswad kabíir. 10 is-safíir il-míSri xoosh rayyáal.

Exercise 4.9

1 The international airport 2 The head office 3 The Egyptian embassy 4 The Kingdom of Saudi Arabia (lit. 'the Saudi Arab Kingdom') 5 The Arabic language 6 An Indian restaurant 7 An Arab film 8 A secondary school 9 A light meal (= 'fast food') 10 An Arab school

Unit 5

Exercise 5.1

1 xamsíin káylo áalu/putáyta 2 sitt u arba9íin xáyshat smiit 3 thaláath
ímya uu sittíin mayl 4 sittíin alf náfar 5 miyatáyn alf diináar 6 fi sánat
alf u tis9 ímya u sitt u sab9íin 7 fi sánat alf u tis9 ímya u sittíin 8 sab9
ímya u xamsíin fils 9 miyatáyn xáyshat 9aysh 10 tis9 u thalathíin sána
u iHdá9shar sháhar

Exercise 5.2

1 bi cham il-burtugáal il yoom? – ímyat fils il-káylo.
2 bi cham il-báSal il-yoom? – xams u xamsíin fils il-káylo.
3 bi cham is-símich il-yoom? – thaláath ímya u xamsíin fils il-káylo.
4 bi cham il-mooz il-yoom? – míya u xams u sab9iin fils id-dárzan.
5 bi cham il-malfúuf il-yoom? – míya u xams u 9ishríin fils il-wáaHid.
6 bi cham il-chaay il-yoom? – sáb9iin fils ir-rub9.
7 bi cham it-támar il-yoom? – tis9 ímyat fils il-káylo.
8 bi cham iT-TamáaTa il-yoom? – xamsíin fils il-chiis.
9 bi cham il-áalu/putáyta il-yoom? – thamaaníin fils il-xáysha.
10 bi cham ir-ruwáyd il-yoom? – ithná9shar fils iS-Súrra.

Exercise 5.3

1 at 1.30 p.m. 2 at 8.40 a.m. 3 at 4.00 p.m. 4 at 8.30 p.m. 5 at 7.15 a.m.

Exercise 5.4

1 ithná9shar u thilth 2 thintáyn illa thilth 3 sítta ílla xams 4 sáb9a u
rub9 5 sáb9a u nuSS u xams 6 9áshra u 9áshar

Dialogue 5.1

A What's your full name please?
B My name is Hussain Muhammad Hassan.
A Fine ... and your nationality?
B Bahraini.
A Social status?
B Married.
A Do you have any children?
B Yes. Two girls and six boys.
A Six boys! That's a lot! And where d'you live?
B I live in Isa Town.
A In what street?
B Street 46. House No. 311.

A OK ... and what is your present job?
B Labourer in the company.
A Which company?
B BAPCO.
A What is your salary?
B 190 dinars per month.
A That's a good salary! And how old are you now?
B About 45.
A You have educational certificates of course?
B Yes. Primary school certificate.
A Is that all? Don't you have secondary?
B No.

Cultural point

The denominations of the banknotes are:

1 míyat báysa 2 riyáal wáaHid 3 diináar wáaHid 4 xámsa riyaaláat

Reading Arabic

The car registration number is 337357, and it is from Qatar. The values of the stamps from left to right are: 500 fils, 100 fils and 3 fils. In Arabic, these are: **xams ímyat fils**, **míyat fils** and **thaláatha fluus**.

The word for 'open' is **maftúuH**. The coffee shop is open from 8.00 a.m (**SabáaHan** 'in the morning') to 3.00 a.m (**láylan** 'at night').

> The business is open from Saturday to Thursday from 9.00 a.m. (**SabáaHan**) to 1.00 p.m. in the afternoon (**DHuhran** 'at noontime'), and from 4.00 p.m. (**9áSran** 'in the afternoon') to 10.00 p.m. (**láylan** 'at night'). On Friday it's open from 4.00 p.m. (**masáa'an** 'in the afternoon') to 10.00 p.m. (**láylan** 'at night'). The telephone numbers are 4361414 and 4362121.

Review Unit I

Exercise RI.1

- Ali, come here!
- Yes?
- Fetch me some cold water please. I'm very thirsty.
- God willing.

Dialogue Rl.1

B   Do I have any appointments tomorrow, Salwa?

S   You have two in the morning ... The first is at nine with official visitors from the Ministry of Foreign Affairs, and the other is at eleven-thirty with the chief engineer of the Antar Company.

B   Fine. Is there anything in the afternoon?

S   No, nothing ... you're free.

B   And in the evening?

S   You have a tennis match with Mr Johnson at six-fifteen ...

9índak thaláatha mawaa9íid iS-SubH ... il-máw9id il-áwwal wiyya SáHafi min jaríidat il-jumhuuríyya fis-sáa9a tís9a u nuSS ... with-tháani wiyya Taalibáyn min il-jáami9a fis-sáa9a 9áshra u rub9 ... with-tháalith fis-sáa9a iHdá9shar wiyya l-muqáawil áHmad 9abd álláh ... uu 9índak Háflat chaay fis-sifáara l-briiTaaníyya il-9áSir fis-sáa9a árba9a ... il-masáa 9índak Háflat 9ásha fil-bayt.

Dialogue Rl.2

A   Hello, Jaasim!

B   Hello, Ahmad! How are you? Well?

A   Fine! How are you?

B   Fine! ... Have some tea!

A   Excuse me, but I've got a bit of work to do at home.

B   What is it?

A   A real headache! My car's broken down.

B   Really? Repairing cars is my business!

A   Is that so?

B   Yes.

A   OK, come with me then!

Exercise Rl.2

My name is Faatima Muhammad Isa. I was born in Manama and I'm living at present in Al-Fadil quarter. I've got four kids – a girl called Nuura and three boys called Jaasim, Mubaarak and Baxayt. My daughter Nuura is 17 and she's a student at the university. She's a lovely girl! My son Jaasim works as a clerk in the Antar Company. He's a nice lad! Mubaarak works as a contractor. He's got a lot of money and a big red car. My third son is Baxayt. He's about 20 years old now, but he hasn't any qualifications or anything.

Exercise Rl.3

hast 9índak Halíib?	… nzáyn, 9áTni thaláath aghráash.
fii bábsi 9índak?	… nzáyn, 9aTni thaláatha kawaartíin.
hast milH?	… nzáyn, 9áTni gúuTi.
hast láHam xarúuf?	… nzáyn, 9áTni káylo.
fii 9índak burtugáal?	… nzáyn, 9áTni nuSS dárzan.
hast áalu il-yoom?	… nzáyn, 9áTni thaláatha kaylowáat.
fii malfúuf il-yoom?	… nzáyn, jiib lii wáaHid.
hast chibríit?	… nzáyn, 9áTni guuTiyyáyn.
fii 9índak jigáara?	… nzáyn, jiib lii xámsa gawáaTi.

Note that the answers in this exercise are only examples of the many acceptable sentences that could be made using **hast/fii**, **9índak**, **jiib**, **9aT**. It has been assumed that the shopkeeper is male.

Unit 6

Exercise 6.1

1 garíib min id-dawwáar. 2 yamm il-mátHaf, fi sháari9 9abdállah. 3 wayn il-másyid? 4 mgáabil shárikat '9ántar' fi sháari9 9uthmáan. 5 ba9íid 9an shárikat '9ántar'. 6 mgáabil il-bank il-wáTani. 7 garíib min il-báriid fi sháari9 9abdállah (or yamm il-baríid, etc.).

Translation:
1 Where is the museum? Near the roundabout. 2 Where is the National Bank? Next to the museum in 'Abdallah Street. 3 Where is the mosque? Behind Abu Bakr school. 4 Where is your home? Opposite the Antar Company in 'Uthman Street. 5 The post office is far away from the Antar Company. 6 Abu Bakr school is opposite the National Bank. 7 Where is the playground/pitch? Near the post office in 'Abdallah Street (or 'next to the post office …'). 8 ismáH lii, wayn il-baríid? yamm il-mál9ab. 9 wayn madrásat abu bakr min fáDlak? mgáabil il-bank il-wáTani. 10 ismáH lii, wayn shárikat '9ántar'? garíib min id-dawwáar fi sháari9 9uthmáan. 11 ismáH lii, wayn il-másyid? wára madrásat abu bakr. 12 wayn is-síinama min fáDlak? garíib min id-dawwáar fi sháari9 9abdállah.

Exercise 6.2

1 9ala l-mayz 2 taHt is-sayyáara 3 foog id-dáray 4 fis-siinama 5 fis-
sayyáara 6 taHt il-báHar 7 9ála (or foog) is-sagf 8 garíib min báyti
9 giddáam il-bank 10 foog il-bayt 11 fil-maay 12 yamm il-gáSir il-jadíid
13 ba9íid 9an il-kuwáyt 14 wara sháari9 il-málik 15 9ala l-jidáar 16
garíib min id-daríisha 17 taHt il-mayz

Exercise 6.3

id-dráywil fi máktabik uu fii rayyáal wiyyáah.

1 il-farráash fi máktabik uu fii rayyáal wiyyáah. 2 sikirtíirtik fi máktabik
uu fii rayyáal wiyyáaha. 3 il-muqáawil fi máktabik uu fii rayyáal wiyyáah.
4 bínti fi máktabik uu fii rayyáal wiyyáaha. 5 il-muhandisíin fi máktabik
uu fii rayyáal wiyyáahum. 6 iS-SaHafiyyíin fi máktabik uu fii rayyáal
wiyyáahum. 7 il-mudárrisa fi máktabik uu fii rayyáal wiyyáaha.

shfiik? ta9báan bas!

8 shfiich? 9aTsháana bas! 9 shfiih? za9laan bas! 10 shfíikum?
yuuwáa9a bas! 11 shfíihum? bardaaníin bas! 12 báyti yamm báytkum.
13 jigáara '9ántar' maa fóogah foog! 14 9alíyyi dyúun u maa 9índi fluus.
15 chayf il-Haal? foog in-náxal! 16 sh-fíiha ith-thaláaja? xarbáana.

Exercise 6.4

1 they heard 2 I/you (m.) stayed 3 you (pl.) played 4 she grew 5 she
filled 6 you (f.) hit 7 they stopped 8 we entered 9 he carried 10 I/you
(m.) filled 11 he broke 12 she heard 13 I/you (m.) stopped 14 they
broke 15 they carried 16 she wrote 17 we hit 18 you (pl.) drank 19 he
grew 20 you (f.) played 21 they sat 22 we grew

Exercise 6.5

1 they heard him 2 I/you (m.) filled it 3 he carried it 4 you (f.) broke it
5 we entered it 6 they broke it 7 we hit him 8 she wrote it 9 they drank
it 10 you (pl.) entered it. 11 simá9tik 12 Dírbatik 13 Hamalnáak
14 Dárabik (or Drábik) 15 sim9óok 16 síma9ik (or smá9ik) 17 Hímlatik
18 sima9náak 19 he hit me 20 they heard me 21 they hit me 22 they
carried me 23 you (pl.) hit me 24 you (f.) hit me 25 she heard me
26 he carried me 27 he heard me 28 she carried me 29 simá9thum
30 sim9óokum 31 Dírabhum 32 kisartóohum 33 Hamaltíihum
34 Darabnáakum 35 tirásthum 36 Dirbóokum

Dialogue 6.1

1 A Ali, have you written the report or not?
  B Sorry, Mr Smith, I haven't written it.
  A How come you haven't written it?
  B Yesterday I had a lot of work. I stayed in the office until 6.00 p.m. but I didn't finish it.
  A All right, never mind.
2 A Haven't you heard the news?
  B What?
  A Salwa passed the exam!
  B My goodness! What about Faatima?
  A She passed as well, but Abdallah failed.
  B And you?
  A I passed!
3 A What was your lunch like today, Ahmad?
  B By God, the best lunch there is ... rice and meat and stew, and we drank red tea.
  A Very nice! And then?
  B We sat in the sitting-room for a little and drank a cup of coffee.
  A Did you have a sleep or not?
  B Yes, we had a sleep in the afternoon.
4 A Hello? This is Ahmad ...
  B How are you Ahmad? Well?
  A God save you! Are the boys in?
  B No, they went out at 11.30 and they haven't returned yet.
  A OK, thanks. Good-bye.
5 A What's the matter, Amina, are you tired?
  B Yes, very tired. This morning I washed the clothes and then did the washing up. In the afternoon I played with the kids for two or three hours.

Reading Arabic

The landmarks are: 1 the National Bank (**il-bank il-wáTani**); 2 Abu Bakr School (**madrásat abúu bakr**); 3 the Antar Company (**shárikat 9ántar**); 4 Uthman Street (**sháari9 9uthmáan**); 5 the museum (**il-mátHaf**); 6 Abdullah Street (**sháari9 9abdállah**).

The Arabic for 'hotel' in the sign is **fúnduq**; the Arabic for 'parking' is **mawáaqif**, which is the plural of **máwqif**, literally 'stopping place'.

Unit 7

Exercise 7.1

1 they slept 2 you (pl.) went 3 you (f.) brought 4 she visited 5 I/you (m.) saw 6 I/you (m.) stole 7 I/you (m.) died 8 we became 9 he was afraid 10 you (pl.) sold 11 he stood up 12 they said 13 you (pl.) hunted (or caught) 14 we sold 15 you (f.) came 16 she became 17 I/you (m.) stood up 18 I/you (m.) visited 19 he died 20 they brought 21 she saw 22 I/you (m.) slept 23 they removed 24 I/you (m.) was 25 we said 26 they went 27 she brought 28 you (f.) were afraid 29 she was 30 he hunted (or caught)

Dialogue 7.1

1 A What happened?
  B They stole the car and sold it!
2 A Where did you go yesterday? We didn't see you.
  B We took the launch and went to a small island. We caught a lot of fish and ate it for dinner.
  A How nice!
3 A Why did they go home?
  B They didn't tell me.
4 A What did you bring from the market?
  B Lots of things ... some good beef and fruit and a few sacks of rice.
5 A Where's Jaasim? I haven't seen him for ages.
  B He's gone to London for the summer holidays.
  A Lucky fellow! how much money did he take with him?
  B 600 dinars.
6 A Where did you have dinner last night?
  B In a Lebanese restaurant called 'The Cedars'. The food was really delicious, and we drank a few bottles of Pepsi.

Exercise 7.2

1 gaal líyyi ínnik axádht rúxSa u riHt id-dáxtar li-ánnik maríiD. 2 gaal líyi ínnich bí9ti l-bayt il-9atíij li'ánnich maa 9índich fluus. 3 gaal líyyi ínnik jibt il-gháda wiyyáak u akált mínnah shwáy. 4 gaal liyyi ínnakum yíitaw min amríika Hagg il-9úTla u yíbtaw hadáaya Hagg il-yiháal. 5 gaal líyyi ínnakum fitáHtaw l-máxzan uu shíltaw l-aaláat mínnah. 6 gaal líyyi ínnich maa shiftíih min zamáan. 7 gaal líyyi ínnah sáakin il-Hiin

wára madrásat ábu bakr, garíib min báyti. 8 gaal líyyi ínnik rijá9t min
ish-shúghul u nimt min waqt li'ánnik ta9báan wáayid. 9 gaal líyyi
ínnakum fisháltaw fil-imtiHaanáat li'ánnakum kaslaaníin. 10 gaal líyyi
ínnik gumt u gilt 'áhlan wa sáhlan'.

Exercise 7.3

1 sa'álni law shift il-ahráam. 2 sa'álni law simá9taw l-xábar. 3 sa'álni
law rijá9t min ish-shúghul. 4 sa'álni law nijáHtaw fil-imtiHaanáat. 5 sa'álni
law kísart il-jaam. 6 sa'álni law búgti l-jánTa.

Dialogue 7.2

A trip to Kuwait

A Hello Abu Khaliil! Glad to see you safely home!
B God save you Hassan!
A How was the trip? You went by plane, didn't you?
B Yes. It was very nice. I got to Kuwait at three in the afternoon and
   I went straight from the airport to Salmiyya.
A Does your family live there?
B Yes. In the old days they used to have an old house in the
   market but they sold it and rented a new house last year. It's a
   lovely house with an interior courtyard in which there are trees,
   and an outer courtyard covered in flowers.
A Nice ... and did you go anywhere else in Kuwait?
B We went to the parks and the markets in the day-time and the
   restaurants at night.
A How was your family?
B In good health. It's a long time since I saw my cousin, and he's
   grown really big now – he's a man. He's clever as well – he came
   out first in the secondary school examinations.

Exercise 7.4

ríHla ila lándan

– yaa hála Hássan! ir-ríHla chayf káanat?
– záyna! wuSálna lándan fis-sáa9a árba9a il-9áSir uu ríHna síida
  min il-maTáar lil-fúnduq. káanat Hijrátna kíllish 96oda liha
  mánDHar jamíil min id-daríisha.
– wayn ríHtaw fi lándan?

- ríHna l-matáaHif, il-guSúur wil-maTáa9im fin-naháar, wil-masáariH wis-siinamáat bil-layl. il-' akil wáayid gháali bin-nísba ila kuwayt, láakin in-naas Tayyibíin wil-jaww báarid.
- cham fluus Saráftaw?
- wáayid! láakin maa 9aláyh! kínna mistaansíin fi lándan!

Reading Arabic

The months are: 1 rájab 2 Sáfar 3 jumáada al-áwwal 4 muHárram 5 shawwáal 6 dhu l-qá9da 7 rabíi9 ath-tháani 8 ramaDáan 9 dhu l-Híjja 10 sha9báan 11 rabíi9 al-áwwal 12 jumáada ath-tháani

The years are: 1 1982; 2 2003; 3 1765; 4 1830; 5 1066; 6 1492; 7 1567; 8 2010; 9 1604

The dates are: 2 jumáada ath-tháani 1008; 23 dhu l-qá9da 1341; 8 muHárram1259; 17 shawwáal 946; 26 rabíi9 al-áwwal 1410

Unit 8

Exercise 8.1

1 mudíir ish-shárika l-mashhúur 2 mudíir il-mádrasa l-míSri 3 baab il-bayt il-barráani 4 suug is-sámach 5 máktab il-Hisaabáat ir-ra'íisi 6 madrásat il-awláad il-kabíira 7 ra'íis il-wuzaráa 8 as9áar il-mawáadd il-gháalya 9 the Ministry of Defence 10 the State of Kuwait 11 the cup of coffee 12 the National Library's books 13 the street lights 14 the company boss's son 15 the daughter of a headmistress 16 the windows of my old house

Exercise 8.2

1 il-mádrasa maal (or máalat) il-banáat – the girls' school 2 il-máktab maal ir-ra'íis – the boss's office 3 iz-zaam maal in-naháar – the day shift 4 il-qamíiS il-áHmar máali – my red shirt 5 id-daráayish máalat il-Híjra l-9óoda – the windows of the big room 6 il-jánTa l-kabíira máaltich – your big case 7 il-jidráan id-daaxilíyya máalat il-gáSir – the palace's interior walls 8 il-maTáabix máalat máT9am il-'arz – the kitchens of the 'Cedars' restaurant 9 iS-SúHuf máalat il-kútub – the pages of the book 10 il-firíij maal il-bagaagíil – the greengrocers' quarter

Exercise 8.3

1 ay, láakin sí9ir is-sámach ághla bá9ad! – Yes, but the price of fish
is even higher! 2 ay, láakin 'ákil il-bayt áHsan bá9ad! (or ázyan bá9ad!)
– Yes, but home cooking is even better! 3 ay, láakin banáat lubnáan
áHla bá9ad! – Yes, but Lebanese girls are even prettier! 4 ay, láakin
sayyáarat axúuk ákbar bá9ad! – Yes, but your brother's car is even
bigger! 5 ay, láakin sikirtíirat ir-ra'íis kasláana ákthar bá9ad! – Yes,
but the boss's secretary is even lazier! 6 ay, láakin dukkáan il-baggáal
áwsax bá9ad! – Yes, but the greengrocer's shop is even dirtier! 7 ay,
láakin ráatib il-farráash agáll bá9ad! – Yes, but the salary of a servant
is even less! 8 ay, láakin sámach il-baHráyn aládhdh bá9ad! – Yes,
but Bahraini fish are even more tasty!

Exercise 8.4

1 la, amíina shúghulha mumárriDa. – No, Amina works as a nurse. 2
la, 9áli wíldah il-ákbar kíllish ghábi. – No, Ali's eldest son is very stupid.
3 la, háli il-bayt máalhum fi firíij il-Hammáam. – No, my family's house
is in Al-Hammaam quarter. 4 la, sálwa jaríimatha ínnaha gítlat zóojha.
– No, Salwa's crime was that she killed her husband. 5 la, il-xáadim
yoomíyyatah sítta danaaníir. – No, a labourer's day-wage is six dinars.
6 la, il-bank Táabiqah ith-tháani maa fiih kandíshan. – No, there's no
air-conditioning on the bank's second floor. 7 la, il-baHráyn bú9dha
9an gíTar thalaathíin mayl. – No, Bahrain is 30 miles from Qatar.

Exercise 8.5

1 In the seventh century AD. 2 Because there are two kinds of water
found there – sweet water and sea-water. 3 It declined. 4 They went
to work in the oil company. 5 About 300,000. 6 It has only a little oil.
7 It is a thousand times more beautiful – the writer thinks that because
Bahrain is his country.

Reading Arabic

The signs say and mean:

1 maTáar al-kuwáyt ad-dáwli – Kuwait International Airport 2 shárikat
'9ántar' as-siyaaHíyya – The Antar Touristic Company 3 qism al-lugháat
al-'ajnabíyya – The Department of Foreign Languages 4 bank al-
baHríyn al-wáTani – The Bahrain National Bank 5 máT9am 'az-záhra'
aS-Síini – The Zahra ('flower') Chinese Restaurant

Unit 9

Exercise 9.1

1 layn ga9ádt, sharábt glaas chaay uu axádht ir-rayúug. 2 bá9admaa
xalláSt ir-rayúug, la9ábt wíyya l-yiháal. 3 garáyt il-jaríida gabilmaa
Talá9t min il-bayt. 4 yoom wuSált il-máktab, riHt síida l-máSna9. 5
ba9admaa kisháft 9ala l-mantuujáat, Hicháyt wíyya t-tindáyl. 6 layn rijá9t
ila l-máktab, jaab líyyi l-farráash chaay. 7 Darábt tilifúun li zóojti gábil
maa riHt il-bank. 8 yoom xalláSt shúghli fil-bank, masháyt 9ala l-sayf
u axádht il-gháda.

Using 3rd person 'he':

1 layn gá9ad ... shárab ... u áxadh 2 bá9admaa xállaS ... lá9ab ...
3 gára ... gábil maa Tála9 ... 4 yoom wúSal ... raaH ... 5 bá9admaa
kíshaf ... Hícha ... 6 layn ríja9 ... jaab lih ... 7 Dárab tilifúun ... gábil
maa raaH ... 8 yoom xállaS ... misha ... uu áxadh ...

Exercise 9.2

1 the first ship 2 the first lesson in the third of the books 3 the twentieth
page of the last report 4 the end of the fourth month 5 the sixteenth
house on the right 6 the fifth street on the left 7 First, I haven't the
money and, second, there isn't enough time. 8 The first time I went to
Saudi Arabia I didn't like it; the second time I liked it better.

Dialogue 9.1

Questions:

1 Saar lih ihdá9shar sána. 2 shúghlah muHáasib ra'íisi fi shárikat tijáara.
3 mállat zóojtah min il-baHráyn uu sáyyid Johnson bá9ad mall mínha.
4 Tárrash risáala li mudíir shárikat is-smíit uu Tálab fíiha waDHíifa
jadíida. 5 il-imaaráat bálad faqíir fil-xamsiináat – maa fíiha maay wala
'ákil. 6 sukkáan il-imaaráat fagáara fil-xamsiináat. 7 fi ra'y is-sayyid
Johnson, il-imaaráat maal il-qadíim áHsan, li'ann gluub is-sukkáan
áHsan min glúubhum il-Hiin.

Translation:

The Emirates in the old days and now

I You've spent a long time in the Gulf, haven't you Mr Johnson?
J Yes indeed, about 17 years. I've been 6 years in Dubai now, but
   I stayed 11 years in Bahrain before that.

I   What were you doing in Bahrain?

J   I was chief accountant in a trading company.

I   So why did you come to the Emirates? Didn't you like Bahrain?

J   Yes, yes, I liked it a lot, but 11 years is a long time ... one day my wife told me she was fed up with the place. I said to her that I'd got fed up with the work at the trading company as well. So I sent a letter to the boss of the Dubai Cement Company, and asked for a new position. When I got the reply I was happy, because they accepted me on the spot, and gave me a better salary than the Bahraini company.

I   What d'you think of the Emirates?

J   The first time I came to the Emirates, about 20 years ago, there was nothing there – no water and no decent food. Frankly Bahrain was 20 times better. But little by little it changed, until, when I returned, it was completely different from before.

I   How was it different?

J   There are enormous buildings everywhere ... banks, apartment blocks, palaces, restaurants ... there's everything available, nothing lacking.

I   Do you like the Emirates of today better than the country you knew in the 1950s, or the other way around?

J   A difficult question. In the old days, people were poor, it's true, but they were good hearted. Now they're not. They've got richer than before – they've got houses furnished with everything, and big American cars ... but in my opinion, there's less companionship than there was.

I   You mean, there's more money but less companionship?

J   That's right ... and more illnesses as well!

Reading Arabic

The dates are:
2 April 1968; 17 October 2003; 31 January 2008; 4 August 1995; 13 October 1982; 10 December 1974; 6 June 1967; 17 July 1845; 14 March 1709; 30 March 2006.

The 'equivalent dates' in the box below are:
17 Rajab 1429 AH, corresponding to 21 July 2008 AD.

Unit 10

Exercise 10.1

ir-rayyáal ílli	shíftah ams	il-muHáasib ir-ra'íisi.
	kitábt lih risáala	muqáawil kabíir.
	Tarrásht lih taqríiri	Sadíig il-Háakim.
	gilt lik 9ánnah	shaxSíyya háamma.
	Hicháyt wiyyáah	náa'ib il-mudíir.
		SáHafi mashhúur.
		náa'ib ra'íis il-wuzaráa.
		il-muhándis ir-ra'íisi.

Exercise 10.2

il-Háfla~lli ríHtha			mashhúura.
il-9úTla~lli gaDáyt fi lándan			záyna/zayníin.
il-mukaanáat ílli zírthum			gháalya.
		káanat wáayid	Hálwa/Halwíin.
il-fanáadiq ílli nizált fíihum	káanaw		raxíiSa.
il-mabáani~lli shífthum			kabíira/kibáar.
il-jáami9a~lli ríHtha			wáasi9a.

Exercise 10.3

	it-tádhkira		
	ir-risáala		
	it-taqríir		Talábtah/ha gábil nuSS sáa9a?
	il-miláffa		ligáytah/ha ams?
wayn	il-ákil	illi	9aTáytik iyyáah/ha?
	il-barqíyya		kitabtah/ha?
	il-gálam		Talábtah/ha gábil subúu9?
	il-kitáab		shiráytah/ha iS-SubH?
	il-Tard		HaTTáytah/ha ihni gábil xams dagáayig?
	il-jaríida		

Exercise 10.4

1 hal-yáahil áshTar min dhaak, etc. 2 háadhi s-sayyáara ághla min dhiich, etc. 3 hal-Híjra áwsa9 min haadhíich, etc. 4 hash-shayb ákbar min dhaak, etc. 5 háadha l-wálad áTwal min haadháak, etc. 6 hal-kútub áqdam min dhayláak, etc. 7 háadhi l-xiyáash áthgal min

haadhayláak, etc. 8 hash-shíqqa árxaS min dhiich, etc. 9 háadhi l-jánTa
axáff min haadhíich, etc. 10 háadha sh-shayx ághna min dhaak, etc.

Suggested adjectives:
1 aghba ('more stupid') from ghábi 2 árxaS 3 áSghar 4 áSghar 5 áqSar
('shorter') from qaSíir 6 ajádd 7 axáff 8 ághla 9 áthgal 10 áfqar (or
agáll il-maal 'less of fortune')

Exercise 10.5

1 háadha húwa l-káatib ílli Tárrash ir-risáala. 2 haadhíich híya l-mára~lli
yaat máktabik. 3 haadhayláyn hum il-masaakíin ílli maa 9índhum fluus.
4 haadhayláyn hum iS-Súwar illi gilt lik 9ánhum. 5 haadháak húwa
sh-shayb illi ligáytah ams. 6 háadha húwa d-dukkáan illi shiráyt hal-
júuti fiih. 7 háadha húwa l-máT9am illi akált fiih ams. 8 háadhi híya
l-bádla illi shiráytha s-subúu9 il-máaDi. 9 háadhi híya l-fluus illi ligáytha
fish-sháari9. 10 haadhayláyn hum il-9ummáal illi Tílbaw fluus ákthar.
11 háadhayláak hum ish-shubbáan illi sharábt wiyyáahum chaay.
12 háadha huwa l-fúnduq illi nizált fiih áaxir márra yiit il-kuwáyt.

Exercise 10.6

1 ir-rayyáal illi shíftah mub ínta. 2 layn ríja9t min il-máktab maa ligáyt
áHad fil-bayt. 3 fii áHad bárra. 4 hádha mub illi bághatah. 5 maa
sháafaw áHad wa la sím9aw shay. 6 maa 9ájabni il-fúnduq – maa káan
naDHíif u kaan fii wáayid Dájja. 7 máHHad ja l-maTáar yoom wuSált.
8 hal-Halíib illi shiráytah mínnik iS-SubH mub Táazij. 9 hal-gúTa9
ghiyáar illi shiráythum mínnik maa fíihum fáyda (or mub mufíida).
10 máHHad gaal líyyi ínnik mawjúud.

Dialogue 10.1

A Hello Jaasim, how are you?
B Hello Abu Khaliil. I'm not feeling well today.
A Why? What's the matter? Are you tired?
B Yes, I've got a bit of a cold ... my head's going round.
A Haven't you been to the doctor?
B Yes I've been, but he didn't give me good medicine. Those
   doctors are useless, you know.
A What did the doctor tell you then?
B Nonsense ... he told me 'Just take this medicine twice a day and
   rest at home.'

A And this medicine he gave you, what is it?
B Just little white pills. When I got home I took one of them but
   the taste was bad – horrible in fact. I haven't taken any more –
   I threw the rest away.
A I've got a good idea!
B Let's hear it!
A There's a medicine that is better than the one he gave you ...
   and it's in my fridge!
B What?
A A freezing cold bottle of Pepsi!

Reading Arabic

The name on the first card is Dr **áHmad bin SáaliH al-Yamáani**; he
is the Rector (**mudíir**, 'director') of Prince Sultan University (**jáami9a**);
he is from the Kingdom of Saudi Arabia; his PO box number is 66833
in Riyadh (postcode 11586); other information given is his office
phone number (454-8350); the main switchboard (**sintráal**) number
(454-8489/454-8011); his fax number (454 8317); and his mobile
(**jawwáal**) number (050 5238765).

On the second card, the name is **muHámmad mubáarak al-múrri**.
The م that precedes it stands for **muhándis** 'engineer', which is used
as a title, like **duktúur** 'Dr', in the Arab World. He is a Deputy Director
(**náa'ib mudíir**) at the Military Engine Workshop (**warsh al-muHarrikáat
al-9askaríyya**) at the Gulf Aircraft Maintenance Co. (**shárikat al-xalíij
li Siyáanat aT-Taa'iráat**). He gives telephone, fax and mobile numbers
(he uses **mutaHárrik** rather than **jawwáal** as the word for 'mobile phone';
both words mean 'moving, mobile, roving around'); and his email, telex
and PO box numbers. He is from Abu Dhabi, United Arab Emirates.

Review Unit II

Exercise RII.1

1 – cham fluus axádht?
   – arba9íin diináar.
   – gilt lik árba9a mub arba9íin!
2 – cham kartúun jigáara shiráyt?
   – ithná9shar kartúun.
   – gilt lik ithnáyn (or kartuunáyn), mub ithná9shar!

3   – cham yoom 9úTla axádht?
    – xamstá9shar yoom.
    – gilt lik xámsa mub xamstá9shar!
4   – cham xáyshat 9aysh shiráyt?
    – sittá9shar xáysha.
    – gilt lik sitt mub sittá9shar!
5   – cham gáfshat dáwa axádht?
    – gafshatáyn (or thintáyn).
    – gilt lik árba9 mub thintáyn!

Exercise RII.2

1   – limán 9aTáyt il-fluus?
    – lil-farráash.
    – gilt lik il-káatib mub il-farráash!
2   – limán bi9t ith-thalláaja?
    – lil-miSríyya.
    – gilt lik il-lubnaaníyya mub il-miSríyya!
3   – limán 9aTáyt il-xábar?
    – li náa'ib il-mudíir.
    – gilt lik il-mudíir, mub náa'ibah!
4   – limán Tarrásht il-barqíyya?
    – li axúuk ílli fi amríika.
    – gilt lik li axúuyi~lli fi ingíltara, mub ílli fi amríika!
5   – limán Tarrásht id-da9wa?
    – li ra'íis shárikat it-tijáara.
    – gilt lik ra'íis wakáalat is-safariyyáat, mub shárikat it-tijáara!

Exercise RII.3

Presents for him

1 qamíiS	kraafáat
2 sáa9a	bádla
3 kitáab	siidíi
4 jawwáal	ráydo
5 jaakáyt	bantalóon

Presents for her

1   – shiráyt líha nafnúuf.
    – háadhi mub il-hádiya~lli baghátha, Tílbat júuti.
    – bas híyya maa gáalat líyyi chidhíi.

2 tannúura	bluus
3 áalat taSwíir	xáatam
4 kambyúutar	sáykal
5 áala Háasiba	gálam

Exercise RII.4

1 – háadhi mádrasa kabíira.
  – ay, láakin hast ákbar min háadhi fi wasT il-madíina.
  – wállah? 9úmri maa shíftha!
2 – háadha firíij faqíir.
  – ay, láakin hast áfqar min háadha garíib min il-jísir.
  – wállah? 9úmri maa shíftah!
3 – háadha másyid jamíil.
  – ay, láakin hast ájmal min háadha mgáabil il-gáSir il-9atíij.
  – wállah? 9úmri maa shíftah!
4 – háadha mábna qadíim.
  – ay, láakin hast áqdam min háadha garíib min maktab il baríid.
  – wállah? 9úmri maa shíftah!
5 – háadha máT9am wásix.
  – ay, láakin hast áwsax min háadha yamm síinama 9ántar.
  – wállah? 9úmri maa shíftah!
6 – háadha sáaHil jamíil.
  – ay, láakin hast ájmal min háadha 9ála bu9d xamst amyáal min íhni.
  – wállah? 9úmri maa shíftah!
7 – háadhi má'dhana Tawíila.
  – ay láakin hast áTwal min háadhi garíiba min il-bank il-9árabi.
  – wállah? 9úmri maa shíftha!
8 – háadha maTáar Hadíith.
  – ay, láakin hast áHdath min háadha fish-shárja.
  – wállah? 9úmri maa shíftah!

Dialogue RII.1

Questions:
1 Tílbaw mázza lubnaaníyya káamla (mujáddara, HúmmuS bi TaHíina, baylinjáan máHshi, etc.). 2 li'ánnahum mub yuwáa9a wáayid. 3 jaab líhum iT-Talabáat maal naas ghayr. 4 li jimáa9a min is-sa9uudiyyíin.

Translation:
M Right, what d'you have that's nice? We're not very hungry.

W We've got everything ... for example roast chicken, and there's rice and fish ... we've got lamb with yoghurt, and meat sandwiches ...

J No, no! All those dishes are Gulf dishes – they're a bit heavy. Don't you have any hummus and stuffed aubergines and fried lentils ... light Lebanese dishes I mean? We're not *that* hungry!

W Yes, we've got as much Lebanese food as you want!

M OK, bring us a big plate of fried lentils and hummus and ... a complete hors d'oeuvres, I mean.

W Yes sir.

J Where's the waiter?

M Here he comes now!

W OK, this is two plates of chicken, and this is the rice and fish you ordered ...

J No, no! This is a mistake! This food isn't for us! It must be for some other people. We ordered a complete hors d'oeuvres, not these things you've brought!

W No, no! What I've brought is correct! Your orders are written on this paper. Look! 'Two plates of chicken –'

M What's the number of this table?

W Sixteen.

M What's the number you've written on this paper?

W 'Six' is written ... oh! Sorry, I'm mistaken, this food isn't yours, it's true, it's for those Saudis sitting over there! And I've given them your hors d'oeuvres!

Unit 11

Exercise 11.1

1 – ... ta9Tíihum? – a9Tíihum ... 2 – ... sittíin diináar ... 3 – ... ta9Tíiha?
– a9Tíiha ... 4 – ... kill subúu9. 5 – ... ta9Tíina? – a9Tíikum ... 6 –
... ta9Tíini? – a9Tíik ... 7 – ... xams u sab9íin diináar ... 8 – ... kill
subuu9áyn.

Exercise 11.2

1 – ... yHibb ...? 2 – 9aysh u símich. 3 – ... tiHibbúun ...? – niHíbb
... 4 – ... ákil inglíizi. 5 – ... tiHibbíin ...? – aHíbb ... 6 – diyáay
máshwi. 7 – ... yiHibbúun ...? – yiHibbúun ... 8 – ... baylinjáan
máHshi.

Exercise 11.3

1 – … míSir ashúuf il-ahráam. 2 – … súuriya ádris 9árabi. 3 – … bitruuHúun …? – binrúuH súuriya nádnis 9árabi. 4 – … biyruuHúun …? – biyrúuHuun súuriya yidirsúun 9árabi. 5 – … biyruuHúun il-báHar yiSiidúun símich. 6 – … biyrúuH …? – … biyrúuH il-báHar yiSíid símich. 7 – … biyrúuH il-jibáal yáaxidh ráaHatah.

Exercise 11.4

1 – … sáa9a thaláatha u nuSS. 2 – … biyúun? – biyúun … 3 – … biyíi? – biyíi … 4 – … sáa9a xámsa ílla rub9. 5 – … bityíin? – bayíi … 6 – … sáa9a ithná9shar. 7 – … bityíi? – bityíi … 8 – … sáa9a thaláatha u thilth.

Exercise 11.5

1 – … chaay? 2 – … gáhwa? 3 – tishirbúun …? – la, maa níshrab. 4 – yíshrab …? – la, maa yíshrab. 5 – … báarid? 6 – … 9aSíir? 7 – tishirbíin …? – la, maa áshrab. 8 – yishirbúun …? – la, maa yishirbúun.

Exercise 11.6

1 – … sayyáara jadíida? 2 – shíraw …? – la, maa shíraw … byishrúun … 3 – shiráyt …? – la, maa shiráyt … báshri … 4 – … gúT9at 'arD jadíida? 5 – … is-subúu9 il-jaay. 6 – shírat …? – la, maa shírat … bitíshri … 7 – … thalláaja jadíida? 8 – shiráyti …? – la, maa shiráyt … báshri …

Exercise 11.7

1 – … il-baHráyn …? – … il-baHráyn …! 2 – maa ta9íbkum …? – … ta9íbna …! ta9íbna …! 3 – … is-sa9uudíyya …? – … is-sa9uudíyya …! 4 – maa ti9íjbah …? – … ti9íjbah …! ti9íjbah …! 5 – maa yi9ijbúunah il-kuwaytiyyíin …? – … yi9ijbúunah …! yi9ijbúunah …! 6 – maa yi9ijbúunha …? – … yi9ijbúunha …! yi9ijbúunha …! 7 – … is-sa9uudiyyíin …? – … is-sa9uudiyyíin! …! 8 – maa yi9ijbúunich …? – … yi9ijbúunni …! yi9ijbúunni …!

Exercise 11.8

1 … il-kúura iT-Táa'ira … 2 … tíila … 3 káanat tíl9ab … híyya Saghíira. 4 káanaw yili9búun … húmma Sigháar. 5 … ytimmúun fil-bayt … 6 … húmma kibáar. 7 … ySiidúun símich … 8 kaan yiSíid símich … húwwa kabíir.

Dialogue 11.1

A Hello.

B Hello ... What can I do for you?

A This car of mine isn't running well. I don't know what's wrong with it ... Maybe something's wrong with the plugs or the carburettor ...

B OK, put the bonnet up and let's have a look inside ... No, nothing wrong with the plugs ... let's see the breaker-points ... a bit dirty, need cleaning, but that's not the cause ... This is a problem ...! When was the last time you put oil in it?

A I don't know exactly ... about two or three months ago ...

B Oh! That's not so good! In this hot weather you must put oil in every month. Let's look at the level ... See! The level's very low. It's almost run out. I'll put a couple of cans in for you and you'll see how well your car goes ... but no, two cans isn't enough ... let's put in one more ... that's OK like that ... finished! That's two and a half dinars please.

A Here's your money ... and thanks.

B Why not take another can? Maybe it'll come in handy on the road!

A That's true ... Give me a big can and I'll put it in the boot.

Dialogue 11.2

1 Jaasim's father. 2 12.15 p.m. 3 2.00 p.m. 4 Jaasim's father. 5 He's ill, and the doctor says he must stay at home. 6 He'll be wearing a yellow suit and a blue shirt.

Reading Arabic

The sign says, at the top, *wáHdat al-baríid* 'Postal Unit' (or 'Post Office') and, below, *wizáarat an-naql wa l-ittiSaaláat* 'Ministry of Transport and Communications'.

Unit 12

Exercise 12.1

1 bagháani arúuH il-bayt. 2 abghíik tigúul lii shay. 3 tabbíih yighásil is-sayyáara. 4 nabbíikum taaklúun hal-akil wiyyáana. 5 tabbíinni agúul lich iS-Sidq? 6 bághaw ydirsúun fil-qáahira. 7 bagháyti tishríin dhaak

il-júuti, muu chidhíi? 8 hal-Híjra tábbi líha tanDHíif. 9 il-baab dhaak yábghi lih taSlíiH. 10 tábbi líha fluus.

Exercise 12.2

1 maa gidárt asíkk il-baab. 2 maa yigdarúun yooSlúun íhni gábil sáa9a tís9a. 3 gidárt tígra il-xaTT máalah? 4 layn shaaf il-ghálaT gaam yíD-Hak. 5 yoom ana 9úmri 9ishríin sána, gumt áshrab jigáayir. 6 bá9ad sáa9a gáamat iT-Tayyáara tánzil. 7 DHalláyt áskin fir-riyáaD sanatáyn bá9ad. 8 támmat tímshi thaláath saa9áat. 9 DHállaw yDirbúun lii tilifúun kill yoom. 10 maa zilt táskin garíib min máktab il-baríid, muu chidhíi? 11 maa zaal yisúug sayyáarat foord. 12 maa zilt ádhkir haadháak il-yoom.

Exercise 12.3

1 ana gáa9id áktib risáala. 2 amíina gáa9da tígra mujálla. 3 gáa9da táknis il-arDíyya. 4 láazim maa tígra hal-xárbuTa. 5 muu láazim yírja9 báachir, muu chidhíi? 6 lázim maa tixáaf min ir-rayyáal dhaak. 7 muu láazim trúuH Háalan. 8 yúmkin yábbi yirúuH. 9 yúmkin maa y9arfúun yigrúun. 10 yúmkin yífraH layn yishúufah, maa~dri.

Exercise 12.4

1 – ...9áshar siníin ... il-kúura iT-Táa'ira.
2 – ... xamstá9shar sána ... yiHíbb dhiich il-bint.
  – ... maa zaal yiHíbbha!
3 – ... 9ishríin sána ... yirúuH is-síi-nama marratáyn fil-yoom.
  – ... maa zaal yirúuH!
4 – ... wáaHid u 9ishríin sána ... yisúug sayyáarat káadilaak.
  – ... maa zaal yisúug!
5 – yoom híya 9úmurha ithná9shar sána káanat tíTbax zayn.
  – Sidj, u maa záalat tíTbax zayn!
6 – ... tisa9tá9shar sána ... tílbas azyáa gharbíyya.
  – ... maa záalat tilbáshum!
7 – ... sitt siníin ... tígra saa9atáyn kill yoom.
  – ... maa záalat tígra saa9atáyn kill yoom.
8 – ... arba9tá9shar sána ... táktib qíSaS.
  – ... maa záalat táktibhum!

Exercise 12.5

yabghíik	– 1 tyiib lih finjáal gáhwa.
	– 2 tighásil sayyáartah.
	– 3 truuH is-suug.
	– 4 tishíil il-wásix min hal-Híjra.
	– 5 tyíi báachir sáa9a árba9a.
shitigúul il-mudíira?	
tabghíich	– 6 tili9bíin wíyya yiháalha.
	– 7 tyiibíin líha glaas maay.
	– 8 tiDirbíin tilifúun lish-shúrTa.
	– 9 tisikkíin il-baab il-barráani.
	– 10 timurríin 9ála l-bank u ta9Tíin risáala lil-mudíir.

Exercise 12.6

1 layn raaH il-kuwáyt, gaam yílbas díshdasha. 2 layn gára l-maqáal, gaam yíD-Hak. 3 layn ríkab il-baaS, gaam yíHchi bi Soot 9áali. 4 layn shaaf il-ghálaT, gaam yíbchi. 5 layn wuSált il-xalíij, gumt áshrab wáayid gáhwa. 6 layn kint fi 9umáan, gumt ámshi fil-jibáal. 7 layn shiráyt tilivizyúun, gumt atímm fil-bayt wáayid. 8 layn riHt il-qáahira, gumt áTla9 wáayid li Hafalát.

Exercise 12.7

1 – laazim trúuH il-bank il-Hiin! – la, mub láazim il-Hiin … barúuH bá9ad shway. 2 – … truuH is-suug …! – … barúuH is-suug … 3 – … tighásil il-mawaa9íin …! – … baghásilhum … 4 – … tígra háadha l-kitáab …! – … bagráah … 5 – … tíTbax il-gháda …! – … ba Tábxah … 6 – … táaxidh had-dáwa …! – … báaxidhah … 7 – … táktib hal-jawáab …! – … bakítbah … 8 – … truuH tyiib iT-Tawáabi9 …! – … barúuH ayíibhum … 9 – … táDrub lih tilifúun …! – … báDrub lih tilifúun … 10 – … timúrr 9aláyha …! – … bamúrr 9aláyha …

Exercise 12.8

1 – … a9Tíih ir-risáala s-subúu9 il-máaDi. – … 9aTáytah iyyáaha …! 2 – … a9Tíik il-xábar ams. – … 9aTáytni iyyáah …! 3 – … a9ázmik lil-Háfla min gábil. – … 9azámtni …! 4 – … a9Tíih il-9aqd ish-sháhar il máaDi. – … 9aTáytah iyyáah …! 5 – … ágra l-maqáal min gábil. – … garáytah …! 6 – … a9Tíik ma9áashik il-báarHa. – … 9aTáytni iyyáah …! 7 – … ágra taqríirha min gábil. – … garáytah …!

Exercise 12.9

1 gilt lih yájlis láakin tamm yóoguf. 2 ... yígra l-kitáab ... yísma9 ir-ráydo. 3 ... yílbas díshdáasha ... yílbas bantalóon. 4 ... yáskit ... yíHchi bi Soot 9áali. 5 ... yiDHíll fil-faráash ... yíg9ad. 6 ... yáakil il-gháda ... yíl9ab fish-sháari9. 7 ... yismá9ni ... yígra jaríidatah. 8 ... yóoguf ... yisúug. 9 ... yárkuD ... yímshi bi búTu'. 10 ... yáaxidh ráaHatah ... yádris.

Exercise 12.10

1 – ... yighásil is-sayyáara Háalan! – ... yíHchi wíyya l-mudíir. 2 – ... iyíi yishúuf háadha ...! – ... yáaxidh Suwar. 3 – ... yáknis il-arDíyya ...! – ... yíSbagh il-baab. 4 – ... yirúuH il-bank ...! – ... yáktib taqríir haamm. 5 – ... yirúuH máktab il-baríid ...! – ... yádris Hagg il-imtiHaanáat.

Exercise 12.11

1 la tóoguf, tóogufi, tóogufu! 2 ruuH, rúuHi, rúuHu l-bayt! 3 la tigúul, tigúuli, tigúulu lii háadha! 4 shiil, shíili, shíilu háadha! 5 9áTni, 9aTíini, 9aTúuni iyyáah! 6 sikk, síkki, síkku l-baab! 7 íTla9, íTla9i (Tíl9i), íTla9u (Tíl9u) bárra! 8 ta9áal, ta9áali, ta9áalu~hni! 9 la tíshrab, tíshrabi (tishírbi) tíshrabu (tishírbu)! 10 la tinsáaha, tinsáyha, tinsúuha! 11 íkilhum, iklíihim, iklúuhum kíllhum! 12 óoguf, óogfi, óogfu garíib min il-bank! 13 la tiHúTTha, tiHuTTíiha, tiHuTTúuha hnáak! 14 yíibhum, yiibíihum, yiibúuhum líyyi! 15 guul, gúuli, gúulu shay! 16 xudh, xúdhi, xúdhu ráaHatik/ich/kum! 17 la tiTíiH, tiTíiHi, tiTíiHu! 18 liff, líffi, líffu yasáar ihni! 19 la tilíff, tilíffi, tilíffu yamíin! 20 íg9ad, íg9adi (gí9di) íg9adu (gí9du) yámmi! 21 íktibha, iktibíiha (kitbíiha), iktibúuha (kitbúuha) bi súr9a! 22 gúTThum, guTTíihum, guTTúuhum!

Note that in all fem. and pl. negative imperative examples, the final **-n** can be retained. So, for example, **la tiguulíin** (f.), **la tiguulúun** (pl.) 'don't say!', etc. are also possible.

Dialogue 12.1

A I want to go to the Arab Bank ... how much d'you want?

B Half a dinar.

A No, that's too much (lit. 'does not happen'). Take three hundred fils!

B Four hundred.

A OK.

B Where is the Arab Bank exactly?
A In Sheikh Salman Street … go round this roundabout … OK …
and take the first street on the right … turn left at the Casino
restaurant … go straight on – no, no! I said turn left not right!
What's the matter with you?
B Sorry. I've only been driving a taxi for three days. Don't get upset!
A It doesn't matter … stop here please … here's your money …
thanks.

B abbi arúuH wizáarat il-xaarijíyya.
A wayn háadha?
B maa tádri? fi sháari9 il-mághrib, garíiba min bank il-kuwáyt.
A diináar wáaHid.
B xudh sab9 ímya u xamsíin fils.
A zayn.
B Tuuf id-dawwáar … zayn … liff yasáar … xudh tháani sháari9
9ala yamíinik … la … la truuH síida! gilt lik táaxidh tháani sháari9
yamíin!
A 9áfwan. maa a9árf hal-mínTaqa dhi.

Exercise 12.12

1 First, take a little rice and pour water over it. 2 Put the saucepan on
the heat and don't forget to add a little salt. 3 Cut up the meat into
small pieces with a sharp knife and brown it with a little oil. 4 Add
spices to taste with a little flour. 5 Pour hot water on the meat and stir
it over the heat until it boils. 6 Cover the saucepan and leave it boiling
for 20 minutes until it is ready. 7 Remove the rice from the heat when
it is ready and shake it dry in a sieve ('sieve it until it dries').

1 xúdhi shwáyyat 9aysh u ghaslíih fi maay báarid. 2 ghaTTíih bi maay
báarid u HúTTi l-jídir 9ála D-Daww. 3 DHíifi nítfat milH. 4 gáSgiSi
d-diyáay Sigháar u Hamríiha. 5 DHíifi nitfat TiHiin u xúuri dagiigatáyn.
6 Súbbi maay Harr 9ala d-diyáay u xúuri bi gáfsha layn yíghli. 7 gháTTi
l-jídir u xáfDi D-Daww. 8 layn yínDHaj il-9aysh, shiilíih min iD-Daww u
shaxlíih, la tixallíin il-9aysh yíghli ákthar min xamstá9shar dagíiga.

Unit 13

Exercise 13.1

1 – Where's the officer who wrote this report?
   – I don't know, I haven't seen him today.

2 – Have you been to Egypt?
  – No, not yet. I'll go next year.
3 – Read the first paragraph on page five, please.
  – Excuse me, sir, my friend who is absent has taken my book!
4 – Watch out for him, he's a very dishonest man!
  – Not just dishonest, he's a thief as well. He's stolen my wallet!
5 – Don't get upset, my friend!
  – Why shouldn't I get upset? Those layabouts beat me with a stick!

Exercise 13.2

1 – wayn HaaTT id-dáftar máali? mub laagíih. – fi d-durj il-yamíin lil-mayz. 2 – wayn bádlatik il-jadíida? – bá9adni muu maaxídhha min il-xayyáaT. 3 – 9áThum glaas chaay! – la, maa yabbúun. kill minhum sháarib glaasáyn. 4 – ir-rayyáal dhaak yaay min wayn? – ana laagíih fish-sháari9. 5 – shloon muu sháayil dhaak il-mayz? – maa ágdar ashíilah, thagíil wáayid.

Exercise 13.3

1 – la, muu maaxídhha bá9ad. 2 – la, muu faahímha bá9ad. 3 – la, muu máaxdhah bá9ad. 4 – la, muu gaaríiha bá9ad. 5 – la, muu waaSílha bá9ad. 6 – la, muu laagyíinha bá9ad. 7 – la, muu Saaydíinah bá9ad. 8 – la, muu jaaybíinah bá9ad. 9 – la, muu raaj9íin bá9ad. 10 – la, muu raayHín bá9ad.

Translation:

1 – Have you got your Secondary School Certificate yet or not?
  – No, not yet.
2 – Do you understand Arabic yet or not?
  – No, not yet.
3 – Have you had breakfast yet or not?
  – No, not yet.
4 – Have you read that paragraph yet or not?
  – No, not yet.
5 – Have you reached the end of the story or not?
  – No, not yet.
6 – Have you found the money that you lost yet or not?
  – No, not yet.
7 – Have they (you) caught the thief yet or not?
  – No, not yet.

8 – Have they brought the food you ordered yet or not?
  – No, not yet.
9 – Have they returned from the trip yet or not?
  – No, not yet.
10– Have they gone to the mosque yet or not?
  – No, not yet.

Exercise 13.4

1 – la, la, táwni shaaríiha! 2 – la, la, táwha ráaj9a! 3 – la, la, táwhum daashshíinha! 4 – la, la, táwwah ráayiH! 5 – la, la, táwni sháayfah! 6 – la, la, táwhum naashríinah! 7 – la, la, tawna maaklíinah! 8 – la, la, táwha ghaaslátha (or ghaasláthum)

Translation:

1 – I thought you bought this suit ages ago.
  – No no, I've just bought it!
2 – I thought Amiina returned from Syria the day before yesterday.
  – No no, she's just returned!
3 – I thought they went into the room three hours ago.
  – No no, they've just gone in!
4 – I thought he went to the doctor's two days ago.
  – No no, he's just gone!
5 – I thought you saw the mistake before me.
  – No no, I've just seen it!
6 – I thought they published the book last year.
  – No no, they've just published it!
7 – I thought you had dinner a short while after you got back.
  – No no, we've just had it!
8 – I thought she did the dishes before she went out.
  – No no, she's just done them!

Exercise 13.5

1 She's a girl who is (well) known in the district. 2 I didn't pick up the skirt from the tailor's because the hem was ripped. 3 This sink is full of water because the pipe from it is blocked up with rubbish. 4 Have you seen the plastic bags dumped on the seashore? The government ought to remove them. 5 I wanted to talk to you on the phone yesterday but the line was engaged all the time. 6 Have you found the money that was lost? No, not yet. 7 What d'you want to eat? I want a boiled egg with a little roast meat. 8 Who is responsible for this mess?

Not us, sir, it's them who are responsible! 9 When we were young, marbles was a very popular game with us. 10 Have you heard the news? The Minister of Defence has been killed! 11 The late Sheikh Salman was a famous ruler. 12 The Arab countries are open to everyone – everyone is allowed entry.

Exercise 13.6

One day, Juha spread out his shirt on the roof. Then he went downstairs, having left it up there to dry. Juha began to cry out. His neighbour hears him and comes out, and he says to him 'What's up Juha?' (Juha) says to him 'My shirt has fallen from the roof to the ground!' So the neighbour says 'So what?' So Juha says 'If I'd been in the shirt I'd have died!'

Reading Arabic

The vegetable tags are, from the top, left to right: carrots 250 per kilo; cabbage 350; beetroot 175; apples 350; oranges 600; and bananas 500. The meat prices are, left to right: beef 900 per kilo; mutton 750; chicken 500; and kebab 425.

Unit 14

Exercise 14.1

1 la tiTárrish haadháak il-wálad! 2 SálliH ith-thalláaja! 3 la twággif is-sayyáara! 4 wáSSilni Il-bayt min fáDlik! 5 fákkir gábil la tsáwwi shay! 6 wáddha l-baríid! 7 rawwúuni Suwárkum! 8 sállif líi xamsíin diináar min fáDlik! 9 la tiHaachíihum! 10 la tiHáawil truuH! 11 He came and put up the picture crookedly but put it straight later. 12 Don't put that tyre on … it's got a puncture. 13 Clean the windows please and repair the broken door. 14 Give me the report and I'll think about the matter. 15 They sent me to school (I was sent to school) when I was five. 16 They travelled to India and stayed there a long time. 17 Don't talk to me in that tone! Lower your voice! 18 When they sacked him from his job at the company, he took up repairing broken down cars. 19 After I'd shown him the present that they'd given me, he remained silently thinking. 20 I'll pass by you (f.) tomorrow and take you to your uncle's. 21 I can't hear you! Speak up! 22 We reduced the prices by 25 per cent. 23 I taught for two years in a government school. 24 Don't put the gear over there! Put it over here!

Exercise 14.2

1 titráyyag kill yoom fis-sáa9a sítta. 2 atghádda fi hal-máT9am kathíir.
3 sáa9a cham nit9áshsha il-láyla? 4 laysh maa titghaddúun wiyyáana
báachir? 5 tiráyyag wiyyáay báachir! 6 hat-tayr maa yitrákkab 9ála
has-sayyáara. 7 baab il-máxzan maa yitbáTTal. 8 il-makaatíib titwádda
bil-yad dáa'iman. 9 has-suug maa yitbánnad ábadan. 10 is-SáHan
il-maksúur maa yitSállaH. 11 xállna nitHáacha shway 9an háadha
l-mawDúu9! 12 xállna nitfáaham fi han-núqTa! 13 xállhum yitsaa9adúun
fi hal-mawDúu9! 14 xállna nitláaga márra tháanya 9ógub báachir! 15
xállhum yitSaalaHúun! 16 laysh maa yitHachchúun? 17 laysh maa
yitzáwwaj? 18 laysh maa tit9állam il-lúgha l-ingliizíyya? 19 laysh maa
nitwáafag 9ála háadha? 20 laysh maa titsaa9adúun ákthar? 21 laysh
maa tit9áwwad 9ála l-ákil?

Note that, in nos. 16–21, **shloon** can equally well be used instead of
laysh.

Exercise 14.3

1 – Haacháyt il-mudíir ams, muu chidhíi? – la muu mHaachíih bá9ad!
2 – SalláHt il-makíina ams, muu chidhíi? – la, muu mSálliHha bá9ad!
3 – naDHDHáft ghúrfat in-noom iS-SubH, muu chidhíi? – la, muu
mnáDHDHifha bá9ad! 4 – Tarrásht il-maktúub áwwal ams, muu chidhíi?
– la muu mTárshah bá9ad! 5 – waafágt 9ála l-mashrúu9 ish-sháhar il-
máaDi, muu chidhíi? – la, muu mwáafig 9aláyh bá9ad! 6 – fattásht il-
máSna9 is-subúu9 il-máaDi, muu chidhíi? – la, muu mfátshah bá9ad!
7 – jarrábt il-máT9am il-jadíid ams, muu chidhíi? – la, muu mjárbah
bá9ad! 8 – fannásht il-9ummáal dhayláak is-subúu9 il-máaDi, muu
chidhíi? – la, muu mfánnishhum bá9ad! 9 – chayyákt mustáwa z-zayt
gábil nuSS sáa9a, muu chidhíi? – la, muu mcháykah bá9ad! 10 –
baddált it-tayráat is-subúu9 il-máaDi, muu chidhíi? – la, muu mbáddilha
bá9ad!

Using the you (f.) form:
1 Haacháyti – mHáachyatah 2 SalláHti – msalliHátta 3 naDHDHáfti
– mnaDHDHifátta 4 Tarráshti – mTárshatah 5 waafágti – mwáafga 6
fattáshti – mfátshatah 7 jarrábti – mjárbatah 8 fannáshti – mfannisháttum
9 chayyákti – mcháykatah 10 baddálti – mbaddilátta

Using the you (pl.) form:
1 Haacháytaw – mHaachíinah 2 SalláHtaw – mSalHíinha 3
naDHDHáftaw – mnaDHfíinha 4 Tarráshtaw – mTarshíinah 5 waafágtaw

– mwaafgíin 6 fattáshtaw – mfatshíinah 7 jarrábtaw – mjarbíinah 8 fannáshtaw – mfanshíinhum 9 chayyáktaw – mchaykíinah 10 baddáltaw – mbadlíinha

Exercise 14.4

Juha went to his radio and turned it on. The one who was singing (on the radio) said 'My darling I'm thirsty!' Juha went and put the radio in the water jug, and pulled it out. It kept on singing 'My darling I'm thirsty!' Juha dunked it in the water again and pulled it out … now he wants to play it and it doesn't work. Juha says to it 'Won't you work now? When you were thirsty I gave you (water) and now you've stopped (working)!'

Note that 'thirsty' is a common locution in Arab love songs meaning 'thirsty for love'.

Reading Arabic

The signs say:

1 Please do not enter. 2 Please lock the door. 3 Please do not pick the flowers. 4 Please keep to the right. 5 Please do not park. 6 Please do not exit. 7 Please do not disturb.

Unit 15

Exercise 15.1

Translation:

1 He didn't agree to help the club. 2 It's prohibited for you to smoke in the bedroom. 3 What they did won't be any use to us at all. 4 Who allowed you (f.) to come in? 5 I get angry merely seeing his face. 6 The inspector ordered the policeman to stop the bus. 7 He sells and buys apartments, that's his business. 8 He smashed the window pane unintentionally.

Using verbal nouns:

1 maa wáafag 9ala musáa9adat in-náadi. 2 it-tadxíin mamnúu9 fi ghúrfat in-noom. 3 tiswáathum maa btifíidna ábadan. 4 mínhu símaH lich id-duxúul? 5 mujárrad shóofat il-wijh máalah tizá99ilni. 6 il-mufáttish 'ámar ish-shúrTi bi tawgíif il-baaS. 7 bay9 u shiráa shiqqáat, haay shúghlah. 8 kássar il-jaam bidúun qaSd.

Translation:

9 hal-kútub tábbi liha gaTáaT. 10 mamnúu9 tawgíif is-sayyaaráat ihni!
11 ma y9árf is-sibáaHa. 12 góolah yábbi lih taHqíiq. 13 tachyíik hal-
Hisaabáat shúghul mút9ib. 14 la tdiir báalak min Háchi n-naas! 15 níshri
agáll min áwwal min zood il-as9áar. 16 shínhu it-taxáSSuS máalik?
tadríis il-lugháat.

Exercise 15.2

1 maa síma9 illa galíil min il-Háchi. 2 la laytáat is-sayyáara wa la l-bítri
máalha mSállaHa. 3 maa 9aTáana tashjíi9 wa la musáa9ada. 4 maa
t9arf tíTbax wa la tábbi tit9állam: bafánnishik! 5 bititHássan bi káthrat
il-mumáarasa. 6 maa aHibb il-musáawama, la fis-suug wa la wíyya
suwwáag it-takáasi. 7 maa gídrat táakil wa la tináam min humúumha.
8 la 'ádab wa la axláaq 9índhum! 9 mub laagyíin wa la mTarrishíin
makaatíib has-subúu9. 10 la ínta wa la gháyrik yígdar yisáa9idni fi
háadha. 11 dawwárt, láakin maa ligáyt burtugáal wa la tufáaH. 12
rayyáal zayn: maa iyíi sh-shúghul mit'áxxir wa la yirúuH gábil niháayat
id-dawáam.

Exercise 15.3

1 saww brúuHik, ana maa basáa9dik! 2 maa bághaw yisaafrúun
brúuHhum. 3 maa biysáa9dik háadha; sáa9id rúuHik! 4 si'látni nafs is-
su'áal – 9aTáytha nafs il-jawáab. 5 shúghlik nafs shúghli (or shúghlatik
nafs shúghlati). 6 maa waddáyt is-saamáan kíllah fi nafs il-mukáan;
waddáyt il-masaamíir fi Sandúug brúuHhum wil-chilaalíib fi chiis
brúuHhum. 7 maa baTTált id-daríisha – tibáTTalat brúuHha. 8 háadha
nafs il-bayt illi dáshshatah l-9ajúuz. 9 il-míHfaDHa l-mabyúuga nafs
háadhi. 10 láazim maa truuHúun il-firíij dhaak brúuHkum – wáayid
xáTar!

Exercise 15.4

The usefulness of fasting

First of all, fasting is useful from the point of view of the body … the
body, erm, is like the engine of a car. If, every six months or every
year you don't take it for servicing, to be checked, cleaned, adjusted
– even if it's a car (costing) sixty or seventy thousand – in the space
of two or three years it'll be ruined. On the other hand, the car that

costs one thousand dinars, if every six months the mechanic checks it, inspects it and sees if it's (working) well and properly – it won't deteriorate. The body is like a car – it needs to be rested and adjusted now and again. These days, disease is on the increase ... why? from overeating ...

Verbal nouns:
- **Soom** from **Saam/yiSúum** 'to fast'
- **fáyda** from **faad/yifíid** 'to give benefit; be useful to (someone)'
- **xídma** from **xádam/yáxdim** 'to serve'
- **tachyíik** from **cháyyak/yicháyyik** 'to check'
- **tanDHíif** from **náDHDHaf/yináDHDHif** 'to clean'
- **ta9díil** from **9áddal/yi9áddil** 'to adjust'
- **amráaD** pl. of **máraD** from **múraD/yímraD** 'to fall, be ill'
- **ákil** from **'ákal/yáakil** 'to eat'

Exercise 15.5

Juha goes to the doctor's

One day, Juha went to the doctor's. He gave him some medicine in a bottle and said to him 'When you take this medicine, shake the bottle.' Juha went home and took the medicine without shaking it. When he remembered what the doctor had told him, he said 'Oo-er!' and began jumping up and down like this. The neighbours said to him 'What's wrong with you Juha?' So Juha said 'I forgot to shake the bottle before I took the medicine – so I'm shaking it up now in my belly!'

Reading Arabic

The signs say:
1 No parking. 2 No smoking. 3 No entry. 4 No exit.

The prohibitions are as follows, and are transliterated according to MSA rather than Gulf Arabic pronunciation:

1 laa tudáxxin. – Do not smoke. 2 laa táqTif az-zuhúur. – Do not pick the flowers. 3 laa túdxul min háadha l-baab. – Do not enter by this door. 4 laa tuláwwith al-fálaj. – Do not pollute the irrigation channel. 5 laa táqif húnaa. – Do not park here. 6 laa táxruj min húnaa. – Do not exit this way (lit. 'from here'). 7 laa tuláwwith al-Hadíiqa. – Do not pollute the park.

Review Unit III

Dialogue RIII.1

T Hello?
E Hello. Good morning!
T Good morning!
E Is that Gulf Aviation?
T Yes.
E May I speak to the general manager please? My name is
   Johnson. I'm the manager of 'New World' travel agency.
T Just a moment, the line is engaged ... (pause) ... I'm sorry Mr
   Johnson, his secretary says he's not there at the moment. He
   went out five minutes ago, she says ...
E When will he be back?
T Just a moment, I'll ask his secretary ... she says she doesn't
   know ...
E Can I leave a message for him with her?
T Please do.
E I want her to tell him that we've agreed to the conditions he
   imposed on us regarding the contract.
T Fine, I'll give her the message and she'll inform him when he gets
   back.
E Thank you.
T Don't mention it.

Exercise RIII.1

(a) haay shárikat il-xalíij lin-nifT?
    lis-smiit?
    lil-bináa?
    lit-taTwíir il-iqtiSáadi?
    lil-mantuujáat iz-ziraa9íyya?
    haay mu'ássasat il-xalíij lin-nifT? etc.
    haay shárikat il-kuwáyt lis-smiit? etc.
    haay il-mu'ássasa l-waTaníyya   li taSdíir in-nifT?
                                     li taSdíir il-asmáak?
                                     li taswíiq il-láHam?
                                     li taSlíih is-sufun?
                                     li San9 il-aaláat iS-Sinaa9íyya?

(b) ana mudíir shárikat   is-smiit '9ántar'.
                          il-bináa 'ziyáad'.
    ana mudíir wakáalat il-anbáa 'ay bii sii'.
                          il-9ámal 'fayrúuz'.
(c) 1 wayn raaH?
     2 9índah mawáa9id ba9ad iDH-DHúhur?
     3 9indah faráagh báachir?
     4 húwwa mashghúul kill il-yoom?
     5 múmkin yigáabilni ba9adáyn?
     6 húwwa gáari taqríiri?
     7 húwwa mHáachi zamíili?
     8 húwwa káatib lína lo bá9ad?
     9 húwwa mwáqqi9 il-9aqd wílla la?
    10 húwwa mitlággi risáalti?
(d) 1 abbíiha tigúul lih ínnana mufakríin fi 9árDah u biná9Ti
        jawáabna is-subúu9 il-qáadim.
     2 ... mufakríin fi 9árDah laakínna raafDíin ish-shurúuT illi hu
        mwaddíiha 9aláyna.
     3 ... muu mwaafgíin 9ala 9árDah fi sháklah il-Háali.
     4 ... muu mwaafgíin 9ala t-taghyiiráat illi hu Táalibha.
     5 ... qaablíin shurúuTah u binjáawib rasmíyyan bá9ad ayyáam
        galíila.

Exercise RIII.2

Old-style marriage

The boy's father would go to the girl's father and betroth her. If they
agreed, we would send those presents we used to send, and clothes,
and we'd send them money, and we'd betroth (them) in the Sheikh's
presence. Then the 'Henna Night' came. They beat drums and clapped
hands rhythmically and (there were) songs. They'd paint 'the bride'
with henna and then they'd slaughter an animal and cook (it). Afterwards, they'd take her, the bride I mean, and wrap her in a rug and
bring her in to her husband.

Unit 16

Exercise 16.1

1 – la, hal-glaasáat maa tinkísir. 2 – la, hat-tayráat maa titrákkab.
3 – dhiich il-Hijáara maa tinsháal! 4 – la, it-taqríir maa yitwádda fíiha.
5 – la, as9áarna maa titxáffaD! 6 – maa yinákil. 7 – hal-baab maa

yitbánnad! 8 – la, hal-maay maa yinshírib. 9 – la, maa insím9aw or maa yinsim9úun. 10 – la, 9aadáathum maa tigháyyarat.

Translation:

1 – You broke the glasses, didn't you? – No, those glasses are unbreakable. 2 – Did you fit the new tyres? – No, these tyres can't be fitted. 3 – Remove those stones! – Those stones can't be removed! (e.g. because they are too heavy.) 4 – You put the report in this envelope, didn't you? – No, the report wouldn't go in it. (e.g. because it was too big.) 5 – Reduce your prices a bit please! – No, our prices can't be reduced! 6 – What do you think about English food? – It's inedible. 7 – Shut the door please! – This door can't be shut! 8 – This is drinking water, isn't it? – No this water isn't drinkable. 9 – Could you hear them from far away? – No, they couldn't be heard. 10 – They changed their customs as time passed, didn't they? – No, their customs didn't change.

Exercise 16.2

1 aSárr 9ala muqáabalat il-wazíir shaxSíyyan. 2 yiHíbb ilqáa muHaaDráat bil-lúgha l-9arabíyya. 3 maa símHaw lii isti9máal il-aaláat maaláthum. 4 iqtiráaHah muu ma9gúul fi rá'yi ána. 5 láazim tachyíik il-makíina gábil tarkíib il-blaagáat.

Translation:

1 He insisted on meeting the minister personally. 2 He likes giving lectures in Arabic. 3 They didn't allow me to use their tools. 4 His suggestion is unreasonable, in my opinion. 5 You must check the engine before fitting the plugs.

Exercise 16.3

1 gaal 'ínnah istafáad wáayid min had-dóora. 2 gáalaw 'ínnahum iHtáajaw ila musáa9ada ázyad láakin maa HaSSalóoha. 3 gáalat 'ínnaha maa tígdar tistághni 9an dhaak il-kitáab. 4 gáalaw 'ínnahum yoom hum Sgháar, ihtámmaw wáayid bi jam9 iT-Tawáabi9. 5 gaal 'ínnah tamm yi9íish hash-shákil Tuul Hayáatah.

Translation:

1 He said he benefited a lot from this course. 2 They said they needed more help but they didn't get it. 3 She said she can't do without that

book. 4 They said that when they were small, they were very interested in collecting stamps. 5 He said that he carried on living this way all his life.

Exercise 16.4

1 ... zirt il-qáahira. 2 ... ta9allámt is-siyáaqa. 3 ... ishtaghált mudárris. 4 ... ishtaráyt máT9am. 5 ... tizawwájt min 9úmri 9ishríin sána. 6 ... ta9allámt is-sibáaHa. 7 ... gilt lih iS-Sidq? 8 ... salláft lih ílli Tálabah? 9 ... 9allámtah yígra 9árabi? 10 ... 9arráftah 9ála r-ra'íis? 11 ... 9aTáytah shúghul? 12 ... saa9ádtah fi diraasáatah? 13 idha/lo/in/chaan/ila táTlubah mínnah ... 14 tixáabrah il-Hiin ... 15 tistá9milah kamáa yájib ... 16 tíqbal shurúuTah ... 17 tiTárrish lih il-bayzáat ... 18 timtíni9 min shurb il-jigáayir ...

Dialogue 16.1

A Before, you used to work in the airport?

B Yes. I spent a whole year at the airport ... and at the bank a year and a few months. Well, I used to work as a machine operator at first, and then I changed to the computer, and after the computer to the Accounts (Department) downstairs ... for those who are opening accounts or who are paying cheques into their accounts ... that kind of thing, that's my job.

A Do you like the college here?

B Really, I wanted to go to university to study Law ...

A Why didn't you go?

B Circumstances were a bit difficult before ... I was obliged to go to work, and I worked at the American Mission Hospital ... I only worked (there) for two years ...

A What was your job?

B Clerk ... I worked two years there and, well, I don't know, office hours were morning and afternoon, and my mother said it was a bother for me to go morning and afternoon, so I should look for another job. But she insisted that I enter the college so I'd become a teacher.

Reading Arabic

The sign says **at-ta'áxxur fii l-wuSúul xáyrun min 9ádam al-wuSúul**, literally 'being late in arriving is better than lack of arriving' or, as we might say, 'Better to arrive late than not at all.'

Unit 17

Exercise 17.1

1 titgáhwa kill yoom gábil la truuH ish-shúghul. 2 nitgáhwa ... nruuH ... 3 9áli yitgáhwa ... yruuH ... 4 yitgahwúun ... yruuHúun ... 5 titgahwúun ... truuHúun ... 6 il-9ummáal yitgahwúun ... yruuHúun ... 7 il-mudíir yitgáhwa ... yruuH ... 8 úmmi titgáhwa ... truuH ... 9 ídha tixallíihum yisawwúun háadha brúuHhum, byitgharbalúun. 10 ... tixallíiha tisáwwi ... brúuHha, bititghárbal. 11 ... tixálli fáaTma tsáwwi ... brúuHa, bititghárbal. 12 ... tixálli d-dráywil ysáwwi ... brúuHah, byitghárbal. 13 ... tixálli sikirtíirtik tisáwwi ... brúuHha, bititghárbal. 14 ... tixálli l-miikáaniki ysáwwi ... brúuHah byitghárbal. 15 ... tixálli hal-yiháal ysawwúun ... brúuHhum, byitgharbalúun. 16 ... tixallíina nsáwwi ... brúuHna, bnitghárbal. 17 Hátta lo 9aTáach qaamúus, chaan maa gidárti titarjimíin hal maqáal. 18 ... 9aTáana ... gidárna nitárjim ... 19 ... 9áTa T-Tulláab ... gídraw yitarjimúun ... 20 ... 9aTáakum ... gidártaw titarjimúun ... 21 ... 9áTa l-bint ... gídrat titárjim ... 22 ... 9áTa zamíili ... gídar yitárjim ... 23 ... 9áTa l-káatib ... gídar yitárjim ... 24 ... 9aTáak ... gidárt titárjim ...

Exercise 17.2

1 ídha tíl9ab wiyyáah yistáanis li'ánnah yiHíbb il-li9b. 2 ... tinákkit ... it-tankíit. 3 ... titmáshsha ... il-máshi. 4 ... tiHádig ... il-Hadáag. 5 ... titHáchcha ... il-Háchi. 6 ... tiqáamir ... il-muqáamra. 7 ... tighánni ... il-ghína.

Exercise 17.3

1 híyya wíddha trúuH il-jáami9a u tádris Huqúuq. 2 húmma wíddhum yiruuHúun il-jáami9a u ydirsúun Huquuq. 3 íHna wíddna nrúuH il-jáami9a u nádris Huqúuq. 4 niHíbb nirúuH il-jáami9a u nádris Huqúuq. 5 yiHíbb yirúuH il-jáami9a u yádris Huqúuq. 6 yiHíbb yirúuH il-jáami9a u yádris hándisa. 7 yiHíbb yirúuH il-jáami9a u yádris riyaaDiyáat. 8 yiHíbb yirúuH il-jáami9a u yádris il-lúgha l-9arabíyya. 9 yi9íjbah yirúuH il-jáami9a u yádris il-lúgha l-9arabíyya. 10 yi9íjbik trúuH il-jáami9a u tádris il-lúgha l-9arabíyya. 11 – yi9íjbah yishtághil fil-imaaráat? – la, maa yi9íjbah. yifáDDil yishtághil fil-kuwáyt. 12 – yi9íjbkum tishtaghlúun ...? – la, maa yi9jíbna. nifáDDil nishtághil ... 13 – yi9jíbhum yishtaghlúun ...? – la, maa yi9jíbhum. yifaDlúun yishtaghlúun ... 14 – yi9jíbha tishtághil ...? – la, maa yi9jíbha. tifáDDil tishtághil ...

15 – yí9jib abúuk yishtághil ...? – la, maa yi9íjbah. yifáDDil yishtághil
... 16 – yi9íjbik tishtághil dráywil? – la, maa yi9jíbni. afáDDil ashtághil
farráash. 17 – ... tizúur il-imaaráat? – ... atímm fil-bayt (or fi biláadi).
18 – ... táakil fi máT9am? – ... astághni 9an il-ákil. 19 – ... tíg9ad
mubákkir? – ... ág9ad mit'áxxir. 20 – ... tit9állam tírkab sáykal? – ...
at9állam asúug sayyáara.

Exercise 17.4

1 háadha húwwa l-kitáab illi rawwáytna iyyáah s-subúu9 il-máaDi?
2 ... rawwóona ...? 3 háadhi híyya sh-sh-sharíiTa ílli rawwóona iyyáaha
...? 4 ... 9aTóoha iyyáaha ...? 5 ... samma9óoha ...? 6 ... sammá9tak
iyyáaha ...?

Exercise 17.5

1 la ta9Tíiha iyyáaha! 2 la trawwíina iyyáahum! 3 la tixárbah iyyáay!
4 la tsammí9ha iyyáaha! 5 la ta9Tíih iyyáaha/iyyáahum! 6 la trawwíini
iyyáah!

Dialogue 17.1

Translation:
A They say a child threw himself from the roof to the ground,
  imitating a strong man he saw on TV.
B Yes, he was imitating Steve.
A Why do children do things like that?
B A child doesn't understand. Every single lad is following that
  serial. Then he thinks he's the same as Steve and leaps from
  house to house and falls ...
A What are the best programmes on now, d'you think?
B I'm in favour of scientific programmes, for example. Now they put
  on a programme every week called 'The First Year in the Life of a
  Child'. That's very good, it's useful. D'you watch films on TV?
A No. There are films on TV with shameless scenes in them that
  are not proper. A girl just wearing a bra and shorts is an unlawful
  thing in Islam. And another thing is that, if young men see such
  things, they're bound to commit bad acts.

Questions:
1 yáhil TaaH min foog sáTah bayt. 2 kaan il yáahil yiqállid rayyáal
sháafah fit-tilivizyúun. 3 ti'áyyid il-baráamij il-9ilmíyya l-mistafíida. 4 hal-
manáaDHir tixallíihum yisawwúun múnkar.

Unit 18

Exercise 18.1

Well, my friend, I began my life in the 1940s. I was a little child – I'd be about five or six, as I remember – God knows! I was happy and would play in our quarter with the little lads, my brothers, happy and without a care in the world. Then one day, before I knew what was happening, my Dad took me and put me in the Qur'anic school ... with the Qur'an teacher called bin Humuud. So I put my trust in God, and went to Qur'anic school ... Well, I stayed there – I don't know how long – a year and a half or two years. I read the Qur'an from cover to cover. I had a lot of friends ... some of them have died, and some I've lost touch with now. I was content at the Qur'anic school for those two years roughly, and then my father said 'We'll send you to the (government) school', so they took me away from the Qur'anic school and sent me to the government school, the west-side school that is today (called) Abu Bakr school. Well, I stayed at the school – they put me in the first class of the kindergarten at first ... yes, that's right ... and after a while they put on dramas and plays at the school ... and some of the teachers would let us act in the plays ... and I became one of them (the actors). And, as far as I remember, the late Sheikh A. bin I., the Minister of Information, would attend these plays ... as would Mr A. il-9. We played our roles well, and Mr A. il-9. would give us presents after we'd finished ... I remember that among these presents he'd give us bottles of orangeade, and those things for geometry – I don't know, I've forgotten, it's gone out of my head what you call them – and drawing books, and an envelope with ten rupees in it and white (sports) shoes – if you don't mind me mentioning such a thing! – and blue shorts with a white stripe ...

Exercise 18.2

There was a robber who went and climbed up on top of a wall, wanting to jump inside. But he fell from the top to the ground and really smashed himself up. They sent him to hospital. The doctor examined him and prescribed just pills – he didn't prescribe him any medicine for his legs. They just said to him 'Go to the chemist's and take this medicine.' So he went to the chemist's and they just gave him pills. He said 'What's written (on the prescription)? What are these pills for?' They told him 'For worms', so he said 'These pills are for worms? Why pills for

worms?' They said 'How should we know? Go and ask the doctor.' So
he went to the doctor and said to him 'I'm all smashed up and you're
giving me pills for worms, for my stomach?' And the doctor said to him
'Yes! If you hadn't had a worm in you, you wouldn't have climbed up
(on to the wall)!'

Unit 19

Exercise 19.1

min tírja9 akúun ...

1 miHáSSil 9ála rúxSat siyáaqa. 2 mitzáwwaj. 3 miSálliH sayyáartik.
4 náajiH fil-imtiHáan. 5 misáafir is-sa9uudíyya. 6 gháasil il-mawaa9íin.
7 miHáSSil shúghul jadíid. 8 mitgháddi.

Note that, in all the above sentences, it is acceptable to use a past-
tense verb instead of the participle, namely: 1 **HaSSált**; 2 **tizawwájt**;
3 **SalláHt**; 4 **nijáHt**; 5 **saafárt**; 6 **ghasált**; 7 **HaSSált** 8 **taghaddáyt**.

9 – ríkab il-baaS ráqam xamstá9shar. – kaan láazim yírkub ir-ráqam
xamsíin! 10 – 9aTáani l-míTraga l-kabíira. – kaan láazim ya9Tíik iS-
Saghíira! 11 – ishtághalaw saa9atáyn awirtáym ams. – kaan láazim
yishtaghlúun thaláath! 12 – istaajárt sayyáara abu daxlatáyn. – kaan
láazim tistáajir wanáyt! 13 – gilt lit-tindáyl iyíi sáa9a thamáanya u nuSS.
– kaan láazim tigúul lih iyíi sáa9a sáb9a! 14 min wuSálna kaan il-fílim
báadi. 15 shífna káanaw mxalSíin shayaláan il-aatháath. 16 min
ríkbat iT-Tayyáara káanat láabsa tannúura xáDra. 17 layn ittaSált fiih,
kaan migháyyir báalah. 18 min wúSlat sayyáarat il-wazíir káanat ish-
shúrTa msáyTira 9ála l-máwqif. 19 kint ahtámm bi aaláat it-taSwíir u
áaxidh Súwar wáayid. 20 áwwalmaa yiit il-xalíij kint ashtághil najjáar.
21 sh-káanaw il-kuwaytiyyíin yaaklúun áwwal? 22 – wayn 9áli? – muu
mawjúud. láazim raaH il-bayt. – kaan láazim yitímm saa9atáyn bá9ad!
23 – múmkin tisallíf líi 9áshra danaaníir? – mit'ássif, Siráft kill ma9áashi.
– kaan láazim maa tíSrufah kíllah! 24 – wayn il-mawaa9íin il-wásxa?
– táwni ghaasílhum. – kaan mub láazim tsáwwi háadha! 25 – cham
DHalláyt 9ind waalidáyk? – yoomáyn bas. kaan láazim nilaagíik.
– kaan mub láazim tista9jilúun hash-shákil! 26 – wayn it-tindáyl?
– láazim raaH il-máxzan. – kaan láazim maa yixálli har-rayaayíil
brúuHhum!

Exercise 19.2

1 kíllmaa tábbi, nígdar niHáSlah. 2 kíllmaa tiHtáaj ila shay, múrr 9alíyyi.
3 maadáam ána íhni, batímm aHáawil attáSil fiih. 4 míthilmaa tádri,
akúun Tarrásht ir-risáala min yírja9. 5 wáynmaa truuH, la tínsa tixálli
9unwáanik 9índi. 6 kíllmin yidíshsh il-mátHaf láazim yídfa9 miyatáyn
u xamsíin fils. 7 shgáddmaa kint yuu9áan, kaan láazim maa táakil
háadha. 8 shkíthirmaa tíSruf, la tiDáyyi9 flúusik bi ashyá maa líha fáyda.

Dialogue 19.1

A If you want to get a driving licence ... a licence ... what d'you
   have to do?
B First you go to – what d'you call it – the (police) fort, and they
   register you and test your sight. After about two days they give
   you the result: if it's six out of six, fine; if it's weak they tell you to
   get glasses, to wear glasses ... that's what they say, anyway, I
   haven't been ...
A And then you take a driving test?
B Yes, the test. You get in the car with a (police) officer and if he
   thinks you're OK you pass, if he doesn't you repeat.
A And does the car have to be the driver's own?
B No, usually it's the instructor's. You take it for an hour, go with
   the officer and pay (the instructor) a fee. If you pass you give him
   (the instructor) a bonus, er, like a present because you've
   passed.

Unit 20

Exercise 20.1

Translation:

Hello, everyone! My name's Muhammad bin Rashid. I married recently
– only 19 years ago! – and I've got no kids ... I looked for a long time
for a job that would leave me in peace ... there are lots of jobs, but
they don't suit me ... I want a job in which there's no bother ... that
leaves me in peace and in which I earn a lot of money ... I sat for
many days thinking about work ... I thought and thought, and then I
had an idea: why not become a doctor? And in the event, I became a
doctor, because, in the old days, our Indian neighbour was a doctor,
and in that way I learnt how they treat people ... but I have a dear

friend from the days of Qur'anic school, but he works as a gravedigger while I'm a doctor. This friend of mine got me into some real trouble, and in this episode and the ones that follow, I want you to listen to the story of me, him and my wife ...

Questions:

1 19 years. 2 No trouble and a lot of money. 3 Medical doctor. 4 His family's neighbour was an Indian doctor. 5 Gravedigger. 6 Since they were both at Qur'anic school.

Dialogue 20.1

Translation:

K I'd hate you to kill yourself ... it's a sin, by God a sin, even though you're my friend and I'll be able to feed my family for five days because of what you're doing. That's my job, what can I do about it?

M So, you want *me* to kill myself so *you* get the benefit! But I'm not going to kill myself!

K All right, don't kill yourself then! Take the bread out of my mouth! Let my children starve to death!

M Well, that's something, isn't it! If *I* don't kill myself *your* children starve!

K Yes, you're the reason for the situation we're in! Before, someone would fall ill for a day or two or three, and on the fourth day he'd kick the bucket, and we'd get the benefit.

M Heavens! What are you on about, Khalid?

K Now *you* come, and give the sick who would die medicine, and keep them alive! And at whose expense? At mine! Why are you so stubborn? Why are you so selfish? Why?

M Look pal, that's my job, what can I do about it?

K Why don't you let us make a truce for just one year? You'll gain from it and so will I!

M Huh! What's this 'truce'?

K Now, every sick person that comes to see you, kill him or give him the wrong medicine, and I'll give you half the money I get for washing the corpse!

M First thing, I'm no butcher, and second, I cannot betray the vocation that has been placed upon my shoulders.

K Hell, anyone hearing you talk would think you were the absolute cat's whiskers!

M And, as well, I have a conscience and I have sensitivity ...

K OK, you've got a conscience and sensitivity, never mind ... every time a sick person comes here tell him there's nothing wrong with him until he feels ashamed and just dies (of his own accord)!

M Please, mate, I can't!

K Blast! I can't get round you, one way or the other!

Questions:

7 By curing people who would, in the old days, have died, Muhammad has reduced the amount of money Khalid makes from his job! 8 Khalid suggests they call a truce: Muhammad will give patients the wrong medicine or no medicine at all, which will result in more deaths and more money for Khalid, which he will split with Muhammad. 9 He refuses because he can't betray his vocation, and he has a conscience and feelings.

Dialogue 20.2

Translation:

M My dear friend, I agree to give you what you've asked for! One thousand! One thousand!

K You're giving it to me? Ten green ones?

M Yes, note on top of note! Ten green ones!

K Green ones, green ones! *Ten* green ones, really *ten*?

M Yes, mate.

K In the name of God the ... (faints).

M Oh! He's gone and fainted again! Get up, get up!

K Where am I? Muhammad! Hold on to me! Help me!

M Get up and be a man! Listen to what I say and leave off falling down. I'm bored with it!

K Please, my friend, don't cheat me! First let me get a thousand green ones, let me get hold of them!

M You'll get them ... but, as I told you –

K I deserve it from you, I want –

M Right, right, and I'll give you a thousand ... but I have one condition ...

K Make your condition! One condition only?

M Just one little tiny condition ...

K By God, if you want me to turn salt water sweet, to bring down
   stars from the sky, to –
M My friend, I want you to kill my wife!

Questions:
10 100 Bahraini dinars. 11 He would change the sea into sweet water
and bring down the stars from the heavens! 12 To kill his wife.

Appendix 1
Variations in pronunciation

The variety of Arabic presented in this book is that which is used by educated Gulf Arabs when talking in a relaxed style. Like all speakers of all languages, Gulf Arabs may speak more or less formally, depending on who they are talking to, what they are talking about, and when and where they are speaking. The differences in the formality of situation are reflected in a number of ways in speech, and it is a good idea to be aware of some of the commonest features of this.

(A) Consonant alternations

k **and** ch

ch is the less formal variant in pairs such as **kam/cham** 'how much?', **kalb/chalb** 'dog', **chibíir/kabíir** 'big; old' and **sámak/símich** 'fish'.

j **and** y

y is the less formal variant. Examples include **jáahil/yáahil** 'child', **ja/ya** 'he came', **jadíid/yidíid** 'new' and **dáraj/dáray** 'steps; ladder'.

q **and** gh

Some speakers regularly substitute **q** for **gh** and vice versa in informal speech (a tendency that is also noticeable on even quite formal occasions), for example they say **qásal** 'he washed' and **múqánni** 'singer' instead of **ghásal** and **mughánni**, and **ghur'áan** 'Qur'an' and **tagháddum** 'progress' instead of **qur'áan** and **taqáddum**. This book reflects usage in which these two consonants are not confused.

f **and** th, d **and** dh

In some parts of the Gulf (especially Bahrain and Qatar), some speakers substitute **f** for **th** and **d** for **dh** quite consistently, for example **faláafa** 'three' and **háadi** 'this (f.)' for **thaláatha** and **háadhi**. Such substitutions rarely occur in educated speech.

D **and** DH

In Literary Arabic, these two sounds are distinguished, as they increasingly are in the speech of educated Gulf Arabs. However, many do not consistently make the distinction and, depending on their origin, some use only **D** for both sounds or only **DH** for both sounds. Thus some speakers pronounce the words for 'he hit' and 'noon' as, respectively, **Dárab** and **Dúhur**, while others say **DHárab** and **DHúhur**. In this book, 'educated' usage is reflected, which makes a distinction between **Dárab** and **DHúhur**. The spelling conventions used in this book distinguish three consonants: **D**, **DH** and **H**. In the rare cases of the juxtaposition of **D** and **H**, a hyphen is inserted between them to distinguish them from **DH**, for example **áD-Ha**.

j **and** g **and** q

In a few words (though some of them are common), three-way variation is possible between **j**, **g** and **q**, for example **jidíim**, **gadíim** and **qadíim** may all be used to mean 'ancient; old', while **mjáabil**, **mgáabil** and **muqáabil** are all possible ways of saying 'opposite'. Of the three variants, **j** is less and less used, being considered uneducated. The **q** variant, on the other hand, is limited to situations where the speaker is deliberately aiming at a 'high' style of speech. The **g** variant is the commonest and most neutral variant, use of which is reflected in this book.

Note on the dialects of Oman

The dialects of Oman are significantly different from the rest of the Gulf in terms of the pronunciation of certain consonants, and to some degree in their vocabulary. The main differences to watch out for are in the Capital Area and the mountainous areas of northern Oman. In these areas:

1 **k** does not change to **ch**, thus **kayf** 'how', not **chayf**.
2 Where the rest of the Gulf has **y** and **j** in free variation in many common words such as **ja/ya** 'he came', **jaab/yaab** 'he brought' and

rayyáal/rajjáal 'man', the Omanis have neither of these variants, but use **g**, thus Omani **ga** 'he came', **gaab** 'he brought' and **raggáal** 'man'.
3 On the other hand, where other Gulf speakers have **g** in words such as **gaal** 'he said', **gara** 'he read' and **suug** 'market', the Omanis have **q** as their normal dialectal sound, thus **qaal**, **qara** and **suuq**.

(B) Vowel alternations and dropped vowels

1 In many words, a short vowel **-a** may be replaced by **-i-** if it occurs in a short open (CV) syllable, for example:

taHáchcha	'he spoke'	varies with	**tiHáchcha**
dárrasat	'she taught'		**dárrisat**
sábab	'reason'		**síbab**
kátab	'he wrote'		**kítab**

2 Unstressed **-i-** and **-u-** in open (CV) syllable are often dropped:

yisawwúun	'they do'	varies with	**ysawwúun**
simá9na	'we heard'		**smá9na**
nirúuH	'we go'		**nrúuH**
tiHáchcha	'he spoke'		**tHáchcha**
			(see B1 above)
muHámmad	'Mohammed'		**mHámmad**

3 A short vowel (usually **i-**) may be put at the beginning of forms such as **nrúuH** to make them easier to pronounce: **itHáchcha** 'he spoke', **ismá9na** 'we heard', etc.

The processes described in B1–3 can lead to alternations of the type **il-kabiir/likbiir** 'the big one':

kabiir 'big'	→	**kibíir** (by B1)
	→	**kbíir** (by B2)
	→	**ikbíir** (by B3)

Definite article:

il-kabíir	varies with	**likbíir** 'the big one'

(C) Consonant cluster reduction

If a 'cluster' of three consonants occurs as a result of the juxtaposition of two words, speakers 'reduce' the cluster by dropping a consonant or, in some cases, by inserting a vowel. Thus:

9ind + hum	'they have'	→	**9ídhum** or **9índahum**
gilt lik	'I told you'	→	**git lik** or **gilt ilik**
Tagg + na	'he hit us'	→	**Tággana**

In some verb forms, clusters arise as a result of the dropping of unstressed **-i** (B2 above):

yidarrisúun	'they teach'	→	**yidarrsúun**

In such cases, the cluster is reduced:

→	**yidarsúun**

And applying the **-i-** dropping rule again, some speakers say:

→	**ydarsúun**

(D) Alternative syllable structures

Many words that have a CV-CV-C(V) or a CVC-CVC syllable structure have alternatives with a CCV-CV(C) structure:

HáTaba	'a piece of wood'	varies with	**HTíba**
kítbat	'she wrote'		**ktíbat**
Dírbaw	'they hit'		**Drúbaw**
rúgba	'neck'		**rgúba**
náxla	'palm tree'		**nxála**
mághrub	'evening'		**mghárb**

(E) Variations in stress placement

1 Words (or combinations of words in phrases) having a CVC-CV-CV syllable structure are sometimes stressed on the first, sometimes the second syllable:

mádrasa	'school'	varies with	madrása
Híjratik	'your room'		Hijrátik
sím9atah	'She heard him'		sim9átah
'ísmaH lii	'Excuse me!'		'ismáH lii

2 Words having a CVV-CVC structure in which the first syllable is stressed according to the rule given in the 'Pronunciation guide' may be stressed on the second syllable if a prepositional phrase or pronoun that begins with a consonant is suffixed:

shaafat + kum	'she saw you'	sháafatkum or shaafátkum
maalat + ha	'belonging to her'	máalatha or maalátha
gaalat + lik	'she told you'	gáalat lik or gaalát lik

Appendix 2
The Arabic script

This short and simplified appendix on the conventions of how Arabic is written is not in any sense a complete guide to how to read Arabic (which is different in many respects from the spoken dialects). It should be used in conjunction with the Reading Arabic sections of each of the 20 main units, and the overall aim of the reading sections and this appendix is limited to acquainting the learner of spoken Gulf Arabic with the writing conventions he or she will need to know when reading street signs, business cards and other straightforward texts encountered in everyday life.

Arabic is written and read from right to left. The script is cursive, which means that the letters are joined to each other, even in print. There are 28 separate letters, although not that many separate letter shapes, because some of the letters are distinguished from one another only by the presence or absence, position and number of dots, under them or above them. The shape of a letter changes slightly depending on whether it is in initial, medial or final position in the word. All the letters join on to a preceding letter, but six letters of the 28 (marked on the chart, see facing page) do not join on to a following letter.

Chart of Arabic letters

Name of letter	Uncon- nected	With preceding letter only	With following letter	With both	Symbol in transcription
'alif	ا	ا	...	...	**aa** (long 'a') or ' (the glottal stop)
baa'	ب	ب	بـ	ـبـ	**b**
taa'	ت	ت	تـ	ـتـ	**t**
thaa'	ث	ث	ثـ	ـثـ	**th**
jiim	ج	ج	جـ	ـجـ	**j**
haa'	ح	ح	حـ	ـحـ	**H**
xaa'	خ	خ	خـ	ـخـ	**x**
daal	د	د	...	...	**d**
dhaal	ذ	ذ	...	...	**dh**
raa'	ر	ر	...	...	**r**
zaa'	ز	ز	...	...	**z**
siin	س	س	سـ	ـسـ	**s**
shiin	ش	ش	شـ	ـشـ	**sh**
Saad	ص	ص	صـ	ـصـ	**S**
Daad	ض	ض	ضـ	ـضـ	**D**
Taa'	ط	ط	طـ	ـطـ	**T**
DHaa'	ظ	ظ	ظـ	ـظـ	**DH**
9ayn	ع	ع	عـ	ـعـ	**9**
ghayn	غ	غ	غـ	ـغـ	**gh**
faa'	ف	ف	فـ	ـفـ	**f**
qaaf	ق	ق	قـ	ـقـ	**q**
kaaf	ك	ك	كـ	ـكـ	**k**
lam	ل	ل	لـ	ـلـ	**l**
miim	م	م	مـ	ـمـ	**m**
nuun	ن	ن	نـ	ـنـ	**n**
haa'	ه	ه	هـ	ـهـ	**h**
waaw	و	و	...	...	**w** or **uu** (long **u**)
yaa'	ي	ي	يـ	ـيـ	**y** or **ii** (long **i**)

Spelling conventions

Written Arabic words can be thought of as 'skeletons', consisting of
consonants and long vowels only. Long 'a' (in the transcription system
in this book written as **aa**) is written as an **alif**, long 'u' (**uu**) as a **waaw**,
and long 'i' (**ii**) as a **yaa'**, though **waaw** and **yaa'** can also function as
consonants, similar in sound to English 'w' and 'y'. When used as
markers of vowel length, they are written after the vowels they lengthen.
The corresponding short vowels, **a** (called in Arabic **fatHa**), **u** (called
Damma) and **i** (called **kasra**) are not normally written, but if they are,
as in the Qur'an and in children's books, they are written either above
(**a**, **u**) or below (**i**) the consonant they follow. Here are some examples
of words written with and without their short vowels:

Without short vowels (normal)	With vowels	
كتب	كَتَبَ	**kataba** 'he wrote'
كتاب	كِتَاب	**kitaab** 'book'
مكتوب	مَكْتُوب	**maktuub** 'letter'
مكاتيب	مَكَاتِيب	**makaatiib** 'letters'

If a letter has no short vowel following it, a small circle (called **sukuun**
'silence') is written above it. If it is 'doubled' (e.g. **bb**, **dd**, **yy**), a sign
that looks like a 'w' (called **shadda** 'strengthening') is written above it.
Again, these signs, like short vowels, are not normally marked in
unvowelled texts, for example:

مكتب	مَكْتَب	**maktab** 'office; desk'
كتاب	كُتَّاب	**kuttaab** 'writers'

You can see from this that the same set of letters, as in كتاب, can be
read in different ways (that is, with different short vowels) depending
on the meaning: you can only tell from the context whether كتاب is to
be read as **kitaab** 'book' or **kuttaab** 'writers'.

There are a few words in which the **alif** that signifies a long **aa** sound is not written in the body of the word, but above the letter it follows, as if it were a short vowel. But since short vowels are not normally written, you will not usually see this **alif**. The two commonest words in everyday usage in this category are:

الله	اللّٰه	**allaah** 'God'
هذا	هٰذَا	**haadhaa** 'this'

As well as marking vowel length, **alif**, like **waaw** and **yaa'**, is used as a 'carrier' (in Arabic **kursii** 'chair') of the glottal stop, **hamza**, which can be written above **alif**, below it, on top of **waaw**, on top of **yaa'** (which in this case has no dots) or on no carrier at all. The rules for how to write **hamza** are complicated and beyond the scope of this guide: all you need to be able to do is recognise **hamza** sitting on its various carriers. The glottal stop is a fully functional consonant in written Arabic, although it has largely disappeared from the Arabic dialects, for example:

on top of **alif**	رأس	رَأْس	**ra's** (in dialect **raas**) 'head'
below **alif**	إرسال	إرسَال	**'irsaal** 'sending'
on **waaw**	سؤال	سُؤَال	**su'aal** 'question'
on **yaa'**	رئيس	رَئِيس	**ra'iis** 'president'
on the line (no carrier)	بناء	بِنَاء	**binaa'** (in dialect **binaa**) 'building'

The **l** of the definite article **al-** (in the Gulf dialect it is usually pronounced **il-**) is assimilated to certain following consonants (see Unit Two), as in **ash-shams** 'the sun'. This assimilation is not marked in unvowelled writing, the definite article being written as an **l** whether or not it is pronounced as one, for example:

الباب	البَاب	**al-baab** 'the door'

| الشمس | الشَّمْس | **ash-shams**
'the sun' |

One final orthographic point is that a word-final long **aa** in certain word classes is written not with an **alif**, but with a dotless **yaa'**, called **alif maqSuura** ('shortened **alif**'), for example:

رمى	رَمَى	**ramaa** 'he threw'
معنى	مَعْنَى	**ma9naa** 'meaning'
أغنى	أَغْنَى	**'aghnaa** 'richer'
كبرى	كُبْرَى	**kubraa** 'bigger, biggest (f.)'

But the above rule of thumb is not true in all cases: when the final **-aa** is preceded by a **yaa'**, the marker of vowel length is **alif**, as normal, for example:

| الدنيا | الدُّنْيَا | **ad-dunyaa**
'the world' |
| عليا | عُلْيَا | **9ulyaa**
'higher, highest (f.)' |

And this spelling is the norm in one or two other cases, for example:

| عصا | عَصَا | **9aSaa**
'stick' |

There are one or two other special conventions:

1 The feminine noun suffix -a

A special letter, a **haa'** with two dots on top of it (ة) (called **taa' marbuuTa**, or 'tied 't') marks the feminine noun suffix. When pronounced in pause (that is, with nothing following it), this letter is simply pronounced as **-a**. But if a noun with this feminine suffix is followed by another noun with which it is in a possessive relationship, for example 'the girls' school' (see Units One and Eight), this **-a** is pronounced **-at**. However it is pronounced, it is always written as (ة), for example:

مدرسة	مَدْرَسَة	**madrasa**
		'school'
مدرسة البنات	مَدْرَسَة البَناَت	**madrasat al-banaat**
		'the girls' school'

2 Case inflection

In written Arabic, but not in any dialect, nouns are inflected for case. This mainly involves changes in the short vowels suffixed to nouns, which are not reflected in unvowelled writing. However, certain categories of indefinite noun and adjective add an **-an** ending when they are in the accusative case, which is reflected in writing by the addition of a final **alif**, above which are written two **fatHa**s. This ending is pronounced **-an**, and is sometimes encountered in public signs, for example outside cinemas, in advertisements for upcoming films one may see:

قريبا	قَريباً	**qariiban**
		'(coming) shortly'

And of course one often sees:

شكرا	شُكْراً	**shukran**
		'thank you!'

3 Redundant **alif**

In certain plural verb forms that otherwise would end in a **waaw**, a redundant **alif** is written that serves simply to mark the end of the word. One is unlikely to see such verb forms in street signs and the like, since imperatives such as 'Do not enter!' and 'Fasten your seat belt!' are normally in the singular, not the plural. A possible example might be the international scouts' motto:

كونوا مستعدين!	كُونُوا مُسْتَعِدِّين!	**kuunuu musta9iddiin!**
		'be prepared!'

Gulf Arabic–English glossary

The order of the glossary follows the English alphabet, with digraphs (**dh**, **gh**, **sh**, **th**) following the entries for **d**, **g**, **s**, **t** and emphatic consonants (**D**, **DH**, **S**, **T**) following their plain counterparts. **9** is the final consonant.

- An asterisk (*) after a feminine noun indicates it as a 'hidden' final **t**, which reappears in construct phrases and when it has a suffix (e.g. the dual **-ayn**).
- 'Broken' noun plurals are separated from their singulars by a slash (/); sound noun plural endings are in brackets (**aat**, **iin**) as are a few other plural suffixes (e.g. (**iyya**)).
- Verbs are listed as past/imperfect. Verbal nouns (where they exist) are placed after the imperfect form for simple verbs only (i.e. where the verbal noun is not predictable). Some basic common imperatives are listed separately.
- Idiomatic phrases are listed under the main word in the phrase, for example **bi xayr** is listed under **xayr**; **bruuH** under **ruuH**; the verb **gaam bi** under **gaam.**
- In a few cases, the regional specificity of a word is indicated in capitals: KWT (Kuwait), BAH (Bahrain), OM (Oman).

A much more detailed Arabic–English glossary running to 600 pages, and based on the Arabic of Bahrain, can be found in Clives Holes, *Dialect, Culture and Society in Eastern Arabia: Volume I: Glossary*, published by Brill in 2001.

a

aab	August
áadmi/awáadim	someone; a human being; (pl.) people
aadháar	March
'áala*(aat)	tool
áala*(aat) Háasiba	calculator
áalat*(aat) taSwíir	camera
áalu	potato(es)
áamin	safe; secure
aatháath	furniture
áaxir	last; latest
ab/ubuháat	father
ábadan	never; not at all
abríil	April
ábyaD/biiD	white
adáar/yidíir	to run; to manage
ádab/aadáab	manners
aDHáaf/yiDHíif	to add
ághna/yíghni	to make (someone) rich
ahl (or **hal**)	family
áhlan wa sáhlan	welcome
il-ahráam	the Pyramids
áHad	someone
il-áHad	Sunday
áHmar/Húmur	red
áHsan	better
aHsant/i/u!	much obliged
aHyáanan	occasionally
bil-'ajáar	on a lease; for rent
'ájnabi	foreign; foreigner
'ákal/yáakil/ákil	to eat
akíid	certain, sure
ákil(aat)	food
'ákkal/yi'ákkil	to feed
aku/máaku (KWT)	there is/are; there isn't/aren't
alf/aaláaf	thousand
álgha/yílghi	to cancel
alláah	God

alló	hello (telephone)
álqa/yílqi muHáaDra*	to give (a lecture)
amáan	security
'ámar/yá'mur/'amr	to order someone to do something
amríika	America
amríiki (yyiin)	American
ams	yesterday
ána	I
anáani	selfish
anáasa	enjoyment; companionship
án9am/yín9im (9ála)	to bestow favours (on)
aráad/yiríid	to want
árba9(a)	four
il-'árba9a	Wednesday
arba9íin	forty
il-arba9iináat	the (19)40s
arba9tá9shar	fourteen
arD (f.)	earth; floor
arDíyya*	floor
arjúu (+ pron.)	I ask, beg …
'arz	cedar tree
áswad/suud	black
aSárr/yiSírr	to insist
áSfar/Súfur	yellow
áSil/uSúul	origin; principle
'áththar/yi'áththir	to have an effect (**fi** on)
athnáa	during
awáaxir	end parts
awáayil	beginning parts
awghústos	August
awirtáym	overtime
áwwal, f. úula	first; first of all
(il-)áwwal	old times
áwwalmaa	when first (conj.)
áwwal ams	the day before yesterday
áwwal il-layl	afternoon (shift)
ax/ixwáan	brother

'áxadh/yáaxidh/   to take
'axdh

axDar/xúDur   green

axíiran   recently

axláaq (pl.)   morals

ay¹   yes

ay²   which?

aylúul   September

ayyáar   May

'áyyad/yi'áyyid   to support; favour

ázrag/zúrug   blue

á9lan/yí9lin   to announce

á9ma/9umyáan   blind

á9waj, f. 9óoja   crooked; bent

á9zab   bachelor

b

baab/abwáab or   door
biibáan

báachir   tomorrow

baag/yibúug/boog   to steal

báagi   remainder; rest

baal   mind

9ála baal (+ pron.)   I/you, etc. think

(diir) báalik!   Mind out! Be careful!

gháyyar il-baal   to change one's mind

báarak/yibáarik   to bless

il-báarHa   yesterday

báarid   cold (weather, manner)

baaS(aat)   bus

báayig/bawáyga   thief

baa9/yibíi9/bay9   to sell

bádalan min   instead of

bádda   to begin
(v. n. tibdáa*)

báddal/yibáddil   to change (e.g. clothes, tyres)

bádla*(aat)   suit of clothes

bágar   cows; cattle

baggáal/bagaagíil   greengrocer

bágha/yábghi or   to want
yábbi or yíbgha/
bághi

baghdáad   Baghdad

báHar/biHáar   sea

il-baHráyn   Bahrain

baHráyni(yyiin)   Bahraini

balá   yes, on the contrary

baláash   free of charge

bálad   country; town

bánchar(aat)   puncture

bánid   bonnet (car)

bank/bunúuk   bank

bannáay/banáani   builder

bánnad/yibánnid   to close

bannid/i/u!   close! (imp.)

bantalóon   pair of trousers

báraz/yábriz   to be ready

bardáan(iin)   cold (feeling)

baríid   post; post office

il-baríid il-jáwwi   airmail

barnáamaj/baráamij   programme

barqíyya*(aat)   telegram

bárra   outside (adv.)

barráani   outer (adj.)

bas   only; just; but

báSal   onion(s)

báTin/buTúun   stomach; guts

báTTal/yibáTTil   to open

baTTíix   watermelon(s)

báTTil/i/u!   open! (imp.)

baxshíish   gratuity; tip

bayb(aat)   pipe

baybfíita   plumber

bayD   egg(s)

baylinjáan   aubergine

bayt/buyúut   house

báyyaD/yibáyyiD   to brighten; lighten

báyyan/yibáyyin   to appear

bayzáat	money
bá9ad[1]	more; as well; still; yet
bá9ad[2]	after (prep.)
fi maa bá9ad	afterwards
ba9adáyn	afterwards
bá9admaa	after (conj.)
ba9D	some of
ba9íid 9an	far from
bháar(aat)	spices
bi	in; at; with
bícha/yíbchi/báchi	to weep
bída/yíbda/bidáaya	to begin
bidúun maa + verb	without ...ing
biláad/buldáan	country
bína/yíbni/bína or bíni	to build
bináa	construction
bináaya*(aat)	building
bint/banáat	girl
binyáan	building
bítri(yaat)	battery
blaag(aat)	sparking plug
blaastíik	plastic
bluus(aat)	blouse
briij/abaaríig	water pot
búga/yíbga	to remain
búghsha*(aat)	envelope
buldáan	countries
burtugáal	orange(s)
búTil/bTáala	bottle
búTu'	slowness
buuz	mouth
bu9d	distance

ch

cháadhib	dishonest
chaay	tea
chalb/chiláab	dog
cham/kam	how much, many?
bi cham	for how much?
chatf/chtúuf	shoulder
chayf/kayf	how?

cháyfmaa	however; in whatever way
cháyyak/yicháyyik	to check
chibríit	matches
chidháak	like that
chídhab/yáchdhib/ chidhb	to lie; cheat
chidhíi	like this
chiis/achyáas	bag
chilláab/chilaalíib	hook
chinn-/kinn-	as if; like

d

dáafa9/yidáafi9 (9an)	to defend
dáara/yidáari	to take care of
dáawa/yidáawi	to treat; give medicine to
dáaxil	inside
dáaxili	internal; interior
dáayir	going round
dábba*(aat)	belly
dabbáasa*(aat)	stapler
dáftar/dafáatir	notebook
daf9	payment
dagg/yidígg/dagg	to knock; hit
dagíiga*/dagáayig	minute
dajáaj/dyáay	chicken
dall/yidíll/daláal	to indicate; show
damm	blood
dára/yídri (bi)/ diráaya	to know (something)
dáraja*(aat)	degree
dáras/yádris/ diráasa	to study
dáray(aat)	steps; ladder
daríisha*/daráayish	window
dárra/yidárri	to make (someone) know
dárras/yidárris	to teach
dars/druus	lesson
dárzan/darázin	dozen

dashsh/yidíshsh/ dáshsha	to enter
dáwa/adwíya	medicine
dáwla/dúwal	nation-state
dáwli or dúwali	international
dáwwar/yidáwwir	to look for
dawwáar(aat)	traffic roundabout
dáxal/yídxul or yídxal/duxúul	to enter
dáxla*(aat)	opening; entrance
dáxtar/daxáatir	doctor
dáxxan/yidáxxin	to smoke
dayn/dyúun	debt
dazz/yidízz/dázza	to push; send
dá9am/yíd9am/ da9áam	to collide (car)
dá9wa*(aat)	invitation
difáa9	defence
dífa9/yidfá9/daf9	to pay
díhin	cooking oil
diináar/danaaníir	dinar
Id-dínya	the world (and its works)
dirhám/daráahim	dirham
disámbar	December
dooláar(aat)	dollar
door/adwáar	role; turn
dóora*(aat)	course (e.g. of training)
dráywil(iyya)	driver
dukkáan/dakaakíin	shop
durj/adráaj	drawer
duud	worms

D

DáabiT/DubbáaT	officer
Daa9/yiDíi9/Dáy9a	to get lost; be missing
DáHak/yíD-Hak/ DaHk	to laugh
Dájja*	noise; clamour
Dárab/yíDrub/ Darb	to hit; to take (crops)
Dárab tilifúun	to telephone

Daww	fire; light
Dáxim	large; enormous
Dáyyaj/yiDáyyij	to irritate; annoy
Dayya9/yiDáyyi9	to waste; squander
Da9íif(iin)	weak
DíHa	forenoon

dh

dhákkar/yidhákkir	to remind
dhíbaH/yídhbaH/ dhibáaH	to slaughter (animal)
dhibíiHa/dhabáayiH	animal killed for eating (esp. at 9iid)
dhíkar/yádhkir/dhikr	to remember; mention
dhíkra	memory (of something); commemoration
dhoog	taste; flavour
dhu l-Híjja	pilgrimage month in the Islamic calendar

DH

biDH-DHabT	exactly
DHall/yiDHíll	to remain
DHamíir	conscience
DHann/yiDHúnn/ DHann	to think
9ála DHann + pron.	I/you, etc. think
DHúhur	noon
DHúhran	at noontime
DHurúuf	circumstances (pl.)

f

fa	then; so
faad/yifíid/fáyda	to be of use
fáarsi	Persian
faat/yifúut/foot	to pass
fáawal/yifáawil (9ála)	to cheat; dupe

fabráayir	February	
fáDDal/yifáDDil	to prefer	
faDl: min fáDlik/ ch/kum	please	
fáham/yífham/fahm	to understand	
fákkar/yifákkir	to think	
fállat/yifállit	to fling; throw	
fann/funúun	art	
fánnash/yifánnish	to sack; fire	
fáqad/yáfqid/faqd	to lose	
fáqara*(aat)	paragraph	
faqíir/fagáara	poor	
faráagh	free time	
faráash(aat)	bed	
fáraH/yífraH/fáraH	to be happy, joyful	
faránsa	France	
farg	difference; gap	
farHáan(iin)	happy	
faríiq/fúruq	team; group (of musicians)	
farr/yifírr/faráara	to flee	
farráash/faraaríish	servant; cleaner	
fattáan	seductive; mischievous	
fáttash/yifáttish	to inspect	
fáyda*	usefulness	
fi	in; at	
fii/maa fii	there is/are; there isn't/aren't	
fíkra*/afkáar	idea; thought	
filasTíini	Palestinian	
fílim/afláam	film	
fils/fluus	fils coin	
finjáal/fanaajíil	(small) coffee cup	
firíij/firgáan	quarter (of a city)	
fítaH/yíftaH/fatH	to open; conquer	
bil-fi9l	indeed; in fact	
flaan(a)	so-and-so	
fluus	money	

foog	above; over; on top of; on; upstairs	
fúnduq/fanáadiq	hotel	
fúrSa*(aat)	opportunity	

g

gáabal/yigáabil	to meet; be opposite to, across from	
gaal/yigúul/gool	to say	
gaam/yigúum/goom	to rise; get up	
gaam (bi)	to undertake	
gaarsóon	waiter	
gáa9id	sitting	
gáa9id (+ verb)	to be in the middle of, in the process of	
(min) gábil	before (adv.)	
gábil la	before (conj.) (with imperf. verb)	
gábilmaa	before (conj.)	
gabr/gubúur	grave; tomb	
gadd	extent	
gadúu9	morning snack	
gáDa/yígDi/gáDa	to spend (time)	
gáDa 9ála	to sentence; condemn	
gáfsha*(aat)	spoon	
gáhwa	coffee	
gáhwa (v.)/yigáhwi	to give someone coffee	
gálab/yíglub/galb	to turn over (something); turn something into something	
gálam/agláam or gláama	pen	
galb/gulúub	heart	
galíil(iin)	few; small in number	
gál9a*(aat)	castle; fort	
gámgam/yigámgim	to nibble	
gára/yígra/giráaya	to read	

gáriib (min)	near (to)
min garíib	recently
gáSgaS/yigáSgiS	to chop up into bits
gáSir/guSúur	palace
gaSSáab/gaSaaSíib	butcher
gáshma*(aat)	spectacles
gaTT/yigúTT/gaTáaT	to throw (esp. 'away')
gáwwa/yigáwwi	to give (someone) strength
gayúula*	noonday heat
gá9ad/yíg9ad/gu9úud	to sit; stay; get up in the morning
gíbal/yígbal/gubúul	to accept
gídar/yígdar/gádar or mágdira	to be able
giddáam	in front of
gílla*	lack; scarcity
gítal/yágtil	to kill
glaas(aat)	glass
gúmruk/gamáarik	Customs
gúT9a*	piece
gúT9a*/gúTa9 ghiyáar	spare part
gúuTi/gawáaTi	packet; box; tin
gúwi/agwiyáa	strong
gúwwa	strength

gh

ghaab/yighíib/ghayb	to be absent
gháali	expensive
ghábi/aghbiyáa	stupid
gháda	lunch
ghála/yíghli/ghalayáan	to boil (intrans.)
ghálab/yíghlib/ghalíiba	to overcome; beat
ghálaT/aghláaT	mistake
ghalTáan(iin)	mistaken
gháni/aghniyáa	rich
ghánna/yighánni/ghína	to sing

gharb	west
ghárbal/yighárbil/ghirbáal	to confuse; upset
ghárbi	western
ghársha*/aghráash	bottle
ghásal/yighásil/ghasáal	to wash
ghassáala*(aat)	washing machine
gháSban 9ála + pron.	unwillingly
gháSub	compulsion; coercion
gháTTa/yigháTTi	to cover
ghawáaS/ghawaawíiS	pearl-diver
ghayr	other than
gháyyar/yigháyyir	to change (trans.)
ghazáal	gazelle
ghooS	pearl-diving
ghúuri	kettle; teapot

h

háadha/dhi	this
haadháak/dhiich	that
haadhayláak	those
haadhayláyn	these
haadhooláak	those
haaf	shorts
haamm	important
haay (short for háadha)	this
háda/yiháda	to give (someone) guidance
hadd/yihídd/hadd	to leave; abandon
hádiya/hadáaya	present; gift
hamm/humúum	cares; worries
hamm/yihímm	to concern; be important (to someone)
wila yihímmik!	Don't worry about it!
hándisa*	engineering; geometry

hast/maa hast (BAH)	there is/are; there isn't/aren't	HáDar/yáHDur/ HuDúur	to attend; be present
háwa	weather; air	HáDDar/yiHáDDir	to make ready (something)
hídna*	truce		
il-híjra*	The Prophet's flight from Makkah to Medina	Hadíiqa*	kindergarten
		Haffáar(iin)	digger
		Háfla*(aat)	party; celebration
híndi/hunúud	Indian	Háflat chaay	tea party
híyya/híya	she	Hagg¹	right (n.)
húmma/hum	they	Hagg²	for; to
hunáak	over there	Hájar/Hijáara*	stone
húwwa/húwa	he	Hajj/yiHíjj/Hajj	to go on the pilgrimage

H

		Hákam/yáHkum/ Hukm (9ála)	to sentence
Háa'iT/HiiTáan	outer wall		
Háacha/yiHáachi	to address (someone)	Haláawa*	sweetness; prettiness
Haadd	sharp	Halíib	milk
Háadtha*/ Hawáadith	accident	Hall/yiHíll/Hall	to solve
HáaDir	at your service	Hálla/yiHálli (v. n. tiHláa*)	to decorate
Háaja*(aat)	need		
Háajaj/yiHáajij	to argue with (someone)	Hálqa*/Halaqáat	episode
		Hálu, (f.) Hálwa	sweet; pretty; handsome
Háakim/Hukkáam	ruler (of a country)	Hámal/yáHmil or yiHámil/Hamáal	to carry
Haal/aHwáal	condition; state		
Háala*/aHwáal	condition; state	il-Hámdu lilláah	Praise be to God
Háalan	on the spot	il-Hámdu lilláah 9ala salámtik!	Welcome back!
Háali	present; current		
Haalíyyan	at the moment	Hammáam(aat)	bathroom; toilet
Háarab/yiHáarib	to fight; make war	Hámmar/yiHámmir	to brown; roast
Haarr	hot	Hánna/yiHánni/ Hanna*	to paint with henna
Háashya*(aat)	hem		
Háawal/yiHáawil	to try; attempt	Haqq/Huqúuq	right; law
Habb/yiHíbb/Hubb	to love; like	Háqqaq/yiHáqqiq	to confirm; verify
Habb/Hbúub	pill		
Hábba*	grain	Haráam	prohibited (by Islam)
Habíib/aHíbbaa	darling; loved one		
Háchi/Hacháawi	talk; gossip	Harb (f.)/Hurúub	war
Hádag/yiHádig/ Hadáag	to fish (with a line)	HárHash/yiHárHish	to cough hoarsely
		Harr	heat
Hadíiqa/Hadáayiq	park; garden	HáSSal/yiHáSSil	to get; obtain
Hadíith	modern	Hátta	until; even

HaTT/yiHúTT/ HaTáaT	to put (on, in)	íjra	fee
Hawáali	approximately	ijtimáa9	meeting; society
Háwwal/yiHáwwil	to get down, out of	ijtimáa9i	social
		ikraamíyya	bonus; honorarium
Hayáa*	life	íla	to; towards
Hayawáan/ Hayaawíin	animal	ílla	except
		illi	which
Haziiráan	June	imáara*(aat)	emirate
Házza*	moment; time	imtána9/yimtíni9 (min)	to abstain (from)
Hícha/yíHchi/Háchi	to talk		
Hicháaya*	story	imtiHáan(aat)	examination; test
HífaDH/yíHfaDH/ HafáaDH	to keep; preserve	inchább/yinchább	to go away (vulg.)
Hiin/aHyáan	time; period	inDámm/ yinDámm (íla)	to join; be joined (to)
il-Hiin	now		
lil-Hiin	up till now	inglíizi(yyiin)	English(man)
Híjra*/Híjar	room	inn	that (conj.)
Hisáab(aat)	(financial) account	insháallah	God willing
		ínta	you (m. sing.)
9ala Hsáab + pron.	at (someone's) expense	intáha/yintíhi	to come to an end
		intáHar/yintíHir	to commit suicide
Hoosh/aHwáash	courtyard	ínti	you (f. sing.)
Húkum	power; judgement	íntu	you (pl.)
Hukúuma*(aat)	government	iqtáraH/yiqtáriH	to suggest
Hukúumi	governmental	iqtiSáad	economy
HúmmuS bi TaHíina	chickpea dip with sesame oil	IqtiSáadi	economic(al)
		irsaalíyya*	mission
Hurríyya*	freedom	ísim/asáami	name
		isláam	Islam
i		isláami	Islamic
ibtidáa	beginning	ismáH/i/u lii!	excuse me, sorry! (imp.)
ibtidáa'i	elementary; primary		
		istáahal/yistáahil	to deserve; merit
ídha	if	istáajar/yistáajir	to rent; hire
ídhan	so; therefore	istáanas/yistáanis	to be happy, content
iDTárr/yiDTárr	to oblige, force		
íhni	here	istafáad/yistafíid (min)	to benefit (from)
ihtámm/yihtámm (bi)	to be interested (in)		
iHdá9shar	eleven	istághna/yistághni (9an)	to do without
íHna	we		
iHsáas	sensitivity	istáHa/yistáHi	to be shamefaced
iHtáaj/yiHtáaj (íla)	to need	istaHáqq/yistaHíqq	to deserve

istaqáam/yistaqíim (9ála)	to live on (e.g. a type of food)
istánfa9/yistánfi9 (min)	to profit; benefit (from)
istáslam/yistáslim	to surrender
istáwa/yistáwi	to happen; become
istá9jal/yistá9jil	to hurry
istá9mal/yistá9mil	to use
ishtághal/yishtághil	to work
ishtáka/yishtáki	to complain
ishtára/yishtíri	to buy
ittájah/yittájih	to direct oneself
ittákal/yittákil (9ála)	to put one's trust (in)
ittáSal/yittáSil (fi)	to get in touch with
ittáxadh/yittáxidh	to take for oneself
Ithnáyn (thintáyn)	two
il-ithnáyn	Monday
ithná9shar	twelve
íxit or uxt/xawáat	sister
ixtálaf/yixtálif	to differ
i9tábar/yi9tábir	to consider
i9táqad/yi9táqid	to believe
i9tibáaran min	with effect from

j

ja(a) or ya(a)/ijíi or iyíi/jíyya or yáyya	to come
ijíi or iyíi	approximately
jaab or yaab/yijíib or iyíib/jáyba or yáyba	to bring
jaam	glass (sheet)
jáami9	main (Friday) mosque
jáami9a*(aat)	university
jáami9i	university (adj.)
jaar/jiiráan	neighbour
jáaza/yijáazi	to reward
jáawab/yijáawib	to answer

jaay or yaay	coming; next
jabáan/jubanáa	coward
jadd or yadd	grandfather
jádda* or yádda*	grandmother
jadíid/jíddad	new
jakáyt(aat)	jacket
jálas/yájlis/julúus	to sit
jálsa*	sitting; session
jamíil	beautiful
jánTa*/janaTáat	bag; case
jára/yájri/jári	to run; flow
járaH/yíjraH/jarH	to wound; injure
jaríida/jaráayid	newspaper
jaríima*/jaráa'im	crime
járrab/yijárrib	to test out; try
jawáab/ajwíba*	answer; reply
jaww	weather
jawwáal	mobile phone
jáwwad/yijáwwid	to grasp; hold on to
jaysh/juyúush	army
jázar	carrots
jazíira*/jízir	island
jíbin	cheese
jidáar/jidráan	wall (interior)
jigáara*	cigarette
min jíhat + noun	from the point of view of ...
jiib/i/u oryiib/i/u!	bring! (imp.)
jild	leather; skin
jílla*(aat)	56 lb basket of dates
jimáa9a*(aat)	community; group of people
jíma9/yíjma9/jam9	to collect
jínay stárlin	pound sterling
jinsíyya*(aat)	nationality
jinúub	south
jinúubi	southern
jísim/ajsáam	body
jísir/jusúur	bridge; causeway
il-jum9a*	Friday
júuti/jawáati	pair of shoes

k

ka + indep. pron.	here's …!
káafi	enough
káamil	complete; perfect
kaan/yikúun	to be; exist
kaanúun il-áwwal	December
kaanúun ith-tháani	January
káatib/kuttáab	clerk
kabíir/kibáar	big; old
káhrab	electricity
kaláafa*	bother; trouble
kaláam	speech; talk
kálima*(aat)	word; utterance
kamáa yájib	correctly, as it should be
kambyúutar(aat)	computer
kámmal/yikámmil	to complete
kandíshan	air-conditioning
kárah/yíkrah/kárah	to hate
karbráytir	carburettor
karíih	horrible
karíim/kiráam	generous; kind
kárram/yikárrim	to honour
kartúun/kawaartíin	carton
kasláan(iin)	lazy
kássar/yikássir	to smash
kathíir(iin)	many; numerous
káthra*	abundance; large amount
9ála kayf + suffix pron.	as … like(s); as … want(s)
káylo (waat)	kilo
kill	all
kíllah	always
kíllah wáaHid	it's all the same; it makes no difference
9ála kíllin	anyway; however that may be
kíllish	completely
kíllmaa	whatever; whenever
kíllmin	whoever
kínas/yáknis	to sweep
kísar/yáksir/kasr	to break
kíshaf/yákshif/ kasháaf (9ála)	to inspect
kitáab/kútub	book
kítab/yáktib/kitáaba	to write
kíthir	number; amount
kraafáat(aat)	necktie
kúbar/yíkbar/kúbur	to grow up; grow old
kúbur	size; age
kúrsi/karáasi	chair
kuub/akwáab	cup
kúura*	ball
il-kúura/iT-Táa'ira	volleyball
kúurat il-qádam	football
kuut	fort; castle
kuwáyti(yyiin)	Kuwaiti

l

la	no
láaga/yiláagi	to meet (by chance)
láakin	but
láazim	necessary
lábbas/yilábbis	to dress (someone)
ladhíidh	delicious
laff/yilíff/laff	to turn
láhja*(aat)	tone of voice; accent; dialect
láHam	meat
láHDHa*(aat)	moment
lakk/likúuk	100,000 rupees (= 10,000 Bahraini dinars)
law or lo	whether; if
layl	night-time (as opposed to 'daytime')
layla/layáali	night
láylan	at night-time
layn	as soon as; until
láysan	driving licence

laysh	why?	mabrúuk	blessed
layt(aat)	light (e.g. of a street, car)	máda in 9ála máda z-zamáan	with the passage of time
lá9ab/yíl9ab/li9ib	to play	madíina*/múdun	town; city
lá9an/yíl9an/la9n	to curse	madrása*/madáaris	school
li	to; for	mafhúum/mafaahíim	concept
li'ann	because	mafrúush	furnished
líbas/yílbas/libs	to dress; wear	mághsala*/ magháasil	sink
líga/yílga	to meet; find		
líHya*/líHa	beard	máhar	bride price
ila l-liqáa	See you soon!	maHDHúuDH(iin)	lucky
lisáan/alsína*	tongue; language	máHHad	no one
li9ba*(aat)	game	maHSúul	crop; profit
lo	if; or	máHshi	stuffed
lóofar (iyya)	layabout	majáal	room; scope
loon/alwáan	colour	majnúun/majaaníin	mad; crazy
lú'lu'/la'áali	pearl	makíina*/makáayin	machine; engine
lubnáan	Lebanon	máktab/makáatib	office; desk
lubnáani	Lebanese	máktab il-baríid	post office
lúgha*(aat)	language	maktúub/makaatíib	letter
		málach/yámlich/ mílcha	to betroth
m			
maa	not	malfúuf	cabbage
maa mish (BAH)	there isn't/aren't	mall/yimíll/málal (min)	to get bored (with)
maa 9aláyh	it doesn't matter; OK, no objection	mál9ab/maláa9ib	pitch; playing field
maadáam	as long as		
máadda*/mawáadd	material; substance	mámlaka	kingdom
		mamnúu9	prohibited
máaDi	past	man/min	who
maal	belonging to	il-manáama	Manama
maal/amwáal	goods; money	mandúub(iin)	delegate
máaras/yimáaris	to practise (a skill)	mánDHar/ manáaDHir	view
maars	March	mantúuj(aat)	product
maat/yimúut/moot	to die	maqáal(aat)	article (newspaper)
maay	water		
máayo	May	mára*/niswáan	woman
maa9úun/ mawaa9íin	dishes; tableware	máraD/amráaD	illness
		máraD/yímraD/ máraD	to be ill; fall ill
má'dhana*/ ma'áadhin	minaret		
		márgad/maráagid	bed; sleeping place
máblagh/mabáaligh	sum of money		
mábna/mabáani	building	márHaba	welcome

márHala*/maráaHil	type of basket; phase (e.g. of a plan)	máxzan/maxáazin	store cupboard; storage place
marHúum	late (i.e. dead)	mayl/amyáal	mile
maríiD/máraDa	sick; ill	máylis/mayáalis	sitting-room (in an Arab-style house)
marr/yimúrr/murúur (9ala)	to call (in on someone)		
márra*(aat)	time; occasion	máywa*	fruit
bil-márra	at all	máyyit	dead
masáa	evening	mayz(aat)	table
masáa'an	in the evening	mázza*	(Lebanese) hors d'oeuvres
mas'úul	responsible	má9a	with
masraHíyya*(aat)	play	ma9áash(aat)	salary
másyid/masáayid	mosque	ma9gúul	reasonable
máSlaHa*/maSáaliH	interest; benefit; business	má9had/ma9áahid	institute; college
		ma9lúum	known (fact)
máSna9/maSáani9	factory	mgáabil	opposite (prep.)
mashghúul(iin)	busy; engaged	miftáaH/mafaatíiH	key; opener
mashhúur	famous	míHfaDHa*/ maHáafiDH	wallet
máshi	on foot		
mashkúur	thanks; grateful	miiláad	birth
mashrúu9/ mashaaríi9	plan; project	mikáaniki (yyiin)	mechanic
		mikrufúun(aat)	microphone
máshsha/ yimáshshi	to progress (a project); drive (e.g. a car)	miláffa*(aat)	file; dossier
		milH	salt
		milyóon/malaayíin	million
máshwi	roast	min¹; mínhu	who?
máshya*	gait; style of walking	min²	from; of
		mináasib	appropriate; convenient
mátHaf/matáaHif	museum		
matíin/amtáan	fat	mína9/yímna9/ man9	to prevent
maTáar(aat)	airport		
máTar/amTáar	rain	minníi	over here
máTbax/maTáabix	kitchen	minnáak	over there
máT9am/maTáa9im	restaurant	mínTaqa*/manáaTiq	area
máthal/amtháal	example; proverb	miskíin/masaakiin	poor; wretched
máthalan	for example	mismáar/masaamíir	nail
máththal/yimáththil	to act; represent	mistáanis(iin)	happy; content
mawDúu9/ mawaaDíi9	subject; topic	míSir	Egypt
		míSri (yyiin)	Egyptian
mawjúud(iin)	present; existent	mísha/yímshi/máshi	to walk
mawlúud	born	mit' ássif(iin)	sorry
máwqif/mawáaqif	situation; position	mit'áxxir	late
máw9id/mawáa9id	appointment; date	mitzáwwij	married

míTraga*/maTáarig	hammer
míthil	for example
míthilmaa	just as
míya*(aat)	hundred
moot/amwáat	death
mooz	banana
mTállag	divorced
mu'ássasa*(aat)	establishment
mubáara*(aat)	match; contest
mubáarak	blessed
mubákkir	early
mudárris(iin)	teacher
múdda*	period of time
mudíir(iin)	boss; director
mughárb	evening; sunset
muhándis(iin)	engineer
muHáaDra*(aat)	lecture
muHáasib(iin)	accountant
muHárram	first month of the Muslim calendar
muHássin(iin)	barber
mujáddara*	dish of lentils
mujálla*(aat)	magazine
mujárrad + noun/verb	the mere ...
mújrim(iin)	criminal
mukáan(aat)	place; spot
mukádda*	job; way of earning money
mumárriDa*(aat)	nurse
múmkin	possible; maybe
bi munaasábat + noun	on the occasion of
múnkar(aat)	atrocity; bad act
muqáabla*(aat)	meeting
muqáawil(iin)	contractor
muqtáraH(aat)	suggestion
murúur	traffic; traffic police
musájjila*(aat)	tape recorder
musálsal	serial (TV, radio, etc.)
mustáshfa(yaat)	hospital

mustáwa(yaat)	level; standard
múshkila*/masháakil	problem
mutárjim(iin)	translator
mút9ib	tiring
muu/mub/múhub	not
muu chidhíi?	isn't that so?
muul	completely; absolutely
muwáDHDHaf(iin)	official; employee
muwállid	generator (electric)
muxx	brain; intelligence
mu9állim(iin)	Qur'an teacher
mu9táqad(aat)	belief

n

náa'ib/nuwwáab	deputy
náadi/nawáadi	club; society
náagiS	lacking
naam/yináam/noom	to sleep
naas	people
náasab/yináasib	to suit; match
naaTúur/nawaaTíir	watchman
náazil	low
nába'/anbáa	piece of news
náDHar	sense of sight
naDHDHáara*(aat)	eyeglasses
náDHDHaf/yináDHDHif	to clean
naDHíif	clean
náfar/anfáar	person
nafnúuf/nafaaníif	dress
nafs + noun/pron.	the same ...
nágla*	burden
naháar	daytime
najáaH	success
nájim/nujúum	star
najjáar/najaajíir	carpenter
nákkat/yinákkit	to joke
natíija/natáa'ij	result
náTaH/yínTaH/náTaH	to butt

naTT/yinúTT	to jump
náxal	palm tree(s)
ná9am	yes
na9íiman	greeting for someone who has just had a bath, haircut, etc.
niDHaj/yínDHaj	to ripen; be ready; be cooked
nífad/yínfad	to run out
nifT	petroleum
niháaya*	end; conclusion
lin-niháaya	extremely
niisáan	April
níjaH/yínjaH/najáaH	to succeed; pass
nísa/yínsa/nisyáan	to forget
bin-nísba íla	in relation to; in comparison to
níshaf/yánshif/nasháaf	to become dry
níshar/yánshir/nashr	to publish
nítfa*	a bit
nízal/yánzil/nuzúul	to stay (in a hotel); go down
nóoba wáHda	in one go; all at once
noo9/anwáa9	type; kind
nufámbar	November
núqTa*/núqaT	point at issue
nuSS	half
nzayn	OK; right

p

pánka(aat)	fan
plaatíin	breaker points (car)
poolíis(iyya)	policeman
putáyta	potato(es)

q

qáadim	next
il-qáahira*	Cairo
qáamar/yiqáamir	to gamble

qaamúus/qawaamíis	dictionary
qábad/yíqbaD/qabD	to arrest; get hold of
qadíim	old (of things)
qadíim iz-zamáan	ancient times
qaDáa	execution; termination
qall/yiqáll/qílla or qaláala	to be little, few; become few
qállad/yiqállid	to imitate; copy
qamíiS/qumSáan	shirt
qarn/qurúun	century
qárya*/qúra	village
qáSad/yáqSud/qaSd	to intend
qíbal/yíqbal/qubúul	to accept
qird/qurúud	monkey
qísim/aqsáam	department
qíSSa*/qíSaS	story
il-qur'áan	the Qur'an

r

ráabi9	fourth
raaH/yirúuH/rooHa or rawáaH	to go
ráaHa*	rest
ráakib/rukkáab	passenger
raas/ruus	head
ráatib/rawáatib	salary
ráayiH: min … ráayiH	from … onwards
ra'íis/ru'asáa	chief; boss (n.)
ra'íisi	chief; main; principal (adj.)
rá'san	directly
rá'y/aráa	opinion
rábba/yirábbi	to bring up; raise (children, animals, etc.)
radd/yirídd/radáad or rdúud	to return; give back; answer; repeat; do again
radd + verb	to do something again

ráfaD/yárfuD/rafD	to refuse; reject
raghab/yirghab (fi)	to desire
rájul/rijáal a9máal	businessman
rákkab/yirákkib	to attach; install
ramaDáan	the Muslim month of fasting
ráqam/arqáam	number
rásim/rusúum	drawing; painting
rásmi	official
raSíid	receipt
ráTib	humid
ráwwa/yiráwwi	to show
raxíiS	cheap
ráydo(waat)	radio
ráyil (or rájil)/rijáal	man; husband (alternative to rayyáal/rayaayíil)
rayúug	breakfast
rayyáal/rayaayíil	man
ráyyaH/yiráyyiH	to relieve; give rest
riDa/yírDa/ríDa	to agree; consent
rifíij/rifgáan	friend
rígad/yárgid/irgáad	to lie down; sleep
ríHla(aat)	trip; outing
riiH (f.)/riyáaH	wind
riil/ryúul	leg
ríja9/yírja9/rujúu9	to return; come back
ríkab/yárkub/rukúub	to get on, in (vehicle)
ríkaD/yárkuD/rakíiD	to run
risáala*/rasáa'il	letter; vocation; mission
rísam/yársim/rásim	to draw; paint
riwáaya*(aat)	drama
riyáaDa*	sport
riyaaDiyáat	mathematics
riyáal(aat)	riyal
rizg (or rizj)	sustenance; food (fig.)
róoba*	yogurt

rubbíya*(aat) or rabáabi	rupee (old currency = 100 fils)
rubyáan	prawns
rub9	quarter
ruuH/i/u	go! (imp.)
bruuH + pron.	by ... self
rúuti	bread roll
ruwáyd	radish(es)
rúxSa	permission (to leave)
rúxSat siyáaqa*	driving licence

s

sáabi9	seventh
sáadis	sixth
sáafar/yisáafir	to travel
saag/yisúug/ syáaga	to drive
sáaHil/sawáaHil	shore
sáakin/sukkáan	living; domiciled; inhabitant
sáalfa*/sawáalif	conversation; chat
is-saalmíyya	Salmiya (in Kuwait)
saamáan	stuff; gear
sáawam/yisáawim	to bargain
sáayig/suwwáag	driver
sáa9a*(aat)	hour; watch; clock
sáa9ad/yisáa9id	to help
sá'al/yís'al	to ask
sábab/asbáab	reason; cause
is-sabt	Saturday
sab9(a)	seven
saba9tá9shar	seventeen
sab9íin	seventy
sadd/yisídd/sadáad	to block
safaríyya*(aat)	journey; travel
safíina*/súfun	ship
safíir/sufaráa	ambassador
sagf/sugúuf	roof
sájjal/yisájjil	to record; register

sakk/yisíkk	to shut
saláam	peace; tranquility
saláama*	safety
sállaf/yisállif	to lend
sámak/asmáak	fish (more formal equivalent of simich)
samíin/simáan	fat
sámma/yisámmi	to name
sammáach/ samaamíich	fisherman
sámma9/yisámmi9	to make (someone) hear
sána*/sanawáat (or siníin)	year
sandawíich	sandwich
saríi9/siráa9	fast; speedy
sáTaH/suTúuH	roof
saww/i/u	make!; do! (imp.)
sáwwa/yisáwwi/ tiswáa*	to make; do
sayf/suyúuf	sword
sáykal	bicycle
sáyTar/yisáyTir/ sáyTara* (9ala)	to dominate; control
sayyáara*/sayaayíir	car
sáyyid/sáada*	Mr
sa9úudi(yyiin)	Saudi Arabian
sibáaq	race (sport)
síbaH/yísbaH/ sibáaHa	to swim
sibtámbar	September
sichchíin/ sachaachíin	knife
sifáara	embassy
síida	straightaway; straight on
siidíi(aat)	CD
siif	seashore
síinama(aat)	cinema
sijill(aat)	register
sijin/sujúun	prison
síkan/yáskin/sákan	to live (in a place)
síkat/yáskit/skúut	to be quiet

sikirtíir(iyya)	secretary
síma	sky
símaH/yísmaH/ samáaH (li)	to permit someone (to)
síma9/yísma9/ samáa9	to listen to; hear
símich	fish (coll.)
smicha/asmaach or simchaan	fish (sing.)
sitt(a)	six
sittá9shar	sixteen
sittíin	sixty
síwa/yíswa	to be worth, equal to
siyáaHa	tourism
siyáaHi	tourist; touristic
siyáaqa*	driving
sí9ir/as9áar	cost; price
smiit	cement
sóolaf/yisóolif	to chat
su'áal/as'ila	question
subúu9/asaabíi9	week
suhúula*	ease
súr9a*	speed
suug/aswáag	market
súuriya	Syria

S

Saabúun	soap
Saad/yiSíid/Sayd	to hunt; catch
SaaH/yiSíiH/SayH	to cry out; shout
SáaHi	sober; awake
SáaHib/aSHáab	owner; possessor
Saaj/Saadgíin	truth-telling
SáaliH	proper; valid; in good order
Saalúuna*	stew; curry
Sáam/yiSúum/ Soom	to fast
Sáamit	silent(ly)
Saar/yiSíir/Sayr	to become; happen
SabáaH	morning

SabáaH il-xayr	Good morning!
SabáaH in-nuur	Good morning! (reply)
SabáaHan	in the morning
Sabb/yiSúbb	to pour
Sádag/yáSdig/Sidg	to tell the truth
Sadíiq/aSdiqáa	friend
Sádir	chest (anat.)
Sadríyya*	bra
Saff/Sufúuf	classroom; row
Saghíir/Sigháar	small; young
SáHafi(yyiin)	journalist
SáHan(a*)/SuHúun	plate
SaHíifa*/SúHuf	page (of a book)
SaHíiH	true; correct
SaHráa	desert
SállaH/yiSálliH	to repair; correct
Sána9/yíSna9/San9	to manufacture
Sandúug/Sanaadíig	box; chest; boot (car); trunk (car)
bi SaráaHa*	frankly
Sáraf/yáSruf/Sarf	to pay; spend
Saydalíyya*(aat)	chemist's
Sayf	summer (n.)
Sáyfi	summer (adj.)
Sá9ab	difficult
Sbay(aan)	lad; boy
Síbagh/yíSbagh/ Sabáagh	to paint
Sidj	that's true!
Sidq	truth
SíHHa*	health
Síini	Chinese
SílaH/yíSlaH/ SaláaH	to be proper; right
Sináa9i	industrial
Soot/aSwaat	voice; noise
SubH	early morning
Súdfatan	by chance
biS-Súdfa	by chance
Súrra*(aat)	bundle; bunch
Súura/Súwar	picture; photo
Su9úuba*	difficulty

sh

sh- (prefix)	what?
sháabb/shubbáan	youth; juvenile
shaaf/yishúuf/ shoof or shóofa	to look, see
shaal/yishíil/shayl or shayaláan	to remove, lift
sháari9/shawáari9	street
sháaTir(iin)	clever; smart
shabáab	youth (in general)
shagg/yishígg/ shagáag	to tear
shághal/yíshghal/ shughl	to busy; occupy
shaghgháal/ shaghaaghíil	hardworking
shághghal/ yishághghil	to operate (a machine, etc.)
shaháada*(aat)	certificate; diploma
sháhar/áshur	month
shájar	trees (coll.)
shájja9/yishájji9	to encourage (someone) to (9ála) do something
shákil/ashkáal	form; shape; type
shakk/shkúuk	doubt
shákkar	sugar
shákwa/shakáawi	complaint
shams (f.)	sun
shárab/yíshrab/ shirb (or shurb)	to drink; smoke (tobacco)
sharg	east
shárgi	eastern
sharíiTa*/sharáa'iT	tape recording
shárika*(aat)	company; firm
sharT/shurúuT	condition; stipulation
sháxal/yíshxal	to sieve
shaxS/ashxáaS	person
sháxSi	personal
shaxSíyya*(aat)	personality

shaxT/shuxúuT	stripe	táasi9	ninth
shay¹/ashyáa	thing	ta'xíir	delay
shay²/maa shay (OM)	there is/are; there isn't/aren't	tádhkira*/tadháakir	ticket
		tafáDDal/i/u	be so kind! (imp.)
shayb/shiyáab	old man	tagháyyar/	to change
shayn	bad; evil	yitgháyyar	(intrans.)
shayx/shuyúux	sheikh	taHáarab/yitHáarab	to fight each other
shá9ar	hair (head)	taHáchcha/	to talk
shgáddmaa	however much	yitHáchcha	
shídda*	strength; intensity	taHámmal/	to take care of;
shífa/yíshfa/shífa	to get better; be cured	yitHámmal (bi) (v. n. Hamáala)	look after
shijáa9a*	bravery	taHt	under; below; right next to
shíkilmaa	like, just as (conj.)		
shimáal	north	tamáam	excellent; perfect
shimáali	northern; left (side)	támar	dates
		tamm/yitímm	to stay; continue
shínhu	what?	tammúuz	July
shíqqa*(aat)	apartment	tamthiiliyya*(aat)	play; drama
shíra/yíshri or yishtíri/shíra	to buy	tanDHíif	cleaning
		tánis	tennis
shkíthirmaa	however much	tannúura*(aat)	skirt
shloon	how?	taqríiban	approximately
shubáaT	February	taqríir/taqaaríir	written report
shúghul/ashgháal	work; job	tárak/yátruk/tark	to leave (someone, a place)
shúghla*/shághla*	job		
shúkran	thank you	tárjam/yitárjim	to translate
shúrTa*	police	tárjama*/taráajim	translation
shúrTi(yyiin)	policeman	taswíiq	marketing
shuuf/i/u!	look! (imp.)	taSdíir	exporting
shuwándar	beetroot	taSlíiH	repair
shuwárma	('doner') kebab	taTwíir	development (economic, etc.)
shwáqtmaa	at whatever time		
shway	for a little while	taw + pron.	to have just ...
shway shway	slowly; little by little	taxállaS/yitxállaS (min)	to get rid (of); be free (of)
bi shwáy	by a small amount	taxáSSaS/ yitxáSSaS (fi)	to specialise (in)
shwáyya*	a little; a bit	taym	hours (office, shift)
t		tayr(aat)	tyre
táaba9/yitáabi9	to follow	ta9áal/i/u	come here! (imp.)
táajir/tujjáar	merchant	ta9áawan/	to cooperate
táali	next; then; after	yit9áawan	

ta9ájjab/yit9ájjab	to be surprised, amazed	tisáa9ad/yitsáa9ad	to help each other
ta9áshsha/ yit9áshsha	to dine	tísa9 (tís9a)	nine
		tisa9tá9shar	nineteen
ta9báan(iin)	tired	tist(aat)	driving test
tibánnad/yitbánnad	to close (intrans.); be closeable	tis9íin	ninety
		tiSáalaH/yitSáalaH	to make peace; call a truce
tibáTTal/yitbáTTal	to open; be openable	tishríin il-áwwal	October
tidhákkar/ yitdhákkar	to remember	tishríin ith-tháani	November
tifáaham/yitfáaham	to understand each other	tiTárrash/ yiTTárrash	to be sent
tigáabal/yitgáabal	to meet each other	tiwáafag/yitwáafag	to mutually agree
tigáhwa/yitgáhwa	to have coffee	tiwáffa/yitwáffa	to pass away; die
tighádda/yitghádda	to have lunch	tiwáqqa9/yitwáqqa9	to expect; anticipate
tighárbal/yitghárbal	to get confused, mixed up	tixárbaT/yitxárbaT	to get mixed up
tiHáacha/yitHáacha	to converse	tizábbar/yitzábbar	to dress up smartly
tiHássan/yitHássan	to improve	tizáwwaj/yitzáwwaj	to get married
tíila	marbles (game)	tí9ab/yít9ab/tá9ab	to get tired
tijáara*	trade; commerce	ti9állam/yit9állam	to learn
tijárraH/yitjárraH	to be hurt, injured	ti9áTTal/yit9áTTal	to break down; be unemployed
tíksi/takáasi or tiksiyáat	taxi	ti9áwwad/ yit9áwwad (9ála)	to get used to
tilaf/yátlif/tálaf	to spoil; go bad	tufáaH	apples
tìlágga/yitlágga	to get; receive	túfga*/tífag	gun
tilifúun(aat)	telephone		
tilivizyúun(aat)	television	**T**	
timáshsha/ yitmáshsha	to stroll	Táabiq/Tawáabiq	storey; floor (of a building)
tináazal/yitnáazal (9an)	to abdicate; relinquish control (of)	Táabi9/Tawáabi9	postage stamp
		Taaf/yiTúuf/Tawáaf	to go round something
tindáyl	foreman	TaaH/yiTíiH/TayH	to fall
tiqáddam/ yitqáddam	to proceed; present oneself	Taal/yiTúul/Tuul	to be long
tirákkab/yitrákkab	to be fixed, installed	Táala9/yiTáali9	to watch; look at
		Táalib/Tulláab	student
tirámmaz/yitrámmaz	to jump up and down	TáayiH	broken; dilapidated
tíras/yátris/tars	to fill	Táazij	fresh
tiráyyag/yitráyyag	to breakfast	Tábbal/yiTábbil	to drum

Tabíib/aTibbáa	medical doctor	thaláath(a)	three
Tábil/Tubúul (n.)	drum	ith-thaláatha*	Tuesday
Tábxa*(aat)	cooked dish	thalaathtá9shar	thirteen
Táb9an	naturally	thalaathíin	thirty
Taffáaya*(aat)	ashtray	thalláaja*(aat)	fridge
Tagg/yiTígg/Tagg	to beat; hit	thamáan(ya)	eight
Tálab/yáTlub/Tálab	to ask for; demand	thamaaníin	eighty
		thamantá9shar	eighteen
Tála9/yíTla9/Tuluu9 or Taláa9	to go out; come out of; turn out; end up being	thilth/athláath	one third
		thoob/thiyáab	clothes (sing. means a man's long shirt)
Tálla9/yiTálli9	to take (something) out of (something)		
TamáaT	tomato(es)	**u**	
Taqs	climate; weather	uktúubar	October
Tard/Truud	parcel	umm/ummaháat	mother
Taríig/Túrug	road	urúbba	Europe
9an Taríig	via; by way of	ustáadh/asáatidha	teacher
Tárrash/yiTárrish	to send	úula	first (f.)
Tawíil/Tiwáal	tall; long	uxt (or íxit)/axawáat	sister
Táwla*(aat)	table		
Tayaráan	aviation	**w**	
TáyHa*(aat)	fall; swoon	wáafag/yiwáafig (9ála)	to agree to (something)
Tayyáara*(aat)	aeroplane	wáaHid	one
Ta9áam	food	waalidáy + pron.	my/your, etc. parents
Tíbax/yíTbax/Tabx or Tabíix	to cook	waalidáyn	parents
Tífil/aTfáal	child	wáasi9	roomy; spacious
TiHíin	flour	wáayid/waajid	a lot; many
Tiib	goodness	wádda/yiwáddi	to put; send
Tiráaz	type; style; fashion	wádda9/yiwáddi9	to bid farewell
Tuul/aTwáal	length; along (prep.)	waDHíifa*/ waDHáayif	duty; job; post
		wággaf/yiwággif	to stop (something)
th			
tháabit	fixed; immovable	waHíid	single; sole
tháalith	third (adj.)	wájab/yájib/wujúub	to be incumbent
tháamin	eighth (adj.)	kamáa yájib	as it must be
tháanawi	secondary (school)	wájba*(aat)	meal; repast
tháani	second (adj.)	wajh/wujúuh	face
thagíil/thigáal	heavy	wakáala*(aat)	agency

wakáalat is-safariyyáat	travel agency	**X**	
wálad/awláad	boy	xáabar/yixáabir	to inform (someone about something)
wálla or wílla	or		
walláahi l-9aDHíim	By the great God (strong oath)	xáadim/xuddáam	servant
		xaaf/yixáaf/xoof	to fear
wállah/walláahi	By God!	xáali	empty
wanáyt(aat)	pick-up truck	xáamis	fifth (adj.)
wáqqa9/yiwáqqi9	to sign	xaan/yixúun/ xiyáana*	to betray
waqt	time		
min waqt	early	xáatam/xawáatim	ring (for the finger)
il-waqt il-HáaDir	the present time		
wára	behind	xaar/yixúur/ xawaráan	to stir
wáraga*/awráag	leaf; piece of paper	xáarij	outside
		xáariji	external; exterior
wársha*(aat)	workshop	xábar/axbáar	piece of news
wásix	dirty	xabbáaz/xabaabíiz	baker
wasT/awsáaT	centre; middle	xabíir/xubaráa	expert
wáSSal/yiwáSSil	to take (someone somewhere); give a lift to (someone)	xaDD/yixúDD/xaDD	to shake (something)
		xáffaD/yixáffiD	to decrease; lower (something)
wáTan	homeland	xáffaS/yixáffiS	to crush; squash
wáTani	national; belonging to one's homeland	xafíif/xifáaf	light (in weight)
		xaláaS	finished; over
wayn	where?	xálfmaa	after (conj.)
wáynmaa	wherever	il-xalíij	(Arabian) Gulf
waysh	what?	xálla/yixálli	to let; allow
wazíir/wuzaráa	minister	xalláa9	shameless; depraved
widd + pron.	to want		
wild	boy; son (often used instead of wálad in phrases such as wíldi 'my son', wíldik 'your son')	xállaS/yixálliS	to finish
		xámar	alcohol
		il-xamíis	Thursday
		xams(a)	five
		xamsíin	fifty
wizáara*(aat)	ministry	ll-xamsiináat	the (19)50s
wúgaf/yóoguf/ wugúuf	to stop; stand	xamstá9shar	fifteen
		xanzíir/xanaazíir	pig
wújad	to find	xaráab	broken down; useless
wúja9/awjáa9	pain		
wúSal/yóoSil/ wuSúul	to arrive	xáraj/yáxruj/xurúuj	to go out
		xarbáan	broken down

xárbaT/yixárbiT	to confuse; mix up (something)
xárbuTa*/xaraabííT	rubbish; nonsense
xárrab/yixárrib	to ruin
xarúuf/xirfáan	lamb; mutton; sheep
xast	lettuce
xáshim	nose
xátam/yáxtim/xatm	to read the Qur'an from cover to cover
xáTa'/axTáa'	mistake
xáTab/yíxTub/ xúTba or xuTúuba	to betroth
xáTar/axTáar	danger
xaTíir	grave; dangerous
xaTT/xuTúuT	handwriting; telephone line
xáTTaT/yixáTTiT	to draw lines; make plans
xáwwaf/yixáwwif	to frighten
xayl (pl.)	horses
xayr	good; bounty; good deed
xayr (min)	better (than)
bi xayr	(feeling) good, well
xáysha*/xiyáash	sack
xayyáaT(iin)	tailor
xídma*(aat)	service
fi xiláal	in the space of (time)
xoosh	nice; good
xub	intensifying particle meaning 'heck!', 'really!'
xúbuz	bread
xudh/i/u	take!

y

yaa	hey; oh
yaa hála!	hello!; welcome!
yaa saláam!	bravo!
yáahil/yiháal or jáahil/jiháal	child
yad or iid/ayáadi	hand
yállah!	let's go!; come on!; hurry up!
yamíin	right-hand side; south
yanáayir	January
yanb or yamm	next to; beside
yasáar	left-hand side
yíbas/yíybas	to dry out
yoom/ayyáam	day
il-yoom	today
yoom	when (conj.)
yóommaa	as soon as
yoom min il-ayyáam	one day
yoomíyya(aat)	day's wages
yúbba	address form: father to child
yúmkin	maybe
yúmma	address form: mother to child
yúulyo	July
yuuníyya*/yawáani	sack
yúunyo	June
yuu9 or juu9	hunger
yuu9áan/yuwáa9a	hungry

z

zaad/yizíid/zood or ziyáada	to increase
zaal/yizáal	to cease
maa zaal + imperf. verb	to still be …
zaam(aat)	shift (of work)
zaar/yizúur/ziyáara	to visit
záari9/zurráa9	farmer
záayir/zuwwáar	visitor
zahra*/zuhúur	flower
záHma*	chaos; bother; trouble
min zamáan	for a long time (up to the present)

ayyáam zamáan	(in) the old days
záman	period; point in time
zamíil/zumaláa	colleague
zára9/yízra9/zar9 or **ziráa9a**	to plant; sow
zawáaj	marriage
zayn/zayníin	good
zayt	oil
zayy/azyáa	fashion
za9láan(iin)	angry; upset
zá99al/yizá99il	to annoy; upset
zíbid	butter
ziráa9a*	agriculture
ziráa9i	agricultural
zitáat	quickly
zí9al/yíz9al/zá9al	to get upset
zooj/azwáaj	husband
zóoja*(aat)	wife
zukáam	head cold
zuulíyya*/zawáali	rug

9

9aad	so; then
9áada*(aat)	custom; tradition
9áadatan	usually
9áadi	ordinary; usual
9áadil	just; fair
9áalam	world
9áali	high; loud
9aam (adj.)	general
9áamil/9ummáal	worker; labourer
9áaqab/yi9áaqib	to punish
9aash/yi9íish/9aysh	to live
9áashir	tenth (adj.)
9abáal + pron.	I thought …
9ádad	number (i.e. total)
9ádam	lack; dearth
9add/yi9ídd/9add	to count; enumerate
9áddal/yi9áddil	to straighten; put right
9ádil	correct; just

9aDHíim	great; enormous
il-9áfu and **9áfwan**	reply to 'thanks': don't mention it!; sorry, pardon?
9ájab/yá9jib or **yi9ájib**	to please (someone)
9ajíib	strange; bizarre
9ajúuz/9ajáayiz	old woman
bil-9aks	on the contrary
9ála	on; against
9álam/yá9lam/9ilm	to know
9álla/yi9álli	to raise
9állam/yi9állim	to teach; instruct
9ámal/a9máal	work; job; employment
9amm/a9máam	paternal uncle
9an	from; away from
9aníid	stubborn
9aqd/9uqúud	contract
9árabi/9árab	Arab; Arabic (pl. means 'Arabs')
9áraf/yi9árf/má9rifa	to know (something or someone)
9arD/9urúuD	offer; proposal
9árra	to put a handle on something
9árraf/yi9árrif	to acquaint someone with (**9ála**) someone; introduce someone to someone
9arúus (f.)/**9aráayis**	bride
9ása + noun/pron.	hopefully …
9áSa	stick
9ásha	dinner
9áshar (9áshra)	ten
9aSíir	pressed fruit juice
9áSr	late afternoon
9áSran	in the late afternoon
9atíij/9itáag	old; ancient (of things)

9aT/i/u!	give! (imp.)	**9iid il-fiTr**	Festival of the Fast-breaking
9áTa/yá9Ti/9áTa	to give		
9aTsháan(iin)	thirsty	**9iid il-áD-Ha**	Festival of the Sacrifice
9áTTal/yi9áTTil	to put out of action; make redundant; stop someone (from working)	**9ilm**	knowledge
		9ílmi	scientific
		9imáara*(aat)	apartment block
		9ínab	grape(s)
9áwwar/yi9áwwir	to cause pain; hurt	**9ind**	with; at (+ pron. 'to have')
9áyal or **9ájal**	well then; so	**9iyáal**	family dependants; children
9ayb/9uyúub	shame; disgrace		
9ayn (f.)/**9uyúun**	eye		
9aysh	rice	**9ógub**	after (prep.)
9áyyan/yi9áyyin	to appoint (someone)	**9ógubmaa**	after (conj.)
		9ood	big; large
9ázam/yi9ázim/ 9ázam or **9azáam**	to invite	**9umr/a9máar**	life (length of)
		9úmri + maa + past tense verb	I've never … in my life
9azíiz	dear; cherished	**9unwáan/9anaawíin**	address
9ídam/yí9dam	to be ruined, spoilt	**9úTla*/9úTal**	holiday; day off
9iid/a9yáad	festival		

English–Gulf Arabic glossary

Phrasal verbs of the form 'to be interested in', 'to be forced to', etc. are listed under 'interested', 'forced', etc.

A

to be able	gídar/yígdar/gádar or mágdira
above	foog
to be absent	ghaab/yighíib/ghayb
abstain (from)	imtána9/yimtíni9 (min)
abundance; large amount	káthra*
accent	láhja*(aat)
accept	gíbal/yígbal/gubúul
accident	Háadtha*/Hawáadith
account; bill (financial)	Hisáab(aat)
accountant	muHáasib(iin)
address (n.)	9unwáan/9anaawíin
address (v.)	Háacha/yiHáachi
add	aDHáaf/yiDHíif
adjust	9áddal/yi9áddil
aeroplane	Tayyáara*(aat)
affect (v.)	'áththar/yi'áththir (fi)
to be afraid	xaaf/yixáaf/xoof
after (prep.)	bá9ad
after (prep., adv.)	9ógub
after (conj.)	bá9admaa; xálfmaa; 9ógubmaa
afternoon (late)	9áSr
in the late afternoon	9áSran

afternoon shift	áwwal il-layl
afterwards	fi maa bá9ad; ba9adáyn
against	9ála
age (length of life)	9umr/a9máar
agency (travel, etc.)	wakáala*(aat)
agree to	wáafag/yiwáafig (9ála)
to come to an agreement	tiwáafag/yitwáafag
agree to; consent to	riDa/yírDa/ríDa
agricultural	ziráa9i
agriculture	ziráa9a*
air	háwa
air-conditioning	kandíshan
airmail	il-barííd il-jáwwi
airport	maTáar(aat)
alcohol	xámar
alive	mawjúud(iin); Hayy/aHyaa
all	kill or kull
allow	símaH/yísmaH/samáaH (li)
along (adv.)	Tuul
always	killah
ambassador	safíir/sufaráa
America	amríika

American	**amríiki (yyiin)**	I ask, beg you; please!	**arjúuk!**
amount	**kíthir**		
angry; upset	**za9láan(iin)**	as long as	**maadáam**
animal	**Hayawáan/ Hayaawíin**	as soon as	**layn**
		as well	**bá9ad**
animal killed for eating (esp. at **9iid**)	**dhibííHa/dhabáayiH**	at	**bi; fi**
		(not) at all	**bil-márra**
announce	**á9lan/yí9lin**	attempt (v.)	**Háawal/yiHáawil**
annoy	**Dáyyaj/yiDáyyij; zá99al/yizá99il**	attend; be present	**HáDar/yáHDur/ HuDúur**
answer (v.)	**jáawab/yijáawib; radd/yirídd/radáad or rdúud**	aubergine	**baylinjáan**
		August	**awghústos; aab**
		aviation; flying	**Tayaráan**
answer; reply (n.)	**jawáab/ajwíba***	awake	**SáaHi**
anticipate	**tiwáqqa9/yitwáqqa9**		
anyway; however that may be	**9ála kíllin**	**B**	
		bachelor	**á9zab**
apartment	**shíqqa*(aat)**	bad; evil	**shayn**
apartment block	**9imáara*(aat)**	bag (hand); case	**jánTa*/janaTáat**
to appear	**báyyan/yibáyyin**	bag (plastic)	**chiis/achyáas**
apples	**tuffáaH**	Baghdad	**baghdáad**
appoint	**9áyyan/yi9áyyin**	Bahrain	**il-baHráyn**
appointment; date	**máw9id/mawáa9id**	Bahraini	**baHráyni(yyiin)**
		baker	**xabbáaz/xabaabíiz**
appropriate	**mináasib**	ball	**kúura***
approximately	**Hawáali; iyíi** or **ijíi; taqríiban**	banana	**mooz**
		bank	**bank/bunúuk**
April	**abríil; niisáan**	barber	**muHássin(iin)**
Arab; Arabic	**9árabi/9árab**	bargain (v.)	**sáawam/yisáawim**
area; region	**mínTaqa*/manáaTiq**	bathroom	**Hammáam(aat)**
argue with (someone)	**Háajaj/yiHáajij**	battery	**bítri(yaat)**
		be; exist	**kaan/yikúun**
army	**jaysh/juyúush**	beard	**líHya*/líHa**
arrest (v.)	**qábad/yíqbaD/qabD**	beat; hit	**Tagg/yiTígg/Tagg**
arrive	**wúSal/yóoSil/ wuSúul**	beat; overcome	**ghálab/yíghlib/ ghalíiba**
art	**fann/funúun**	beautiful	**jamíil**
article (newspaper)	**maqáal(aat)**	because	**li'ann**
to be ashamed	**istáHa/yistáHi**	become; turn into	**istáwa/yistáwi; Saar/yiSíir/Sayr**
ashtray	**Taffáaya*(aat)**	bed	**faráash(aat); márgad/maráagid**
as if	**chinn-/kinn-**		
ask	**sá'al/yís'al**	beetroot	**shuwándar**
ask for	**Tálab/yáTlub/Talab**	before (adv.)	**(min) gábil**

before (conj.) (with imperf. v.)	gábil la	boil (v. intrans.)	ghála/yíghli/ ghalayáan
before (conj.) (with perf. v.)	gábilmaa	bonnet; hood (car)	bánid
belonging to	Hagg	bonus; honorarium	ikraamíyya
begin	bída/yíbda/bidáaya; bádda (v. n. tibdáa*)	book (n.)	kitáab/kútub
beginning	ibtidáa	boot (car)	Sandúug/Sanaadíig
beginning parts	awáayil	to get bored	mall/yimíll/málal (min)
behind (prep.)	wára	born	mawlúud
belief	mu9táqad(aat)	boss	mudíir(iin); nóoxadha (lit. 'sea captain')
believe; think (that)	i9táqad/yi9táqid		
belonging to	maal	bother; trouble (n.)	kaláafa*; záHma*
below	taHt		
benefit (from)	istafáad/yistafíid (min)	bottle (n.)	ghársha*/aghráash; búTil/bTáala
bestow favours (on)	án9am/yín9im (9ála)	box	Sandúug/Sanaadíig
belly	dábba*(aat)	boy	wálad/awláad; Sbay(aan)
beside; next to	yanb or yamm	bra; bikini top	Sadríyya*
betray	xaan/yixúun/ xiyáana*	brain; intelligence	muxx
betroth (a woman to a man)	málach/yámlich/ mílcha	bravery	shijáa9a*
		bravo!	yaa saláam!
better (than)	aHsan; xayr (min)	bread	xúbuz
to get better; improve	tiHássan/yitHássan	bread roll	rúuti
		break; snap	kísar/yáksir/kasr
to get better (be cured of illness)	shífa/yíshfa/shífa	break down	ti9áTTal/yit9áTTal
		breakfast	rayúug
bicycle	sáykal	to have breakfast	tiráyyag/yitráyyag
birth	miiláad	bride	9arúus (f.)/9aráayis
big	kabíir/kibáar; 9ood	bride-price	máhar
bit; small piece	nítfa*; shwáyya*	bridge; causeway	jísir/jusúur
black	áswad/suud	brighten; lighten	báyyaD/yibáyyiD
bless	báarak/yibáarik	bring	jaab or yaab/yijíib or iyíib/jáyba or yáyba
blessed	mubáarak		
blind	á9ma/9umyáan		
block (v.)	sadd/yisídd/sadáad	bring! (imp.)	jiib/i/u or yiib/i/u!
blood	damm	bring up; raise (children, animals)	rábba/yirábbi
blouse	bluus(aat)	broken; out of order	xaráab; xarbáan
blue	ázrag/zúrug		
body	jísim/ajsáam	brother	ax/ixwáan

brown (colour)	ásmar/súmur	cause (n.)	sábab/asbáab
brown; roast; fry (meat)	Hámmar/yiHámmir	CD	siidíi(aat)
		cedar tree	'arz
build	bína/yíbni/bína or bíni	ceiling	sagf/sugúuf
		cement	smiit
builder	bannáay/banáani	centre; middle	wasT/awsáaT
building	bináaya*(aat)/ binyáan; mábna/ mabáani	century	qarn/qurúun
		certain; sure	akíid
bunch; bundle (n.)	Súrra*(aat)	certificate; diploma	shaháada*(aat)
burden	nágla*		
bus	baaS(aat)	chair	kúrsi/karáasi
businessman	rájul/rijáal a9máal	by chance	Súdfatan; biS-Súdfa
busy	mashghúul(iin)	change (v. trans.)	gháyyar/yigháyyir
but	láakin	change (v. intrans.)	tagháyyar/ yitgháyyar
butcher	gaSSáab/gaSaaSíib		
butt (v.)	náTaH/yínTaH/ náTaH	change (e.g. clothes, tyres)	báddal/yibáddil
butter	zíbid		
buy	ishtára/yishtíri; shíra/yíshri	change one's mind	gháyyar il-baal or il-afkáar
		chat; tell stories	sóolaf/yisóolif
		cheap	raxíiS
C		cheat; dupe	fáawal/yifáawil (9ála)
cabbage	malfúuf		
Cairo	il-qáahira*	check (v.)	cháyyak/yicháyyik
calculator	áala*(aat) Háasiba	cheese	jíbin
call; drop in (on someone)	marr/yimúrr/murúur (9ala)	chest (anat.)	Sádir
		chest (box)	Sandúug/ Sanaadíig
camera	áalat*(aat) taSwíir		
can; tin	gúuTi/gawáaTi	chicken	dajáaj/dyáay
cancel	álgha/yílghi	chickpea dip with sesame oil	HúmmuS bi TaHíina
car	sayyáara*/sayaayíir		
carburettor	karbráytir	chief; boss	ra'íis/ru'asáa
care; worry	hamm/humúum	chief; main (adj.)	ra'iisi
(be) careful!	(diir) báalik!	child; baby	yáahil/yiháal or jáahil/jiháal; Tífil/aTfáal
to take care of; look after	dáara/yidáari; taHámmal/ yitHámmal (bi) (v. n. Hamáala)		
		Chinese	Síini
carpenter	najjáar/najaajíir	chop up into bits	gáSgaS/yigáSgiS
carrots	jázar	cigarette	jigáara*/jigáayir
carry	Hámal/yáHmil or yiHámil/Hamáal	cinema	síinama(aat)
		circumstances (pl.)	DHurúuf
carton; large box	kartúun/kawaartíin		
catch (v.)	Saad/yiSíid/Sayd	city	madíina*/múdun

class; classroom (school)	**Saff/Sufúuf**	computer	**kambyúutar(aat)**
		concept	**mafhúum/mafaahíim**
clean (adj.)	**naDHíif**	concern;	**hamm/yihímm**
clean (v.)	**náDHDHaf/ yináDHDHif**	be important (to someone)	
cleaning	**tanDHíif**	as far as … is concerned	**bin-nísba íla**
clerk; writer	**káatib/kuttáab**		
clever; smart	**sháaTir(iin)**	condition (state)	**Haal** or **Háala*/ aHwáal**
climate	**Taqs**		
clock	**sáa9a*(aat)**	condition (stipulation)	**sharT/shurúuT**
close (v. trans.)	**bánnad/yibánnid**		
close (v. intrans.)	**tibánnad/yitbánnad**	confirm; verify	**Háqqaq/yiHáqqiq**
close! (imp.)	**bannid/i/u!**	confuse; upset	**ghárbal/yighárbil/ ghirbáal**
club; society	**náadi/nawáadi**		
coffee	**gáhwa**	confuse; make a mess of; mix up	**xárbaT/yixárbiT**
to give someone coffee	**gáhwa (v.)/yigáhwi**		
		to get confused	**tighárbal/yitghárbal**
to have coffee	**tigáhwa/yitgáhwa**	congratulations!	**mabrúuk!**
cold (drink, weather, manner)	**báarid**	conquer	**fítaH/yíftaH/fatH**
		conscience	**DHamíir**
cold (feeling)	**bardáan(iin)**	consent (v.)	**riDa/yírDa/ríDa**
cold (head)	**zukáam**	consider	**i9tábar/yi9tábir**
colleague	**zamíil/zumaláa**	construction	**bináa**
collect	**jíma9/yíjma9/jam9**	contact (v.)	**ittáSal/yittáSil (fi)**
colour; type	**loon/alwáan**	content	**mistáanis(iin)**
come	**ja(a)** or **ya(a)/íiji** or **iyíi/jíyya** or **yáyya**	contract (n.)	**9aqd/9uqúud**
		contractor	**muqáawil(iin)**
come here (imp.)!	**ta9áal/i/u!**	on the contrary	**bil-9aks**
come out; emerge	**Tála9/yíTla9/Tulúu9** or **Taláa9**	control (v.)	**sáyTar/yisáyTir/ sáyTara* (9ála)**
comfort	**ráaHa***	convenient	**mináasib**
commerce	**tijáara***	to be convenient	**náasab/yináasib**
community; group of people	**jimáa9a*(aat)**	conversation; chat	**sáalfa*/sawáalif**
		converse; chat; talk to one another	**tiHáacha/ yitHáacha**
companion	**rifíij/rifgáan**		
company; firm	**shárika*(aat)**	cook (v.)	**Tíbax/yíTbax/Tabx** or **Tabíix**
complain	**ishtáka/yishtáki**		
complaint	**shákwa/shakáawi**	to be cooked; ready (to eat)	**niDHaj/yínDHaj**
complete (adj.)	**káamil**		
complete (v.)	**kámmal/yikámmil**	cooking oil	**díhin**
completely	**kíllish; muul**	cooperate	**ta9áawan/yit9áawan**
(by) compulsion; coercion	**(bil-)gháSub**	copy; imitate	**qállad/yiqállid**
		correct (adj.)	**SaHíiH; 9ádil**

correct (v.)	SáHHaH/yiSáHHiH	dead	máyyit
correctly	kamáa yájib	dear (adj.)	9azíiz
cost; price	sí9ir/as9áar	dear; darling; loved one	Habíib/aHíbbaa
cough hoarsely	HárHash/yiHárHish		
count; enumerate	9add/yi9ídd/9add	death	moot/amwáat
country	biláad/buldáan	debt	dayn/dyúun
course (e.g. of training)	dóora*(aat)	December	disámbar; kaanúun il-áwwal
of course!	Táb9an	decorate	Hálla/yiHálli (v. n. tiHláa*)
courtyard (of a house)	Hoosh/aHwáash	decrease	xáffaD/yixáffiD
cover (v.)	gháTTa/yigháTTi	defence	difáa9
coward	jabáan/jubanáa	defend	dáafa9/yidáafi9 (9an)
cows; cattle	bágar		
crash; collide (car)	dá9am/yíd9am/da9áam	degree	dáraja*(aat)
crazy	majnúun/majaaníin	delay (n.)	ta'xíir
crime	jaríima*/jaráa'im	delegate (n.)	mandúub(iin)
criminal	mújrim(iin)	delicious	ladhíidh
crooked; bent	á9waj, f. 9óoja	demand (v.)	Tálab/yáTlub/Tálab
crop; yield	maHSúul	department	qísim/aqsáam
crush; squash	xáffaS/yixáffiS	deputy	náa'ib/nuwwáab
cup	kuub/akwáab	descend	nízal/yánzil/nuzúul
(small coffee) cup	finjáal/fanaajíil	desert (n.)	SaHráa
to be cured	shifa/yíshfa/shífa	deserve; merit	istáahal/yistáahil; istaHáqq/yistaHíqq
curry; stew	Saalúuna*		
curse (v.)	lá9an/yíl9an/la9n	desire (v.)	raghab/yirghab (fi)
custom; tradition	9áada(aat)	desk	máktab/makáatib
customs (at airport, etc.)	gúmruk/gamáarik	destroy	xárrab/yixárrib
		development (economic, etc.)	taTwíir
cut (v.)	gaSS/yiguSS; gáTa9/yígTa9/gaT9		
		dialect	láhja*(aat)
		dictionary	qaamúus/qawaamíis
		die	maat/yimúut/moot; tiwáffa/yitwáffa

D

danger	xáTar/axTáar	differ	ixtálaf/yixtálif
dangerous	xaTíir	difference; gap	farg
dates	támar	it makes no difference; it's all one	kíllah wáaHid
daughter	bint/banáat		
day	yoom/ayyáam		
one day	yoom min il-ayyáam	difficult	Sá9ab
the day before yesterday	áwwal ams	difficulty	Su9úuba*
		digger	Haffáar(iin)
daytime	naháar	dinar	diináar/danaaníir

dine	ta9áshsha/ yit9áshsha	driving	siyáaqa*
dinner	9ásha	driving licence	láysan; rúxSat siyáaqa*
direct oneself; go	ittájah/yittájih	drum (n.)	Tábil/Tubúul
directly	síida; rá'san	drum (v.)	Tábbal/yiTábbil
dirham	dirhám/daráahim	dry (adj.)	yáabis
dirty	wásix	to become dry	níshaf/yánshif/ nasháaf
dish (cooked)	Tábxa*(aat)		
dishes; tableware	maa9úun/ mawaa9íin	to dry out	yíbas/yíybas
dishonest	cháadhib	during	athnáa
disorder; chaos	záHma*	duty	waDHíifa*/ waDHáayif
distance	bu9d		
divorced	mTállag	**E**	
do	sáwwa/yisáwwi/ tiswáa	early	mubákkir; min waqt
do! (imp.)	saww/i/u!	earth; floor	arD (f.)
do without	istághna/yistághni (9an)	ease	suhúula*
		east	sharg
doctor	dáxtar/daxáatir; Tabíib/aTibbáa	eastern	shárgi
		easy	sahil
dog	chalb/chiláab	eat	'ákal/yáakil/ákil
dollar	dooláar(aat)	economic(al)	iqtiSáadi
door	baab/abwáab or biibáan	economy	iqtiSáad
		with effect from	i9tibáaran min
dot	núqTa*/núqaT	egg(s)	bayD
doubt	shakk/shkúuk	eggplant	baylinjáan
down; downstairs	taHt	Egypt	míSir
dowry	máhar	Egyptian	míSri (yyiin)
dozen	dárzan/darázin	eight	thamáan(ya)
draw (v.)	rísam/yársim/rásim	eighteen	thamantá9shar
drawer	durj/adráaj	eighth	tháamin
drawing	rásim/rusúum	electricity	káhrab
dress (n.)	thoob/thiyáab	elementary; primary (school)	ibtidáa'i
dress (woman's)	nafnúuf/nafaaníif		
dress (oneself)	líbas/yílbas/libs	eleven	iHdá9shar
dress (someone)	lábbas/yilábbis	embassy	sifáara
to get dressed up	tizábbar/yitzábbar	emirate	imáara*(aat)
drink; smoke	shárab/yíshrab/shirb	employee	muwáDHDHaf(iin)
drive (a car)	saag/yisúug/syáaga	empty	xáali
drive (a car); progress (a project)	máshsha/yimáshshi	encourage	shájja9/yishájji9
		end (n.)	niháaya*
driver	dráywil(iyya); sáayig/suwwáag	end parts; later parts (of a month, year)	awáaxir

to come to an end	intáha/yintíhi	external; exterior (adj.)	xáariji
to get engaged to someone	xáTab/yíxTub/ xúTba or xuTúuba	extremely	lin-niháaya
engine	makíina*/makáayin	eye	9ayn (f.)/9uyúun

F

engineer	muhándis(iin)	face (n.)	wajh/wujúuh
engineering	hándisa*	factory	máSna9/maSáani9
English; Englishman	inglíizi(yyiin)	fair; just	9áadil
		fall (v.)	TaaH/yiTíiH/TayH
enjoy (oneself)	istáanas/yistáanis	fall; swoon (n.)	TáyHa*(aat)
enjoyment; companionship	anáasa	family (dependants)	9iyáal
enormous	Dáxim	family; kin	ahl or hal
enough	káafi	famous	mashhúur
enter	dashsh/yidíshsh/ dáshsha; dáxal/ yídxul or yídxal/ duxúul	fan	pánka(aat)
		far (from)	ba9íid (9an)
		to bid farewell; say goodbye	wádda9/yiwáddi9
entrance	dáxla*(aat)		
envelope	búghsha*(aat)	farm	mazrá9a/mazáari9
episode	Hálqa*/Halaqáat	farmer; farmworker	záari9/zurráa9
to be equal to	síwa/yíswa		
establishment	mu'ássasa*(aat)	farming	ziráa9a*
Europe	urúbba	fashion; style	Tiráaz
even	Hátta	fashions (clothes)	zayy/azyáa
evening	masáa; mughárb	fast (v.)	Sáam/yiSúum/Soom
in the evening	masáa'an	fast; speedy	saríi9/siráa9
evil	shayn	fat; plump	matíin/amtáan; samíin/simáan
exactly	biDH-DHabT		
examination; test	imtiHáan(aat)	father	ab/ubuháat
example	máthal/amtháal	fear (v.)	xaaf/yixáaf/xoof
for example	míthil; máthalan	February	fabráayir; shubáaT
excellent	tamáam	fee	íjra
except	ílla	feed (v.)	'ákkal/yi'ákkil
excuse me!; sorry! (imp.)	ismáH/i/u lii!	feelings; sensitivity	iHsáas
expect; anticipate	tiwáqqa9/ yitwáqqa9	festival; holiday	9iid/a9yáad
		few; small in number	galíil(iin)
at (someone's) expense	9ala Hsáab + pron.		
expensive	gháali	to be few or small in number	qall/yiqáll/qílla or qaláala
expert	xabíir/xubaráa		
export(ing) (n.)	taSdíir	fifteen	xamstá9shar
extent	gadd	fifth (adj.)	xáamis

fifty	**xamsíin**	forget	**nísa/yínsa/nisyáan**
the (19)50s	**il-xamsiináat**	form; shape; type	**shákil/ashkáal**
fight; make war on	**Háarab/yiHáarib**	former	**qadíim**
fight one another	**taHáarab/yitHáarab**	fort	**gál9a*(aat)**
file; dossier	**miláffa*(aat)**	forty	**arba9íin**
fill	**tíras/yátris/tars**	the (19)40s	**il-arba9iináat**
film	**fílim/afláam**	to go forward; proceed	**tiqáddam/ yitqáddam**
find (v.)	**líga/yílga**	four	**árba9(a)**
finish; complete	**xállaS/yixálliS**	fourteen	**arba9tá9shar**
finished; done; over	**xaláaS!**	fourth (adj.)	**ráabi9**
fire (n.)	**Daww**	France	**faránsa**
fire (v.); sack (someone)	**fánnash/yifánnish**	frankly	**bi SaráaHa***
first; first of all	**áwwal, f. úula**	freedom	**Hurríyya***
fish (n.)	**sámak/asmáak** or **símich/asmáach**	free of charge	**baláash**
		free time; spare time	**faráagh**
fish (v.) (with a line)	**Hádag/yiHádig/ Hadáag**	to be free (of); escape (from)	**taxállaS/yitxállaS (min)**
fisherman	**sammáach/ samaamíich**	fresh	**Táazij**
		Friday	**il-jum9a***
five	**xams(a)**	friend	**rifíij/rifgáan; Sadíiq/aSdiqáa** or **Sadíig/Sidgáan**
fixed; stable	**tháabit**		
to be fixed, installed	**tirákkab/yitrákkab**		
flavour	**dhoog**	frighten	**xáwwaf/yixáwwif**
flee	**farr/yifírr/faráara**	from; away from	**min; 9an**
floor	**arDíyya***	in front of	**giddáam**
floor (of a building)	**Táabiq/Tawáabiq**	fruit (but not dates)	**máywa***
flour	**TiHíin**	full	**matrúus**
flower	**zahra*/zuhúur**	furnished	**mafrúush**
follow	**táaba9/yitáabi9**	furniture	**aatháath**
food	**ákil(aat); Ta9áam**		
on foot	**máshi**	**G**	
football	**kúurat il-qádam**	gait; way of walking	**máshya***
for	**Hagg; li**		
to force, oblige	**iDTárr/yiDTárr**	gamble	**qáamar/yiqáamir**
foreign; foreigner	**'ájnabi**	game	**lí9ba*(aat)**
foreman	**tindáyl**	gazelle	**ghazáal**
forenoon; late morning	**DíHa**	general (adj.)	**9aam**
		generator (electric)	**muwállid**
		generous; kind	**karíim/kiráam**

geometry	handísa*	greengrocer	baggáal/bagaagíil
get; obtain	HáSSal/yiHáSSil	grow up; grow old	kúbar/yíkbar/kubr
get down from, out of (e.g. bus, car)	Háwwal/ yiHáwwil	guide (give guidance)	háda/yiháda/ hidáaya
get on, in (e.g. car, bus, boat)	ríkab/yárkub/ rukúub	(Arabian) Gulf	il-xalíij
get to one's feet	gaam/yigúum/goom	(hand) gun	túfga*/tífag
girl	bint/banáat		
give	9áTa/yá9Ti/9áTa	**H**	
give (imp.)!	9aT/i/u!!	hair	shá9ar
give back	radd/yirídd/radáad or rdúud	half	nuSS
		hammer	míTraga*/maTáarig
glass (drinking)	glaas(aat)	hand	yad or iid/ayáadi
glass (sheet of)	jaam	handsome	Hálu, f. Hálwa
go; leave	raaH/yirúuH/rooHa or rawáaH	happen; turn out; come to pass	Saar/yiSíir/Sayr
go! (imp.)	ruuH/i/u!	happy	farHáan(iin); mistáanis(iin)
go away (vulg.)	inchább/yinchább	to be happy, joyful	fáraH/yífraH/fáraH
go out; exit	xáraj/yáxruj/xurúuj; Tála9/yíTla9/Tulúu9	have	9ind + pron.
in one go; all at once	nóoba wáHda	he	húwwa or húwa
God	alláah	head	raas/ruus
by God!	wállah/walláahi	health	SíHHa*
God willing	insháallah	hear	síma9/yísma9/ samáa9
going round	dáayir	heart	galb/gulúub
good	zayn/zayníin; xoosh	heat	Harr or Haráara*
goodness; kindness	Tiib	heavy	thagíil/thigáal
good thing; good deed	xayr	hello!	yaa hála!
		hello? (telephone)	alló?
government	Hukúuma*(aat)	help (v.)	sáa9ad/yisáa9id
governmental	Hukúumi	help each other	tisáa9ad/yitsáa9ad
grain (of rice, etc.)	Hábba*	hem	Háashya*(aat)
		henna (v.)	Hánna/yiHánni/ Hanna*
grapes	9ínab	here	íhni
grandfather	jadd or yadd	here's …!	ka + indep. pron.
grandmother	jádda* or yádda*	hey!	yaa
grasp; hold on to	jáwwad/yijáwwid	hit (v.)	dagg/yidígg/dagg; Dárab/yíDrub/Darb; Tagg/yiTígg/Tagg
gratuity	baxshíish		
grave; tomb	gabr/gubúur		
great; grand	9aDHíim	to get hold of, possession of	qábad/yíqbaD/qabD
green	axDar/xúDur		

holiday	**9úTla*/9úTal**	immediately;	**Háalan**
honour (v.)	**kárram/yikárrim**	on the spot	
hook (n.)	**chilláab/chilaalíib**	in	**bi; fi**
hopefully …	**9ása + noun/pron.**	increase (v.)	**zaad/yizíid/zood** or
horrible	**karíih**		**ziyáada**
hors d'oeuvres	**mázza***	indeed; in fact	**bil-fi9l**
(Lebanese-style)		Indian	**híndi/hunúud**
horses	**xayl** (pl.)	indicate; show	**dall/yidíll/daláal**
hospital	**mustáshfa(yaat)**	industrial	**Sináa9i**
hot	**Haarr**	industry	**Sináa9a**
hotel	**fúnduq/fanáadiq**	inform	**xáabar/yixáabir**
hour	**sáa9a*(aat)**	(someone about	
house	**bayt/buyúut**	something)	
how?	**chayf/kayf; shloon**	inhabitant	**sáakin/sukkáan**
however; in	**cháyfmaa**	inside	**dáaxil**
whatever way		insist	**aSárr/yiSírr**
however much	**shgáddmaa;**	inspect	**fáttash/yifáttish;**
	shkíthirmaa		**kíshaf/yákshif/**
how much,	**cham/kam**		**kasháaf (9ála)**
many?		install	**rákkab/yirákkib**
for how much?	**bi cham**	to be installed	**tirákkab/yitrákkab**
humid	**ráTib**	instead of	**bádalan min**
hundred	**míya*(aat)**	institute; college	**má9had/ma9áahid**
hunger	**yuu9** or **juu9**	instruct	**9állam/yi9állim**
hungry	**yuu9áan/yuwáa9a** or	intend	**qáSad/yáqSud/qaSd**
	juu9áan/juwáa9a	intensity	**shídda***
hunt	**Saad/yiSíid/Sayd**	interest; benefit;	**máSlaHa*/maSáaliH**
hurry	**istá9jal/yistá9jil**	business	
hurt; cause	**9áwwar/yi9áwwir**	to be interested	**ihtámm/yihtámm**
pain to		(in)	**(bi)**
to be hurt, injured	**tijárraH/yitjárraH**	internal; interior	**dáaxili**
husband	**zooj/azwáaj; ráyil**	international	**dáwli** or **dúwali**
	(or **rájil**)/**rijáal**	interview	**muqáabla*(aat)**
		introduce	**9árraf/yi9árrif**
I		(someone to	
		someone)	
I; me	**ána**	invitation	**dá9wa*(aat)**
idea; thought	**fíkra*/afkáar**	invite	**9ázam/yi9ázim/**
if	**Ídha; law** or **lo**		**9ázam** or **9azáam**
ill	**maríiD/máraDa**	irritate	**Dáyyaj/yiDáyyij**
illness	**máraD/amráaD**	Islam	**isláam**
to be ill; fall ill	**máraD/yímraD/**	Islamic	**isláami**
	máraD	island	**jazíira*/jízir**
imitate	**qállad/yiqállid**		

J

jacket	jakáyt(aat)
January	yanáayir; kaanúun ith-tháani
job	shúghul/ashgháal; 9ámal/a9máal
job; piece of work	shúghla*/shághla*
job; 'earner'; way of earning money	mukádda*
join; be joined to	inDámm/yinDámm (íla)
joke (v.)	nákkat/yinákkit
journalist	SáHafi(yyiin)
journey	safaríyya*(aat)
to pass judgement; sentence	Hákam/yáHkum/ Hukm (9ála)
juice (fruit)	9aSíir
July	yúulyo; tammúuz
jump; hop (v.)	naTT/yinúTT
jump up and down	tirámmaz/ yitrámmaz
June	yúunyo; Haziiráan
just; fair	9áadil
just as (conj.)	míthilmaa; shíkilmaa
to have just done something	taw + pron. + verb

K

kebab (doner)	shuwárma
keep doing something	tamm/yitimm + imp. verb
key	miftáaH/mafaatíiH
kill	gítal/yágtil/gátl
kilogram	káylo (waat)
kin	ahl (or hal)
kingdom	mámlaka
kitchen	máTbax/maTáabix
knife	sichchíin/ sachaachíin
knock; hit (v.)	dagg/yidígg/dagg

know (someone or something)	9áraf/yi9árf/ má9rifa
know (something to be the case)	dára/yídri (bi)/ diráaya; 9álam/ yá9lam/9ilm
knowledge; science	9ilm
known (fact)	ma9lúum
Kuwaiti	kuwáyti(yyiin)

L

lack; absence	9ádam
lack; scarcity	gílla*
lacking	náagiS
(step)ladder	dáray(aat)
language	lúgha(aat); lisáan/ alsína*
last; latest	áaxir
late	mit'áxxir(iin)
late (dead)	marHúum
laugh (v.)	DáHak/yíD-Hak/ DaHk
layabout; good-for-nothing	lóofar (iyya)
lazy	kasláan(iin)
leaf	wáraga*/awráag
learn	ti9állam/yit9állam
leather	jild
leave (abandon)	hadd/yihídd/hadd
leave (someone; a place)	tárak/yátruk/tark
Lebanon	lubnáan
Lebanese	lubnáani
lecture	muHáaDra*
to give a lecture	álqa/yílqi muHáaDra*
left (opp. of right)	yasáar; shimáal
left (side)	shimáali
leg	riil/ryúul or rijl/rjúul
lend	sállaf/yisállif
length	Tuul/aTwáal
lesson	dars/druus
let; allow	xálla/yixálli

letter	maktúub/makaatíib; risáala*/rasáa'il	loud (voice, etc.)	9áali
letter (of the alphabet)	Harf/Hrúuf	low	náazil
		lower (prices, etc.)	xáffaD/yixáffiD
lettuce	xast	lucky	maHDHúuDH(iin)
level	mustáwa(yaat)	lunch	gháda
lie (v.)	chídhab/yáchdhib/ chidhb	to have lunch	tighádda/yitghádda
lie down	rígad/yárgid/irgáad		
life	Hayáa*	**M**	
to give a lift to someone	wáSSal/yiwáSSil	machine	makíina*/makáayin
		mad; crazy	majnúun/majaaníin
light (in weight)	xafíif/xifáaf	magazine	mujálla*(aat)
light (n.)	Daww; nuur	main; principal (adj.)	ra'iisi
light (street, car, etc.)	layt(aat)	make	sáwwa/yisáwwi/ tiswáa*
like; love	Habb/yiHíbb/Hubb	make! (imp.)	saww/i/u!
like that	chidháak	make/allow (someone) to hear	sámma9/yisámmi9
like this	chidhíi		
as ... like(s); as ... want(s)	9ála kayf + suffix pron.	make/allow (someone) to know	dárra/yidárri
line; stripe; telephone line	xaTT/xuTúuT	make (someone do something)	xálla/yixálli
link (in a chain)	Hálqa*/Halaqáat	man	rayyáal/rayaayíil or rajjáal/rajaajíil
listen	síma9/yísma9/ samáa9	man; husband	ráyil (or rájil)/rijáal
(a) little	shwáyya*	old man	shayb/shiyáab
little by little	shway shway	manager	mudíir(iin)
live	9aash/yi9íish/9aysh	Manama	il-manáama
live (in a place)	síkan/yáskin/sákan	manners	ádab/aadáab
living; domiciled	sáakin/sukkáan	manufacture; make	Sána9/yíSna9/San9
long	Tawíil/Tiwáal	many; numerous	waajid or waayid; kathíir(iin)
to be long, tall	Taal/yiTúul/Tuul		
look (at)	shaaf/yishúuf/shoof or shóofa	marbles (game)	tíila
		March (month)	maars; aadháar
look! (imp.)	shuuf/i/u!	market	suug/aswáag
look after	dáara/yidáari; taHámmal/ yitHámmal (bi) (v. n. Hamáala)	marketing	taswíiq
		marriage	zawáaj
		married	mitzáwwij
look for	dáwwar/yidáwwir	to get married	tizáwwaj/yitzáwwaj
lose	fáqad/yáfqid/faqd	match; contest	mubáara*(aat)
to get lost; be missing	Daa9/yiDíi9/Dáy9a	matches	chibríit
a lot	waajid or waayid	material	máadda*/mawáadd

mathematics	riyaaDiyáat	mistake	ghálaT/aghláaT; xáTa'/axTáa'
it doesn't matter; OK; never mind	maa 9aláyh	mistaken	ghalTáan(iin)
May (month)	máayo; ayyáar	to get mixed up, confused	tixárbaT/yitxárbaT
maybe	múmkin; yúmkin		
meal	wájba*(aat)	mobile phone	jawwáal
meat	láHam	modern	Hadíith
mechanic	mikáaniki (yyin)	moment; occasion	Házza*
medicine	dáwa/adwíya	at the moment	Haalíyyan
meet; be opposite to, across from	gáabal/yigáabil	(just a) moment	láHDHa*(aat)
		Monday	il-ithnáyn
meet one another	tigáabal/yitgáabal	money	bayzáat; fluus; maal
meet (by chance)	láaga/yiláagi	monkey	qird/qurúud
meeting	ijtimáa9	month	sháhar/áshur
meeting (interview)	muqáabla*(aat)	moon	gúmar
		morals	axláaq (pl.)
memory (of something); commemoration	dhíkra	more	bá9ad
		morning	SabáaH
		early morning	SubH
mention	dhíkar/yádhkir/ dhikr	good morning!	SabáaH il-xayr
		good morning! (reply)	SabáaH in-nuur
merchant	táajir/tujjáar		
(the) mere ...	mujárrad + noun/verb	in the morning	SabáaHan
		morning snack	gadúu9
message	xábar/axbáar	mosque	másyid/masáayid
mess up	xárbaT/yixárbiT	main (Friday) mosque	jáami9
microphone	mikrufúun(aat)		
middle	wasT/awsáaT	mother	umm/ummaháat
to be in the middle of, in the process of	gáa9id (+ verb)	mouth	buuz
		MP	náa'ib/nuwwáab
		Mr	sáyyid/sáada*
mile	mayl/amyáal	Mrs	sáyyida(aat)
milk	Halíib	museum	mátHaf/matáaHif
million	milyóon/malaayíin	must; have to	láazim + verb
minaret	má'dhana*/ ma'áadhin	as it must/ should be	kamáa yájib
		mutton	xarúuf/xirfáan
mind	baal		
mind out!	báalik!	**N**	
minister	wazíir/wuzaráa		
ministry	wizáara*(aat)	nail	mismáar/masaamíir
minute (of time)	dagíiga*/dagáayig	name (n.)	ísim/asáami
miserable; wretched (person)	miskíin/masaakíin	name (v.)	sámma/yisámmi
mission	irsaalíyya*		

nation; homeland	**wáTan**	no one	**máHHad**
national	**wáTani**	north	**shimáal**
nationality	**jinsíyya*(aat)**	northern	**shimáali**
nation-state	**dáwla/dúwal**	nose	**xáshim**
naturally	**Táb9an**	not (with verbs)	**maa**
near (to)	**gáriib (min)**	not (with adj.,	**muu/mub/múhub**
necessary	**láazim**	n., pron., adv.)	
to be necessary	**wájab/yájib/wujúub**	notebook	**dáftar/dafáatir**
(for), incumbent	**(9ála)**	November	**nufámbar; tishríin**
(on)			**ith-tháani**
necktie	**kraafáat(aat)**	now	**il-Hiin**
need (n.)	**Háaja*(aat)**	up till now	**lil-Hiin**
need (v.)	**iHtáaj/yiHtáaj (íla)**	number; digit	**ráqam/arqáam**
neighbour	**jaar/jiiráan**	number (total)	**9ádad**
neighbourhood	**faríij/furgáan**	nurse	**mumárriDa*(aat)**
never; not at all	**ábadan**		
I've never …	**9úmri + maa +**	**O**	
in my life	past tense verb		
new	**jadíid/jíddad**	to be obligatory	**wájab/yájib/wujúub**
news (piece of)	**nába'/anbáa;**	(for)	**(9ála)**
	xábar/axbáar	(much) obliged;	**aHsant/i/u**
newspaper	**jaríida/jaráayid**	thank you (lit. you	
next; after that	**táali**	have done well)	
(adv.)		occasion; time	**márra*(aat)**
next; coming	**jaay** or **yaay;**	occasionally	**aHyáanan**
(adj.)	**qáadim**	on the occasion	**bi munaasábat**
next to	**yanb** or **yamm; taHt**	of …	**+ noun**
nibble (v.)	**gámgam/yigámgim**	occupy; to busy	**shághal/yíshghal/**
nice	**xoosh**		**shughl**
night	**layla/layáali**	October	**tishríin il-áwwal;**
night-time	**layl**		**uktúubar**
(as opposed to		of	**min**
'daytime')		offer; proposal	**9arD/9urúuD**
at night-time	**láylan**	office	**máktab/makáatib**
nine	**tísa9 (tís9a)**	officer	**DáabiT/DubbáaT**
nineteen	**tisa9tá9shar**	official (n.)	**muwáDHDHaf(iin)**
ninety	**tis9íin**	official (adj.)	**rásmi**
ninth (adj.)	**táasi9**	oil (fuel or edible)	**zayt**
no	**la**	oil (petroleum)	**nifT**
noise; clamour	**Dájja***	OK!	**nzayn**
nonsense; rubbish	**xárbuTa*/xaraabíiT**	old (of a person)	**kabíir/kibáar; 9ood**
noon	**DHúhur**	old; ancient	**qadíim;**
noon-day heat	**gayúula***	(of things); former	**9atíij/9itáag**
at noontime	**DHúhran**	old man	**shayb** or **sháayib/**
			shiyáab

old times	(il-)áwwal	palace	gáSir/guSúur
old woman	9ajúuz/9ajáayiz	Palestinian	filasTíini
on; on top of	foog; 9ála	palm trees	náxal
one	wáaHid(a)	paper (piece of)	wáraga*/awráag
onions	báSal	paragraph	fáqara*(aat)
only	bas	parcel	Tard/Truud
from ... onwards	min ... ráayiH	parents	waalidáyn
open (v. trans.)	báTTal/yibáTTil;	park; garden;	Hadíiqa/Hadáayiq
	fítaH/yíftaH/fatH	kindergarten	
open (v. intrans.)	tibáTTal/yitbáTTal	park (car)	wággaf/yiwággif
open! (imp.)	báTTil/i/u!	party; celebration	Háfla*(aat)
opener	miftáaH/mafaatíiH	tea party	Háflat chaay
opening	dáxla	pass (v.)	faat/yifúut/foot
operate; turn on	shághghal/	pass away; die	tiwáffa/yitwáffa
(machine, etc.)	yishághghil	passenger; rider	ráakib/rukkáab
opinion; view	rá'y/aráa	past (time)	máaDi
opposite (prep.)	mgáabil	pay (v.)	dífa9/yídfa9/daf9
or	wálla or wílla; lo	peace	saláam
orange(s)	burtugáal	to make peace;	tiSáalaH/
order (v.)	Tálab/yáTlub/Tálab	call a truce	yitSáalaH
(food, etc.)		pearl	lú'lu'/la'áali
order someone	'ámar/yá'mur/'amr	pearl-diver	ghawáaS/
to do something	(bi)		ghawaawííS
out of order	xarbáan	pearl-diving	ghooS
ordinary	9áadi	pen	gálam/agláam or
origin; principle	áSil/uSúul		gláama
other than	ghayr	people	naas; awáadim
outer (adj.)	barráani	perfect (adj.)	káamil
outside	bárra; xáarij	perfect!	tamáam!
over (above)	foog	perhaps	yúmkin
over here	minníi	period; point of	Hiin/aHyáan;
over there	minnáak	time	múdda*; záman
overtime	awirtáym	permit (v.)	símaH/yísmaH/
owner	SáaHib/aSHáab		samáaH (li)
		permission;	rúxSa
P		licence	
packet	gúuTi/gawáaTi	Persian	fáarsi
page	SaHíifa*/SúHuf	person	náfar/anfáar;
(of a book, etc.)			shaxS/ashxáaS
pain	wúja9/awjáa9	personal	sháxSi
paint; dye (v.)	Síbagh/yíSbagh/	personality	shaxSíyya*(aat)
	Sabáagh	petroleum; oil	nifT
paint (a picture)	rísam/yársim/rásim	pharmacy	Saydalíyya*(aat)
painting; picture	rásim/rusúum		

phase (of a plan, etc.)	márHala*/maráaHil	poor	faqíir/fagáara
photograph	Súura/Súwar	position (job)	waDHíifa*/ waDHáayif
pick-up truck	wanáyt(aat)	possible	múmkin
picture; image	Súura/Súwar	post; mail	baríid
piece	gúT9a*	postage stamp	Táabi9/Tawáabi9
pig; hog	xanzíir/xanaazíir	post office	máktab il-baríid
pilgrimage month in the Islamic calendar	dhu l-Híjja	potato	putáyta; áalu
		pound sterling	jínay stárlin
to go on the pilgrimage	Hajj/yiHíjj/Hajj	pour	Sabb/yiSúbb
		power (political)	Húkum
pill	Habb/Hbúub	practise (a skill)	máaras/yimáaris
pipe	bayb(aat)	Praise be to God	il-Hámdu lilláah
pitch; (tennis) court	mál9ab/maláa9ib	prawns	rubyáan
		prefer	fáDDal/yifáDDil
place; spot	mukáan(aat)	prepare; make ready	HáDDar/yiHáDDir
plan; project (n.)	mashrúu9/ mashaaríi9		
		present; current	Háali
plan (v.)	xáTTaT/yixáTTiT	present; existent; there; alive	mawjúud(iin)
plant (v.)	zára9/yízra9/zar9 or ziráa9a		
		present; gift	hádiya/hadáaya
plastic	blaastíik	preserve	HífaDH/yíHfaDH/ HafáaDH
plate	SáHan(a*)/SuHúun		
play (v.)	lá9ab/yíl9ab/li9ib	prettiness	Haláawa*
playing field	mál9ab/maláa9ib	pretty	Hálu, f. Hálwa
play; drama	masraHíyya*(aat); tamthiilíyya*(aat)	prevent	mína9/yímna9/man9
		price	sí9ir/as9áar
please (someone)	9ájab/yá9jib or yi9ájib	prison	síjin/sujúun
		problem	múshkila*/ masháakil
please (when asking someone to do something)	min fáDlik/ch/kum	product	mantúuj(aat)
		progress (a project)	máshsha/ yimáshshi
please …! (imp.) (when offering something or inviting someone to do something)	tafáDDal/i/u!	project (n.)	mashrúu9/ mashaaríi9
		to be proper, right, suitable	SílaH/yíSlaH/ SaláaH
(spark) plug	blaag(aat)	property	maal/amwáal
plumber	baybfíita	profit; benefit (from)	istánfa9/yistánfi9 (min)
point (at issue)	núqTa*/núqaT		
from the point of view of …	min jíhat + noun	programme	barnáamaj/baráamij
police	shúrTa*	prohibited	mamnúu9
policeman	poolíis(iyya); shúrTi(yyiin)	prohibited (by Islam)	Haráam

proverb	máthal/amtháal	refrigerator	thalláaja*(aat)
public (adj.)	9aam	refuse; reject (v.)	ráfaD/yárfuD/rafD
publish	níshar/yánshir/nashr	register; log (n.)	síjill(aat)
puncture	bánchar(aat)	register (v.)	sájjal/yisájjil
punish	9áaqab/yi9áaqib	in relation to …	bin-nísba íla
push	dazz/yidízz/dázza	relieve; make	ráyyaH/yiráyyiH
put (down,	HaTT/yiHúTT/	comfortable	
on, in)	HaTáaT	relinquish control	tináazal/yitnáazal
put (in, on)	wádda/yiwáddi	of; step down	(9an)
Pyramids	il-ahráam	from	
		rely on; put one's	ittákal/yittákil
Q		trust in (esp. God)	(9ála)
quarter	rub9	remain	búga/yíbga;
quarter;	firíij/firgáan		DHall/yiDHíll
neighbourhood		remainder; rest	báagi
(of a city)		remember	dhíkar/yádhkir/dhikr;
question	su'áal/as'ila		tidhákkar/yitdhákkar
quiet; soft	háadi'	remind	dhákkar/yidhákkir
(voice, etc.)		remove	shaal/yishíil/shayl or
quiet; silent	sáakit		shayaláan
to be/keep quiet	síkat/yáskit/skúut	rent; hire (v.)	istáajar/yistáajir
quickly	zitáat	rented; leased	bil-'ajáar
Qur'an	il-qur'áan	repair (n.)	taSlíiH
		repair (v.)	SállaH/yiSálliH
R		repeat; do again	radd + verb
race (sport)	sibáaq	report (written)	taqríir/taqaaríir
radio	ráydo(waat)	reprehensible (act)	múnkar(aat)
radish(es)	ruwáyd		
rain	máTar/amTáar	represent	máththal/yimáththil
raise (children,	rábba/yirábbi	responsible	mas'úul
animals)		rest; relief	ráaHa*
raise (voice, etc.)	9álla/yi9álli	restaurant	máT9am/maTáa9im
read	gára/yígra/giráaya	result	natíija/natáa'ij
ready	báariz	return; come/go	radd/yirídd/radáad
to be ready	báraz/yábriz	back	or rdúud; ríja9/
reason	sábab/asbáab		yírja9/rujúu9
reasonable	ma9gúul	reward (of God)	jáaza/yijáazi
receipt	raSíid	rice	9aysh
receive	tìlágga/yitlágga	rich	gháni/aghniyáa
recently	axíiran; min garíib	to make	ághna/yíghni
record (v.)	sájjal/yisájjil	(someone) rich	
red	áHmar/Húmur	to get rid (of)	taxállaS/yitxállaS
referee	Hákam		(min)
		ride	ríkab/yárkub/rukúub

right; entitlement	**Hagg/Hugúug**	salt	**milH**
right; right hand	**yamíin**	the same …	**nafs** + noun/pron.
ring (for the finger)	**xáatam/xawáatim**	it's all the same; it makes no difference	**kíllah wáaHid**
rip	**shagg/yishígg/ shagáag**	sandwich	**sandawíich(aat)**
ripen; be ready	**niDHaj/yínDHaj**	Saturday	**is-sabt**
rise; get up	**gaam/yigúum/goom**	Saudi Arabian	**sa9úudi(yyiin)**
road	**Taríig/Túrug**	say	**gaal/yigúul/gool**
roast; barbecued (meat)	**máshwi**	school	**madrása*/madáaris**
role; turn	**door/adwáar**	science	**9ílm/9ulúum**
roof	**sagf/sugúuf**	scientific	**9ílmi**
roof (flat); surface	**sáTaH/suTúuH**	scream (v.)	**SaaH/yiSíiH/SayH**
room (in a house)	**Híjra*/Híjar**	sea	**báHar/biHáar**
room; scope	**majáal**	seashore	**siif**
room (space)	**mukáan(aat)**	second (adj.)	**tháani**
roomy; spacious	**wáasi9**	secondary (school, etc.)	**tháanawi**
to go round something; circumambulate	**Taaf/yiTúuf/Tawáaf**	secretary	**sikirtíir(iyya)**
		security	**amáan**
roundabout (traffic)	**dawwáar(aat)**	seductive	**fattáan**
		see	**shaaf/yishúuf/shoof** or **shóofa**
row (n.)	**Saff/Sufúuf**	see you soon!	**ila l-liqáa!**
rug	**zuulíyya*/zawáali**	by … self	**bruuH** + pron.
ruin (n.)	**xaráab**	selfish	**anáani**
ruin; destroy	**xárrab/yixárrib**	sell	**baa9/yibíi9/bay9**
to be ruined, spoilt	**9ídam/yí9dam**	send	**dazz/yidízz/dázza**
ruler (of a country)	**Háakim/Hukkáam**	send (esp. a messenger)	**Tárrash/yiTárrish**
run	**ríkaD/yárkuD/rakíiD**	to be sent (esp. a messenger)	**tiTárrash/yiTTárrash**
run (flow)	**jára/yájri/jári**	sentence; condemn	**gáDa 9ála**
run (manage)	**adáar/yidíir**	September	**aylúul; sibtámbar**
run out	**nífad/yínfad**	serial (TV)	**musálsal**
in the long run	**9ála máda z-zamáan**	servant; cleaner; messenger	**farráash/faraaríish; xáadim/xuddáam**
S		service	**xídma*(aat)**
sack	**xáysha*/xiyáash; yuuníyya*/yawáani**	at your service	**HáaDir**
		seven	**sab9(a)**
safe; secure	**áamin**	seventeen	**saba9tá9shar**
safety	**saláama***	seventh (adj.)	**sáabi9**
salary	**ma9áash(aat); ráatib/rawáatib**	seventy	**sab9íin**

shake	xaDD/yixúDD/xaDD	sitting room (Arab style)	máylis/mayáalis
shame; disgrace	9ayb/9uyúub	situation; position	máwqif/mawáaqif
shameless; depraved	xalláa9	six	sitt(a)
shape	shákil/ashkáal	sixteen	sittá9shar
sharp	Haadd	sixth (adj.)	sáadis
she	híyya or híya	sixty	sittíin
sheep	xarúuf/xirfáan	size	kúbur
sheikh; old man	shayx/shuyúux	skin	jild
shift (at work)	zaam(aat)	skirt	tannúura*(aat)
ship	safíina*/súfun	sky	síma
shirt (man's long Arab-style)	thoob/thyaab (BAH, QAT); dishdáasha/ dashaadíish (KWT, OM); kandúura/ kanaadíir (UAE)	slaughter (an animal)	DhíbaH/yídhbaH/ dhibáaH
		sleep (v.)	naam/yináam/noom; rígad/yárgid/irgáad
shirt (Western-style)	qamíiS/qumSáan	slowly	shway shway
shoes (pair of)	júuti/jawáati	slowness	búTu'
shop (small)	dukkáan/dakaakíin	small; young	Saghíir/Sigháar
shopping	taswíiq	smash	kássar/yikássir
shore	sáaHil/sawáaHil; siif	smoke (v.)	dáxxan/yidáxxin; shárab/yíshrab/ shirb
shorts	haaf		
shoulder	chatf/chtúuf	so; then …	fa; ídhan
shout (v.)	SaaH/yiSíiH/SayH	Isn't that so?	muu chidhíi?
show (v.)	ráwwa/yiráwwi	so-and-so	flaan(a)
shut (v.)	sakk/yisíkk	soap	Saabúun
sick	maríiD/máraDa	social	ijtimáa9i
sieve (v.)	sháxal/yíshxal	society (human)	ijtimáa9; mujtáma9
sight (sense)	náDHar	society (club)	náadi/nawáadi
sign (v.)	wáqqa9/yiwáqqi9	sole	waHíid
silent	Sáamit	solve	Hall/yiHíll/Hall
sing	ghánna/yighánni/ ghína	some (of)	ba9D
		someone	áHad
single; sole	waHíid	someone; a human being	áadmi/awáadim
sink	mághsala*/ magháasil		
		son	wild
sister	íxit/xawáat	soon	bá9ad shway
sit; stay	gá9ad/yíg9ad/ gu9úud; jálas/yájlis/ julúus	as soon as	yóommaa
		south	jinúub
		sort; type; kind	noo9/anwáa9
sitting (adj.)	gáa9id	sorry (adj.)	mit' ássif(iin)
sitting (n.); session	jálsa*	Sorry! Pardon me!	il-9áfu or 9áfwan

sound; proper; thorough	**SáaliH**	store cupboard; storage place	**máxzan/maxáazin**
south	**yamíin; jinúub**	storey; floor	**Táabiq/Tawáabiq**
southern	**jinúubi**	story; yarn	**Hicháaya*;**
spacious	**wáasi9**		**qíSSa*/qíSaS**
spare part	**gúT9a*/gúTa9 ghiyáar**	straight; straightaway	**síida**
speak	**taHáchcha/ yitHáchcha**	straighten; adjust	**9áddal/yi9áddil**
specialise (in)	**taxáSSaS/yitxáSSaS (fi)**	strange; bizarre	**9ajíib**
		street	**sháari9/shawáari9**
spectacles	**gáshma*(aat); naDHDHáara*(aat)**	strength; intensity	**shídda***
		strength; power	**gúwwa**
speech; talk	**kaláam**	strengthen	**gáwwa/yigáwwi**
speed	**súr9a***	stripe	**shaxT/shuxúuT**
spend (money)	**Sáraf/yáSruf/Sarf**	stroll (v.)	**timáshsha/ yitmáshsha**
spend (time)	**gáDa/yígDi/gáDa**		
spices	**bháar(aat)**	strong	**gúwi/agwiyáa**
spoil (intrans.); go bad	**tilaf/yátlif/tálaf**	stubborn	**9aníid**
		student	**Táalib/Tulláab**
spoon	**gáfsha*(aat)**	study (v.)	**dáras/yádris/diráasa**
sport	**riyáaDa***	stuff; things; gear	**saamáan**
stable; immovable	**tháabit**	stuffed (vegetable, etc.)	**máHshi**
stand (up)	**wúgaf/yóoguf/ wugúuf**		
		stupid	**ghábi/aghbiyáa**
standard (n.)	**mustáwa(yaat)**	succeed	**níjaH/yínjaH/najáaH**
stapler	**dabbáasa*(aat)**	success	**najáaH**
star	**nájim/nujúum**	suit (v.)	**náasab/yináasib**
stay (v.)	**tamm/yitímm**	subject; topic	**mawDúu9/ mawaaDíi9**
stay (in a hotel) (v.)	**nízal/yánzil/nuzúul**		
		substance	**máadda*/mawáadd**
steal	**baag/yibúug/boog**	sugar	**shákkar** or **súkkar**
steps; ladder	**dáray(aat)**	suggest	**iqtáraH/yiqtáriH**
stick (n.)	**9áSa**	suggestion	**muqtáraH(aat)**
still	**bá9ad**	to commit suicide	**intáHar/yintíHir**
to still be/do something	**maa zaal/yizáal + adj. or imperf. verb**	suit of clothes	**bádla*(aat)**
		sum (of money)	**máblagh/mabáaligh**
stir (liquids)	**xaar/yixúur/ xawaráan**	summer	**Sayf**
		summer (adj.)	**Sáyfi**
stomach	**báTin/buTúun**	sun	**shams** (f.)
stone	**Hájar/Hijáara***	sunset	**mughárb**
stop (something); park (car)	**wággaf/yiwággif**	Sunday	**il-áHad**
		support; favour (v.)	**'áyyad/yi'áyyid**
to (come to a) stop	**wúgaf/yóoguf/ wugúuf**		

surface (n.)	**sáTaH/suTúuH**	team; group (of musicians)	**faríiq/fúruq**
to be surprised, amazed	**ta9ájjab/yit9ájjab**	tear; rip (v.)	**shagg/yishígg/ shagáag**
surrender	**istáslam/yistáslim**		
sustenance; food	**rizg (or rizj)**	telegram	**barqíyya*(aat)**
sweep	**kínas/yáknis**	telephone (n.)	**tilifúun(aat)**
sweet	**Hálu, f. Hálwa**	telephone (v.)	**Dárab tilifúun**
sweetness	**Haláawa***	television	**tilivizyúun(aat)**
swim (v.)	**síbaH/yísbaH/ sibáaHa**	tell (say to)	**gaal/yigúul/gool**
		tell stories	**sóolaf/yisóolif**
sword	**sayf/suyúuf**	ten	**9áshar (9áshra)**
Syria	**súuriya**	tenth (adj.)	**9áashir**
		tennis	**tánis**
T		termination; putting an end to	**qaDáa (9ala)**
table	**mayz(aat)** or **Táwla*(aat)**	test (driving)	**tist(aat)**
tailor	**xayyáaT(iin)**	test out; try	**járrab/yijárrib**
take	**'áxadh/yáaxidh/ 'axdh**	thank you	**shúkran**
		thank you (lit. (you are) praiseworthy)	**mashkúur**
take! (imp.)	**xudh/i/u!**		
take for oneself	**ittáxadh/yittáxidh**		
take out; remove	**Tálla9/yiTálli9**	that	**haadháak/dhiich**
take to; send to	**wádda/yiwáddi**	that (conj.)	**inn**
talk (v.)	**taHáchcha/ yitHáchcha; Hícha/ yíHchi/ Háchi**	then; next; after that	**táali**
		there is/are; there isn't/ aren't	**fii/maa fii; aku/máaku (KWT); hast/maa hast; maa mish (BAH); shay/maa shay (OM)**
talk; gossip (n.)	**Háchi/Hacháawi**		
tall	**Tawíil/Tiwáal**		
to be tall	**Taal/yiTúul/Tuul**		
tape	**sharíiTa*/sharáa'iT**	(over) there	**hunáak**
tape recorder	**musájjila*(aat)**	therefore	**ídhan**
taste	**dhoog**	these	**haadhayláyn**
taxi	**tíksi/takáasi** or **tiksiyáat**	they	**húmma** or **hum**
		thief	**báayig/bawáyga**
tea	**chaay**	thing	**shay/ashyáa**
teach	**dárras/yidárris; 9állam/yi9állim**	think; be of the opinion; suspect	**DHann/yiDHúnn/ DHann**
		think; ponder	**fákkar/yifákkir**
teacher	**mudárris(iin)**	I/you, etc. think/ are of the opinion that …	**9ála baal + pron.; 9ála DHann + pron.**
teacher (esp. Qur'an school)	**mu9állim(iin)**		
teacher! (as an address form); professor	**ustáadh/asáatidha**	third (adj.)	**tháalith**
		(one) third (n.)	**thilth/athláath**

thirsty	9aTsháan(iin)	translator	mutárjim(iin)
thirteen	thalaathtá9shar	transport	wáSSal/yiwáSSil
thirty	thalaathíin	someone	
this	háadha/dhi; haay	somewhere	
those	haadhayláak;	travel (v.)	sáafar/yisáafir
	haadhooláak	travel agency	wakáalat is-
three	thaláath(a)		safariyyáat
throw (v.)	fállat/yifállit	treat (medically)	dáawa/yidáawi
throw	gaTT/yigúTT/gaTáaT	(a) tree; shrub	shájara
(esp. throw away)		trees; shrubs	shájar
ticket	tádhkira*/tadháakir	trip; journey	ríHla(aat)
tip (taxi, etc.)	baxshíish	trousers (pair of)	bantalóon
tired	ta9báan(iin)	truce	hídna*
to get tired	tí9ab/yít9ab/tá9ab	that's true!	Sidj!
thought	fíkra*/afkáar	trunk (car)	Sandúug/Sanaadíig
thousand	alf/aaláaf	truth	Sidq or Sidg
Thursday	il-xamíis	to tell the truth	Sádag/yáSdig/Sidg
time	waqt	truthful	Saaj/Saadgíin
at whatever time	shwáqtmaa	try; attempt (v.)	Háawal/yiHáawil
for a long time;	min zamáan	Tuesday	ith-thaláatha*
for ages (up to		turn (n.)	door/adwáar
the present time)		turn (the corner)	laff/yilíff/laff
in old times	qadíim iz-zamáan	turn on (engine,	shághghal/
the present time	il-waqt il-HáaDir	machine, etc.)	yishághghil
(what's the) time?	kam is-sáa9a*(aat)?	turn out; end up	Tála9/yíTla9/Tulúu9
tiring	mút9ib	being	or Taláa9
today	il-yoom	turn over	gálab/yíglub/galb
tomatoes	TamáaT	(something); turn	
to; towards	íla; li	something into	
toilet	Hammáam(aat)	something	
tomorrow	báachir	twelve	ithná9shar
tongue	lisáan/alsína*	two	Ithnáyn (thintáyn)
tool	'áala*(aat)	type; kind	noo9/anwáa9; Tiráaz
tourism	siyáaHa	tyre	tayr(aat)
tourist(ic)	siyáaHi		
town	bálad; madíina*/	**U**	
	múdun	uncle (paternal)	9amm/a9máam
trade	tijáara*	under	taHt
trader	táajir/tujjáar	understand	fáham/yífham/fahm
traffic; traffic	murúur	to reach a	tifáaham/yitfáaham
police		(mutual)	
translate	tárjam/yitárjim	understanding	
translation	tárjama*/taráajim	undertake	gaam (bi)
		(a task)	

to be unemployed	ti9áTTal/yit9áTTal
uniform (police, military)	zayy
university (n.)	jáami9a*(aat)
university (adj.)	jáami9i
until	Hátta; layn
unwillingly	gháSban 9ála + pron.
up; upstairs	foog
upset	za9láan(iin)
upset (someone)	zá99al/yizá99il
to get upset	zí9al/yíz9al/zá9al
use (v.)	istá9mal/yistá9mil
to be useful	faad/yifíid/fáyda
to get used to	ti9áwwad/yit9áwwad (9ála)
usefulness	fáyda*
usual; ordinary	9áadi
usually	9áadatan

V

valid	SáaliH
view; panorama	mánDHar/ manáaDHir
village	qárya*/qúra
visit (v.)	zaar/yizúur/ziyáara
visitor	záayir/zuwwáar
voice; vote	Soot/aSwaat
volleyball	il-kúura iT-Táa'ira

W

wages; salary	ma9áash; ráatib
day's wages	yoomíyya(aat)
waiter	gaarsóon
walk; march; go	mísha/yímshi/máshi
wall	Háa'iT/HiiTáan
wall (interior)	jidáar/jidráan
wallet	míHfaDHa*/ maHáafiDH
want	bágha/yábghi or yábbi or yíbgha/ bághi; aráad/yiríid; widd + pron.

war	Harb (f.)/Hurúub
wash (v.)	ghásal/yighásil/ ghasáal
washing machine	ghassáala*(aat)
waste (v.)	Dayya9/yiDáyyi9
watch; look at	Táala9/yiTáali9
watchman; guard	naaTúur/nawaaTíir
water	maay
water pot	briij/abaaríig
watermelon(s)	baTTíix
by way of; by means of	9an Taríig
we	íHna
weak	Da9íif(iin)
wear (clothes)	líbas/yílbas/libs
weather	jaww; Taqs
Wednesday	il-'árba9a
week	subúu9/asaabíi9
weep	bícha/yíbchi/báchi
welcome!	áhlan wa sáhlan!; márHaba!; yaa hála!
welcome back! (from a journey)	il-Hámdu lilláah 9ala salámtik!
well; in good shape	bi xayr
well; so; then …	9áyal or 9ájal
well done!	yaa saláam!
west	gharb
western	ghárbi
what?	sh- (prefix); shínhu; waysh
whatever; whenever	kíllmaa
at whatever time	shwáqtmaa
when?	míta
when (conj.)	yoom
when first … (conj.)	áwwalmaa
where?	wayn
wherever	wáynmaa
whether	law or lo
which; the one that	ílli

which?	**ay**	the world (and its works)	**id-dínya**
(for) a little while; for a bit	**shway**	worms	**duud**
white	**ábyaD/biiD**	don't worry about it!	**wila yihímmik!**
who?	**man/min/minhu**	to be worth	**síwa/yíswa**
whoever; anyone who	**kíllmin**	wound; injure	**járaH/yíjraH/jarH**
why?	**laysh**	wristwatch	**sáa9a*(aat)**
wife	**zóoja*(aat)**	write	**kítab/yáktib/kitáaba**
wind	**háwa; riiH** (f.)/**riyáaH**	(hand)writing	**xaTT/xuTúuT**
window	**daríisha*/daráayish**		
with	**bi; má9a; 9ind**	**Y**	
within (a period of time)	**fi xiláal**	year	**sána*/sanawáat** (or **siníin**)
without ... ing	**bidúun maa** + verb	yellow	**áSfar/Súfur**
woman	**mára*/niswáan; Húrma/Haríim**	yes	**ay; ná9am**
old woman	**9ajúuz/9ajáayiz**	yes, on the contrary	**balá**
word; utterance	**kálima*(aat)**	yesterday	**ams; il-báarHa**
work (n.)	**shúghul/ashgháal; 9ámal/a9máal**	yet	**bá9ad**
work (v.)	**ishtághal/yishtághil**	yoghurt	**roob** or **róoba***
worker; labourer	**9áamil/9ummáal**	you (f. sing.)	**ínti**
working hours; shift hours	**taym**	you (m. sing.)	**ínta**
hardworking	**shaghgháal/ shaghaaghíil**	you (pl.)	**íntu**
		young	**Saghíir/Sigháar**
workshop	**wársha*(aat)**	youth (time of life); young men	**shabáab**
world	**9áalam**	(a) youth; young man	**sháabb/shubbáan**